Beiträge zur historischen Theologie

Edited by
Albrecht Beutel

146

Hilary Anne-Marie Mooney

# Theophany

The Appearing of God According to the Writings
of Johannes Scottus Eriugena

Mohr Siebeck

Hilary Anne-Marie Mooney, born 1962; studied philosophy, classical languages, and theology in Dublin; 1991 Ph.D.; 2003 Habilitation; apl. Professor at the University of Freiburg; she currently teaches at the University of Education in Weingarten.

ISBN 978-3-16-149089-7
ISSN 0340-6741 (Beiträge zur historischen Theologie)

Die Deutsche Bibliothek lists this publication in the Deutsche Nationalbibliographie; detailed bibliographic data is available on the Internet at *http://dnb.d-nb.de*.

The book was typeset by Martin Fischer in Tübingen using Adobe Garamond typeface, printed by Gulde-Druck in Tübingen on non-aging paper and bound by Großbuchbinderei Josef Spinner in Ottersweier.

Printed in Germany.

ΟΙ ϹΤΙΧΟΙ ΤΟΙ ΙΩΑΝΝΟΥ ΤΩ ΚΥΡΡΙΩ ΑΙΤΟΥ
ΤΟ ΑΝΑΚΤΟ ΚΑΡΟΛΩ

Fons medium finis, genitum de lumine lumen,
Est, non est, super est, quo praestitit omnibus esse,
Qui regit atque tenet totum, quod condidit ipse
Totus per totum qui nullis partibus haeret,
Cuius summa procul cunctis natura remota,
Cum sit cunctorum substans essentia simplex
…
Nec minus in caelis prosunt mysteria Christi
Quam terris: merito, cum sit deus omnibus unus:
Illic angelicas patefecit lumine mentes
Ac tenebrosa suae uirtutis prodidit ipsis.
Nulla quidem uirtus potuit dinoscere pure
Quem pater occultum gremio uelabat opaco;
Sed caro nunc uerbum factum – mirabile dictu –
Clare se cunctis hominemque deumque reuoluit.
ΝΟΥϹ ΤΕ ΛΟΓΟϹ ΤΕ capit quem nullus uiderat ante:
ϹΑΡΚΙΚΑ nam ΦΥϹΙϹ diuinas temperat ΑΥΓΑϹ.*

---

* Lines 30–35 and 43–52 from Poem 8, ΟΙ ϹΤΙΧΟΙ ΤΟΙ ΙΩΑΝΝΟΥ ΤΩ ΚΥΡΡΙΩ ΑΙΓΟΥ
ΤΟ ΑΝΑΚΤΟ ΚΑΡΟΛΩ / Lines by John to his Lord Charles, in: Michael Herren (ed.), *Iohannis Scotti Eriugenae, Carmina*, Dublin: School of Celtic Studies / Dublin Institute for Advanced Studies, 1993, p. 84–86.

# Acknowledgements

I owe a dept of gratitude to the late Brian McNamara SJ who first introduced to me Eriugena. On hearing of my project, Dominic O'Meara, John J. O'Meara and Dermot Moran offered me early encouragement. Peter Walter undertook to foster the research and accept the project as a Habilitation-project at the Theology Department of the Albert-Ludwigs-Universität Freiburg. His deep knowledge of the history of theology was a great help to me. While working in Freiburg at the office of the late Karl Suso Frank (Early Church History and Patrology) I learned much about the fathers and Prof. Frank kindly undertook the second reference for the Habilitation.

Willemien Otten, a true expert on Eriugena, was again and again very generous with her time and advice. Without her expertise there would be many more mistakes in this work and without her encouragement the project might not have been completed. The mistakes which remain are my responsibility.

I am grateful to the Adolf Messer Stiftung for initial funding and to the Deutsche Forschungsgemeinschaft for a habilitation scholarship. I thank the Archdiocese of Freiburg and the Diocese of Rottenburg-Stuttgart for contributing to the cost of publishing my research.

I am grateful to Prof. Dr. Albrecht Beutel for accepting my manuscript for publication in the series, Beiträge zur historischen Theologie. I am sincerely grateful to Dr. Henning Ziebritzki and to Jana Trispel at Mohr Siebeck for their competent advice and help in preparing my manuscript for publication. Thanks to Isabelle Cartwright and Tobias Lamp for proofreading much of the text.

I am deeply grateful to my husband Paul-Stefan Roß. This book is dedicated to him.

*Stuttgart, February 2009*                                    *Hilary Anne-Marie Mooney*

# Table of Contents

# Introduction

I

# Presentation of Eriugena's understanding of the appearing of God

## 43

# Reflection on Eriugena's understanding of the appearing of God

185

# Introduction

# Preliminaries

## 1. The issue at hand and the aim of the investigation

### *1.1 'Divine appearing' or 'divine revelation'?*

"For everything that is understood and sensed is nothing else but the apparition of what is not apparent, the manifestation of the hidden, the affirmation of the negated, the comprehension of the incomprehensible …"[1]. The appearing of the

---

[1] "*Omne enim quod intelligitur et sensitur nihil aliud est nisi non apparentis apparitio, occulti manifestatio, negati affirmatio, incomprehensibilis comprehensio …*", É. Jeauneau (ed.), Periphyseon III, Corpus Christianorum Continuatio Mediaeualis CLXIII, 589–591, Turnhout: Brepols, 1999, p. 22, (= PL 122 633A). English from I. P. Sheldon-Williams / J. J. O'Meara, *Iohannis Scotti Eriugenae Periphyseon (De Diuisione Naturae) Liber Tertius,* Dublin: The Dublin Institute for Advanced Studies, 1981, Scriptores Latini Hiberniae XI, p. 59.

In the course of my research I have consulted the translations of Eriugena's works listed in the bibliography. In those cases where I could adopt an existing translation I have always named the translator(s) and given the source. In those cases where a translation is offered but no translator is named, the translation is my own.

*Periphyseon* is becoming available in a critical edition within two series: in Scriptores Latini Hiberniae and in Corpus Christianorum Continuatio Mediaeualis.

*Iohannis Scotti Eriugenae Periphyseon (De Diuisione Naturae) Liber Primus; Liber Secundus; Liber Tertius,* I. P. Sheldon-Williams / Ludwig Bieler, (ed.), Dublin: The Dublin Institute for Advanced Studies, reprint 1978, first published 1968; 1972; 1981, (= Scriptores Latini Hiberniae, vols. VII, IX, XI). *Iohannis Scotti Eriugenae Periphyseon (De Diuisione naturae) Liber Quartus,* Édouard Jeauneau (ed.) / with the assistance of Mark A. Zier, Dublin: The Dublin Institute for Advanced Studies, 1995, (= Scriptores Latini Hiberniae, vol. XIII).

Influenced by the experience of editing the Latin text of book four of *Periphyseon* for the Latin / English format of the Scriptores Latini Hiberniae series, Jeauneau recognised anew the need for a critical, genetic edition such as Traube had in his day desired. It was too late to realise this through the edition in Scriptores Latini Hiberniae which was nearly complete. Jeauneau is therefore edited a new edition of *Periphyseon* for Corpus Christianorum Continuatio Mediaeualis. This edition both shows the various stages in the emergence of *Periphyseon* as a text, and provides a standard critical edition of the text. All five volumes are now available: *Iohannis Scotti Eriugenae Periphyseon, Liber Primus; Liber Secundus; Liber Tertius; Liber Quartus; Liber Quintus, Editionem nouam a supposticiis quidem additamentis purgatam, ditatam uero apppendice in qua uicissitudines operis synoptice exhibentur,* Édouard Jeauneau (ed.), Turnhout: Brepols, 1996; 1997; 1999; 2000; 2003 (= Corpus Christianorum Continuatio Mediaeualis, vols. CLXI, CLXII, CLXIII, CLXIV, CLXV). In the fourth chapter of the introduction to the first volume in the Corpus Christianorum edition Jeauneau explains how he embarked on this edition and how it is structured, CCCM CLXI, pp. LXXXI–XC; see too É. Jeauneau, "L'édition du livre IV du Periphyseon", in: Claudio Leonardi und Enrico Menestò, (ed.), *Giovanni Scoto nel suo tempo. L'organizzazione del sapere in età carolingia. Atti del XXIV Convegno storico internazionale, Todi, 11–14 ottobre, 1987,* Spoleto: Centro Italiano di studi

hidden God is the theme of this study. The expression "the appearing of God" in the title has been carefully chosen.[2] It is an open formulation accommodating many nuances of meaning. For example the expression 'the appearing of God' leaves open the question of the carrier or carriers of the appearing: it does not take a position on the relative value of the disclosure of God in nature, in the human self, or in Jesus Christ. Rather 'the appearing of God' leaves open the question of the means or media whereby this disclosure takes place: indeed, as clearly intended by this study, it facilitates a discussion of these issues. The participial form suggests a processual understanding of the appearing. While a high point (in the sense of a privileged act of appearing with decisive consequences for all that follows) is not excluded, the participial form nevertheless conjures up an ongoing becoming apparent. Furthermore the expression 'appearing' displays an openness with regard to the form the divine disclosure takes: it is open to an sensual appearing or an appearing which is only perceived by the intellect.

This study considers Eriugena's thought on the appearing of God as this thought emerged in his writings. Eriugena's writings are in dialogue with his contemporaries and discuss the central issues at hand against the background of the authors of the patristic period. The investigation seeks to avoid an anachronistic treatment of Eriugena's thought and the title bears witness to this. Thus it represents a conscious decision not to focus the study on the concept of 'the revelation of God' in Eriugena's writings. The term 'revelation' became popular relatively late, much later than the ninth century in which Eriugena lived. It is not a frequent term in his writings[3]. The term 'revelation' has connotations which it has acquired throughout the later history of theological thinking (for example the distinction between general revelation and supernatural revelation[4]). Furthermore the meaning of the term

---

sull'alto medioevo, 1989, (= Atti dei Convegni dell'Accademia Tudertina e del Centro di studi sulla spiritualità medievale, Nuova serie; 1), pp. 469–486, esp. pp. 480–486.

[2] A correspondence might be established to the complex of words centring on the verb '*appareo*' in Eriugena's writings. However, this study is thematically oriented, and not narrowly centred on any one linguistic complex.

[3] This applies above all to the Latin term '*revelatio*'. The *indices generales* of G. H. ALLARD *Johannis Scoti Eriugenae. Periphyseon. Indices generales,* Montréal: Institut d'études médiévales, Université de Montréal, 1983 based on the Migne edition, gives an indication of the relative frequency with which words occur in *Periphyseon.* Thus the verb '*revelare*' and the noun '*revelatio*' are both used very sparingly in *Periphyseon,* together, according to the indices of Allard, 19 times. On the contrary Allard lists 214 places where forms of the verb '*appareo*' or the noun '*apparitio*' occur. Allard lists 132 occurrences of the verb '*manifesto*' and related words.

[4] On the distinction between general revelation / supernatural revelation see: AVERY DULLES, *The Assurance of Things Hoped for. A Theology of Christian Faith,* New York / Oxford: Oxford University Press, 1994, pp. 189, 263. In the context of a contemporary theological reflection writers such as John Milbank, Catherine Pickstock and Graham Ward have found occasion to argue against a reason / revelation duality, see JOHN MILBANK, "Knowledge. The theological critique of philosophy in Hamann and Jacobi", in: JOHN MILBANK, CATHERINE PICKSTOCK and GRAHAM WARD (ed.), *Radical Orthodoxy. A New Theology,* London: Routledge, 1999, pp. 21–37, esp. p. 24. For an astute assessment of the theological movement 'Radical ORTHODOXY' and its epistemological claims see JAMES

'revelation' in magisterial categories was not a burning issue in Eriugena's lifetime[5]. The expression 'appearing' is not accompanied by so specific a history[6]. The use of the expression 'the appearing of God' in the title of the book is thus in keeping with Eriugena's own terminology and the questions which occupied the thoughts and writings of his contemporaries. It indicates that a particular section of the history of the theological issue of the disclosure of the divine is being investigated in this study and that this issue is presented in terms of the discussion preceding Eriugena and those current in his times. However, in the last chapter of this study, in the final assessment of Eriugena's position, matters are raised which pertain to the understanding of revelation in contemporary theology.

## 1.2 *The emergence of the issue*

The belief in Jesus Christ, the Word incarnate, did not emerge in a religious or cultural vacuum. The Christian tradition emerged in close and inevitable dialogue with the cultures, and religious heritages of the first individual Christians.

The very first Christians were monotheistic Jews who believed in the revealing of Yahweh through his word[7]. This revealing was understood to issue from a free divine

---

HANVEY, "Conclusion: Continuing the Conversation", in L. P. HEMMING (ed.), *Radical Orthodoxy – A Catholic Enquiry? A Catholic Enquiry,* Aldershot, Ashgate, 2000, pp. 149–171, esp. p. 162/3.

[5] See JOSEF SCHMITZ, "Das Christentum als Offenbarungsreligion im kirchlichen Bekenntnis", in: WALTER KERN et al. (ed.), Handbuch für Fundamentaltheologie, pp. 1–12. Among the important documents from the catholic magisterium are *Dei Filius* from the first Vatican Council, and *Dei Verbum* and *Gaudium et Spes* from the second Vatican council, *Fides et ratio* from POPE JOHN PAUL THE SECOND.

[6] On "revelation" see WALTER KERN et al., *Handbuch der Fundamentaltheologie, vol. 2, Traktat Offenbarung,* Tübingen: Francke Verlag, second emended edition, 2000, (= UTB für Wissenschaft / Große Reihe); HORST BÜRKLE, CHRISTOPH DOHMEN, THOMAS SÖDING, JOHANN MAIER, WERNER SCHLÜSSLER, JÜRGEN WERBICK, "Offenbarung", in: WALTER KASPER et al. (ed.), *Lexikon für Theologie und Kirche,* vol. 7, *Maximilian bis Pazzi,* Freiburg: Herder, 1998, col. 983–995; GABRIEL DALY, "Revelation in the Theology of the Roman Catholic Church", in: PAUL AVIS (ed.), *Divine Revelation,* London: Darton, Longman and Todd Ltd., 1997, pp. 23–44; WOLFHART PANNENBERG, *Systematische Theologie, vol. I* Göttingen: Vandenhoeck & Ruprecht, 1988, esp. chapter four: Die Offenbarung Gottes, pp. 207–281; PETER EICHER, *Offenbarung. Prinzip neuzeitlicher Theologie,* Munich: Kösel Verlag, 1977. Compare GERNOT WEISSNER, HORST DIETRICH PREUSS, BRIGITTE (RIVKA) KERN-ULMER, HORST BALZ, EILERT HERMS, "*Offenbarung*", in: HORST BALZ et al. (ed.), *Theologische Realenzyklopädie, vol. XXV, Ochino-Parapsychologie,* Berlin: Walter de Gruyter, 1995, pp. 109–210, I disagree with Eilert Herms who here attributes a "*Suffizienz der Schöpfungsoffenbarung*" to Eriugena.
On how various, historically determined understandings of revelation influenced the emergence of fundamental theology as a discipline see FRANCIS SCHÜSSLER FIORENZA, *Foundational Theology. Jesus and the Church,* New York: Crossroad, 1986, chapter 9, pp. 251–264, "The Emergence of Fundamental Theology"; On the understanding of revelation in the documents of the Second Vatican Council see GERALD O'COLLINS, *Retrieving Fundamental Theology. The Three Styles of Contemporary Theology,* London: Geoffrey Chapman, 1993, p. 48–78.

[7] On the disclosure of God as presented in the writings of the Old and New Testaments see RENÉ LATOURELLE, *Theology of Revelation,* New York: Alba House, 1966 (= *Théologie de la Révelation,*

choice, from the decision to communicate with a chosen people. The word of God initiated this history through creation, encountered the chosen people in covenant and regulated their lives as law. What was made known was a living, personal, powerful God, a God who enters into covenant with the chosen people, and who addresses them through the prophets. Created reality too was held to disclose God, and events of visible nature (the parting of the Red Sea, the theophany on Sinai, the plagues in Egypt) were interpreted as manifestational. Nor was the God of the first converts to Christianity perceived only as the creator God, as the initiator of this world in the past, but rather, the God of these Jewish Christians was perceived as here and now active with a plan for history. Yahweh was understood as the Lord of history.

In the creation story of the Priestly tradition, the human beings, man and woman, are presented as special carriers of the revelation of God: "So God created man in his own image, in the image of God he created him; male and female he created them." Gen. 1: 27[8]. Here the human creature alone of all the creatures is said to be created in the image of God. This is a unique affirmation of the disclosing function of human nature. And yet even in the context of this strong affirmation of manifestation, here, as elsewhere in the writings of the Old Testament, the transcendence of God was always preserved. This was achieved by the emphasis on the ongoing divine initiative in whatever appearing takes place, and the emphasis on the residual mystery which is preserved even in the great theophanies[9].

The first Christians had to understand the revealing of God in the single human Jesus within the framework of their inherited religious heritage. The emerging Christian faith had to balance a traditional Jewish belief in the manifestation of God in the salvation history of the people Israel, in the law, and indeed in privileged events of visible nature as carriers of God's own self-disclosure, with the additional insight of the special revealing of God in the Word made flesh. The various writings of the New Testament bear witness to different attempts to articulate how the uniqueness of the new covenant in Jesus Christ is to be reconciled with the 'old' covenant with Yahweh. The letter to the Hebrews is one attempt to reflect upon the relationship of the old and the new covenant, an attempt which makes substantial use of the literary device of contrast: "Πολυμερῶς καὶ πολυτρόπως πάλαι ὁ θεὸς λαλήσας τοῖς πατράσιν ἐν τοῖς προφήταις ἐπ᾽ ἐσχάτου τῶν ἡμερῶν τούτων ἐλάλησεν ἡμῖν ἐν υἱῷ ..."[10]

---

Desclée de Brouwer), pp. 21–81; CHRISTOPH DOHMEN, "Offenbarung II. Biblisch-theologisch: 1. Altes Testament", in: LThK, vol. 7, col. 985–6 and James D. G. DUNN, "Biblical Concepts of Revelation", in: PAUL AVIS (ed.), Divine Revelation, pp. 1–22, an article which focusses on the means or media of revelation in both testaments of the Bible.

[8] Here and elsewhere the English translation is according to the Revised Standard Version of the Bible.

[9] Compare HORST DIETRICH PREUSS, Offenbarung II. Altes Testament, in H. BALZ (ed.) TRE, vol. XXV, p. 127: "'Offenbarungen' *JHWHs* / Gottes geschehen folglich nach dem Zeugnis des Alten Testaments niemals als völlige Selbstoffenbarung *JHWHs*, ...".

[10] Heb. 1:1–2: "In many and various ways God spoke of old to our fathers by the prophets; but in the last days he has spoken to us by a Son, ..."

In all epiphanic events, the dialectic of revealed and yet still hidden is preserved. This is perceivable in those texts in which Christ is spoken of as the mystery of God[11]. In the theology of the Johannine community, this dialectic is subsumed within the theology of the unknowable Father to whom we have access through the Son[12]. The revealing is presented in the terms of generation (the Son from the Father), a category which is to feed the trinitarian reflection of the following centuries.

An awareness of the manifestation of God in the cosmos is also to be observed in the authors of the New Testament: "τὰ γὰρ ἀόρατα αὐτοῦ ἀπὸ κτίσεως κόσμου τοῖς ποιήμασιν νοούμενα καθορᾶται"[13]. But this cosmological appearing too is sublated within a new context. It is presented as culminating in a Christological context: "εἰς οἰκονομίαν τοῦ πληρώματος τῶν καιρῶν, ἀνακεφαλαιώσασθαι τὰ πάντα ἐν τῷ Χριστῷ"[14]. The creation of all humans in the image of God is also Christologically reformed and reappears within the notion of the creation of the proto-human Jesus Christ as image of God (Col. 1:15 He is the image of the invisible God, the first-born of all creation)[15].

The later generations of Christians, and in particular those who enjoyed a certain level of education, were influenced by the philosophical currents of the Mediterranean world. Among these were the Hellenic influences of Middle Platonism and, in its turn, the so-called Neoplatonism. It is worthwhile to briefly consider how the question of the manifestation of the absolute is approached in these systems[16].

---

[11] Col. 2:2: "μυστηρίου τοῦ θεοῦ, Χριστοῦ" and see Rom. 16: 25–26; Col. 1: 25–26; 1 Tim. 3: 16; 1 Cor. 2: 7. See JOSEPH A. FITZMYER, "Pauline Theology", in: RAYMOND BROWN et al. (ed.), *The New Jerome Biblical Commentary*, Englewood Cliffs, New Jersey, Prentice Hall, revised edition, 1990, (first published 1969 under the title *The Jerome Biblical Commentary*), Part Two, pp. 1382–1416: "In presenting the gospel as 'mystery,' Paul is implying that it is never fully made known by ordinary means of communication. As something revealed, it is apprehended only in faith; and even when revealed, the opacity of the divine wisdom is never completely dispelled", p. 1389.

[12] Jn 1:18 and see Jn. 6:46; 7:29; 8:55; 16:27;17:8. "Of all the New Testament writings it is John's Gospel which brings out most fully and clearly the force of Jesus as the revelation of God. ... As the Logos (Word), like Wisdom, he reveals the mind of God in creation (John. 1:1–4). As the descending Son of Man he reveals the secrets of heaven (3:11–13). In his healing and teaching he shows what the Father's works are (5:19–21; 10:32). As the Son sent from heaven he reveals the Father (6:46; 14:9). As the first Paraclete he sends the other Paraclete who will guide unto all the truth (16:13). As the summoner of disciples he makes known God's name (17:6). As the 'I am' in repeated self-affirmations he expresses the character of God. Thematic for the whole Gospel is the climax to the prologue: 'No one has ever seen God. It is God the only Son, who is close to the Father's heart, who has expounded him' (1:18)." JAMES D. G. DUNN, Biblical concepts of revelation, p. 20. I have devoted more attention to the disclosure of God according to the Pauline and Johannine writings because these had the most influence on Eriugena's writings.

[13] Rom. 1: 20. "Ever since the creation of the world his invisible nature, ..., has been clearly perceived in the things that have been made."

[14] Eph. 1:10 and see Heb. 12:18–24.

[15] "ὅς ἐστιν εἰκὼν τοῦ θεοῦ τοῦ ἀοράτου, πρωτότοκος πάσης κτίσεως", Col. 1:15 and see Col. 1:15–20.

[16] See MARKUS ENDERS, *Natürliche Theologie im Denken der Griechen*, Frankfurt: Knecht, 2000, (= Fuldaer Hochschulschriften; 36); On Plotinus see the classic account of H.–R. SCHWYZER, "Plotin", in: *Paulys Realencyclopädie der klassischen Altertumswissenschaft*, Vol. XXI, 1951, col. 471–592.

The theology of Middle Platonism as it flourished in the second century of the Christian era is characterised by the fact that it posits a supreme principle or God at the head of the hierarchy of being, as the first principle of all subsequent reality.[17] Middle Platonism with its sources in Platonic and Aristotelian philosophy, identified this first principle with Plato's Good. In the Neoplatonic philosophy of Plotinus and Proclus the radical unity of the First Principle was even more strongly heightened[18]. Plotinus and later Proclus increasingly presented the Absolute as unknowable[19].

According to Proclus the scope of our knowledge of this One, and about this One is radically limited. The One is so unknowable to us that we do not even know whether it is knowable or unknowable in itself:

καὶ οὐχ ἡμῖν μὲν ἄγνωστον, ἑαυτῷ δὲ γνωστόν ἐστιν. εἰ γὰρ ἐστιν ὅλως ἡμῖν ἄγνωστον, οὐδὲ αὐτὸ τοῦτο γιγνώσκομεν ὅτι ἑαυτῷ γνωστόν ἐστιν, ἀλλὰ καὶ τοῦτο ἀγνοοῦμεν· …[20]

For Plotinus the One is beyond Mind and indeed beyond Being. It cannot be known nor spoken of. He explicitly excludes that it has self-knowledge. The One, he argues, is radically simple, and self-knowledge would involve it in multiplicity. Therefore we must exclude the possibility of it knowing itself. It does not need this self knowledge anyway:

τί γὰρ καὶ μαθήσεται νοῆσαν; πρὸ γὰρ τοῦ νοῆσαι ὑπάρξει ὅπερ ἐστὶν ἑαυτῷ. καὶ γὰρ αὖ πόθος τις καί ἡ γνῶσις ἐστι καὶ οἷον ζητήσαντος εὕρεσις. τὸ τοίνυν διάφορον πάντη αὐτὸ πρὸς αὐτὸ μένει, καὶ οὐδὲν ζετεῖ περὶ αὐτοῦ, ὃ δ'ἐξελίττει ἑαυτό, καὶ πολλὰ ἂν εἴη.[21]

---

[17] A. H. ARMSTRONG, *An Introduction to Ancient Philosophy*, London: Methuen, ³1977, (first published 1947), p. 149.

[18] On the negative theology of Middle Platonism and that of Plotin and Proclus, see DEIRDRE CARABINE, *The Unknown God. Negative Theology in the Platonic Tradition: Plato to Eriugena*, Louvain: Peeters Press, 1995, (= Louvain Theological & Pastoral Monographs; 19), pp. 51–187; and RAOUL MORTLEY, *From Word to Silence I. The Rise and Fall of Logos*, Bonn: P. Hanstein, 1986, (= Theophaneia; 30).

[19] See CARABINE, The Unknown God, pp. 103–187.

[20] *Proclus, Commentarium in Platonis Parmenidem*, Book VI, 1108, lines 25–29, VICTOR COUSIN (ed.), Hildesheim: Olms, 1961, (reprint of 1864 edition from Paris; = Procli Philosophi Platonici Opera inedita; 3); "and it is not the case that it is unknowable to us while being knowable to itself; for if it is absolutely unknowable to us, we do not even know this, that it is knowable to itself, but of even this we are ignorant; …" Translation from GLENN R. MORROW / JOHN M. DILLON, *Proclus' Commentary on Plato's Parmenides, with introduction and notes by John M. Dillon*, paperback printing, with corrections, Princeton: Princeton University Press, 1992, p. 453; see CARABINE, The Unknown God, p. 164 and the extensive study of Proclus carried out by WERNER BEIERWALTES, *Proklos. Grundzüge seiner Metaphysik*, Frankfurt / Main: Klostermann, 1979, (= Philosophische Abhandlungen; vol. 24).

[21] Enneas, V, 3, 10, 47–52, Plotinus. Opera, PAUL HENRY and HANS-RUDOLF SCHWYZER, (ed), vol. II, Enneades IV–V, 1977, Oxford: University Press, 1977, pp. 221–222. A. H. Armstrong translation, in: *Plotinus with an English translation* by A. H. ARMSTRONG, vol. V, (Enneads V. 1–9), Cambridge / Harvard University Press / London: William Heinemann Ltd, 1984, (= The Loeb Classical Library, Vol. 444) p. 109: "… for what will it learn by thinking itself? For what it is will belong to itself before Intellect thinks. Also, knowledge is a kind of longing for the absent, and like the

While his emphasis is definitely on the unknowableness of the One, Plotinus does not fully abandon the dialectic of knowing / not knowing the Absolute. He strongly recommends the search for the Absolute. This search takes the form of a turning inward. In Plotinus' system, and the systems of the philosophers and theologians alike who are influenced by him, the human interior life becomes the focus of attention[22]. Through this inward gaze the presence of intellect in the human soul is understood, and an ascent may be initiated which intends the absolute referred to as the One as its ultimate goal.[23] The soul is then said (in especially privileged moments) to suddenly take light; the Absolute suddenly appears[24]. The One is said to appear suddenly ἐξαίφνης. Aphairesis (taking away or abstraction) is the method or programme by which one prepares for the appearing of the One.

γένοιτο δ᾽ ἂν τοῦτο ἴσως καὶ ταύτῃ, εἰ ἀφέλοις πρῶτον τὸ σῶμα ἀπὸ τοῦ ἀνθρώπου καὶ δηλονότι σαυτοῦ, εἶτα καὶ τὴν πλάττουσαν τοῦτο ψυχὴν καὶ τὴν αἴσθησιν δὲ εὖ μάλα, ἐπιθυμίας δὲ καὶ θυμοὺς καὶ τὰς ἄλλας τὰς τοιαύτας φλυαρίας, ὡς πρὸς τὸ θνητὸν νενούσας καὶ πάνυ. τό δὴ λοιπὸν αὐτῆς τοῦτό ἐστιν, ὃ εἰκόνα ἔφαμεν νοῦ σῴζουσάν τι φῶς ἐκείνου, οἷον ἡλίου μετὰ τὴν τοῦ μεγέθους σφαῖραν τὸ περὶ αὐτὴν ἐξ αὐτῆς λάμπον.[25]

In this state one may wait for the appearing of the One. Porphyry, Plotinus' biographer claims that his master experienced the appearing of the One only four times when he was with him. One sees how Plotinus' injunction to take or to strip everything away (ἄφελε πάντα)[26] can at best be seen as preparation for these mo-

---

discovery made by a seeker. But that which is absolutely different remains itself by itself, and seeks nothing about itself; but that which explicates itself must be many." See Carabine, The Unknown God, pp. 135–137 and p. 148 when speaking of the novum of negative theology in Plotinus in comparison to earlier writers she writes: "Plotinus's distinctive originality is that he proposed the notion that neither the human intellect nor the One itself, can have any knowledge about the One."

[22] Augustine's account of the interior life of the human is indebted to a Plotinus and Porphyry reception which was effected through the translations of Marius Victorinus. See P. F. Beatrice, "*Quosdam Platonicorum Libros.* The Platonic Reading of Augustine in Milan", in: *Vigiliae Christianae* 43 (1989) 248–281.

[23] This is clearly expressed in texts taken from Ennead V, 3. "It is probable, then, that he who intends to know what Intellect really is must know soul, and the most divine part of soul." Ψυχὴν οὖν, ὡς ἔοικε, καὶ τὸ ψυχῆς θειότατον κατιδεῖν δεῖ τὸν μέλλοντα νοῦν εἴσεσθαι ὅ τι ἐστί. Enneas V, 3, 9, 1–2, Henry-Schwyzer (ed.), p. 218. See also Enneas V, 3 section 2, Henry-Schwyzer (ed.), pp. 207–208.

[24] See Enneas V, 3, 17, Henry-Schwyzer (ed.), pp. 231–233.

[25] Enneas V, 3, 9, 2–10, Henry-Schwyzer (ed.), p. 218: "This could happen also in this way, if you first of all separated the body from man (and, obviously, from yourself), and then the soul which forms it and, very thoroughly, sense-perception and desires and passions and all the rest of such fooleries, since they incline so very much towards the mortal. What remains of soul is this which we said was an image of Intellect preserving something of its light, like the light of the sun which, beyond its spherical mass, shines around it and from it." English translation from A. H. Armstrong, Plotinus with an English translation, Vol. V, p. 101. See W. Beierwaltes, *Denken des Einen. Studien zur Neuplatonischen Philosophie und ihrer Wirkungsgeschichte,* Frankfurt / Main: Klostermann, 1985, p. 108ff and p. 129ff; Idem, *Selbsterkenntnis und Erfahrung der Einheit. Plotins Enneade V 3. Text, Übersetzung, Interpretation, Erläuterung,* Frankfurt, 1991.

[26] Enneas, V, 3, 17, 38, Henry-Schwyzer (ed.), p. 233.

ments not as a method which forces the One to appear. The question of the role of human contribution (be it through effort, or virtue, or asceticism) in facilitating the appearing of the divine is one which must be faced in all attempts to reflect on the manifestation of the divine.

In the writings of Plotinus we find the consideration of another question which must be raised in an account of the disclosure of the divine: how may the experience of the manifestation of God or the Absolute be conceptualised, or indeed expressed in words? The difficulty of a conceptual appropriation of this vision or indeed its subsequent verbal description is recognised by Plotinus as being extremely difficult!

ἐπιθέουσα γὰρ πᾶσι τοῖς ἀληθέσι καὶ ὧν μετέχομεν ἀληθῶν ὅμως ἐκφεύγει, εἴ τις βούλοιτο εἰπεῖν καὶ διανοηθῆναι, ἐπείπερ δεῖ τὴν διάνοιαν, ἵνα τι εἴπῃ, ἄλλο καὶ ἄλλο λαβεῖν· οὕτω γὰρ καὶ διέξοδος· ἐν δὲ πάντῃ ἁπλῷ διέξοδος τίς ἐστιν; ἀλλ᾽ ἀρκεῖ κἂν νοερῶς ἐφάψασθαι· ἐφαψάμενον δέ, ὅτε ἐφάπτεται, πάντῃ μηδὲν μήτε δύνασθαι μήτε σχολὴν ἄγειν λέγειν, ὕστερον δὲ περὶ αὐτοῦ συλλογίζεσθαι. τότε δὲ χρὴ ἑωρακέναι πιστεύειν, ὅταν ἡ ψυχὴ ἐξαίφνης φῶς λάβῃ·[27]

Thus in this long quotation we can catch a glimpse of two issues arising in the reflection on the appearing of God as this reflection emerged in history. In the first place: is, or *how* is the conceptual appropriation of the divine manifestation possible? Secondly: can this appropriation of divine manifestation be subsequently expressed in words?

These are questions which the Christian authors of the early centuries also had to address. While to some extent it may be said that the philosophy of Plotinus provided them with a philosophical apparatus with which to approach these questions, the system could not simply be transferred into a Christian setting. It could not simply be adopted in all respects by Christian thinkers. In particular, the question of the disclosure of God in the concrete human Jesus Christ is difficult to voice from within a purely Plotinian perspective. Further the rationality of a trinitarian God seems to be challenged by the Plotinian insistence on the ultimate unity of the Absolute.

In the fourth century bishop, Gregory of Nyssa, we have a person whose writings were a direct source for Eriugena and who is certainly one of the most important media through whom the issues of the theological and philosophical tradition on the appearing of God and the possibility of knowing God were transmitted to

---

[27] Enneas V, 3, 17, 21–29, HENRY-SCHWYZER (ed.), pp. 232–233.

"The soul runs over all truths, and all the same shuns the truths we know if someone tries to express them in words and discursive thought; for discursive thought, in order to express anything in words, had to consider one thing after another: this is the method of description; but how can one describe the absolutely simple? But it is enough if the intellect comes into contact with it; but when it has done so, while the contact lasts, it is absolutely impossible, nor has it time, to speak; but it is afterwards that it is able to reason about it. One must believe one has seen, when the soul suddenly takes light: ...", English translation from A. H. ARMSTRONG, Plotinus with an English translation, pp. 133–135.

Eriugena[28]. Early Christian writers such as Justin, Irenaeus, Clement of Alexandria, Origen, while presenting the appearing of God in creation and Jesus Christ, all stressed the ultimate mystery that God is. In the fourth century Gregory of Nyssa and the other Cappadocians had to defend this unknowableness of the divine essence[29]. The position which Gregory developed represents a negative theology stressing the ultimate unknowableness not only of the divine essence in itself, but also of the human *ousia*. Nature can tell us that God exists, but what God is[30], is not revealed to us either by the natural world in general nor the human as image of God. The revelation of God in Jesus Christ is repeatedly presented in terms of the Pauline mystery, the mystery of the salvific plan of God in which Christ is the key to the mystery of the human race and to the whole of creation alike. The writer known to us as Ps. Dionysius Areopagita who wrote at the end of the fifth century and at the beginning of the sixth century was also heir to the Neoplatonic reflection on God[31]. His emphasis on the superessentiality of the divine essence also fed into Eriugena's understanding of an ultimately nameless God[32]. Ps. Dionysius' theory of hierarchic mediation of knowledge and being is also an important precursor of the Eriugenian account of the encounter with the appearing God as theophany. But the philosophical heritage of Eriugena spans East and West. The theme of the manifestation of God through the likeness of the trinity in the triple motion of the soul in the human mind is bequeathed to Eriugena from another direct source, the great Augustine of Hippo. Further, the seventh century Eastern writer Maximus Confessor bequeathed Eriugena a complementary set of concepts with which to investigate divine manifestation and the answering human assent: the loving descent of God in the incarnation (συγκατάβασις) and the 'theosis' or deification of the conscious appropriation of this truth.

   Johannes Scottus Eriugena was an academic of the Carolingian renaissance and he inherited this issue of the appearing of the divine from earlier authors. As a teacher he was challenged by the task of explaining all that is. His starting point is the *universum:* all that presents itself for explanation, all that falls within the horizon

---

[28] GREGORY himself reflects on his use of philosophical reflection, see for example *Gregorii Nysseni De Vita Moysis,* HUBERTUS MUSURILLO (ed.), Leiden: Brill, 1964, II 115, p. 68, 14–17, (= Gregorii Nysseni Opera, vol. VII, pars I). For an introduction to Gregory of Nyssa and his contribution to the theological tradition see ANTHONY MEREDITH, *The Cappadocians,* London: Geoffrey Chapman, 1995, pp. 52–127.

[29] The ecclesiastical writers Gregory of Nyssa, Ps. Dionysius, Augustine of Hippo and Maximus Confessor are only briefly mentioned here in order to illustrate the issue which is being investigated in this study. Eriugena's debt to these thinkers will be considered in more detail in chapter six of this study.

[30] Important for the emergence of this distinction are the writings of Philo of Alexandria.

[31] The Neoplatonic heritage in particular of Proclus is one of the most important factors in the academic attempts to date his writing and has contributed to our dating the Ps. Dionysian Corpus to the end of the fifth or beginning of the sixth century.

[32] For an introduction to the person and works of Ps. Dionysius Areopagite see, ANDREW LOUTH, *Denys the Areopagite,* London: Geoffrey Chapman, 1989).

of human questioning. He was sensitive to the heart of the matter: the self-revealing of the divine essence out of its superessential nothingness into all that is and is not. His answer, I will argue, contains a Christological heart and an anthropological centring that both stem from his understanding of incarnation. However, just as the church fathers used the spoils of Egypt, so too Eriugena thought it fitting to use the methods of dialectic to explain the whole scope of reality in a comprehensive account of the so-called divisions of nature. The thesis which this investigation proposes is the following: whether he is speaking from the perspective of dialectic or from the perspective of a christian theology, the key to interpreting Eriugena's account of the disclosure of God is the notion of theophany.

## *1.3 The aim of the investigation*

Eriugena's work is thus approached through the canon of questions which can be addressed to all purportedly comprehensive accounts of the appearing of God: In which creatures is God made manifest and what is the relation of the appearing of God in one creature to the appearing of God in another? How is God presented as revealed in nature as a whole (a question inherited not only from Christian thinkers in the Genesis tradition, but also from the tradition of philosophical cosmology)? To what extent is the human subject a medium of divine manifestation? To these more general questions come the specifically Christian questions: How is God revealed in the Word made flesh, in Jesus Christ? How is the divine trinity mirrored in creation as a whole, and in the functions of the human spirit in particular?

The appearing of God has an objective side referring to structures in reality concerning the absolute which is to appear, and a subjective or epistemological side. Belonging to an adequate investigation of the objective side are issues such as whether God appears as one or three and a consideration of the ontological structure which lies behind the unknowableness of God. An investigation of the subjective side of the manifestation of God must include some treatment of themes such as the possibility of union with God in this life in contrast to the situation of the blessed in the next life; and, the mutual relationship of cognitive union and moral discipleship[33]. Eriugena's contribution to this complex of questions is the matter examined in this thesis.

The study claims to detect a structure which recurs in all Eriugena's accounts of encounter with God, that is, whether these accounts focus on the subjective presuppositions on the part of the human or on the objective presuppositions. In both contexts, it will be argued, Theophany is the notion which connotes this recurring pattern.

---

[33] It is significant that in Michael Sells' much read account of mystical language, Eriugena is devoted a chapter: see MICHAEL A. SELLS, *Mystical Languages of Unsaying*, Chicago: Chicago University Press, 1994, pp. 34–62.

To the systematic complex of questions, come questions concerning Johannes Scottus Eriugena's own academic method. While the main aim of this investigation lies in the systematic field, the study does nevertheless attempt to make transparent Eriugena's theological method. From a methodological point of view his interpretation of the Bible and his use of the patristic tradition are analysed.

## 2. Past research: its achievements and deficits

Eriugena was rediscovered by the academic community through the writings of nineteenth century German speaking scholars, scholars heavily indebted to Hegelian philosophy. In this century the studies of Hjort, Staudenmaier, Christlieb, Kaulich, Huber, and Noack appeared[34]. The academic inquiry into Eriugena's writing received a new impetus through the publication of Maïeul Cappuyns relatively comprehensive study which was published in 1933[35]. This study is characterised by its attempt to situate Eriugena's thought within the historical setting in which the Carolingian writer lived and within which his writings arose. Cappuyns' study soon was recognised as a classic and it has served as the point of departure for countless other studies, encyclopaedia and lexicon articles.

Since 1970 a series of conferences have been organised under the auspices of the Society for the Promotion of Eriugenian Studies (SPES). The publication of the papers read at these conferences has substantially promoted research on Eriugena[36].

---

[34] P. HJORT, *Johan Scotus Erigena oder von dem Ursprung einer christlichen Philosophie und ihrem heiligen Beruf,* Copenhagen: 1823. F. A. STAUDENMAIER, *Johannes Scotus Erigena und die Wissenschaft seiner Zeit. Mit allgemeinen Entwicklungen der Hauptwahrheiten auf dem Gebiete der Philosophie und Religion, und Grundzügen zu einer Geschichte der speculativen Theologie,* vol.1, Frankfurt on Main: Andreäische Buchhandlung, 1834. T. CHRISTLIEB, *Leben u. Lehre des Johannes Scotus Eriugena in ihrem Zusammenhang mit der vorhergehenden und unter Angabe ihre Berührungspuncte mit der neueren Theologie,* Gotha: Besser, 1860. W. KAULICH, *Das spekulative System des Johannes Scotus Eriugena,* Prag: Gerzabek, 1860. J. HUBER, *Johannes Scotus Erigena. Ein Beitrag zur Geschichte der Philosophie und Theologie im MA,* Munich: Lentner, 1861. W. KAULICH, *Die Entwicklung der scholastischen Philosophie von Johannes Scotus Erigena bis Abälard,* Prag: 1863. L. NOACK, *Johannes Scotus Erigena. Sein Leben u. seine Schriften, die Wissenschaft u. Bildung seiner Zeit, die Voraussetzungen seines Denkens u. Wissens u. der Gehalt seiner Weltanschauung,* Leipzig: Koschny, 1876.

[35] MAÏEUL CAPPUYNS, O. S. B., *Jean Scot Érigène. Sa vie, son oeuvre, sa pensée,* Louvain: Abbaye du Mont César and Paris: Desclée de Brouwer, 1933, (= Universitas Catholica Lovaniensis. Dissertationes ad gradum magistri in Facultate Theologica consequendum conscriptae, Series II. Tomus 26).

[36] JOHN J. O'MEARA, and LUDWIG BIELER (ed.), *The Mind of Eriugena. Papers of a Colloquium Dublin, 14–18 July 1970,* Dublin: Irish University Press, 1973. RENÉ ROQUES (ed.): *Jean Scot Érigène et l'histoire de la philosophie. Laon 7–12 juillet 1975,* Paris: Éditions du Centre National de la Recherche Scientifique, 1977, (= Actes du Colloque International No 561, Colloques Internationaux du Centre National de la Recherche Scientifique). WERNER BEIERWALTES, (ed.), *Eriugena. Studien zu seinen Quellen. Vorträge des III. Eriugena-Colloquiums Freiburg im Breisgau, 27.–30. August 1979,* Heidelberg: Carl Winter Verlag, 1980, (= Abhandlungen der Heidelberger Akademie der Wissenschaften, Philosophisch-historische Klasse; Jg. 1980, Abh. 3). G.-H. ALLARD, (ed.), *Jean Scot écrivain. Actes*

Many of the most important articles on Eriugena have appeared within these collected volumes. In recent years three important clusters of essays on Eriugena have appeared: a special issue of the *American Philosophical Quarterly* from 2005; in 2006, a collection of articles edited by STEPHEN GERSH and DERMOT MORAN under the title: *Eriugena, Berkeley, and the Idealist Tradition;* and, in 2007 a Festschrift for Robert D. Crouse[37].

Édouard Jeauneau, the editor of many of the critical editions of Eriugena's writings, published the essays which he wrote between 1969 and 1985 on Eriugena in a collection in 1987[38]. These essays contribute greatly to an adequate interpretation of the cultural, philosophical and theological significance of the Eriugenian oeuvre. The research of the scholar Werner Beierwaltes has also been published in an essay-collection which appeared in 1994 and which bears witness to the long term commitment of this world-renowned expert on Neoplatonism to the interpretation of the writings of Eriugena[39].

The textual basis for the investigation of Eriugena's thought is improving from year to year[40]. Of special significance for the study at hand is the publication of a critical edition of Eriugena's most important work, *Periphyseon*[41].

---

*du IVe colloque international. Montréal 28 août–2 septembre 1983.* Montréal / Paris: Cahiers d'études médiévales. Cahier spécial 1, 1986. WERNER BEIERWALTES, *Eriugena Redivivus. Zur Wirkungsgeschichte seines Denkens im Mittelalter und im Übergang zur Neuzeit. Vorträge des V. Internationalen Eriugena-Colloquiums Werner-Reimers-Stiftung Bad Homburg, 26.–30. August 1985,* Heidelberg: Carl Winter Universitätsverlag, 1987. CLAUDIO LEONARDI and ENRICO MENESTÒ, (ed.), Giovanni Scoto nel suo tempo. WERNER BEIERWALTES, (ed.), *Begriff und Metapher. Sprachform des Denkens bei Eriugena. Vorträge des VII. Internationalen Eriugena-Colloquiums Werner-Reimers-Stiftung Bad Homburg 26.–29. Juli 1989,* Heidelberg: Carl Winter Universitätsverlag, 1990, (= Abhandlungen der Heidelberger Akademie der Wissenschaften, Philosophisch-historische Klasse; Jg. 1990, Abh. 3). BERNARD MCGINN and WILLEMIEN OTTEN (ed.), *Eriugena. East and West. Papers of the Eighth International Colloquium of the Society for the Promotion of Eriugenian Studies, Chicago and Notre Dame 18–20 October 1991,* Notre Dame, Indiana: Univ. of Notre Dame Press, 1994, (= Notre Dame Conferences in Medieval Studies, No 5). GERD VAN RIEL, CARLOS STEEL and J. MCEVOY (ed.), *Iohannes Scottus Eriugena. The Bible and Hermeneutics,* Leuven: Leuven University Press, 1996. JAMES MCEVOY and MICHAEL DUNNE, (ed.) *History and Eschatology in John Scottus Eriugena and his Time,* Leuven: Leuven University Press, 2002, (= Ancient and Medieval Philosophy. De Wulf-Mansion Centre, Series 1; 30).

[37] *American Catholic Philosophical Quarterly* 79 (2005); GERSH, STEPHEN and DERMOT MORAN (ed.). *Eriugena, Berkeley, and the Idealist Tradition,* Notre Dame: Notre Dame University Press, 2006; MICHAEL TRESCHOW, WILLEMIEN OTTEN, WALTER HANNAM (ed.), *Divine creation in ancient, medieval, and early modern thought. Essays presented to the Reverend Robert D. Crouse,* Leiden: Brill, 2007, (= Brill's Studies in Intellectual History; 151).

[38] ÉDOUARD JEAUNEAU, *Études Érigéniennes,* Paris: Études Augustiniennes, 1987.

[39] WERNER BEIERWALTES, *Eriugena. Grundzüge seines Denkens,* Frankfurt: Klostermann, 1994.

[40] *Joannis Scoti opera quae supersunt omnia,* H. J. FLOSS (ed.), Paris: Migne, 1853, 1865, (= Patrologiae Cursus Completus, Series Latina CXXII). *Iohannis Scotti Annotationes in Marcianum,* CORA E. LUTZ (ed.), Cambridge, Massachusetts: The Mediaeval Academy of America, 1939, reprint 1987. Le Commentaire érigénien sur Martianus Capella, De nuptiis Lib. I, d'après le manuscrit d'Oxford Bodl. Lib. Auct. T. 2. 19, fol. 1–31, E. JEAUNEAU (ed.), in: *Quatre thèmes érigéniens* (Conférence Albert-le-Grand 1974) Montréal / Paris: 1978, pp. 101–186.

Since the beginning of the eighties a series of monographs has appeared among which the studies of Gangolf Schrimpf, Carlo Riccati, John J. O'Meara, Dermot Moran, Ulrich Rudnick, Willemien Otten, Dirk Ansorge and Sebastian Weiner deserve special mention[42]. The studies completed by Otten and Ansorge were originally submitted as doctoral theses in theology[43]. For this reason they are devoted special attention in what follows.

---

*Iohannis Scotti De diuina praedestinatione,* G. MADEC (ed.), Turnhout, 1978, (= Corpus Christianorum. Continuatio Mediaeualis L).

JOANNES SCOTUS, *Versio operum S. Dionysii Areopagitae,* in: PL 122.

*Maximi Confessoris Quaestiones ad Thalassium, una cum latina interpretatione Ioannis Scotti Eriugenae,* CARL LAGA und CARLOS STEEL (ed.), Turnhout: 1980; 1990, (= Corpus Christianorum, Series Graeca 7; 22).

*Maximi Confessoris Ambigua ad Iohannem, iuxta Iohannis Scotti Eriugenae Latinam interpretationem,* ÉDOUARD JEAUNEAU, (ed.), Turnhout: Brepols / Leuven: Leuven University Press, 1988, (= Corpus Christianorum, Series Graeca, 18.).

"Le '*De Imagine*' de Grégoire de Nysse traduit par Jean Scot Érigène", MAÏEUL CAPPUYNS, (ed.), in: *Revue de théologie ancienne et médiévale* 32 (1965) 205–262.

*Iohannis Scoti Eriugenae, Expositiones in ierarchiam coelestem,* J. BARBET, (ed.), Turnhout: Brepols, 1975, (= Corpus Christianorum Continuatio Mediaeualis 31).

Ioannis Scotti Eriugenae Carmina, MICHAEL HERREN, (ed.), Dublin: School of Celtic Studies / Dublin Institute for Advanced Studies, 1993, (= Scriptores Latini Hiberniae, vol. XII).

*Jean Scot. Homélie sur le Prologue de Jean,* ÉDOUARD JEAUNEAU (ed.), Paris: CERF, 1969, (= Sources Chrétiennes 151).

*Jean Scot. Commentaire sur l'évangile de Jean,* ÉDOUARD JEAUNEAU (ed.), Paris: CERF, 1972, (= Sources Chrétiennes 180).

*Widmungsbrief zu De Praedestinatione,* E. DÜMMLER, (ed.), in: *Monumenta Germaniae historica* Epist. V 630 and following.

Widmungsbriefe zu den Übersetzungen des Ps. Dionysius und des Maximus Confessor, E. DÜMMLER (ed.), in: *Monumenta Germaniae historica* Epist. VI 158–162.

*Glossae Divinae Historiae. The Biblical Glosses of John Scottus Eriugena,* edited with an introduction by JOHN J. CONTRENI and PÁDRAIG P. Ó NÉILL, Florence: SISMEL–Edizioni del Galluzzo, 1997.

[41] See my p. 2, footnote 1 for information on the critical editions of *Periphyseon*. See also DAVID C.GREETHAM, "Édouard Jeauneau's edition of the 'Periphyseon' in light of contemporary editorial theory", in: *American Catholic Philosophical Quarterly* 79 (2005) 527–548.

[42] GANGOLF SCHRIMPF, *Das Werk des Johannes Scottus Eriugena im Rahmen des Wissenschaftsverständnisses seiner Zeit. Eine Hinführung zu Periphyseon,* Münster: Aschendorff, 1982, (= Beiträge zur Geschichte der Philosophie und Theologie des Mittelalters, Neue Folge vol. 23). CARLO RICCATI, *'Processio' et 'Explicatio'. La doctrine de la création chez Jean Scot et Nicolas de Cues,* Naples: Bibliopolis, 1983, (= Istituto italiano per gli studi filosofici, Serie Studi, VI). JOHN J. O'MEARA, *Eriugena.* New York: Clarendon Press, Oxford University Press, 1988. DERMOT MORAN, *The Philosophy of John Scottus Eriugena. A Study of Idealism in the Middle Ages,* Cambridge: Cambridge University Press, 1989. ULRICH RUDNICK, *Das System des Johannes Scottus Eriugena. Eine theologisch-philosophische Studie zu seinem Werk.* Frankfurt-Bern-New York-Paris: Peter Lang, 1990. WILLEMIEN OTTEN, *The anthropology of Johannes Scottus Eriugena.* Leiden: Brill, 1991, (= Brill's studies in intellectual history, vol. 20). DIRK ANSORGE, *Johannes Scottus Eriugena. Wahrheit als Prozeß. Eine theologische Interpretation von "Periphyseon",* Innsbruck: Tyrolia Verlag, 1996 (= Innsbrucker theologische Studien, 44). WEINER, SEBASTIAN FLORIAN. *Eriugenas negative Ontologie,* Amsterdam / Philadelphia: B. R. Grüner, 2007, (= Bochumer Studien zur Philosophie; 46).

[43] RUDNICK too refers to his dissertation in its subtitle as "*eine theologisch-philosophische Studie*". The study, however, owes much to the methods of the philosophy of religion and led to the conferral

Many academic investigations of Eriugenian thought, be they monographs or articles, concentrate their attention on Eriugena's method. For example, the *Habilitationsschrift* of Gangolf Schrimpf is mainly concerned with Eriugena's academic intention or goal. Rudnick too is more concerned with a methodological aim, one that shows the "*Verwandtschaft Eriugenas mit dem irisch-keltischen Denken*"[44], than with a presentation of the contents of his teaching.

There are some studies which focus on Eriugena's presentation of specific themes. Here we may distinguish between those which investigate a particular limited theme as handled by Eriugena (of these there are hundreds)[45] and, on the other hand, the series of attempts to encapsulate his central doctrine or to identify the key to interpreting his system as a whole (or at least *Periphyseon* as his major work).

Taking into account that *Periphyseon* deals extensively with the first three chapters of Genesis, G.-H. Allard suggested in an important essay that one could interpret *Periphyseon* as a whole as an example of 'hexaemeral' literature[46]. His analysis has difficulty in explaining the role of book one within *Periphyseon*. It is difficult to explain that book's investigation of the possibility of an application of the Aristotelian categories to God within the logic of a Hexaemeron. Nevertheless this interpretation of Eriugena's theology in terms of creation functioned as an inspiring impetus for further studies.

Carlo Riccati's doctoral dissertation also devoted much attention to the creational aspect of Eriugena's synthesis[47]. He linked the theme of the creation of the world with that of its return to the creator at the end of time. Riccati was more interested in Eriugena's heirs in the history of thought rather than in those authors who served as sources for him. He thus extensively compared Eriugena with Cusanus. Riccati's interpretation tended to concentrate on Eriugena as a philosopher not a theologian, a tendency already criticised by Werner Beierwaltes[48].

---

of a doctorate in philosophy. F. WEINER's study *Eriugenas negative Ontologie* understands itself as an investigation of Eriugena's philosophy: "*Doch was ist seine philosophische Leistung, aufgrund der er als bedeutender Philosoph zu gelten hat?*", WEINER, p. 3. Weiner's investigation concentrates on the first book of *Periphyseon*.

[44] RUDNICK, Das System des Johannes Scottus Eriugena, p. 344.

[45] See MARY BRENNAN, *Guide des études érigéniennes. Bibliographie commentée des publications 1930–1987/A Guide to Eriugenian Studies. A Survey of Publications 1930–1987*, Fribourg (Switzerland): Éditions Universitaire, 1989, (= Vestigia, vol. 5). Two supplements to this bibliography has been compiled by GERD VAN RIEL, "A Bibliographical Survey of Eriugenian Studies 1987–1995", in: GERD VAN RIEL et.al., (ed.), Iohannes Scottus Eriugena. The Bible and Hermeneutics, pp. 367–400; GERD VAN RIEL, "Eriugenian Studies 1995–2000," in: JAMES McEVOY, MICHAEL DUNNE, (ed.), *History and Eschatology in John Scottus Eriugena and his time*, pp. 611–626.

[46] GUY-H. ALLARD, "La structure littéraire de la composition du *De diuisione naturae*", in: JOHN J. O'MEARA and LUDWIG BIELER (ed.), The Mind of Eriugena, pp. 147–157.

[47] CARLO RICCATI, 'Processio' et 'Explicatio'.

[48] Compare WERNER BEIERWALTES book review of Riccati's study, in: *Mitteilungen und Forschungsbeiträge der Cusanus-Gesellschaft* 17 (1986) 272–277. Beierwaltes writes: "*Den sogenannten christlichen Platonismus beider Autoren betrachtet Riccati offensichtlich als reine Philosophie ... Die*

Brian Stock's article from 1967 and Willemien Otten's dissertation from 1991 represent the two most significant studies of Eriugena's anthropology[49]. Willemien Otten presents anthropology as the key to Eriugena's synthesis. In her book she draws attention to the fact that for Eriugena the appearing of God in the human is an apex of divine manifestation. Otten correctly points out that for all Eriugena's emphasis on the appearing of God in nature as a whole, the appearing of God in the human person retains a special priority within his system. Through this insight she has had a marked and lasting influence on Eriugenian research. Otten's study with its investigation of two main carriers of the manifestation of God, i. e. the human person and nature as a whole, is an important point of reference for my own study. However, her research is in need of a supplementary consideration of Eriugena's understanding of the appearing of God in Jesus Christ. Furthermore, not all her conclusions on those aspects of his thought to which she does devote attention, are beyond question. For example in her conclusion she relates the notions of theophany, the infinitude of the universe, the infinity of God and human rationality in a synthesis with which I am not fully in agreement[50]. She suggests that the role of the cognitive ability of the human creature as thinking subject is not only devoted more attention by Eriugena in books four and five of *Periphyseon,* but attains a different status with respect to the initiative of God in self-revelation through *natura.* The ascending, returning human reason is assigned an initiating and measuring role which was not communicated by the notion of theophany as used in the earlier books. Here, Otten wrote: "Eriugena introduced the concept of theophany to express the indefinable divine presence in the universe. Thus the outstretched universe became the very instrument by which knowledge of the divine was communicated to created nature, especially to man. All the while the initiative was clearly on the side of the divine essence itself. It was God's will to manifest himself in created nature."[51] She views Eriugena's notion of theophany as unsuccessful: "In a sense, the notion of theophany could only imply its own failure. Be that as it may, after our anthropological reading of the *Periphyseon* the theophanic spell of the universe has in fact been broken, for man seems to impose his rational standards on the universe he investigates rather than letting himself be intimidated by something that from the very start would transcend his human capacities."[52] Again on the eschatological level she wrote, "In the paradisiacal theophanies to which man will return it appears that it is a human hand, viz. Eriugena's, as it writes the *Periphyseon,* that controls the manifestation of God just as much as

---

*spezifischen Gehalte christlicher Religion seien verdeckt oder verfremdet, es gebe z. B. wenig Raum für einen 'personalen', sich gnadenhaft eröffnenden Gott, Inkarnation werde zu Symbol oder Metapher herabgestuft. Diese These halte ich in ihrer extremem Form nicht für angemessen.",* p. 276.

[49] BRIAN STOCK, "The Philosophical Anthropology of Johannes Scottus Eriugena", in: *Studi Mediaevali,* 3a Serie, 8 (1967) 1–57; W. OTTEN, The Anthropology of Johannes Scottus Eriugena.

[50] See WILLEMIEN OTTEN, The Anthropology of Johannes Scottus Eriugena, pp. 214–219.

[51] W. OTTEN, The Anthropology of Johannes Scottus Eriugena, p. 214.

[52] W. OTTEN, The Anthropology of Johannes Scottus Eriugena, p. 215.

God himself does."[53] Otten's study invites the reaction of further studies and gives rise to some questions. May not the Eriugenian notion of theophany and the concept of the appearing of God in the human person be somewhat differently related? Is the moment of divine initiative not more strongly preserved even in the later books of *Periphyseon* than Otten's conclusion suggests?[54] Further, one must go beyond Otten's *Periphyseon*-centred book to raise the question of Eriugena's sources for his manifestational anthropology. A detailed investigation of the influence of Gregory of Nyssa on Eriugena sheds new light on how the Carolingian author understood God to appear in the human as created in the image of God[55].

A second theological investigation which attempts to present a comprehensive interpretation of *Periphyseon* is Dirk Ansorge's dissertation, published in 1996[56]. Ansorge tried to present the impetus which inspired Eriugena's thought: "*die Eriugenas Denken bewegende Sache*"[57]. According to Ansorge, Eriugena's central insight is that the world exists as creation and that all individual beings reveal God as their creative cause[58].

From the point of view of this central theme the study may be linked to a chain of writings which attempt to present Eriugena's understanding of creation[59]. Ansorge is heir to the writings of Hoeps[60], Brueren[61], Moran[62] and Beierwaltes[63] on

---

[53] W. OTTEN, The Anthropology of Johannes Scottus Eriugena, p. 218.

[54] It is mainly in chapter four of my study that I analyse these questions. Further, I reflect on the relative roles of the notion of theophany and the appearing of God in, and through, the human person in my chapter six.

[55] For example since 2004 help in understanding the influence of Gregory is provided by José Antonio Pachas' well documented summary of common ground between the thought of Gregory of Nyssa and Eriugena: JOSÉ ANTONIO PACHAS. "Influencia de Gregorio de Nisa sobre Juan Escoto Eriúgena: aproximación a partir del "Periphyseon", in: *Teología y vida* 45 (2004) 539–563.

[56] DIRK ANSORGE, Johannes Scottus Eriugena. Wahrheit als Prozeß.

[57] DIRK ANSORGE, Johannes Scottus Eriugena. Wahrheit als Prozeß, p. 334.

[58] "Diese Grundidee ist Eriugenas Annahme, daß die Welt 'Schöpfung' und alles Seiende Erscheinung Gottes als des schöpferischen Ursprungs von allem ist.", ANSORGE, Johannes Scottus Eriugena. Wahrheit als Prozeß, p. 334.

[59] Ansorge refers to the publications of many previous interpreters of Eriugena, he does not however enter into dialogue with the results of their research. For example, in his footnotes he gives many references to the dissertation of Willemien Otten, but nowhere does he discuss her ideas or her thesis on the relationship between the human person and nature as a whole as carriers of divine manifestation. Ansorge's dissertation thus fails to take account of a stage in the interpretation of this issue which has been accepted as a milestone in academic circles.

In Ansorge's own conclusion we observe that Eriugena's understanding of creation and his understanding of truth are both of central importance for his dissertation. This reveals that his academic concerns are similar to those of CARLO RICCATI in his treatment of Eriugena (Processio et Explicatio). Ansorge only makes one passing reference to this work (ANSORGE, Johannes Scottus Eriugena. Wahrheit als Prozeß, p. 292).

[60] REINHARD HOEPS, "Theophanie und Schöpfungsgrund. Der Beitrag des Johannes Scottus Eriugena zum Verständnis der *creatio ex nihilo*", in: *Theologie und Philosophie* 67 (1992) 161–191.

[61] RAINIER BRUEREN, "Die Schrift als Paradigma der Wahrheit. Gedanken zum Vorbegriff der Metaphysik bei Johannes Scotus Eriugena", in: WERNER BEIERWALTES, (ed.), Begriff und Metapher, pp. 187–201.

this subject matter, his own hermeneutic is however, as he himself admits, heavily influenced by the philosophy of Husserl, Heidegger and Gadamer[64].

Ansorge's main aim is however, not the presentation of a particular individual thematic, but the investigation of how *Periphyseon* may be grasped as a whole. He goes through the books of *Periphyseon* and relates them to the theme of creation. He succeeds in showing how creation is a central theme for books one to three of Periphyseon[65]. The threads with which he links the contents of books four and five with the central idea which he ascribes to Eriugena are less densely spun. He gravely minimises the systematic content of book four and five. He writes: "Auf eine Analyse der Ausführungen zu den ersten fünf Schöpfungstagen, mit denen Eriugena seine im zweiten Buch von PERIPHYSEON begonnene Auslegung von Gen. 1–3 fortsetzt, wird im Folgenden verzichtet. Inhaltlich gehen diese Ausführungen nicht über bereits Bekanntes hinaus. In ihrer Orientierung am Text des biblischen Schöpfungsberichtes stellen sie keinen systematisch eigenständigen Entwurf dar."[66] He applies this not only to parts of book three but to the remaining books of *Periphyseon* too.[67] Must we not ask whether the aim which he set himself of demonstrating the unity and wholeness of *Periphyseon* is not jeopardised by this?

In undertaking to produce a theological interpretation of *Periphyseon* Ansorge certainly identified a deficit in the research on Eriugena: there is no comprehensive assessment of Eriugena precisely as a theologian. However, the question must be raised whether his own attempt really removes this desideratum. His dissertation is certainly theocentric. He orbits around what he perceives as the hidden presence, the "*Entzogene Anwesenheit*" of God in all creation. His investigation is however not theological in the sense that it examines or assesses Eriugena's method precisely as theological. Ansorge does not independently investigate Eriugena's orientation to Scripture nor his hermeneutic of ecclesial writers[68]. The criterion according to which he passes judgement on *Periphyseon* is reduced to that which he has in common with a philosophising interpreter: Ansorge investigates whether *Periphyseon* may be read as a coherent unity or whole.

---

[62] Dermot Moran, The Philosophy of John Scottus Eriugena.

[63] Many of Beierwaltes' publications are mentioned by Ansorge.

[64] See D. Ansorge, Johannes Scottus Eriugena. Wahrheit als Prozeß, p. 38, footnote 67.

[65] Although Ansorge seems to experience some difficulty in his 47 page long attempt to show how the account of the ten categories in book one is not a digression!

[66] D. Ansorge, Johannes Scottus Eriugena. Wahrheit als Prozeß, p. 248.

[67] "Dies gilt im übrigen auch für die beiden verbleibenden Bücher IV und V von PERIPHYSEON. Allein Eriugenas Ausführungen über das Erkennen des Menschen im vierten Buch von PERIPHYSEON können noch einmal als ein systematisch einheitlicher Entwurf gelesen werden." D. Ansorge, Johannes Scottus Eriugena. Wahrheit als Prozeß, p. 248, footnote 113.

[68] He makes approving references to the work of Rainier Brueren on the Scripture as the paradigm of truth in Eriugena's thought and the positive position of Scripture in Eriugena's writings. Ansorge's own dissertation contains few places where he himself reflects on the role of Scripture in Eriugena's method. See Rainier Brueren, Die Schrift als Paradigma der Wahrheit, pp. 187–201, see D. Ansorge, Johannes Scottus Eriugena. Wahrheit als Methode, pp. 32–33; 248–49.

We may conclude that there already exist studies, compiled in the past and more recently, which shed some light on the chosen topic, the appearing of God according to Eriugena. Still I suggest, that however helpful the research to date is, it has not yet given an adequate account of all the carriers of the divine manifestation as they appear in the writings of Eriugena, in their individual functions and in their mutual relations. Thus the aim of the study as outlined above, not only retains its legitimacy in the face of the research to date, but indeed is inspired by the work of other scholars (and, indeed, their shortcomings) to pursue further the theme of the appearing of God.

Nor is an additional assessment of the method of Eriugena as a biblically oriented theologian redundant. Precisely when we consider those studies which have treated the manifestation of God in Eriugena we notice that they are very often carried through by scholars who have a philosophical background. It is often experts on the philosophy of Neoplatonism who take up Eriugena's writings and bring the questions of a philosopher to them[69]. And yet the thematic of the divine manifestation itself, precisely as it is handled by Eriugena, demands to be considered from a theological perspective. The following are two brief exemplary reasons for insisting on a theological interpretation of his writings on this matter:

In the first place, Eriugena's presentation of the manifestation of God in creation follows the biblical account of the creation of the world and culminates in a theological anthropology which centres on the biblically rooted understanding of the human person as created in the image of God. The dynamic of Eriugena's system and the movement of the biblical account concur. The appearing of God in the human is a very important facet of Eriugena's system as a whole. An adequate reflection on Eriugena's presentation of the appearing of God in the human person must explicitly consider his exegesis and interpretation of scripture.

---

[69] Among the relevant secondary literature are the titles:

WERNER BEIERWALTES, "Negati Affirmatio. Welt als Metapher. Zur Grundlegung einer mittelalterlichen Äesthetik durch Johannes Scotus Eriugena", in: RENÉ ROQUES (ed), Jean Scot Érigène et l'histoire de la philosophie, pp. 263–276; B. BOŠNJAK, "Dialektik der Theophanie. Über den Begriff der Natur bei J. S. Eriugena", in: *La Filosofia della Natura nel Medioevo* (Atti del Terzo congresso internazionale di filosofia medioevale, Passo della Mendola (Trento) 31 agosto–5 settembre 1964), Milan: 1966, pp. 264–271; DONALD F. DUCLOW, "Pseudo-Dionysius, John Scotus Eriugena, Nicholas of Cusa. An Approach to the Hermeneutic of the Divine Names", in: *International Philosophical Quarterly* 12 (1972) 260–278; TULLIO GREGORY, "Note sulla dottrina delle 'teofanie' in Giovanni Scoto Eriugena", in: *Studi medievali* 3a ser. IV (1963) 75–91; R. HOEPS, "Theophanie und Schöpfungsgrund"; R. ROQUES, I. Théophanie et nature chez Jean Scot Erigène; II. Explication de textes érigéniens et pseudo-dionysiens, *École Pratique des Hautes Études. Section des sciences religieuses. Annuaire 1965–66,* Paris: 1965, pp. 156–161; R. ROQUES, I. Théophanie et nature chez Jean Scot Erigène; II. Explication de quelques passages du De divisione naturae, *École Pratique des Hautes Études. Section des sciences religieuses. Annuaire 1966–67,* Paris: 1967, pp. 162–167; J. TROUILLARD, "Eriugène et la théophanie créatrice", in: J. J. O'MEARA and L. BIELER (ed.), The Mind of Eriugena, pp. 98–113; J. TROUILLARD, "La notion de 'théophanie' chez Erigène", in: S. BRÉTON et. al. *Manifestation et révélation,* Paris: Institut Catholique de Paris, 1976, pp. 15–39, (= *Philosophie* I).

Secondly, in his presentation of the perception of the manifestation of the divine, Eriugena draws not only on the *'ascensio mentis in divina mysteria'*[70] of the Pseudo-Dionysius but also on the divine *descensus* as emphasised in the writings of Maximus Confessor[71] as categories to describe the encounter. Maximus' account of the encounter with God in theophany is radically Christological and stresses the initiative and condescension of God to us in Christ. Eriugena's thought, heir to the writings of Maximus on the preconditions of the divine appearing, must also be approached from a theological perspective sensitive to the Christological context of this divine condescension.

## 3. The *ductus* of the investigation

Following on the preliminary clarifications (issue and aim of the study, report on research to date, outline of the *ductus* of the investigation, indication of the methods adopted in the investigation) the first chapter deals with the development which Eriugena's own thought experienced in the course of his writing career. Then follow chapters two to five which present Eriugena's understanding of the chosen thematic, the appearing of God. Chapter six is a three-fold reflection on Eriugena's system. There is a so-called historical reflection in which the author's appropriation of material from his sources is assessed. A reflection on his academic methods follows. Here the central question of the theological character of his writings will be raised. Finally, the systematic reflection reviews the various facets of Eriugena's understanding of the appearing of God.

## 4. A note on the methods adopted in the investigation

Since this study investigates a specific theme in a thinker of the past it must employ a spectrum of historical and systematic methods.

### *4.1 Historical methods*

The ultimate aim of this study is a theological assessment of Eriugena's system, that is, an assessment of the chosen thematic with a sensitivity to the author as a writer

---

[70] *Expositiones in ierarchiam coelestem,* J. Barbet (ed.), Cap. I, 262–263, p. 8, (= PL 122 132D).

[71] See PP I, JEAUNEAU (ed.), CCCM CLXI, 325–326, p. 14, (PL 122 449D).

In the following the five books of *Periphyseon* shall be abbreviated as PP I, PP II, PP III, PP IV, PP V. Books one to five are quoted according to the edition of Édouard Jeauneau in Corpus Christianorum (see my p. 2, footnote 1). (Since the same editor, Jeauneau, is responsible for two editions of book four, the one in Scriptores Latini Hiberniae, the other in Corpus Christianorum, in the case of a reference to book four, the series is always explicitly mentioned.) The numeration in Migne, *Patrologiae cursus completus, series latina* (PL) is always given in brackets.

within the Christian tradition and as one who is oriented to an interpretation of that religion's sacred scripture. This study can, however, in no way dispense with historical research on the Carolingian period[72]. The interest of the theologically trained eye may grasp its subject matter more precisely, when it can determine just what in the object of its attention is a response to the inspiring scripture, and what is a cultural common-place of the ninth century[73]. Eriugena's thought has to be situated in the context of the learning of his day and his contemporary school system. The Carolingian school system has been the object of the research of such scholars as Pierre Riché[74] and indeed Eriugena's scientific method in it's relationship to, and distinction from, the scientific self-understanding of the surrounding educational system has been analysed in Gangolf Schrimpf's work[75]. Other scholars (for example, J. M. Wallace-Hadrill, John Contreni, and Rosamond McKitterick[76]) have opted to situate Eriugena more clearly within the circle of scholars of his time than Schrimpf's writings have done.

Nor is the study of Eriugena's sources, that is, of writers who lived before him, an 'optional extra'. Even if the investigation at hand focuses on a particular theme as expounded by our author, that is, it is primarily interested in his internal systematic, we can only adequately grasp this inner logic when the historical preconditions of the elements of which the system consists have been considered. Now Eriugena stood at a very interesting juncture of the Christian reception of Neoplatonic philosophy. The writers Gregory of Nyssa, Ps. Dionysius, Augustine of Hippo and Maximus Confessor had thoroughly imbued the 'platonic' philosophy encountered in their formal education. They had however transformed it each in their own way within their syntheses. Eriugena in turn was heir to this 'theologised' Neoplaton-

---

[72] Nor is a distinction between secular historical research and church history relevant here: Church history may indicate a focus of interest – events are selected for attention because of their relevance for the emerging christian community and they are related to this Christian community – the discipline does not however offer the researcher different facts to her / his secular counterpart. Compare NORBERT BROX, "Fragen zur 'Denkform' der Kirchengeschichte", in: *Zeitschrift für Kirchengeschichte* 90 Vierte Folge 28 (1979) 1–21, especially pp. 12–13.

[73] This is not to suggest that all cultural baggage may be cleanly severed away from a pristine Christian carrier. We may however say something about the historical conditions which favoured one form of expression of a Christian truth which has experienced several successive cultural appropriations and expressions.

[74] PIERRE RICHÉ, *Écoles et enseignement dans le Haut Moyen Age de la fin du Ve au milieu du XIe siècle*, Paris, 1979.

[75] GANGOLF SCHRIMPF, Das Werk des Johannes Scottus Eriugena.

[76] "Eriugena belonged to a circle, however much he might tower within it. ... Eriugena shared a common background in the liberal arts with Wulfad, Heiric, Hildebold, Hincmar, Lupus and many others, ..." J. M. WALLACE-HADRILL, *The Frankish Church*, Oxford: Clarendon Press, 1983, (= Oxford History of the Christian Church), p. 376; JOHN J. CONTRENI, *Carolingian Learning, Masters and Manuscripts*. London: Variorum Reprints, 1992. ROSAMOND MCKITTERICK, "The Palace School of Charles the Bald", in: MARGARET GIBSON and JANET NELSON, (ed.), Charles the Bald: Court and Kingdom, pp. 385–400. See too PIERRE RICHÉ, "Charles le Chauve et la culture de son temps", in: R. ROQUES, Jean Scot Érigène et l'histoire de la philosophie, pp. 37–46 and compare the essays in CLAUDIO LEONARDI and ENRICO MENESTÒ, (ed.), Giovanni Scoto nel suo tempo.

ism[77]. "*Das 'Neuplatonische' in Eriugenas 'Philosophie' ist ihm ausschließlich durch seine <u>theologischen</u> 'auctoritates' vermittelt und so gegenüber dem ursprünglichen Aspekt dieses Denkens in einer theologisch schon modifizierten Form des philosophischen Gedankens.*"[78] It is not clear that he had direct contact with philosophical writings. My investigation has thus been limited to an explicit investigation of those writers who influenced him directly, that is, those authors to whose writings we believe that he had direct access. However, I hope to have preserved a sensibility to the "philosophical implications" (to use Werner Beierwaltes' expression) of certain moments in their writings and Eriugena's own writings[79].

The second criterion for the selection of the sources who receive extensive attention in chapter six, is that they have influenced Eriugena precisely in this grasp of the thematic with which this investigation is concerned: that is, they have influenced his understanding of the appearing of God. Within chapter six these sources are handled in the order in which Eriugena engaged in an intense confrontation with their writings (in the case of Augustine), or, in the case of the Greek thinkers, the order in which he translated them into Latin.

## 4.2 Systematic methods

Eriugena neither separated theology and philosophy nor distinguished their methods from each other. In the words of Werner Beierwaltes:

*'Philosophie' und 'Theologie' machen in diesem Denken eine dialektisch sich einander bedingende Einheit aus: ursprünglich Philosophisches ist in die Intention der Theologie aufgehoben, primär Theologisches (etwa ein durch die Heilige Schrift initiierter oder geforderter Gedanke) ist durch philosophische Reflexion und Argumentation in die Dimension des Begriffs eingeführt; das, was in der Theologiegeschichte – durch die Inkarnation des Gottes als ein eschatologischer Prozeß bestimmt – Bild oder Symbol ist, hat im philosophischen Gedanken seine Reflexionsform gefunden; diese wiederum schließt das geoffenbarte Wort in einer Weise auch sachlich bestimmend auf, wozu es von ihm selbst her nicht imstande wäre.*[80]

It falls, however, to a study of his thought from the perspective of the 21st century to lay open those methods which the study itself employs, and to make some distinctions between the respective methods of these disciplines.

---

[77] "*Wenn man die geringen Folgen eines <u>direkten</u> Bezugs Eriugenas zu griechischer Philosophie im Blick hat, so ergibt sich für das "Philosophische" in ihm ohne Zweifel dies: Nicht Platonisches, nicht Aristotelisches, sondern der <u>Neuplatonismus</u> ist die methodisch und sachlich bestimmende Grundstruktur von Eriugenas philosphischer Theologie. Allerdings wird sich ein direkter, historisch verifizierbarer Bezug Eriugenas zu <u>genuin</u>-neuplatonischen Quellen, also etwa zu Plotin, Porphyrios oder Proklos, schwerlich nachweisen lassen.*", W. BEIERWALTES, "*Plato philosophantium de mundo maximus*", in: IDEM, Eriugena. Grundzüge, pp. 32–51, here p. 35.

[78] Ibidem.

[79] See WERNER BEIERWALTES, Eriugena. Grundzüge, p. 34.

[80] W. BEIERWALTES, "Plato philosophantium de mundo maximus", p. 32.

Beierwaltes' thoughts, speaking albeit of Eriugena's synthesis, provide an excellent starting position: one may make a tentative distinction between the *origins* of certain ideas (occurrence in philosophical discourse / initiation through the scripture). Such a distinction is, of course, limited by the factual circumincession of biblical and platonic ideas not only in the ninth century but indeed in most epochs of Western culture. Beierwaltes is, of course, as the quotation shows, fully aware of this *factual* interdependence. Of interest is that he also speaks of ideas which are demanded by Scripture. Here their 'theological' primacy is not merely an account of their occurrence in a certain category of texts but of the fact that they are logically presupposed by the Word of revelation. Beierwaltes' distinctions are very helpful for investigating Eriugena's synthesis.

A complementary approach to the issue of the interdependance and autonomy of theology and philosophy arises from a consideration of their methods, and in particular from a consideration of the criteria according to which they proceed. This is the approach adopted in the study at hand. For this reason it is devoted a relatively extended treatment in what follows.

When one undertakes to analyse and assess a system of thought one may ask whether the system is logically coherent and whether the terms and arguments used within the system are consistently used. Coherence and consistency are two well established criteria for establishing the truth of a theory and they are common to philosophical and theological investigations. They shall be employed in assessing the system of Eriugena in this book.

Further, whether an explanatory system is intrinsically philosophical or intrinsically theological, it must attempt adequately to shed light on the existential questions of those persons whose assent it courts: the peak and trough experiences of the addressee demand an interpretation and explanation. At this juncture one may ask whether a system is not only coherent and consistent, but in addition whether it is *comprehensive,* that is, whether it may explain all human experiences (the full spectrum of human experiences at any one time and the train of successive experiences as they emerge in history). Here we may observe how a criterion which is of great importance for the study of religion and religious texts emerges. When the experience of religiously oriented persons is in question, then the measure against which the comprehensiveness of a system is measured does not consist in non-specific human experience (after all, there is no fully abstract human experience; instead there exist the concrete experiences of humans in their individual life-stories and value systems). Rather it consists in experience that is already informed by the attempt to live out a religious conviction. For example one may test the comprehensiveness of an explanatory system against its success (or lack thereof) in explaining lived religious experience.[81] The criterion of comprehensiveness, also a criterion

---

[81] One of the few academic studies of Eriugena which has attempted to integrate this criterion within its assessment of Eriugena is the dissertation of BRIAN McNAMARA, S.J., Emanation and re-

common to philosophical and theological assessments, is among those employed in the final assessment of Eriugena's position in the closing chapters of this study[82].

Christian *theology* is not only a speculative but also a positive science. It is concerned with the interpretation of the sacred scripture and the historical train of theologies which have emerged as the believing community interprets the bible. Thus a further criterion emerges with the question of whether a system is compatible with the content of the Scriptures[83]. This question emerges in a particularly visible form when the system of thought itself uses Scriptural quotations as premises in its argumentation. The question of the compatibility with scripture also emerges with respect to those accounts which do not explicitly refer to Scripture. The study at hand raises the question whether Eriugena has a clear biblical hermeneutic. This is approached above all in chapter six. With regard to the issue of the appearing of God, the question emerges whether Eriugena gives sufficient weight to the biblical accounts of the manifestation of God (including the Christological culmination as witnessed to by the New Testament).

One may also ask to what extent, and how, Eriugena integrates the theological tradition produced by earlier writers. His de facto appropriation of his sources with regard to the theme of the appearing of God is summarised in (6.1). The question of Eriugena's hermeneutic of his many sources is also raised as a methodological question (6.2). In this context the question of his understanding of the authority of the sources is touched upon.

The study at hand avails of methods and employs criteria which are common to philosophical and theological investigations alike. It also employs some methods and criteria which are specifically theological. It thus represents a primarily theological investigation and interpretation of Eriugena's system.

---

turn. A study of the relations between the Creator and man in the later work of Johannes Eriugena, (= A Dissertation submitted to the Faculty of Theology in partial fulfilment of the requirements for the Degree of Doctor, Faculty of Theology, St. Patrick's College Maynooth, Ireland), 1983. Due to the early death of Father McNamara this study has not been published. The following article may however be consulted: BRIAN McNAMARA, S. J., "The Ascent to Truth. Methodological Factors in the Writings of John Scotus Eriugena", in: *Milltown Studies* (1985) 1–31.

[82] For example, it might be asked to what extent Eriugena's account of the correlation between 'spiritual crucifixion' as in Gal. 6:14 and access to higher theophanies may adequately explain the religious experience of advancing in the spiritual life, see Comm. I, XXXII, 33–38, ÉDOUARD JEAUNEAU (ed.), p. 182.

[83] Implied is a dialogue with the findings of the current critical biblical exegesis and interpretation.

# Chapter 1

# The dynamic intellectual formation
# of Johannes Scottus Eriugena

The philosophical and theological edifice which Eriugena erected was the work of a lifetime. It is possible to trace the stages in the development of his thought. While this study is primarily concerned with Eriugena's mature position, it is advisable to consider the genesis of this synthesis in order to explain how passages from different stages of his writing, which at first glance might seem to be contradictory, are really steps in a development.

## 1. Eriugena: the historical context within which he lived

It is important to handle these topics because although the study at hand presents a theological interpretation of Eriugena, this interpretation is rooted in an appreciation of the author's own time and cultural circle. It is not however on the level of biography that the thesis seeks to make its main contribution. For this reason the main points are merely mentioned and footnote references to more detailed studies are indicated.

### 1.1 The sources for the reconstruction of a biography

Unfortunately a contemporary biography of the Irish scholar Johannes Scottus Eriugena does not exist[1]. What we do have are passing remarks about him found in the writings of several historical figures. In her 1986 collection of materials[2] relevant to the biography of Eriugena, Mary Brennan presents 37 testimonies to Eriugena, 11 of which stem from the ninth, and 3 from the tenth centuries.

His own writings too shed some light on his life story. For example his various poems or *Carmina* succeed in throwing light on his relationship to his patron, Charles the Bald, one of Charlemagne's grandsons.[3] Since John Contreni has es-

---

[1] The *Annals of St. Bertin,* the contemporary chronicle of the court of the emperor does not mention him; see MARY BRENNAN, "Materials for the Biography of Johannes Scottus Eriugena", in: *Studi Medievali* 27 (1986) 413–460, p. 413.

[2] MARY BRENNAN, "Materials for the Biography of Johannes Scottus Eriugena".

[3] See PAUL E. DUTTON, "Eriugena the Royal Poet", in: G.-H. ALLARD (ed.) *Jean Scot Écrivain,* pp. 51–80.

tablished the Eriugenian authorship of a set of Latin glosses on the Old Testament[4] further research has tried to extract possible clues about Eriugena's Irish origins from these glosses[5]. At the end of his major work *Periphyseon* Eriugena entrusts the manuscript to a certain Wulfad, probably the Abbot at Saint-Medard in Soissons, for examination and correction[6]. Such references also helps us to situate Eriugena within the network of scholars co-operating in the mid-ninth century[7].

In addition to his research on Eriugena's own writings, Contreni's research on Irish scholarship in general in the ninth century and the sources thereof, has shed much light on Eriugena and his role within the Irish academic community active in continental Europe[8].

On the basis of these sources what can we say about the life, context and work of Eriugena?

## *1.2 Eriugena and ninth century Ireland*[9]

The author of *Periphyseon* seems regularly to have called himself simply 'Iohannes'[10]. His contemporaries often referred to him with the additional term 'Scotus', thus Bishop Pardulus of Laon mention: "... *Scotum illum ... Joannem nomine* ..."[11]. At the beginning of his translation of the writings of Dionysius the pseudo Areopagite

---

[4] J. CONTRENI and P. Ó NÉILL, (ed.), *Glossae Divinae Historiae;* see JOHN CONTRENI, "The Biblical Glosses of Haimo of Auxerre and John Scottus Eriugena", in: *Speculum* 51 (1976) 411–434.

[5] See PÁDRAIG O'NÉILL, "The Old-Irish Words in Eriugena's Biblical Glosses", in: G.-H. ALLARD (ed.), *Jean Scot Écrivain,* pp. 287–297.

[6] PP V, 7363–7370, p. 227, (= PL 122 1022A).

[7] See JOHN MARENBON, "Wulfad, Charles the Bald and John Scottus Eriugena", in: MARGARET GIBSON and JANET NELSON (ed.), *Charles the Bald: Court and Kingdom. Papers based on a Colloquium held in London in April 1979,* Oxford: BAR, 1981, (= BAR International Series 101), pp. 375–383.

[8] See JOHN J. CONTRENI, *The Cathedral School of Laon from 850–930. Its Manuscripts and Masters,* Munich: Bei der Arbeo-Gesellschaft, 1978; IDEM, "Masters and Medicine in Northern France during the Reign of Charles the Bald", in: M. GIBSON and J. NELSON, Charles the Bald, pp. 333–350; IDEM, "The Irish 'Colony' at Laon during the time of John Scottus", in: R. ROQUES, Jean Scot Érigène et l'histoire de la Philosophie, pp. 59–67.

[9] The most recent detailed account of the relevant material is to be found in JOHN J. CONTRENI and PÁDRAIG P. Ó NÉILL's introduction to Glossae Divinae Historiae, pp. 11–85. See too MICHAEL HERREN's review of the material in his introduction to Iohannis Scotti Eriugenae Carmina, pp. 1–55. Compare the general accounts in: MAÏEUL CAPPUYNS O. S. B., Jean Scot Érigène, pp. 3–29; JOHN J. O'MEARA, Eriugena, pp. 1–9; DERMOT MORAN, The Philosophy of John Scottus Eriugena, pp. 2–7; JOHN J. O'MEARA and LUDWIG BIELER (ed.), The Mind of Eriugena, pp. ix–x.

[10] CAPPUYNS, Jean Scot Érigène, p. 5. On the names that other Irish emigrants called themselves on the continent see the introduction to JOHN J. CONTRENI AND PÁDRAIG P. Ó NÉILL (ed.), Glossae Divinae Historiae, p. 82.

[11] "*Sed quia haec inter se valde dissentiebant, Scotum illum qui est in palatio regis, Joannem nomine scribere coegimus*", quoted from S. REMIGIUS Lugdunensis Episcopus, *Liber de tribus Epistolis,* PL 121 1051D–1052A.

he is called 'Iohannes Eriugena'[12]. In the seventeenth century, the editor Thomas Gale popularised the combined form 'Scotus Eriugena': his edition of the *Periphyseon* was entitled *Joannis Scoti Erigenae de divisione naturae*[13]. The way of naming him is pleonastic because both the names '*Scotus*'[14] and '*Eriugena*'[15] reveal the Irish nationality of their bearer. Likewise Bishop Prudentius' remarks on the author as originating in '*Hibernia*' ("*Te solum omnium acutissimum Galliae transmisit Hibernia, ...*"[16]) also reveal the Irish origins of Eriugena.

More difficult is the matter of establishing Eriugena's date of birth. We can only estimate that it occurred some time in the first quarter of the ninth century[17]. Similarly difficult is the question of where in Ireland he was born or educated. Contreni hoped that the examinations of the old Irish words in Eriugena's biblical glosses might help locate his place of birth or where he was reared[18]. However, the Irish used in the glosses is the standard dialect-free form used by an educated class which toured around Ireland[19]. This standard form did not vary from area to area. The glosses do

---

[12] JOANNIS SCOTUS, *Versio operum S. Dionysii Areopagitae, De caelesti Ierarchia*, PL 122,1035–1036A, where the editor FLOSS gives precedence to the manuscripts with 'IERUGENA'. Cappuyns prefers 'Eriugena' arguing that it appears in the oldest testimonies; he likewise rejects 'Erigena' which appeared in a thirteenth century manuscript; see CAPPUYNS, Jean Scot Érigène, p. 5 together with footnotes 9 and 10, and p. 6 together with footnotes 1 and 2.

[13] Oxford, 1681. A previous use of the double form is attributed to Archbishop J. USSHER in his *Veterum epistolarum Hibernicarum sylloge*, Dublin: 1632 p. 57, see CAPPUYNS, Jean Scot Érigène, p. 7, footnote 1. On this point see also MARY BRENNAN, "Materials for the Biography of Johannes Scottus Eriugena", p. 414; O'MEARA, *Eriugena*, p. 1.

[14] In the ninth century '*Scottia*' indicated Ireland and only later in the wake of emigration from Ireland to Scotland did the latter take over the name, see CAPPUYNS, *Jean Scot Érigène*, p. 8. 'Scotus' was originally attributed to John, not so much as a proper surname, but more as an indication of nationality, thus Bishop PRUDENTIUS referred to him in his *De Praedestinatione* of 851 as 'a certain Scot' ("*ex libro cujusdam Scoti*", S. Prudentius Trecensis Episcopus, *De Praedestinatione contra Erigenam*, PL 115 1010C). 'Scotus' also appeared in the usage '*Scotigena*', used for example by ANASTASIUS BIBIOTHECARIUS in 875 ("*Mirandum est quoque, quomodo vir ille barbarus, qui in finibus mundi positus, quanto ab nominibus conversatione, tanto credi potuit alterius linguae dictione longinquus, talia intellectu capere, in aliamque linguam transferre valuerit: Joannem innuo Scotigenam, virum, quem auditu comperi per omnia sanctum.*", *Epistola ad Carolum*, PL 122 1027–1028.

[15] See CAPPUYNS, Jean Scot Érigène, pp. 7–8: '*Eriu*' is an Old-Irish word from which 'Ireland' was eventually derived. J. O'MEARA agrees with Cappuyns in rejecting the theories that 'Eriu' might refer to Ayr in Scotland (so G. MacKenzie in 1708) or Eriuven in Herefordshire (so T. Gale in 1681); he also rejects with Cappuyns the theory that it indicates 'born in the East' (so Schaarschmitt); for O'Meara's discussion of the issue see O'MEARA, Eriugena, pp. 2–3.

[16] S. PRUDENTIUS Trecensis Episcopus, *De Praedestinatione contra Erigenam*, 14, PL 115 1194A.

[17] For discussions of this point see CONTRENI / Ó NÉILL, introduction, Glossae Divinae Historiae, p. 80–81; CAPPUYNS, *Jean Scot Érigène*, pp. 9–11; O'MEARA, Eriugena, p. 2; MORAN, The Philosophy of John Scottus Eriugena, p. 35.

[18] CONTRENI, "The Biblical Glosses of Haimo of Auxerre and John Scottus Eriugena", p. 424.

[19] "Unfortunately, the linguistic evidence offers no assistance in determining the dialect or provenance of John's Old Irish, because Classical O. Ir. such as John writes was a literary *koiné* used in Ireland by both the secular learned class of the *filid* and the monastic *literati*. The fact that both groups moved about the country freely, and cultivated a written, standard language removed

however reveal that he was not only born but also reared in Ireland[20] and that he received an education there which included familiarity with the contemporary Irish legal system and with Irish literature[21]. He must have acquired this education in an Irish monastery since these were centres where both secular and religious learning had already long been integrated[22]. We must not, however, conclude that Eriugena must have been a monk, as these centres were also open to lay scholars[23].

The Ireland to which Eriugena belonged has been described as a tribal, rural, hierarchical and familiar society[24]. While the eighth century may be seen as a golden age for Irish culture and learning, the ninth century cannot, for various reasons, be praised in such glowing terms. Within the culture itself the synthesis of secular and Latin literature was giving way to a predominance, even within some of the monasteries, of secular learning[25]. An external threat to the former societal and cultural order came with the invasions of Vikings. The first Viking expedition to Ireland took place in 795, while the raids of the following forty years were sporadic, from 835 on the Viking interest in Ireland took on more organised forms[26]. Now it is precisely at this time that the first report of Eriugena on the mainland arises! Fleeing from the Vikings raiders is a possible explanation for his emigration, it remains however only a theory[27]. The true or full explanation for his 'exile' may not be ascertained. Perhaps having exhausted the possibilities in Ireland, it was potential for better academic prospects which drew him to the continental centres of learning. O'Néill has suggested the further possibility that he fled from the impending dominance of secular learning[28].

To what extent had Eriugena already attained his education in Ireland? Which cultural goods and what learning did Eriugena bring with him to the continent?[29] Latin

---

from common speech undoubtedly prevented the development of dialectical or local pecularities." PÁDRAIG P. O'NÉILL, "The Old-Irish Words in Eriugena's Biblical Glosses", p. 293.

[20] His knowledge of Irish flora and fauna can only be explained in this way, see O'NEILL, "The Old-Irish Words in Eriugena's Biblical Glosses", p. 295.

[21] See O'NEILL, "The Old-Irish Words in Eriugena's Biblical Glosses", p. 295/6.

[22] See O'NEILL, "The Old-Irish Words in Eriugena's Biblical Glosses", p. 296; cf. P. HARBISON, "Irland. C. Monastisches und kirchliches Leben", in: *LMA,* vol. V, 1991, pp. 660–662.

[23] Indeed this lack of orders was used as an occasion to criticise him by his opponents in theological controversy.

[24] See DANIEL A. BINCHY, "The Passing of the Old Order", in: BRIAN O' CUIV, *The Impact of the Scandinavian Invasions on the Celtic-speaking Peoples c. 800–1100 A. D. Introductory Papers read at Plenary Sessions of the International Congress of Celtic Studies held in Dublin, 6–10 July, 1959,* Dublin: Institiúid Ard-Léinn, 1975, pp. 119–132, p. 121.

[25] See O'NÉILL, "The Old-Irish Words in Eriugena's Biblical Glosses", p. 295.

[26] See O'MEARA, Eriugena, p. 5.

[27] T. M. CHARLES-EDWARDS distances himself from this possibility in his account of Eriugena and the Ireland of his day in *Early Christian Ireland,* Cambridge: Cambridge University Press, 2000, p. 591.

[28] O'NÉILL, "The Old-Irish Words in Eriugena's Biblical Glosses", p. 295.

[29] For discussions of this point see among others: O'MEARA, Eriugena, pp. 6–9; MORAN, The philosophy of John Scottus Eriugena, pp. 2–7; CAPPUYNS, Jean Scot Érigène, pp. 27–29.

learning was widespread in Ireland and tended to concentrate on ecclesiastical writers: Ambrose, Jerome, Augustine, Gregory the Great and Isidore of Seville[30]. While we may be certain that he acquired his Latin in Ireland, Eriugena's Latin prose is said to be remarkably free from 'Hibernian' stylistic influences[31]. It is more difficult to account for Eriugena's knowledge of the Greek language. His biblical glosses, one of his earliest works to be completed after reaching the continent, already show that he had a knowledge of Greek[32] so he probably had acquired at least a rudimentary knowledge of it in Ireland[33]. However, we must also bear in mind that the translations of the Greek fathers which he completed later on in his academic career demanded an extensive knowledge of the Greek language. This combined with the presumption that the knowledge of Greek grammar available in Ireland at the time was relatively poor, has led some scholars such as Bernard Bischoff to postulate that Eriugena must have availed of a Greek language native speaker as his teacher after he arrived on the continent[34]. Just how extensive the knowledge of Greek in Ireland was in the early middle ages is a disputed point[35]. A fragmentary knowledge of Greek seems to have been widely available in the middle ages from biblical exegesis[36]. Yet it appears that the Irish read the Greek fathers mainly in translation[37]. Scholars agree that the Irish had an early knowledge of Greek *vocabulary*[38]. More contentious is the issue of their

---

[30] See JOSEPH F. KELLY, "Hiberno-Latin Theology", in: H. LÖWE (ed.), *Die Iren und Europa im früheren Mittelalter,* Stuttgart: Klett-Cotta, vol. 2, 1982, (= Veröffentlichungen des Europa-Zentrums Tübingen: Kulturwiss. Reihe), pp. 549–567, esp. pp. 560–564; O'MEARA, Eriugena, p. 8.

[31] See LUDWIG BIELER, "Remarks on Eriugena's Original Latin Prose", in: J.J. O'MEARA und L. BIELER (ed.), The Mind of Eriugena, pp. 140–146, pp. 142–143.

[32] Certain glosses could only have been written by someone with an independent knowledge of Greek, see CONTRENI, "The Biblical Glosses of Haimo of Auxerre and John Scottus Eriugena", pp. 423–424.

[33] CAPPUYNS minimises this knowledge of Greek: "Mais sur un point nous devons être fermes: l'Irlande du haut moyen âge n'a pas connu véritablement le grec.", Jean Scot Érigène, p. 28. Cappuyns held that Eriugena learned his Greek on the continent, Jean Scot Érigène, p. 29.

[34] See BERNARD BISCHOFF, "Das griechische Element in der abendländischen Bildung", in: *Mittelalterliche Studien. Ausgewählte Aufsätze zur Schriftkunde und Literaturgeschichte,* vol. II, Stuttgart: Anton Hiersemann, 1967, pp. 246–275, esp. p. 265.

[35] See WALTER BERSCHIN, "Griechisches bei den Iren", in: H. LÖWE (ed.), Die Iren und Europa, vol. 1, pp. 501–510; MICHAEL HERREN, "The Commentary on Martianus Attributted to John Scottus: its Hiberno-Latin Background", in: G.-H. ALLARD (ed.), Jean Scot écrivain, pp. 265–286; JOSEPH F. KELLY, "Hiberno-Latin Theology", in: H. LÖWE, (ed.), Die Iren und Europa, vol. 2, pp. 549–567, pp. 561–2.

[36] See R. LE BOURDELLÈS, "Connaissance du grec et méthodes de traduction dans le monde carolingien jusqu'à Scot Érigène", in: RENÉ ROQUES (ed.), Jean Scot Érigène et l'histoire de la Philosophie, pp. 117–123, esp. p. 117.

[37] "The Irish as a group used the Greek fathers in Latin translation. The appearance of Greek words or phrases in Irish texts, such as *cata Iohannem* in a Lucan commentary, can probably best be explained by copying from older authors. There are also occasional examples of a falsified knowledge of Greek, and a knowledge of Greek became a hagiographical motif.", JOSEPH F. KELLY, "Hiberno-Latin Theology", p. 562.

[38] See WALTER BERSCHIN, "Griechisches bei den Iren", in: H. LÖWE (ed.), *Die Iren und Europa im früheren Mittelalter,* vol. 1, pp. 501–510, p. 510, (whereby Berschin's article concentrates on the

knowledge of Greek grammar and grammatical paradigms. Making the explicit distinction between the ninth century and earlier centuries Michael Herren writes: "The Greek grammatical notes of several Irish masters, named and anonymous, from the ninth century demonstrate the availability of paradigms by this period."[39]

The expression 'Hiberno-Latin theology' has been used to refer to the theology of Irish writers who wrote in Latin from the fifth century down to the absorption of this stream of theology within the larger western theological tradition in the ninth century[40]. It is thus of interest here as the native cradle of Eriugena's thought. Joseph F. Kelly has characterised this theology as conservative and not very speculative[41]. The Irish exegesis of the period exhibited among other traits, a noticeable preference for Matthew's Gospel[42] and little formal reflection on biblical hermeneutics[43]. These characteristics are of interest because Eriugena's preoccupation with the Johannine writings in his exegetical writings, and his speculative tendency (especially in the *Periphyseon*) stand in contrast to those of his predecessors in Ireland. Perhaps the contemporary academic climate in Ireland was too stifling for the intellectual curiosity and innovative spirit of Eriugena.

At the end of this reflection on the cultural inheritance which Eriugena brought with him to the continent we can mention the old question of a 'Celtic' influence. This question formerly dealt with by Dempf[44], Hauer[45], and Bommersheim[46], has been raised again recently by K.-H. Ohlig[47] and Ulrich Rudnick[48]. Rudnick

---

seventh and eighth centuries); MICHAEL HERREN, "The Commentary on Martianus Attributted to John Scottus: its Hiberno-Latin Background", in: G.-H. ALLARD (ed.), Jean Scot écrivain., pp. 265–286, p. 285.

[39] MICHAEL HERREN, "The Commentary on Martianus Attributted to John Scottus: its Hiberno-Latin Background", in: G.-H. ALLARD (ed.), *Jean Scot écrivain.*, pp. 265–286, p. 285.

[40] JOSEPH F. KELLY, "Hiberno-Latin Theology", p. 549; JOHN J. CONTRENI, "The Irish 'Colony' at Laon during the time of John Scottus", pp. 59–67; MICHAEL HERREN, "The Commentary on Martianus Attributed to John Scottus: its Hiberno-Latin Background"; BERNHARD BISCHOFF, "Das griechische Element in der abendländischen Bildung", and Idem, "Irische Schreiber im Karolingerreich", in: R. ROQUES, Jean Scot Érigène et l'histoire de la philosophie, pp. 47–57; WALTER BERSCHIN, "Griechisches bei den Iren"; LOUIS HOLTZ, "Grammairiens irlandais au temps de Jean Scot: quelques aspects de leur pédagogie", in: RENÉ Roque*s* (ed.) Jean Scot Érigène et l'histoire de la philosophie, pp. 69–78.

[41] JOSEPH F. KELLY, "Hiberno-Latin Theology", p. 550.

[42] KELLY, "Hiberno-Latin Theology", p. 560.

[43] See KELLY, "Hiberno-Latin Theology", p. 560.

[44] A. DEMPF, "Johannes Eriugena und die Metaphysik der Karolingerzeit", in: DEMPF, *Metaphysik des Mittelalters,* Part I, Munich: R. Oldenbourg, 1971, reprint of edition from 1934.

[45] J. W. HAUER, "Der nordische Geist im christlichen Frühmittelalter", in: *Deutscher Glaube* 4 (1937) 394–405.

[46] P. BOMMERSHEIM, "Johannes Scottus Eriugena und die Dynamik des Nordens", in: *Deutsche Vierteljahresschrift für Literaturwissenschaft und Geistesgeschichte* 21 (1943) 395–416.

[47] See K.-H. OHLIG, *Fundamentalchristologie. Im Spannungsfeld von Christentum und Kultur,* München: Kösel, 1986.

[48] ULRICH RUDNICK, *Das System des Johannes Scottus Eriugena.* See pp. 344–5 where he discusses the positions of Dempf, Hauer and Bommersheim, and pp. 337/8 on Ohlig.

attempts an '*ideengeschichtlichen Vergleich*' between a reconstruction of what Celtic elements might have survived into the ninth century on the one hand, and the system of Eriugena on the other[49]. He thus proposes common ground such as concern with the dynamic and the processual, a tendency to organic thinking, an emphasis on freedom, and an affinity with Johannine thought[50]. While there is indeed some evidence for these traits in the writings of Eriugena, the attribution of these and other characteristics to a general Celtic influence must remain very tentative and speculative[51]. As Rudnick himself admits it is hard to pin down textually the Celtic essence on which his comparison stands[52].

## 1.3 Eriugena and ninth century continental Europe[53]

The most significant early references to Eriugena occur within documents which arose in connection with the predestination debate of the 850s[54]. Eriugena had at this point in time probably already spent some time on the continent, otherwise he would not have established the reputation which occasioned his advice being sought in the predestination debate. The tentative dating of one of his earliest continental works, his biblical glosses[55], reinforces the speculation that he probably arrived in

---

[49] ULRICH RUDNICK, Das System des Johannes Scottus Eriugena, p. 338.

[50] See ULRICH RUDNICK, Das System des Johannes Scottus Eriugena, pp. 344–355.

[51] For example Rudnick suggests that the Irish monks' thinking had a particular affinity with Johannine thought, RUDNICK, *Das System des Johannes Scottus Eriugena,* pp. 354–355. This indeed fits in with Eriugena's interest in the fourth Gospel. Yet textual evidence which has survived suggests that the Irish exegetes as a whole were more interested in *Matthew's* Gospel, see KELLY, "Hiberno-Latin Theology", esp. pp. 558–559. Either Eriugena's Celtic roots were deeper than those of his contemporaries, including those who stayed at home (which seems unlikely!), or his preference for John's Gospel may perhaps be attributed to his interest in Greek speculative thought rather than to these Celtic roots. In support of the latter is the late date of his writings on John, that is they were completed after his treatment of the Ps. Dionysius and the Greek fathers. Rudnick's argumentation remains highly speculative because it must argue from generalities such as general celtic trends. In the case at hand he even employs this speculation against documented facts i.e. what we actually know from extant written sources about the interests of Hiberno-Latin exegesis.

[52] ULRICH RUDNICK, Das System des Johannes Scottus Eriugena, p. 338.

[53] The most recent detailed account of the relevant material is to be found in JOHN J. CONTRENI and PÁDRAIG P. Ó NÉILL's introduction to Glossae Divinae Historiae, pp. 11–85. See too MICHAEL HERREN's review of the material in his introduction to Iohannis Scotti Eriugenae Carmina, pp. 1–55. See JOHN J. CONTRENI, The Cathedral School of Laon from 850–930; "Masters and Medicine in Northern France during the Reign of Charles the Bald"; "The Irish 'Colony' at Laon during the time of John Scottus" and compare the general accounts in: MAÏEUL CAPPUYNS O. S. B., Jean Scot Érigène, pp. 30–80; JOHN J. O'MEARA, Eriugena, pp. 9–15; DERMOT MORAN, The Philosophy of John Scottus Eriugena, pp. 7–26; JOHN J. O'MEARA and LUDWIG BIELER, (ed.) The Mind of Eriugena, 1973, p. x.

[54] See for example the 851 text, S. PRUDENTIUS Trecensis Episcopus, *De Praedestinatione contra Erigenam,* PL 115 1009–1352 already quoted from above (see my p. 27, footnote 14).

[55] See PÁDRAIG O'NÉILL, "The Old-Irish Words in Eriugena's Biblical Glosses"; on the glosses he writes, "… their linguistic forms, … belong to the first half rather than the middle or second half of the ninth century, …", p. 296. My use of the glosses to date Eriugena's arrival in France presupposes

what we now know as France around the year 840. If the '*Johannes medicus*' mentioned in Charles the Bald's charter for Notre-Dame of Reims dating from the first
of October 845 may be identified with Eriugena, then we have another testimony
which supports the theory that Eriugena was already established in continental
circles by the mid 840's[56].

Between 838 and 843 Charles the Bald consolidated a kingdom in the western
parts of what we now call France[57]. He continued to foster education as his grand-
father had done and his kingdom was acquainted with such scholars as Eriugena,
Lupus of Ferrières, Ratramnus of Corbie, Hincmar of Rheims, Martin of Laon,
Haimon of Auxerre and Godescalc of Orbais[58]. Charles the Bald supported the
study of the *artes liberales*[59] and was outstanding in his interest in, and patronage,
of the Greek language.

From the texts of Heiric of Auxerre[60], Hincmar of Rheims and Pardulus of
Laon we know that some form of a school was associated with the court of Charles
the Bald. We know little of its constitution[61], where it was situated, or whether it
had a settled venue at all[62]. Thus for example even Pardulus' explicit testimony to
Eriugena's activity in the palace school[63] does not lead us very far in our search for
Eriugena's geographic sphere of activity. It has been postulated that Eriugena arrived
at the palace after having spent some time at Schuttern near Strasbourg[64]. Whether
Laon is to be identified with the palace school or not, there is some evidence that
Eriugena had contact with that town[65].

---

that he wrote the glosses while already living on the continent. For the arguments in favour of an
original audience of Irish expatriate scholars, see O'NÉILL, p. 290.

[56] See the decree of October 1, 845 reproduced in *Recueil des Actes de Charles II le Chauve Roi
de France,* I, Paris: Imprimerie Nationale, 1943, pp. 210–213, No. 75, edited by GEORGES TESSIER.
JOHN J. CONTRENI has collected, in part edited, and commented on various texts which may link
Eriugena to medical studies; see JOHN J. CONTRENI, "Masters and Medicine in Northern France
during the Reign of Charles the Bald".

[57] See J. M. WALLACE-HADRILL, *The Frankish Church,* pp. 241–257.

[58] See PIERRE RICHÉ, "Charles le Chauve et la culture de son temps"; ROSAMOND McKITTER-
ICK, "The Palace School of Charles the Bald".

[59] See pp. 23–48, of GANGOLF SCHRIMPF, Das Werk des Johannes Scottus Eriugena.

[60] "... ita, ut merito vocitetur scola palatium, cuius apex non minus scolaribus quam militaribus
consuescit cotidie disciplinis." HEIRIC OF AUXERRE, in: *Vitae S. Germani Commendatio, MGH,
Poetae Latini aevi Carolini, (III),* LUDWIG TRAUBE (ed.), 1896, (= Poetae Latini Medii Aevi, Bd. 3),
p. 429.

[61] See PIERRE RICHÉ, "Charles le Chauve et la culture de son temps", pp. 38–9.

[62] See JOHN J. CONTRENI, The Cathedral School of Laon, pp. 83–5, where he argues against
Laon as the site of the palace school; ROSAMOND McKITTERICK, "The Palace School of Charles the
Bald, pp. 385–400, where Compiègne is favoured as location of the palace school; see also MAÏEUL
CAPPUYNS, O. S. B., Jean Scot Érigène, pp. 65–66 for a discussion of Laon as location.

[63] See S. REMIGIUS Lugdunensis Episcopus, *Liber de tribus Epistolis,* PL 121 1051D–1052A, as
quoted above on my p. 26, footnote 11.

[64] See JOHN CONTRENI The Cathedral School of Laon, pp. 85–6.

[65] See JOHN J. CONTRENI, "The Irish 'Colony' at Laon during the time of John Scottus; IDEM,
The Cathedral School of Laon, p. 87 where he remarks reservedly: "The most that this evidence

Eriugena's poetry seem to reveal a close relationship with the person of the emperor; he had perhaps absolved an oath of fealty to Charles[66]. Dutton has in this context described Eriugena as a 'royal' poet as opposed to a primarily 'court' poet: "Whereas the poets at the courts of Charlemagne and Louis the Pious had composed poems about the life of the court, its prominent personages, its lively debates, and its intrigues, Eriugena's poems almost exclusively speak to and about Charles the Bald."[67] It is Eriugena's poetry too which may offer us the last date on which we know that Eriugena was alive: if we accept that his poem *Aulae sidereae* refers to the dedication of the church Notre-Dame de Compiègne, then we can date this work to 877[68].

## 2. Eriugena's early writings

The first mention of Eriugena in theological debate occurs in connection with the debate on predestination in the 840s and 850s[69]. In 850 or 851 Pardulus the bishop of Laon, acting in the name of the archbishop Hincmar of Rheims, commissioned Eriugena to produce a theological position paper[70] on the already burning issue of the divine predestination of the human. (Hincmar was a close adviser of Charles the Bald and Charles is mentioned by Eriugena in glowing tones in the dedicatory letter and in the first chapter of *De praedestinatione*[71].)

---

suggests is that John was a familiar figure at Laon as he was at the palace, Reims, Soissons, and doubtless other centers. ... While John might be a member of a loosely defined Irish 'colony' at Laon, it would go beyond the bounds of the available evidence to tie him intimately to Laon."

[66] See PAUL E. DUTTON, "Eriugena the Royal Poet", p. 61. Dutton draws attention to Eriugena's reference to himself as the king's '*uotifer*', vow-bearer; see: "*Munera uotiferi sint tibi grata tui.*", Iohannis Scotti Eriugenae Carmina, MICHAEL W. HERREN, (ed.), 20, 4, p. 108, (PL 122 1029).

[67] PAUL E. DUTTON, "Eriugena the Royal Poet", pp. 64/5.

[68] Compare MAÏEUL CAPPUYNS O.S.B., Jean Scot Érigène, pp. 233–238 who holds that the poem *Aulae sidereae* refers to the dedication, not of Notre-Dame de Compiègne in 877, but of the Marian church at Rheims in 862. PAUL E. DUTTON, "Eriugena the Royal Poet", p. 62 discusses the possibility that the poem refers to the dedication in Compiègne and lists authors who support this claim in footnote 46. A new study of the poem by MICHAEL HERREN, "Eriugena's 'Aulae Sidereae', the 'Codex Aureus', and the Palatine Church of St. Mary at Compiègne", in: *Studi Medievali*, ser. 3 28 (1987) 593–608 suggests a dating around 870.

[69] On the ninth century debate on predestination see, DAVID GANZ, "The Debate on Predestination", in: M. GIBSON AND J. NELSON, Charles the Bald, pp. 353–373. On Eriugena's role within this debate see GANGOLF SCHRIMPF, Das Werk des Johannes Scottus Eriugena, pp. 72–84.

[70] *Iohannis Scotti De diuina praedestinatione liber*, GOULVEN MADEC (ed.); ERIUGENA, Widmungsbrief zu De Praedestinatione, E. DÜMMLER, (ed.), in: MGH Epist. V, pp. 630-631; *Eriugena, Johannes Scottus, Treatise on Divine Predestination*, transl. MARY BRENNAN, University of Notre Dame Press: Notre Dame, Indiana, 1999, (= Notre Dame Texts in Medieval Culture; vol. 5).

[71] De Praedestinatione, praefatio, E. DÜMMLER (ed.), MGH Epist. V, p. 631, reproduced in *De divina praedestinatione liber*, G. MADEC (ed.) p. 5, 66–70, (PL 122, 357 B–C); and De praedestinatione chap. 1, 2, MADEC (ed.), p. 7, 40–44, (PL 122 358 B–C).

The occasion was provided by the writings of the former monk Gottschalk who, relying on certain Augustinian texts (for example the anti-pelagian texts), played down the role of human freedom in co-operating with divine grace and suggested that God predestines all humans, some positively to eternal happiness, and some negatively to eternal damnation. Eriugena countered his arguments with other Augustinian texts but above all by his own sharp argumentation. Gottschalk had spoken of a "*gemina praedestinatio*", one divine act which had two opposing consequences: salvation or damnation. Eriugena argued that a twofold predestination (*gemina*) in Gottschalk's sense of this expression, including a positive divine predestination of some individuals to hell, would mitigate against the divine justice. Whereas Gottschalk had attacked the idea that humans still have the freedom to do good, the heart of Eriugena's argumentation is that this divine justice demands the ongoing subsistence of a free human will. Thus the defence of human freedom occupies a central place in the work. Chapters six to eight are concerned with the free choice of the will[72]. In chapter eight he speaks of the immeasurable gift that human freedom is, a gift according to the text, granted only to the human amongst the living:

*Cui debemus ineffabiles gratias reddere, non solum quod naturam nostrae mentis bonitatis suae copia condiderit rationalem, liberam, uoluntariam, mobilem, sed quod nobis largitatis suae munere concessit, proprio nostro nutu rationabiliter, libere, uoluntarie posse nos mouere. Qui motus nulli animalium praeter hominem concessus est.[73]*

A further aspect of the human freedom as described in this work is its function in mirroring or imaging God. In chapter four we read of God's creation:

*Eo enim modo iustissimo benignissimoque pulchritudinis totius uniuersitatis consuluit naturae, quam ad imaginem et similitudinem suam creauit, ut sibi uoluntate non necessitate seruiret, rectissimo quidem diuinae sapientiae moderamine. Non enim aliter debuit fieri rationalis uita nisi uoluntaria, cum ab ea uoluntate quae est causa omnium creata sit ad imaginem et similitudinem sui. Aut quomodo eam diuina uoluntas, summa uidelicet uniuersitatis ratio, quae nulla necessitate stringitur, quoniam sua liberrima potentia potitur, imaginem sui similem faceret, si non eius substantiam crearet uoluntatem liberam rationalem?[74]*

---

[72] In these chapters Eriugena quotes extensively from Augustine's *De libero arbitrio*.

[73] ERIUGENA, De praedestinatione, chapter 8, 7, MADEC (ed.), p. 53, (PL 122 388, B–C). "To him we owe it to return inexpressible thanks not only for creating, by the abundance of his goodness, the nature of our mind as rational, free, voluntary and mobile, but also because by the favour of his bounty he arranged that we could move at our own pleasure rationally, freely and voluntarily. This movement is granted to no living thing apart from man.", translation from MARY BRENNAN, Treatise on Divine Predestination, p. 55.

[74] ERIUGENA, De praedestinatione, chapter 4, 5, MADEC (ed.), p. 31, (PL 122 373 A–B). "For in such a very just and most beneficent manner he had regard for the nature of the whole world, which he made to his own image and likeness, that it should serve him by will, not by necessity, indeed by the most just governance of divine wisdom. For rational life was bound not to have been made otherwise than voluntary, since by that will which is the cause of all things it was created in his own image and likeness. Otherwise how would the divine will, that is to say the highest reason of the universe, being unrestricted by any necessity as in the greatest freedom it possesses its own power,

The role of human freedom in mirroring the divine sovereignty emerges more clearly in this work than in any other of Eriugena's writings. This is perhaps the most important aspect of this early writing of Eriugena when we review his work from the standpoint of the theme of the appearing of God. It is significant that this apparitional role of human freedom emerges here in a systematic context: it is affirmed as part of Eriugena's own argumentation[75].

It would have been unlikely that a completely unknown author would be called upon to produce such an strategically important document as the *De praedestinatione*. And indeed we do discover that Eriugena had already produced an earlier work, a commentary on the *De Nuptiis Philologiae et Mercurii* of Martianus Capella, to which, in part, his reputation as a teacher of the liberal arts was due.

Eriugena's glosses on the *De Nuptiis Philologiae et Mercurii* present the author's encounter with the world of classical pagan culture and religion. In the *De Nuptiis Philologiae et Mercurii*,[76] a mythical account of the marriage between Philology and Mercury provides the narrative framework for a compendium of the liberal arts[77]. The god Mercury offers his bride Philology seven handmaids as a marriage gift. Each maiden represents one of the liberal arts: Grammar, Dialectic, and Rhetoric constituting the *trivium;* and Geometry, Arithmetic, Astronomy and Harmony constituting the *quadrivium*. As each handmaid introduces herself a handbook of the arts results[78]. Its author was Martianus Mineus Felix Capella who lived in Carthage[79]. In the first two hundred years after its composition it was used as a textbook in North Africa, Italy, Gaul and Spain[80]. In the early middle ages it be-

---

how could he make it to his own image and likeness if he did not create its substance a free rational will?", translation from MARY BRENNAN, Treatise on Divine Predestination, p. 29.

[75] At some stage in his career Eriugena encountered the idea of the imaging function of the human freedom in the writings of Gregory of Nyssa. Circa 860 Eriugena began to translate the Greek ecclesiastical writers into Latin, starting with the works of the Pseudo-Dionysius. Some scholars however suggest that even before this (or indeed perhaps even before he wrote the *De praedestinatione*) he was already familiar with their writings. See MARY BRENNAN, "Foreword" in: Treatise on Divine Predestination, p. xii.

[76] The text has been edited by ADOLF DICK, *Martianus Capella,* Leipzig: Teubner, 1925 and again by JAMES WILLIS, *Martianus Capella,* Leipzig: BSB B.G Teubner Verlagsgesellschaft, 1983, (= Bibliotheca Scriptorum Graecorum et Romanorum Teubneriana).

[77] A review of some studies of the *De Nuptiis* up to 1975 is given by JEAN PRÉAUX, "Jean Scot et Martin de Laon en face du *De Nuptiis* de Martianus Capella" in: RENÉ ROQUES (ed.), Jean Scot Érigène et l'histoire de la philosophie, pp. 161–170, pp. 161–162.

[78] The precise date of composition is still a matter of debate, see JEAN PRÉAUX, "Jean Scot et Martin de Laon en face du De Nuptiis de Martianus Capella", in: RENÉ ROQUES (ed.) Jean Scot Érigène et l'histoire de la philosophie, pp. 162/3. William Stahl gives the common consensus as between 410 and 439, see WILLIAM STAHL, RICHARD JOHNSON, E. L. BURGE *Martianus Capella and the Seven Liberal Arts*. Vol. I The Quadrivium of Martianus Capella. Latin Traditions in the Mathematical Sciences 50 B.C.–A.D. 1250 by WILLIAM HARRIS STAHL. With a Study of the Allegory and the Verbal Disciplines by RICHARD JOHNSON with E. L. BURGE. New York: Columbia University Press, 1971, (= Records of Civilization: Sources and Studies LXXXIV), pp. 12–15.

[79] See, W. STAHL, R. JOHNSON, E. L. BURGE, Martianus Capella, Vol. I, pp. 9–20.

[80] W. STAHL, R. JOHNSON, E. L. BURGE, Martianus Capella, Vol. I, p. 56.

came one of the standard texts within the school system. In the opinion of Gangolf
Schrimpf its reception provided the search for a suitable manual of the liberal arts
with a provisional result[81]. A commentary on the *De Nuptiis* attributed to Eriugena
was instrumental in focusing attention on the text.

Since 1862 the ninth century Martian glosses contained in the manuscript Paris
B. N. lat. 12960, f. 47$^r$–115$^v$ which originated in Corbie has been ascribed to Eriugena[82]. Cora Lutz's edition of the commentary which appeared in 1939 is based
on this Corbie manuscript[83]. Since 1943 an important further manuscript, Bodl.
Auct. T II 19 originating in Metz, has been made known[84]. Édouard Jeauneau has
published an edition of the first book of the commentary according to the Metz
manuscript.[85] From the second book onwards, the Metz version of the glosses is
similar to, although not identical with, the Corbie version. However, the text of
book one differs significantly from that in the Corbie manuscript. The lemmata
selected are in part different. Some of those lemmata which occur in both texts
exhibit different commentaries, others differ according to the words used even
where the content of the commentary is very similar.[86] The central question which
arises with respect to these manuscripts is that of the relationship of the Corbie and
Metz texts. It is debated whether they are directly related to each other or are both
transcripts of Eriugena's lessons on the *De Nuptiis*.

The commentary as presented in both the major manuscripts takes the form of
a series of glosses on individual phrases of the *De Nuptiis*. This does not rule out
the possibility that Eriugena may have originally written his glosses in the margins
or between the lines of a *De Nuptiis* text. The books are unequally glossed, the
books one and two (the story which frames the exposition), four (on dialectic) and
eight (on astronomy) receiving the most attention. Correspondingly, of thematic
interest are the comments on the status of the liberal arts in the first two books, the
cosmological references in book eight and the extended commentary on dialectic
in the commentary on book four[87].

---

[81] See GANGOLF SCHRIMPF, "Johannes Scottus Eriugena und die Rezeption des Martianus
Capella im karolingischen Bildungswesen", in: WERNER BEIERWALTES (ed.), Eriugena. Studien zu
seinen Quellen, pp. 135–148, pp. 137–138.

[82] For a treatment of the authenticity of the glosses see GANGOLF SCHRIMPF, "Zur Frage der
Authentizität unserer Texte von Johannes Scottus' 'Annotationes in Martianum'", in: J. J. O'MEARA
und L. BIELER (ed.), *The Mind of Eriugena*, pp. 125–139.

[83] CORA E. LUTZ (ed.), Iohannis Scotti Annotationes in Marcianum. On the manuscript see,
pp. xxviii–xxx.

[84] See GANGOLF SCHRIMPF, Zur Frage der Authentizität, p. 126 where the identification is attributed to L. Labowsky.

[85] ÉDOUARD JEAUNEAU, Quatre Thèmes Érigéniens, pp. 101–166.

[86] E. g. the commentaries on PALESTRA in *De Nuptiis* 6, 11.

[87] In the time of Louis the Pius and Charles the Bald interest was shown in dialectic not just in
grammar and rhetoric, see CLAUDIO LEONARDI, "Martianus Capella et Jean Scot. Nouvelle Présentation d'un vieux problème", in: G.-H. ALLARD, Jean Scot Écrivain, pp. 187–207, p. 200.

It is the relevance of the work for Eriugena's methodology which has attracted recent scholarly attention. Eriugena's understanding of dialectic and its importance for the method he uses in his subsequent works has been explored by D'Onofrio[88]. Schrimpf's *Habilitationsschrift* highlights the central role of dialectic in the argumentation of *Periphyseon*. Schrimpf sees this interest emerging in the commentary on the *De Nuptiis,* developing in the *De praedestinatione* and enduring in the chief work, *Periphyseon.*

Finally, we reiterate that to Eriugena's early writings belong the collection of 660 biblical glosses, almost all on the Old Testament, probably completed soon after he reached the continent, perhaps used in the instruction of Irish monks living on the mainland. These glosses edited and examined by John J. Contreni and Pádraig Ó'Néill have already been mentioned because of their biographical interest[89]. They also reveal much on the Carolingian system of learning, on the sources which fed into Eriugena's learning, and on the version of scripture available to Eriugena[90]. In terms of Eriugena's intellectual development they bear witness, not only to a significant early preoccupation with the scriptures, but also to the fact that, even at this early stage in his career, Eriugena was uniquely at pains to avail of the most advanced version of the scriptures available within his cultural sphere[91].

### 3. The encounter with the writings of the Greek ecclesiastical authors

The controversial debate on predestination had introduced Eriugena to ecclesiastical controversy. He emerged from the controversy with a strong supporter from the secular field. Charles the Bald was a lover not only of learning in general, but of all things Greek in particular. In 827 the Byzantine Emperor Michael had sent a manuscript of the writings of the Pseudo-Dionysius Areopagita as a gift to Louis the Pious. Hilduin had already been commissioned to translate the *Corpus Dionysiacum* into Latin. The resultant translation was wanting in many respects. Now Charles requested Eriugena to undertake a new translation. With this commission began a

---

[88] G. D'ONOFRIO, ""Disputandi disciplina" Procédés dialectiques et "logica vetus" dans le langage philosophique de Jean Scot", in: G.-H. ALLARD, Jean Scot Écrivain, pp. 229–263.

[89] *Glossae Divinae Historia.* JOHN J. CONTRENI and PÁDRAIG P. Ó NÉILL, (ed.). The long introduction gives an excellent account of the cultural world out of which these glosses emerged.

[90] J. J. CONTRENI / P. P. Ó NÉILL think that Eriugena was using Theodulf of Orléan's recension of the Bible, see the introduction to Glossae Divinae Historia, p. 38.

[91] See J. J. CONTRENI / P. P. Ó NÉILL, Introduction, Glossae Divinae Historiae, p. 39: "The *Glossae diuinae historiae* appears to be the only medieval work influenced by Theodulf's Bible. That in itself is a significant finding. It might even be a startling finding if we turn the phrase around to state that Theodulf's Bible was a major influence in John Scottus's work and teaching – startling, that is, because in his biblical glosses, probably in his earliest and most 'Irish' work, John shows himself to be a Carolingian scholar thoroughly at home with the most advanced traditions in contemporary continental biblical scholarship."

period of intense preoccupation with the works of the Greek writers. This is not to suggest that Eriugena had not read the Greek fathers before this point in time. It is more likely that he received the commission to translate Dionysius precisely because of his familiarity with them. Contreni comments on the influence of a knowledge of Maximus Confessor's *Quaestiones ad Thalassium* on him as writer of the biblical glosses[92]. Hans Liebeschütz had already suggested some influence of Gregory of Nyssa's *De hominis opificio* on the *Annotationes in Marcianum*[93]. The encounter with the Greek sources must then be considered to have been a gradual and ongoing process within which periods of more concentrated study occurred. The translation of works of the Pseudo-Dionysius (860–864; revision 865–870), then of Gregory of Nyssa (*De imagine*[94] 862–864) and of Maximus Confessor (*Ambigua ad Iohannem* 862–864; *Quaestiones ad Thalassium* 864–866) must be considered as such concentrated periods[95]. The order in which Eriugena is believed to have translated these works is reflected in the ordering of the patristic reflection in (6.1) of this study. There too his debt to Augustine of Hippo will also be considered. In common with other cultured Western scholars of the ninth century, Eriugena had of course read not only Augustine, but also Ambrose of Milan, Hilary, Isidore, Jerome, and Gregory the Great[96]. However, it was in the world of the Greek fathers that Eriugena encountered the decisive versions of such themes as the unknowableness of God, the ultimately Christocentric heart of a theological anthropology, and the spirituality of 'theosis' or deification in the specifically eastern form which he was to make his own. It is indeed one of his greatest gifts to posterity to have transferred these themes with their Eastern nuances to the Carolingian world. While the standard Latin authors provided his educational background (and thus constituted ground common to him and many other scholars) it is nonetheless correct to highlight the

---

[92] See J. J. CONTRENI / P. P. Ó NÉILL, Introduction, Glossae Divinae Historiae, p. 26/7.

[93] HANS LIEBESCHÜTZ in "The Place of the Martianus *Glossae* in the Development of Eriugena's Thought", in: J. J. O'MEARA / L. BIELER (ed.). The Mind of Eriugena, pp. 49–58, p. 53–55.

[94] Eriugena's Latin title for the work otherwise referred to as *De hominis opificio*.

[95] Dates according to the list in J. J. CONTRENI / P. P. Ó NÉILL, Introduction, Glossae Divinae Historiae, pp. 74/5. The chronology of Eriugena's works given on these pages is not however adopted with respect to all Eriugena's works. For example on page 74 the *De diuinae praedestinatione liber* is presented as predating the *Annotationes in Marcianum*. I prefer to follow Contreni / Ó Néill's own reference (footnote 272 with reference to footnote 292) to what is called the "more plausible dating" of the *Annotationes* suggested by HANS LIEBESCHÜTZ in "The Place of the Martianus *Glossae* in the Development of Eriugena's Thought". Liebeschütz differentiates between the Annotationes as we find them in the Oxford text and in the Paris text: "… the Oxford version represents more closely the teaching of the court grammarian during the 840s, while the Paris text would be dated after the literary controversy about predestination.", pp. 52/3.

[96] See the collection of essays, GOULVEN MADEC, *Jean Scot et ses auteurs. Annotationes érigéniennes*, Paris: Études Augustiniennes, 1988 and more recently J. J. CONTRENI / P. P. Ó NÉILL, Introduction, *Glossae Divinae Historiae*, pp. 29–36 and the wide spectrum of authors and works listed in the *index fontium* pp. 221–231.

encounter with certain Eastern writers within the activity of translation as a special stage in the dynamic of his intellectual formation[97].

## 4. Periphyseon

At the close of *Periphyseon* Eriugena addresses the monk Wulfad and writes:

"… *hoc opus primo omnium deo, qui dixit: 'Petite et dabitur uobis, quaerite et inuenietis, pulsate et aperietur uobis', subinde dilectissimo tibi frater in Christo et in studiis sapientiae cooperatori, Vulfade, examinandum offero et corrigendum committo.*"[98] This dedication to Wulfad, who was Abbot of St. Medard in Soissons up until 866 may help us to date the point of time before which Eriugena finished his masterpiece. Indeed the year 866 is repeatedly suggested as the *terminus ad quem* for the completion of *Periphyseon*[99]. John Contreni and Pádraig Ó Néill have however now suggested that the contact between Eriugena and Wulfad must not necessarily have ended abruptly in 866 and suggest that this year be viewed as a "soft" date for the completion of the work[100]. It is suggested that even after this date Eriugena could have continued to make adjustments to the work. In any case, the fact that the work emerges over a span of time is important and that not only scribes influenced by his thinking, or acting on his orders, but that Eriugena himself adjusted the text[101]. Furthermore it is very significant that at least the later work on the book was carried out during and indeed for the most part after, the above described intense encounter with Greek thought.

---

[97] His knowledge of Greek had given him access to the writings of Basil of Caesarea and Epiphanius. It is probable that he completed a translation of the *Ancoratus* of EPIPHANIUS but it has not survived.

[98] "… I dedicate this book in the first place to God, Who has said: 'Ask and it shall be given unto you, seek and ye shall find, knock and it shall be opened unto you,' and in the second place to you, most beloved brother in Christ, and collaborator in my studies, Wulfad, entrusting to you the examination and correction of it.", PP V, 7366–7370, (= PL 122 1022A), here the English translation of Sheldon-Williams / O'Meara, p. 714 has been modified by Hilary Mooney taking acount of Jeauneau's new critical edition of book five in CCCM CLXV. On Eriugena's contact with Wulfad see, JOHN J. MARENBON, "Wulfad, Charles the Bald and John Scottus Eriugena".

[99] See M. CAPPUYNS, Jean Scot Érigène, p. 189 and I. P. SHELDON-WILLIAMS in his "Introduction" to Iohannis Scotti Eriugenae Periphyseon (De Diuisione Naturae, Liber Primus), p. 7.

[100] See J. J. CONTRENI / P. P. Ó NÉILL, Introduction, Glossae Divinae Historiae, p. 76

[101] See ÉDOUARD JEAUNEAU / PAUL E. DUTTON, *The Autograph of Eriugena*, Turnhout: Brepols, 1996, (= Autographa Medii Aeui III).

### 4.1 Periphyseon *as text*

In his commentary on the Celestial Hierarchy of the Pseudo-Dionysius Eriugena refers to his earlier major work as follows: "*in libris ΠΕΡΙ ΦΥΣΕΩΝ*"[102]. To some extent the title reveals the initial programme for the work. At the outset of *Periphyseon* Eriugena appears to have a clear plan for the work, envisaging four books each book corresponding to one of his so called divisions of nature[103]. In the course of the work he changes his plan and completes his work in five books. Thus in book four we read: "*Et quoniam prolixitas huius uoluminis quaedam ex his, de quibus in eius exordio nos dicturos esse promisimus, nunc exponere non admittit, in alium librum differenda sunt.*"[104] Now Eriugena explains his decision with reference to the breadth and difficulty of the material book four has had to cover.[105]

Now it is precisely the biblical account of creation with its emphasis on the manifestational role of the human as the image of God which occasions his change of plan. This is significant. *Periphyseon* is a work with several organisational principles: the fourfold division of nature, the *exitus / reditus* movement; the biblical account of creation. It is significant that precisely the biblical account of the role of the human in the manifestation of the divine is dominant enough to cause Eriugena to change his plan.

*Periphyseon* has been transmitted to us through many manuscripts and their contents are far from identical. The multiplicity of versions bears witness to recension and editing. The research of Jeauneau and Dutton has established that at least some of the alterations have been added by the hand of an Irish scribe known in academic circles as i[1] and who is to be identified with Eriugena himself. The fact that Eriugena himself corrected and improved his work is of significance for every attempt to interpret *Periphyseon*. Eriugena was a thinker whose thought was in constant development. As a result, *Periphyseon* may not be regarded as a static, finished object but as a stage in the development of his work. It grew out of the studies in dialectic attested to in the early writers, it is fertilised by the encounter with great theological and Christological themes of Greek patristic thought, and it leads on to an ever increasing preoccupation with the specifically biblical themes attested to in the biblical commentaries. *Periphyseon* can only be interpreted within the wider context of his *oeuvre* as a whole with its intrinsic dynamic and within the

---

[102] *Expositiones in ierarchiam coelestem,* JEANNE BARBET (ed.), (CCCM 31): IV, 100–101, p. 68 (not in PL 122) "*De quibus rationibus in libris ΠΕΡΙ ΦΥΣΕΩΝ satis tractauimus, ut opinor.*"; see also II, 1038, p. 48 (PL 122 168A ) and XI, 102–103, p. 10 (PL 122 230B).

[103] See PP I, PL 122 441B–442B

[104] PP IV, CCCM CLXIV, 5164–5166, p. 167, (PL 122 860A–B) "As there are certain things which at the beginning of this book we promised to discuss, but which its lengthiness has prevented us from mentioning, we must postpone the examination of them to the next volume." English from J.J. O'MEARA, SLH XIII, p. 273.

[105] See PP IV, CCCM CLXIV, 66–70, p. 5, (PL 122 743D–744A).

chronological development of his academic pursuits inspired by his encounter with privileged sources from the tradition.

### 4.2 Periphyseon: *one source among many?*

This investigation is systematically structured. With regard to the theme of the appearing of God, it follows that I investigate the motives relevant to this theme as they occur in the various writings of Eriugena. As his main work, *Periphyseon* has a special role to play. However, this investigation neither attempts to give a synopsis of the *Periphyseon* nor to present a key to this work. There have been enough attempts to systematise *Periphyseon*. Nor is this systematisation necessary for an adequate treatment of the theme of the appearing of God. Rather I argue that *Periphyseon* eludes an 'over-systematisation'. All attempts at systematisation in the past have had to deal with sections of the work which do not fit into the respective analyses. I place the genesis of the work within the larger dynamic of the intellectual formation of the author and explain shifts in emphasis and organisational principles in these terms. I let *Periphyseon* be what it is, a work which not only revises its own plan but also is revised by its author[106]. I bring the systematic questions of the appearing of God to bear on this work of Eriugena just as I have searched among his other writings for relevant insights.

## 5. Eriugena's later works

At the close of his life Eriugena's attention seems to have focused on the interpretation and commentary on Biblical texts. We have a fragmentary commentary on the Gospel according to John and a complete Homily on the prologue to this Gospel.[107] These works are vitally important for a presentation of the appearing of God according to Eriugena. Themes such as the Word of God appearing; the book of nature and the book of scripture; theophany and growth in moral virtue; theophany and the appearing of Christ, receive here their most mature treatment. To this last period too belongs his commentary on the Celestial Hierarchy of the Ps. Dionysius, an author to whom in the eyes of Eriugena an almost apostolic status adhered.

---

[106] When a text from *Periphyseon* is quoted, it is made clear whether it belongs to the main argumentative text or occurs in a textual addition. Jeauneau's edition for the Corpus Christianorum series provides the basis for these distinctions.

[107] GUSTAVO PIEMONTE has attributed a commentary on the Gospel according to Matthew to Eriugena but suggests that the work was completed relatively early in his academic career. See "Recherches sur les 'Tractatus in Matheum' attribué à Jean Scot", in: GERD VAN RIEL et al. (ed.), Iohannes Scottus Eriugena. The Bible and Hermeneutics, pp. 321–350.

## 6. Conclusion on Eriugena's intellectual
## formation and the methodology of this study

In this chapter the processual formation of Eriugena's thought has been considered. This is significant for the study as a whole. This study addresses Eriugena's writings with a systematic question: how did Eriugena understand and present the appearing of the divine? This question is addressed to the whole of Eriugena's *oeuvre*. The form in which the question is raised is dictated by the subject matter itself (that is the question of the manifestation of the divine as it emerged in history and under consideration of the recurring issues connected with this matter) and by the interaction between this subject matter and the answer, or answers, Eriugena gives. The titles of the chapters of this study emerge out of this interaction. *Periphyseon* is the author's most comprehensive contribution to the matter raised and accordingly receives extensive attention. However, this work too is flanked by earlier and later works and its contributions are thus constantly qualified and complemented by the other texts.

Presentation of Eriugena's understanding
of the appearing of God

CHAPTER 2:

# The question of the possibility of speaking about God

This study attributes an account of the appearing of God to Eriugena: it thereby presupposes that the author affirms at least a minimal ability to make statements about God[1]. The second chapter investigates the teaching of Eriugena on the divine nature. In a first step his presentation of the formal (or methodological) aspects of the question are investigated, that is, the parameters within which the question of the divine nature is raised are explained. In a second step, Eriugena's resultant account of the divine is reviewed. This account emerges from Eriugena's attempt to reconcile his academic conception of the divine nature as '*ea quae creat et non creatur*' with the biblical account of God.

## 1. The parameters within which the question is raised by Eriugena

On the basis of Eriugena's writings we can reflect 1) on the possible scope of our talk about God; 2) on the 'division' of all reality ('*natura*') in terms of the grammatical forms of the verb to create; 3) on Eriugena's understanding of the modes in which something may be said to be or not to be; finally, 4) on the importance of the emergence of the position that God 'appears'.

### 1.1 The scope of Eriugena's academic quest

The extent to which God, or the divine nature, may be the object of discourse is reflected upon extensively by Eriugena in the opening passage of the first book of *Periphyseon*.

*Saepe mihi cogitanti diligentiusque quantum uires suppetunt inquirenti rerum omnium quae uel animo percipi possunt uel intentionem eius superant primam summamque diuisionem esse in ea quae sunt et in ea quae non sunt horum omnium generale uocabulum occurrit quod graece ΦΥCIC, latine uero natura uocitatur.*[2]

---

[1] Compare DOMINIC J. O'MEARA, "The Problem of Speaking about God in John Scottus Eriugena", in: U.-R. BLUMENTHAL (ed.), *Carolingian Essays. Andrew W. Mellon Lectures in Early Christian Studies*. Washington, D.C.: The Catholic University of America Press, 1983, pp. 151–167.

[2] "As I frequently ponder and, so far as my talents allow, ever more carefully investigate the fact that the first and fundamental division of all things which either can be grasped by the mind or lie

*Periphyseon* takes its point of departure from the Greek term phusis (φύσις), and its Latin counterpart, the term 'natura.'[3]. *Natura* functions for Eriugena as a general name for all things that are and all things that are not, and so is capable of covering everything we can think of, and indeed that which eludes our limited human understanding[4]. It is the 'double expression' within the phrase (*nomen ... omnium quae sunt et quae non sunt*)[5] which most merits our attention both from the point of view of identifying Eriugena's sources, and from the point of view of the development of the theme of the present study.

G. Piemonte has pointed out that similar formulations are to be found in the writings of Marius Victorinus[6]. Dominic O'Meara has not only confirmed the influence of the writings of Boethius[7] he also considers the Dionysian roots of the expression that things which are and the things which are not[8].

We have already mentioned that which is innovative in Eriugena's writings when compared with Boethius' use of natura (i.e. the extension of the scope of the term 'natura' to cover the things which the mind cannot grasp). We must now consider the advance which this position makes when compared with that of the Pseudo-Dionysius. Drawing on the Pseudo-Dionysius Eriugena adopts the expression 'the things that are not'[9]. Now whereas in the writings of the Pseudo-Dionysius it is

---

beyond its grasp is into those that are and those that are not, there comes to mind as a general term for them all what in Greek is called Φύσις and in Latin Natura." PP I, 1–6, p. 3, (= PL 122 441A), English from I. P. Sheldon-Williams, SLH VII, p. 37.

[3] D. O'Meara has drawn attention to the Boethian roots of this use of natura as a term which may embrace created reality *and* God. See D. O'Meara, The Problem of Speaking about God, p. 128/9 with reference to Boethius, *Contra Eutychen et Nestorium,* chapter one. Cappuyns had earlier identified Boethius *Contra Eutychen et Nestorium,* as the source for Eriugena's use of the word at the beginning of *Periphyseon* see Maïeul Cappuyns O. S.B, *Jean Scot Érigène,* p. 312–313.

[4] In the Boethian work the use of natura was limited to what the mind can grasp, (not that which eludes the mind too). See D. O'Meara, The Problem of Speaking about God, p. 129–131.

[5] PP I, 9–10, p. 3, (= PL 122, 441A).

[6] See G. Piemonte, "L'expression quae sunt et quae non sunt. Jean Scot et Marius Victorinus", in: G. -H. Allard (ed.), Jean Scot écrivain, p. 81–113. This article compares Eriugena with Marius Victorinus and demonstrates similar formulations in both authors; see the tables on p. 95 and 98. In his footnote 38 on pp. 89/91 Piemonte reviews the research of other authors who mention or omit the parallels between Eriugena and Marius Victorinus. He concludes that although he can cite no place in Eriugena's works where Marius Victorinus is mentioned by name, nevertheless it is his opinion that Eriugena was most probably not only influenced by the ideas of Marius Victorinus but probably adopted preformulated elements from his writings, p. 108/9.

[7] See Dominic J. O'Meara, "The Concept of *Natura* in John Scottus Eriugena (De divisione naturae Book I)", in: *Vivarium* XIX(1981) 126–145. The article suggests Boethius' writings as a source for Eriugena's use of the term 'natura'. For a comparison of what the term means in the two authors, see p. 130/131.

[8] See D. O'Meara, The Concept of Natura, p. 131 with reference, for example to *De divinis nominibus,* Suchla (ed.), Berlin: Walter de Gruyter, 1990, (= Patristische Texte und Studien, vol. 33), IV, 10, p. 155, 3–4, (= PG 3 708A).

[9] D. O'Meara points out that the use of "those that are not" to refer to transcendent realities is in itself not altogether without precedent, The Concept of Natura, p. 132, footnote 19. He mentions Proclus and makes a reference to Elem. theol. 115, 123. In my opinion section 123 offers the most

completely clear that God is said not to be (αὐτὸ δὲ μὴ ὄν)[10] it is not so clear that when he uses the plural formulation in the expression 'the things that are not' that he intends this to include God[11]. It is sometimes used by this author to indicate the created order which depends on God, (πάντα τὰ οὐκ ὄντα ὑπερουσίως ἐν τῷ καλῷ καὶ ἀγαθῷ[12]) but which God (the Good) transcends (ὑπερβάλλουσα τὰ ὄντα καὶ οὐκ ὄντα)[13]. Following O'Meara we can say that at the very least an openness remains in his thought. Eriugena too sometimes uses the expression in this sense attested to by the Dionysian writings. However, it is also true that in Eriugena's writings the expression 'the things that are not' definitely may be, and explicitly is, applied in a way which includes God[14]. He thus makes explicit something implicit in Dionysius' thought. Below we shall see that the context within which Eriugena does this is that of the appearing of higher realities.

This apparitional contextualisation of the things which are not is significant not only because it makes explicit something left implicit in the writings of the pseudo Areopagite. It is also of specific thematic interest for the investigation at hand. The research on Eriugena is divided on the matter whether the so called first division, the distinction between the things that are and the things that are not is intended by Eriugena to be an ontological division or an epistemological one. I, however, agree with Dominic O'Meara[15] and Gangolf Schrimpf[16] that this division is to

---

support for O'Meara's observation. In section 123, lines 31–32 of F. R. Dodds edition, *Proclus. The Elements of Theology. A revised text with translation, introduction and commentary*, Oxford: Oxford University Press, ²1963, reprint 1977, p. 108 we read: οἱ δὲ θεοὶ πάντων εἰσὶν ἐπέκεινα τῶν ὄντων. In these sections it is not only stated that God transcends being, but also the divine things transcend being.

[10] κατὰ μηδὲν τῶν ὄντων οὖσα καὶ αἴτιον μὲν τοῦ εἶναι πᾶσιν, αὐτὸ δὲ μὴ ὂν ὡς πάσης οὐσίας ἐπέκεινα … *De divinis nominibus*, I, 1, SUCHLA (ed.), p. 109, 15–16, (= PG 3, 588B). I find Colm Luibheid's English translation of these lines is misleading: (*Pseudo-Dionysius. The Complete Works*, translated by COLM LUIBHEID, foreword, notes, and translation collaboration by PAUL ROREM, Mahwah, New York: Paulist Press, 1987. He translates "It is and it is as no other being is. Cause of all existence, and therefore itself transcending existence, …", p. 50. I prefer to translate " existing according to none of the beings, and although the cause of the existence of all, it itself however does not exist, for it transcends all existence …".

[11] See D. O'MEARA, The Concept of Natura, p. 131 and footnote 15 where he gives Proclus and Porphyry as the sources for Ps. Dionysius' use of the expression.

[12] *De divinis nominibus*, IV, 10, SUCHLA (ed.), p. 155, 4, (= PG 3, 708A ).

[13] *De divinis nominibus*, IV, 35, SUCHLA (ed.), p. 180, 4–5, (= PG 3, 736B).

[14] See PP I, 55–59, p. 5, (= PL 122 443A–B): "*ea uero quae per excellentiam suae naturae non solum sensum sed etiam omnem intellectum rationemque fugiunt iure uideri non esse, quae non nisi in solo deo et in omnium rerum quae ab eo condita sunt rationibus atque essentiis recte intelliguntur.*" Eriugena will speak of the nothing out of which everything is created as the superessential divine nature in the third book of *Periphyseon*, see his account of the question of the creation out of nothing in PP III, 633–2946, pp. 23–101, (= PL 122 634A–690B).

[15] See D. O'MEARA, The Concept of Natura, p. 129: "It seems from this then that Eriugena modified Boethius' use of *natura* as a term for a totality of all that is, making it function now as a comprehensive term for another totality constituted of all that the mind grasps and that transcends its grasp."

[16] See GANGOLF SCHRIMPF, "Die Systematische Bedeutung der beiden logischen Einteilungen

be understood against an epistemological background, that is that it is ultimately underpinned by the distinction between the things that may be known and the things which transcend our knowledge. For Eriugena the structure of being and the conditions of our thinking this being are closely interrelated. In order to understand how God is conceived as appearing in 'nature' he must first consider the divisions which this concept of nature supports. A further prerequisite for understanding the conception of the appearing of God is a differentiation of the senses in which, according to Eriugena, something may be said to be. Therefore Eriugena proceeds to handle both what he calls the *divisions* of nature and the *modes* with which our thought and speech can appropriate nature by affirming that it exists. This reflection on the modes of interpreting being contains a strong affirmation that the first logical division is to be understood as saying something about the objects we can know or which transcend our knowledge and not principally something about the beings in themselves. For our theme this means that here, in the prologue of *Periphyseon,* the preconditions for a theory of manifestation are already being established. The importance of the dialectic of the appearing and the non appearing of being, and of the more than real depths of being, is already evident here.

The distinction between the things which are and the things which are not occurs in other writings of Eriugena too. In his commentary on John's Gospel it occurs in a passage which as an interpretation of Rom. 4:17[17] has an intrinsically trinitarian form: "*Ipse* [the Son- H. M.] *enim uocat ea quae sunt tanquam quae non sunt, quia per ipsum deus pater clamauit, id est creauit cuncta quae fieri uoluit*".[18] Here however the expression is used in the Dionysian sense of created reality in its dependence on a transcending God.

*1.2 The species of nature considered in terms of creation*

In late antiquity and the early middle ages division was employed as a grammatical device deemed suitable for using in order to approach the meaning of a word which in itself eluded definition.[19]

---

(*divisiones*) zu Beginn von *Periphyseon*", in Claudio Leonardi and Enrico Menestò, (ed.), Giovanni Scoto nel suo tempo, pp. 113–151, here p. 126 following.

[17] "God ... who gives life to the dead and calls into existence the things that do not exist." Quoted from the R. S. V. See Édouard Jeauneau in his critical edition of Eriugena's Commentary on John's Gospel footnote 20, p. 142/3.

[18] Comm., I, XXVII, 94–96, É. Jeauneau (ed.), p. 142, (= PL 122 304D). See too Hom. I, 6–12, É. Jeauneau (ed.), pp. 202–204, (= PL 122 283B–C); *Expositiones in ierarchiam coelestem*, IV, 78–79, J. Barbet (ed.), p. 67 (chapter four is not available in PL 122).

[19] See D'Onofrio, G. "Über die Natur der Einteilung. Die dialektische Entfaltung von Eriugenas Denken", in: W. Beierwaltes (ed.), Begriff und Metapher, pp. 17–38. In this significant article D'Onofrio compares Eriugena's method of division with the logical methods of other thinkers.

The term natura Eriugena tells us may be considered as a genus and it may be divided into four species by means of four differentiations[20]. These four species may be listed as follows:

The first species is that which creates and is not created (*quae creat et non creatur*);

the second is that which is created and creates (*quae et creatur et creat*);

the third is that which is created and does not create (*quae creatur et non creat*);

and the fourth is that which neither creates nor is created (*quae nec creat nec creatur*).

Thus a fourfold division of nature[21] results. The first and the third species are said to be in opposition, as are the second and the fourth. The fourth species belongs to the class of things which are said to be 'impossibles' because their existence is impossible[22].

As a logical device division had a long history in such figures as Socrates, Porphyry, Augustine and Eriugena's near contemporaries Theodulf of Orléans and Alcuin[23]. Striking in Eriugena's use of the method is the way it combines his undertaking to present a systematic account of all that is. It is however above all his choice of the

---

[20] In his note on PP I lines 19/26, p. 3 of the critical edition, É. JEAUNEAU reports that Bett attributed this four fold division to AUGUSTINE, *De ciuitate dei*, V, 9, 4; CCSL 47, p. 139, 138–144; (= PL 41, 151). In my opinion it is important to point out that here Augustine is discussing *efficient* causality in dialogue with Cicero's *De Fato*. A corresponding fourth species, essential to Eriugena's eschatological perspective is missing in the Augustinian text. É. Jeauneau himself prefers to point out the affinity to the division of numbers in Philo and Martianus Capella and offers the following references: PHILO of Alexandria, *De opificio mundi*, 99, L. COHN – P. WENDLAND (ed.), editio minor, Berlin, 1886, p. 27, 28–31 and MARTIANUS CAPELLA, De Nuptiis, VII, 738, J. WILLIS (ed.), Leipzig, 1983, p. 266, line 17–p. 267, line 5. I consulted not the editio minor of Philo's works, but the standard edition with critical apparatus: PHILO OF ALEXANDRIA, *De opificio mundi*, 99, L. COHN–P. WENDLAND (ed.),, Berlin, 1896, p. 34, 1–4: ἐκείνων γὰρ οἱ μὲν γεννῶσιν οὐ γεννώμενοι, οἱ δὲ γεννῶνται μὲν, οὐ γεννῶσι δέ, οἱ δὲ ἀμφότερα καὶ γεννῶσι καὶ γεννῶνται· μόνη δ᾽ ἑβδομὰς ἐν οὐδενὶ μέρει θεωρεῖται. "for of these [numbers within the decade – H. M.] some beget without being begotten, some are begotten but do not beget, some do both these, both beget and are begotten: 7 alone is found in no such category.", English translation from F. H. COLSON, and G. H. WHITAKER, *Philo in ten volumes (and two supplementary volumes)*, Vol. I, London: Heinemann Ltd, 1966, p. 79. In Philo a four-fold division is reported. His text goes to speak of the number seven alone as neither begetting nor being begotten: μόνας δ᾽ ὡς ἔφην ὁ ἑπτὰ οὔτε γεννᾶν πέφυκεν οὔτε γεννᾶσθαι. De opif. mun. 100, p. 34, 9–10. So I agree that this four-fold division may indeed have inspired Eriugena.

 The link to Martianus Capella is promising too. Eriugena was certainly familiar with the passage in De Nuptiis. In this reflection on the numbers in the decade MARTIANUS CAPELLA even uses in part the terminology *creat/creatur*: "*tetras autem et creat et creatur*", De Nuptiis, VII, 738, J. WILLIS (ed.), p. 267, line 3.

[21] The expression *diuisio naturae* has been taken over a name for the work as a whole which has often been referred to as *De diuisione naturae*.

[22] "*Videtur mihi diuisio naturae per quattuor differentias quattuor species recipere, quarum prima est in eam quae creat et non creatur, secunda in eam quae et creatur et creat, tertia in eam quae creatur et non creat, quarta quae nec creat nec creatur. Harum uero quattuor binae sibi inuicem opponuntur. Nam tertia opponitur primae, quarta uero secundae; sed quarta inter impossibilia ponitur, cuius esse est non posse esse.*", PP I, 19 -25, pp. 3–4, (= PL 122, 441B–442A).

[23] See D'ONOFRIO, Über die Natur der Einteilung pp. 34 -35. The author situates Eriugena's account of division within an extensive history of logic. GANGOLF SCHRIMPF, Das Werk des Johannes Scottus Eriugena, concentrates on logic and dialectic as exercised in the *Carolingian Renaissance*.

verb according to which the general term of nature is divided into species which merits attention. Eriugena does not choose other available verbs such as to cause / be caused but rather the theologically hued verb to create / to be created[24]. In choosing this verb he adopts a tool which is open not only to Genesis chapters one to three, but to the full riches of the Judaeo-Christian scriptures; indeed in the course of *Periphyseon* we witness a process whereby the specific biblical themes interact with the more logical ordering[25]. His choice of verb is deliberate and is in accord with his identity as an interpreter of the Bible. Elsewhere Eriugena explicitly reflects on the other possibilities, more precisely on the infinite number of other possibilities, for dividing the *universitas* along the line of participated being and participating being[26].

Eriugena identifies the first species with God as cause of all that is; the second he identifies with the primordial causes; the third with the things which come into being in times and places. The fourth species is perhaps the most puzzling, in any case the second speaker of Periphyseon, the Alumnus is perturbed by what he calls the 'addition' of the fourth species, God as end of all things[27].

The Alumnus' request introduces the need to consider each of the divisions in turn. Thus the original programme for the work *Periphyseon* (in which each book handles a division and thus four books are planned) emerges[28].

---

[24] Compare D'ONOFRIO, Über die Natur der Einteilung, p. 2 on Eriugena's early use of logical methods within theology in *Div. praedestinatione*. Compare too GANGOLF SCHRIMPF, Das Werk des Johannes Scottus Eriugena, p. 72–108 on dialectic and *Div. praed.*

[25] The prime example of this being the necessitation of five books instead of four occasioned by the biblical understanding of the creation of the human in the image of God.

[26] "*Nam uniuersalis boni prima sectio est in illud unum ac summum incommutabile per se et substantiale bonum, ex quo omne bonum manat, et in illud bonum quod participatione summi et incommutabilis boni bonum est. Similiter uniuersalis essentiae, universalis uitae, uniuersalis sapientiae, uniuersalis uirtutis eadem principalis diuisio est.*" PP III, 83–88, pp. 5–6, (= PL 122 621 A–B). See D'ONOFRIO, Über die Natur der Einteilung, p. 32.

[27] *Periphyseon* takes the form of a dialogue between the two speakers, Nutritor and Alumnus. In this study when I quote from passages assigned to the Alumnus, this is explicitly indicated.
In this passage we see the Alumnus depending heavily on AUGUSTINE who, on the formal level, in *De civitate dei* worked with a three fold division and who, on the thematic level, spoke in *De Genesi ad litteram* VI, 10 and 11 of the primordial causes or primordial reasons CSEL 28, 1, JOSEPH ZYCHA (ed.), p. 182, 24 and p. 185, 5–6, (= PL 34, 346 and 347)). The 'addition' of a fourth species is however not original to Eriugena. The divisions of Philo and Martianus Capella already mentioned are four-fold. Sheldon-Williams traced the fourfold division back through Macrobius to a theory familiar to the Neoplatonists attributed by Philo to the Pythagoreans, see I. P. SHELDON-WILLIAMS note 10 on *Periphyseon* Book I, PL 122 444A, SLH edition, p. 38, line 2.

[28] D'ONOFRIO, Über die Natur der Einteilung, pp. 26/7 on the problem posed by the relationship of the two-fold division (*quae sunt / quae non sunt*) to the four-fold one: "Der Einfachheit des porphyrianischen Verfahrens widerspricht zuerst das Nebeneinander von zwei verschiedenen Einteilungen, wobei beide in demselben Text als Haupteinteilungen, des gleichen Begriffes *natura* eingeführt werden …". In this article he resolves this difficulty in terms of the distinction between the different ways of apprehending the one reality by *nous* and by *ratio:* "die Spaltung zwischen *ratio* und *intellectus* ist der Grund, aus dem das Nebeneinander von zwei verschiedenen Formen der Einteilung, die nicht gleichen Regeln folgen, in bezug auf denselben logischen Gegenstand

In these opening passages of *Periphyseon* we see how creation is emerging as the basic relation of the world to God. Eriugena attempts to give a rational account of this relationship within the limited possibility of speaking of God. The author draws on Scripture and thus has what, from a philosophical point of view, may be considered a contingent starting point. Eriugena does not explicitly defend his choice of the term 'creation'. It flows from his belief in, and familiarity with, the Judaeo-Christian scriptures. He thus exercises his method in terms of a theology of the world-God relationship as creation. This, as Schrimpf has shown, may be viewed as a confirmation of the methodology used by Eriugena in *De divina praedestinatione*. Here the methods of logic were also imbued with theological contents. In that work it was not a world-God relationship which was the subject matter but a Christian anthropology and ethics[29]. The basic 'circumincession' of logical and theological methods (to which the choice of 'creation' as key to the division of nature bears witness) was, however, already apparent in that early work.

### 1.3 Modes of Understanding Existence

Eriugena once again returns to the division of all things into the things that are and the things that are not and proceeds to present five modes of interpreting this basic difference (*primordialis differentia*). This presentation of the five modes of interpretation confirms in my opinion, the epistemological nature of the first primordial division. Even those interpreters of *Periphyseon* who see the first discussion of the things that are and the things that are not, as an ontological distinction must admit that the distinction is subsequently 'epistemologically' interpreted by Eriugena.

The first mode of interpretation is that in which reason differentiates between that which can be perceived by corporeal sense or grasped by reason (*corporeo sensui uel intelligentiae perceptioni*) and is thus said to be, while the things which, because of the excellence of their nature, elude not only sense but also all intellect and reason are said not to be[30]. Eriugena says that this is true because God is the essence of all things. Eriugena supports this first mode of interpretation with a quote from Ps. Dionysius to the effect that God is the existence of all things and with a reference

---

gerechtfertigt werden kann.", pp. 30/31. Compare GANGOLF SCHRIMPF, "Die systematische Bedeutung der beiden logischen Einteilungen (*divisiones*) zu Beginn von *Periphyseon*". In this article Schrimpf reviews other earlier scholar's views on why there are two logical schemes presented at the start of *Periphyseon*.

[29] See GANGOLF SCHRIMPF, Das Werk des Johannes Scottus Eriugena, pp. 114–131.

[30] SCHRIMPF (in "Die systematische Bedeutung") sees in this first mode of interpretation a confirmation for taking the distinction (between the things that are and the things that are not) epistemologically, I agree with this interpretation which is also supported by Dominic O'Meara's analysis (see my p. 46, footnote 15). In D'ONOFRIO's article "Über die Natur der Einteilung" the epistemological import of the first division is not even questioned. Rather D'Onofrio concentrated on clarifying why Eriugena needs two divisional schemes ascribing the first to a noetic intuition, the second to a reasoned intention of nature.

to Gregory of Nazianzus[31]. From Gregory he gains the confirmation that for many reasons no substance or essence of any creature may be fully comprehended by the intellect or reason.

Eriugena goes on to give a theological reason for the incomprehensibility of the creaturely essences: he argues, just as God is not comprehended when as God is in God's very Self beyond all creatures, so is God not comprehended in the innermost depths of creatures which have been made by God and which exist in God. We may note that Eriugena does not here rule out the knowledge that God holds the creature in existence. But he seems to tie the incomprehensibility of the creature positively to this divine inherence. Negatively speaking, the creaturely essence is only indirectly accessible through the accidents. Through quality, quantity, form, matter or difference, or place or time we learn not what a thing is in its essence but that it is.

This first mode of interpreting the division of things which are and are not is held by Eriugena to be the most fundamental: "*Iste igitur modus primus ac summus est diuisionis eorum quae dicuntur esse et non esse …*"[32]. This remark is of immense significance for the methodology of the work as a whole and our theme in particular.

The second mode of interpretation concerns the orders of, and differences between, various types of creature. Each order can be said to be and not to be. When compared to the order above it or below it, it may be said not to be.[33] The affirmation of the lower order is the negation of the higher order and vice versa. The very highest order represents an exception. In this case the existence of no higher order is implied by its negation. Again the very lowest order does not say anything about a lower order because it is not followed by any other.

Eriugena then adds another reason why each order is said to be and not to be: each order is insofar as it is known by the orders above it and by itself; it is not insofar as it does not permit itself to be known by those below it.

The third mode of interpretation seems to broach the domain of theology in its contents and its sources. It is a presentation of the Augustinian theology of the seminal power[34]. It is seen in the fullness of created things as they appear in the visible world and as they are hidden in their causes in the most secret folds of nature which precede them. Those things which are known in matter and form, generated in time and place are said by human convention to be. Those things which are 'still' within the folds of nature and which do not appear in any accidents are said not to be. Eriugena says that of the many examples available, the example of human nature

---

[31] *Gregory of Nazianzus, Oratio 28,* PAUL GALLAY (ed.), MAURICE JOURJON (collaboration), S.C, 250, p. 108–110, (= PG 36, 32B–C). Most probably Eriugena encountered this text through it's citation by Maximus Confessor.

[32] PP I, 73–74, p. 5, (= PL 122 443C).

[33] Compare AUGUSTINUS, *Confessiones,* XI, 4, L. VERHEIJEN (ed.), CCSL, 27, p. 197, 8–10, = (PL 32 811), "*Nec ita pulchra sunt nec ita bona sunt nec ita sunt, sicut tu conditor eorum, quo comparato nec pulchra sunt nec bona sunt nec sunt.*"

[34] See for example AUGUSTINUS, *In Iohannis euangelium tractatus,* IX, 5, R. WILLEMS (ed.), CCSL 36, p. 93, 15–16, (= PL 35, 1460): "*ex occultis creaturae sinibus*".

is most clear. He then gives a theological interpretation of the coming into existence of the human race. God established all human beings in God's image in the first human being although all humans do not appear at the same time. Those who have become visible in the world are said to be, those who up to now have been hidden but who will appear in the future are said not to be.

The fourth mode of interpretation is that by which the philosophers[35] say, not improbably Eriugena adds, that only that which is grasped by the intellect is to be said to really be, those things which are generated in time, space and matter etc., for example bodies which are born and pass away, are said not to be.

The fifth mode of interpretation is said to apply only to the nature of human beings. Reason observes that human nature which was made in the image of God lost this dignity when it sinned, in this sense it lost being and therefore is said not to be. When however human nature is restored to the pristine condition of its substance through the grace of the only begotten son of God, it begins to be, and moreover in him who is established in the image of God it begins to *live*.

For Eriugena those who were lost in the first man and who fell into a certain loss of subsistence, are called by God the Father through faith in his Son. He calls them to be as those who have already been reborn in Christ. Eriugena is giving an interpretation of the Scriptural verse Rom. 4:17.

Eriugena then goes on to say that this may be said of the things which God daily calls forth from the secret folds of nature (something already treated in his third mode of interpretation) things which seem not to be, are able to appear in form and matter and other conditions in which hidden things are able to become manifest. He thus retrospectively affirms a trinitarian perspective on the emergence of all things from their secret reasons. Does the fifth mode of interpretation have a proper characteristic? Yes, the sense of being which is communicated by the metaphor of 'life', and which redeemed humans are held to experience.

Eriugena explicitly states that this listing of the modes of interpretation in *Periphyseon* is not necessarily exhaustive[36]. As a consequence we may conclude that he has presented us with the most significant modes of interpretation from the point of view of understanding the divisions of nature which he has presented to us.

The two-fold division of nature, the four-fold division of nature and the listing of five modes of interpreting *esse* are important parameters of Eriugena's system. They provide rudimentary epistemological and methodological parameters for any possible discourse about God. Of particular importance for the topic at hand is

---

[35] See PLATO, *Timaeus*, 27D–28A, according to Calcidius in: *Timaeus a Calcidio translatus commentarioque instructus*, J. H. WASZINK (ed.), (P. J. JENSEN collaboration), London: 1952, 2a edition, 1975, (= Corpus Platonicum medii aevi, Plato latinus vol. IV), p. 20, 15–20: "*Est igitur, ut mihi quidem uidetur, in primis diuidendum, quid sit quod semper est, carens generatione, quod item quod gignitur nec est semper, alterum intellectu perceptibile ductu et inuestigatione rationis, semper idem, porro alterum opinione cum inrationabili sensu opinabile proptereaque incertum, nascens et occidens neque umquam in existendi condicione constanti et rata perseuerans.*"

[36] PP I, 151–3, p. 8, (= PL 122 445D–446A).

the understanding of God and the God-world relationship which here emerges in terms of the bible theological term of creation. The four divisions of nature, coined as they are in terms of creation, make explicit the basic relationship between the world and God. The world is created by an uncreated God. The world and the *causae primordiales* are first and foremost created realities; that means that they are realities which are from, and are dependant on, a free, fashioning other.

The first and the fourth division within the four fold scheme are identified with God. God is creator and God is the end of a return of all being to its creator. All details on the divine nature which emerge further in *Periphyseon* and Eriugena's subsequent writings are integrated within this understanding of God.

The modes of being, here cryptic in the brevity with which they are handled, are however of utmost importance in correctly interpreting the further books in *Periphyseon*. That which is beyond comprehension is not; here we see a foundation stone in the edifice of negative theology which Eriugena will erect on the basis of a consideration of *creatio ex nihilo* later on. The observation of the hierarchic structure within which higher levels are said to have more real existence than the lower, is too a prerequisite for his treatment of *creatio ex nihilo*. The manifested cause is: this explicitly apparitional statement feeds into all that he says about God becoming in appearing. The position that the being of the enduring is; that of the becoming (and above all of the passing away) is not, will play an important role in Eriugena's eschatology. Finally, in the fifth mode of interpreting being, the human is considered as a special case, as a unique creature. Here the setting is that of fall and grace. Thus the perspective of salvation history is not merely present in his more biblically oriented works but here in *Periphyseon*. Nor is this perspective added on in the more explicitly biblically oriented analyses in *Periphyseon,* but is already present here in this first indication of the significant possibilities of interpreting the things that are and the things that are not.

## 1.4 God appearing: Theophania

The consideration of the modes of being is, in various ways, relevant to the topic investigated by this study: In particular the third mode of being, being through manifestation, is a sign post for what is to come. The manifested effect is, it exists, the 'non-manifested' cause is not. The theme of becoming through appearing will be expanded later on in *Periphyseon* and elsewhere[37]. Here it is introduced in a foundational setting, presenting this understanding of being as a legitimate one, but also admitting that it is one among many.

---

[37] In the conclusion to his article "The Concept of Natura", DOMINIC O'MEARA draws attention to an already emerging specificum of Eriugena's 'metaphysics'. Of Eriugena's so called *physiologia* he writes: "*Physiologia* is metaphysics, then, in its attention to the being fundamental and common to all things, but this being is understood as an appearing pointing 'inwards' to that of which it is an appearing but which is not the appearing, i. e. what 'is not', what is 'beyond being'", p. 144.

Within this fundamental consideration of the modes of being, questions arise which directly touch the theme of the divine appearing. A question concerning the appearing of God to humans and angels in the beatific vision is raised by the dialogue partner known as Alumnus. What first appears to be a limited objection turns out to be the occasion of an affirmation of the apparitional perspective.

The Alumnus considers it a problem that Augustine in his Hexaemeron says that even the angels know the primordial causes, that is, the primary exemplars which the Greeks call *prototypa* (πρωτότυπα), of others and of themselves, first in God, then in themselves and then in creatures themselves. But how can they know their own primordial causes before these have proceeded into their own species? The question arises in Alumnus' opinion because, according to the third mode of interpretation, the causes are not yet if they have not yet proceeded.

Whereas the question on the objects of human and angelic knowledge of the divine (God in God's-Self / the primordial causes) fails to appreciate the sense of 'not being' in the third mode of interpretation, the answer of the Nutritor does not fall back behind the level of reflection that has already been achieved through the account of this mode and the other four modes of interpretation. This answer is in terms of *the way* creaturely knowledge of the divine takes place, that is, as theophany.

It is interesting to observe Nutritor's procedure in dealing with this problem. Significantly Eriugena steers his way to Scripture in his answer. Thus he doesn't handle the problem as a problem between his theory and Augustine's theory as the Alumnus had suggested, but makes it into a problem between Augustine, the opinion of a teacher of highest and sacred authority, and the apostle. The leading scriptural quote which determines the problem is Phil. 4:7: "*et pax Dei quae exsuperat omnem sensum custodiat corda vestra et intelligentias vestras in Christo Iesu*" (Vulgata). The apostle's position seems to suggest an incomprehensibility of God: Augustine's passage seems to suggest a knowableness of the primordial causes in God. The strategy of the speaker Nutritor is to seek the correct middle way between them. He stresses that both are firmly to be held[38].

---

[38] Eriugena's method is interesting also from the point of view of the interweaving of scripturally based theology and reflective philosophy. He explains the first scriptural quotation in explicitly reflective terms: the cause of all things which surpasses all intellect does not allow itself to be known by a caused nature. Then he expands this argument scripturally where it is now not God as cause which is unknowable but the intellect of the Lord (Rom. 11:34) and the *pax Dei* (Phil. 4:7). With this verse '*pax Dei … in Christo Iesu*' we are firmly in the realm of salvation history not of abstract metaphysics.

He does then return to explicitly philosophical terms: if the cause of all things is so inaccessible, then the reasons of all things which exist eternally and immutably in it are utterly inaccessible to all things of which they are the reasons. (I. P. SHELDON-WILLIAMS / L. BIELER translate '*rationes*' in this way. See SLH VII, note 34, p. 225 "… *ratio* of a created thing is that in it which is perfect and eternal in accordance with which it is created". The note maintains that neither the word 'principle' nor the word 'essence' alone have all the necessary connotations).

Nutritor then goes on to suggest a solution to the problem which he has outlined *and in the terms in which he has outlined it.* Nutritor says that it is true to say that in the intellects of angels there exist certain theophanies[39] of these reasons. By theophanies are meant certain appearances graspable by the intellectual nature, not however the reasons themselves, that is the primary exemplars.

Before lower orders of creatures proceeded into their species the angels knew these theophanies. There is more than one meaning to the expression 'in God'. To say that the angels knew the principal causes of lower creatures first 'in God' does not mean that they comprehended the divine nature itself. For not only the divine nature itself is indicated by 'God' but also, as is often the case in Scripture, the way that it shows itself in a certain way to the intellectual and rational creature according to their various capacities[40]. Eriugena writes that the Greeks are accustomed to call this mode theophania (that is the appearance of God)[41].

Eriugena can then conclude that nothing speaks against the position that those things which are above the comprehension of all reason and the intellect are said not to be and those things which may be grasped by intellect or reason are said to be. Thus Alumnus' objection has provided him with an occasion to defend his first and third modes of interpretation alike.

Scriptural quotations which recurr in his work when he speaks of the theophanic appearing of God include I Jn: 3:2 *"Scimus quia filii dei sumus et nondum apparuit quid erimus. Cum autem apparuerit, similes ei erimus, uidebimus enim eum sicuti est"* and 1 Cor. 13:12 *"Nunc uidimus per speculum et aenigmate, tunc autem facie ad faciem"* both of which deal with the appearing of God to the blessed in heaven[42].

---

[39] See too ERIUGENA, Comm. I, XXV, 78–85, É. JEAUNEAU (ed.) p. 122–124 ; PL. 122 302AB: *"Quid, inquam, uident homines et angeli, uel uisuri sunt, dum apertissime et sanctus Ambrosius et Dionysius ariopagita absque ulla cunctatione inculcant deum, summam dico trinitatem, nulli per se ipsam umquam apparuisse, nunquam apparere, nunquam apparituram? Apparebit itaque in theophaniis suis, hoc est in diuinis apparitionibus, in quibus iuxta altitudinem puritatis et uirtutis uniuscuiusque deus apparebit."* Here we are not only given information on the form in which it is possible to speak of the trinitarian God appearing, i.e. in theophanies, but this form is linked to the individual virtue and purity of the beholder. The Ps. DIONYSIUS is definitely a source for Eriugena in this description of knowledge: *De coelesti hierarchia* IV, 3, G. HEIL (ed.), Berlin: De Gruyter, 1991, (= Patristische Texte und Studien, vol., 36), p. 22, 1–5; PG 3, 180C. The Ps. Dionysian text too is an attempt to reconcile the biblical accounts of an appearing of God to pious humans with biblical affirmations of the incomprehensibility of God. It speaks of an appearing to the pious which is nevertheless in accord with the divinity: θεοφάνειαι δὲ τοῖς ὁσίοις γεγόνασι κατὰ τὰς πρέπουσας θεῷ.

[40] Eriugena agrees with the theory that the angel possesses a threefold knowledge. The first is a higher knowledge of the eternal reasons as just described. The second is when the angel makes an image of this image in its memory. Thirdly, the angel has knowledge of the things below it. On *'imago imaginis'* see GREGORY OF NYSSA, De imagine, 12 (13), (= PG 44, 164 A), (in ERIUGENA's translation *"ueluti quaedam imago imaginis est"*, CAPPUYNS (ed.), p. 225, 10, (= PL 122, 790A)).

[41] See Ps. DIONYSIUS *De coelesti hierarchia* IV, 3, G. HEIL (ed.), p. 22, 1–22, (= PG 3, 180C–181A).

[42] See AUGUSTINE, *De civitate dei* XXII, 29, 182–213, B. DOMBART, A. KALB, (ed.), CCSL 48, p. 861–862, (= PL 41, 800–801) that the blessed in heaven will contemplate God with translucent clarity in the bodies we will put on and in every body we see. Which, even taking into account that

The absolute limitation of creaturely knowledge of God (be it angelic or human ) is investigated and affirmed by Eriugena, be it in this life or the next. The theophanic nature of our limited knowledge of God is affirmed in this 'heavenly' context too. In heaven all creatures who are lucky enough to enjoy eternal happiness experience theophanies which are reproduced out of the divine essence and by it in the intellectual nature. The theophanies are said to be reproduced (*exprimuntur*) in the intellectual nature out of the divine essence and from it and also are called 'God'.[43] A lengthy account of theophany occurs too in the fourth chapter of Eriugena's commentary on Dionysius' The Celestial Hierarchy. Here he speaks of those who seek to be formed by that form which God is and which they desire[44].

An emphasis on the divine generosity (Eriugena uses the expression *largietur* in the following) with which theophany is bestowed merits mention. Speaking of the form which is desired he writes in *Periphyseon*: "*Quae, dum sit una eademque incommutabilisque permaneat, multiplex tamen uidebitur his quibus in se habitare largietur.*"[45] A strictly theological contextualisation in terms of the trinitarian God and the work of grace follows: "*... unusquisque ... unigeniti dei uerbi notitiam in se ipso possidebit, quantum ei gratia donabitur.*"[46] The multiplication of divine theophanies corresponds to the number of holy souls in heaven: "*Quot enim numerus est electorum, tot erit numerus mansionum. Quanta fuerit sanctarum animarum multiplicatio, tanta erit diuinarum theophaniarum possessio.*"[47]

Eriugena is indebted to several sources for his account of the theophanic appearing of God. Nutritor's report that Maximus spoke most deeply and subtly about these matters is reflected in the extensive Maximus '*Rezeption*' in *Periphyseon* book one[48]. Eriugena approvingly assigns to Maximus[49] the position that *as far as* the

---

here risen bodies are in question, is nevertheless a significantly aesthetic position and which may have influenced Eriugena on the perception of the risen Body of Christ by the blessed.

[43] PP I, 256–259, p. 11, (= PL 122 448B).

[44] "*Propterea, inquit, celestes essentie reliquas post se substitutas precedunt, causeque omnium proxime sunt, quoniam inuisibiliter seipsas in diuinam similitudinem naturali modo, diuina cooperante gratia, conformant, et ad diuinam imitationem supra mundum intellectualem suam speciem, que Deus est, aspiciunt et ea formari se appetunt, hoc est ab ipsa formari desiderant, et pulchre copiosiores ceteris creaturis ad eam, speciem uidelicet ad quam formantur omnia, habent comuniones.*", ERIUGENA, *Expositiones in ierarchiam coelestem*, IV, 251–259, J. BARBET (ed.), pp. 71–72, (in PL 122 this passage of text is not available).

[45] PP I, 274–276, p. 12, (= PL 122 448C). See HILARY MOONEY, "The Notion of the Liberality of God in Gregory of Nyssa and Johannes Scottus Eriugena", in: M. F. WILES, E. J. YARNOLD (ed.), P. M. PARVIS (assistance), *Studia Patristica, vol. XXXVII*, papers presented at the *Thirteenth International Conference on Patristic Studies held in Oxford 1999*, Leuven: Peeters, 2001.

[46] PP I, 276–278, p. 12, (= PL 122 448C )

[47] PP I, 278–280, p. 12, (= PL 122 448C–D )

[48] Here in PP I, 294, p. 13 following, (PL 122, 449A following ) the '*Rezeption*' is presented as such, that is as the ideas of another albeit one with whom Eriugena, obviously agrees. Later on in this work and other writings the ideas will be integrated within his own synthesis and more clearly presented as is own.

[49] See ERIUGENA's translation, MAXIMUS CONFESSOR, *Ambigua ad Iohannem*, VI, 140–145, É. JEAUNEAU (ed.), CCSG 18, p. 48–49; (= PG 91, 1113B–C).

human intellect ascends through '*caritas*' *so far* does the divine wisdom descend through compassion ('*misericordia*') and that this dynamic is the cause and the substance of all the virtues. "*In quantum enim, ut ait Maximus, humanus intellectus ascendit per caritatem, in tantum diuina sapientia descendit per misericordiam; et haec est causa omnium uirtutum et substantia.*"[50]

Eriugena then links virtue and being gifted with theophanic encounter with God.

*Igitur omnis theophania, id est omnis uirtus, et in hac uita in qua adhuc incipit in his qui digni sunt formari, et in futura uita perfectionem diuinae beatitudinis accepturi, non extra se sed in se et ex deo et ex se ipsis efficitur.*[51]

Every theophany is here related to virtue, a human moral reality. The *intimate* nature of theophany as an encounter between God and the human person is stressed, an encounter *in* the human subject.

The preparatory role of grace is made specific through the naming of the three grades of illumination:

*Ex deo itaque theophaniae in natura angelica atque humana illuminata, purgata, perfecta per gratiam fiunt ex descensione diuinae sapientiae et ascensione humanae intelligentiae.*[52]

Here the three grades *illuminata, purgata, perfecta* show that we are dealing with a '*heilsgeschichtliche*' perspective. They are also listed in the Commentary on John's Gospel: "*quae purgabitur prius per fidem, illuminabitur per scientiam, perficietur per deificationem ...*"[53]. They also occur in Eriugena's dedicatory letter[54] accompanying his translation of the works of the Pseudo-Dionysius and indeed the terms occur within the Dionysian corpus. For Dionysius they are the grades by which one ascends to deification: katharsis, photismos, teleiosis (κάθαρσις, φωτισμὸς, τελείωσις).[55]

Eriugena proposes the principle that whatever the intellect is able to comprehend, that it becomes.[56] He expands: to the extent that the soul comprehends virtue it becomes virtue. Eriugena uses the Maximian illustration for this, the picture of sunlight in air[57]. Air is illuminated by the sun. The air then seems to be nothing other than light, not because it loses its own nature, but because the light prevails in it so that it, the air, may be held to be light. So too human nature joined to God is said to be God through and through (*per omnia*), not because it lacks (its own)

---

[50] PP I, 317–320, p. 14 (= PL 122 449C).

[51] PP I, 320–323, p. 14, (= PL 122 449C–D).

[52] PP I, 324–326, p. 14, (= PL 122, 449D).

[53] Comm. IV,7, 52–54, É. Jeauneau (ed.), p. 316–318; (= PL 122, 338D–339 A).

[54] PL 122, 1031A.

[55] De coel. hier., III, 2, G. Heil (ed.), p. 19, 3–8; (= PG 3, 165C). See also VII, 3; VIII, 2.

[56] Eriugena presents this Aristotelian teaching as the fruit of his reading Maximus.

[57] Maximus Confessor, *Ambigua ad Iohannem*, III, 120–130, É. Jeauneau (ed.), p. 25, (= PG 91, 1073C–1076A).

nature but because it receives a share (*participationem*) in Divinity so that only God appears to be in it.

*Sicut enim aer a sole illuminatus nihil aliud uidetur esse nisi lux, non quia sui naturam perdat, sed quia lux in eo praeualeat ut id ipsum luci esse aestimetur, sic humana natura deo adiuncta deus per omnia dicitur esse, non quod desinat esse natura, sed quod diuinitatis participationem accipiat ut solus in ea deus esse uideatur.*[58]

In his image both the light and the air are separately invisible and only become visible when they come together. He then develops the case of the light of the sun as an image for the becoming manifest of the in-itself-incomprehensible Divine Essence. This latter becomes manifest when it is joined to the intellect of an intellectual creature so that the Divine essence is seen alone (*sola in ea*) in the intellectual creature:

*Ac per hoc intellige diuinam essentiam per se incomprehensibilem esse, adiunctam uero intellectuali creaturae mirabili modo apparere ita ut ipsa, diuina dico essentia, sola in ea, creatura intellectuali uidelicet, appareat.*[59]

'Alone' here means this is the only way that God is 'known'; not by comprehension but in another. It does not mean that God only appears in *intellectual* creatures. This is clear from the sentence which follows: there Eriugena speaks about God appearing in *all* things. Nothing else is presented to those that have this understanding but the ineffable excellence of the divine essence: "*Ipsius enim ineffabilis excellentia omnem naturam sui participem superat ut nil aliud in omnibus praeter ipsam intelligentibus occurrat, dum per se ipsam, ut diximus, nullo modo appareat.*"[60]

The appearing of God in all things is elucidated by Eriugena by means of a dialogue with Augustine. A text from *De ciuitate dei* is interpreted. The text, as cited by Eriugena, reads "*Per corpora quae gestabimus in omni corpore quodcunque uidebimus quaquauersum oculos nostri corporis duxerimus ipsum deum perspicua claritate contemplabimur.*"[61] For Eriugena the important phrases are *per corpora/ in omni corpore*. We shall not see God in God's Self but through bodies in bodies. This is the setting of knowledge of God: it is through the bodies which we shall put on. This is a radically aesthetic position: even in the afterlife our risen bodies are a means of receiving the divine and the occasion of the revealing of the divine for others. There then appears the puzzling sentence "*Similiter per intellectum in intellectibus, per rationem in rationibus, non per se ipsam diuina essentia apparebit.*"[62] Eriugena's concern is to defend the incomprehensibility of the divine essence at all levels of cognition. Yet far from presenting this as something negative, as if it were some unfortunate consequence of the magnitude of the divine essence, he presents

---

[58] PP I, 331–336, p. 14, (= PL 122 450A).

[59] PP I, 340–344, pp. 14–15, (= PL 122 450B).

[60] PP I, 344–347, p. 15, (= PL 122 450B).

[61] See AUGUSTINE, *De ciuitate dei*, XXII, 29, B. DOMBART and A. KALB (ed.), 185–197, p. 861; (= PL 41, 800).

[62] PP I, 359–361, p. 15, (= PL 122 450C).

it positively: so great is the excellence of the divine power that it alone shall be manifest in all things in the future. Eriugena ties this to the biblical verse 1 Cor. 15:28 that God will be all in all[63]. He uses this text in a theophanic context, not in terms of a pantheistic ontology. This presentation is still informed by the image of the light of the sun in the air where it was explicitly stated that the air does not lose its own nature. He confirms the aesthetic orientation of his argumentation by adding a reference to Job 19:29: "*Et in carne mea uidebo deum*". Eriugena gives a very specific interpretation of this verse of Job: Job says that in this body which is inflicted with so many trials, the same measure of glory shall be realised in the future, so that just as now nothing appears in it except death and corruption (*nihil in ea nunc apparet nisi mors et corruptio*), in the future life nothing shall appear to me in it except God alone, who is life and immortality and incorruptibility (*qui uere uita est et immortalitas et incorruptio*).

A quotation from the writer he calls Gregory the theologian occurs within this context:

*Praesertim cum, ut ait magnus Gregorius theologus, corpora sanctorum in rationem, ratio in intellectum, intellectus in deum, ac per hoc tota illorum natura in ipsum deum mutabitur*[64].

The context is not pantheistic. The strength of the fore-going image of light and air again endures. '*Mutabitur*' in this context is to be understood in the sense of 'will let shine through'.

He refers back to the image of the air and light and goes on to give another image, that of iron in fire[65].

*Sicut ergo totus aer lux, totumque ferrum liquefactum, ut diximus, igneum, immo etiam ignis apparet, manentibus tamen eorum substantiis, ita sano intellectu accipiendum quia post finem huius mundi omnis natura siue corporea siue incorporea solus deus esse uidebitur, naturae integritate permanente, ut et deus, qui per se ipsum incomprehensibilis est, in creatura quodam modo comprehendatur, ipsa uero creatura ineffabili miraculo in deum uertatur.*[66]

---

[63] PP I, 364–365, p. 15 (= PL 122 450D).

[64] PP I, 372–375, p. 15, (= PL 122 451A). Eriugena applies this epithet to Gregory of Nyssa and to Gregory of Nazianzus.

[65] In the endnote 57 of the SLH edition, vol. VII, p. 227 I. P. Sheldon-Williams / L. Bieler mention that the image is used by Origen in De princ. ii 6. I presume he is referring to De princ. 2, 6, 6. Sheldon-Williams quotes the "soul plunged in the Word", when "all that it feels, all that it wills, all that it does, is God". This corresponds in the Latin of Rufinus' translation to "*Hoc ergo modo etiam illa anima, quae quasi ferrum in igne sic semper in uerbo, semper in sapientia, semper in deo posita est, omne quod agit, quod sentit, quod intellegit, deus est …*" Origenes, De princ. 2, 6, 6, 192–195, H. Crouzel / M. Simonetti (ed.), SC 252, p. 320 Yet this passage entails, in my opinion, a different usage of the image of the iron in the fire. In Origen the discussion is immediately of what the soul experiences; in Eriugena it seems to me to be primarily a discussion of what the soul mediates, that is, lets shine through it. Only the context in the Origenian text where the image *of viewing* iron in fire is expanded, supports the comparison. Furthermore Origen is primarily speaking of the soul of Christ in the hypostatic union and only secondarily about other human souls.

[66] PP I, 382–389, p. 16, (= PL 122 451B).

The verb *'uidebitur'* shows that here *'uertatur'* is to be taken on the cognitive level of the appearing of God not on an ontological level which might suggest pantheism.

## 2. The Divine Nature: *ea quae creat et non creatur* and the God of the bible and tradition

Eriugena sets himself the task of accounting for God using the instrument of the four-fold division. As we have already noted the verb which he chooses for structuring this division is the biblical notion of creating. In his account of the divine, the relationship between the description of the divine nature as *ea quae creat et non creatur* and the names for God explicitly mentioned in the bible becomes the focus of attention.

### 2.1 God within the four-fold division

Eriugena's doctrine of God takes its rise from the first difference in accordance with which that which both creates and is uncreated is identified with God. Eriugena, in line with his plan for *Periphyseon,* undertakes to expound this division of nature in the first book of *Periphyseon.* Yet very early on in his exposition, he has to consider other factors which seem to mitigate against this way of reflecting on the absolute, or at least to demand that one show that they are compatible with his analysis. Above all he has to deal with the biblical accounts of God and their interpretation by the theological tradition. He has, for example, to account for those texts which seem to suggest that God is made; he has to deal with those texts which describe God as triune; he has to consider within which form of theology the biblical names for God may be accommodated; and he has to deal with specially privileged names for God such as amor, visio, motus. Thus the whole account of God in *Periphyseon* book I may be read as an interaction of various schemes of reference: an adaptation of the four-fold divisional scheme already centring on the creator-creation relationship to other aspects of the biblical message on God. It is a highly differentiated theological attempt to embrace progressively the systematic starting point of the four-fold division, and the contents of the Judaeo-Christian scriptures, the questions raised by the philosophical doctrine of the ten categories and its interpretation by the church fathers.

The first difference of the divisions of nature was identified as that which creates and is not created. This species is said to be properly predicated of God alone, who creates everything and is understood to be ANAPXOC (anarchos)[67]. Eriugena explains this Greek term as "without beginning". He finds it fitting because God alone is the principal cause of all things which are made from God and through God.

---

[67] PP I, 405, p. 16, (= PL 122, 451C). Compare PP I, 3167, p. 101, (= PL 122, 516A).

God is also the end of all things which are from God; for all things desire God. In this sense God is therefore the beginning and the middle and the end. For all things which partake of essence are from God; God is the middle because in God and through God they subsist and are moved; God is the end because it is towards God that all things which are seeking rest from their motion, and the stability of their perfection are moved. Thus Eriugena expands on his concept of God within the framework suggested by his four-fold division of the species of nature, above all in terms of God's not being created, and God as being in-God's-self without beginning, but being the beginning, middle and end of all things. A doctrine of God emerges which includes ideas whose heritage goes back to a wide range of thinkers, but which is in Eriugena's writings proximately influenced by his reading of the Ps. Dionysius[68].

## 2.2 *The problem raised by traditional ways of predicating terms of God*

Eriugena must deal with the apparent problem posed by the fact that in his opinion the fathers frequently refer to the divine nature not only as creating but being created: "*Ea siquidem, ut aiunt, facit et fit, et creat et creatur.*"[69] He must reconcile his preferred means of analysing reality with an apparent contradiction with the theological tradition in general, and the writings of the Pseudo- Dionysius in particular. Eriugena himself admits his dependence on the Pseudo-Dionysius on this point: "*Deus est itaque omne quod uere est, quoniam ipse facit omnia, ut fit in omnibus, ut ait sanctus Dionysius Ariopagita.*"[70] De div. nom. V, 8, indeed seems to be an important source for the idea of God becoming. Here we find not only such expressions as that God was, and is, but even that God 'will become' (γενήσεται): καὶ τὸ ἦν ἐπ' αὐτοῦ καὶ τὸ ἔστι καὶ τὸ ἔσται καὶ τὸ ἐγένετο καὶ γίνεται καὶ γενήσεται κυρίως ὑμνεῖται[71].

The Pseudo-Dionysian treatise is an investigation of biblical predication of terms of God, chapter five centring on the sense in which being is predicated of God. Eriugena too investigates the biblical naming of God considering different predications. He prefaces the particular problem at hand (that of God's becoming or, in Eriugena's terms, being created) with an investigation of the name which he says is

---

[68] See Ps. DIONYSIUS: *De div. nom.*, IV, 4, B. SUCHLA (ed.), p. 148, 8–11, (= PG 3, 700A) (ἀρχή, συνοχή, τέλος). Here Ps. Dionysius also worked with the image of the sun and its light and uses it with respect to the notion of the Good.

See too De div. nom. V, 8, p. 187, 3, and 14–15 (= PG 3, 824A and B). In the first text the key phrase is: ἀρχὴ καὶ μεσότης καὶ τελευτή. Further on in the chapter: ἀρχὰς καὶ μέσα καὶ τέλη τῶν ὄντων.

See also De div. nom. V, 10, p. 189, 7, (= PG 3, 825B ) for God as beginning and end of all things.

[69] PP I, 420–421, p. 17, (= PL 122 452A).

[70] PP III, 586–588, p. 22, (= PL 122 633A ).

[71] De div. nom., B. SUCHLA (ed.), p. 187, 5–6, (= PG 3, 824A).

most usually used in Holy Scripture, that is 'God' (ΘEOC).[72] He has recourse to a commonplace etymological position in terms of the verbs to see, ΘEΩPΩ[73] and to run, ΘEΩ[74]and via these verbs[75] (above all the second with its seeming implication of motion) he moves on to a preliminary consideration of the question whether motion may be predicated of God.

Important observations on the metaphorical nature of our predication of God emerge in this preliminary discussion of motion. Eriugena is clear that motion cannot be predicated of God in the proper sense of the word. The notion of motion is then first internalised and then psychologised: "*Deum moueri non extra se dixi, sed a se ipso in se ipso ad se ipsum*"[76]. God's 'motion' is internal. Next it is presented in terms of the divine will (*uoluntatis appetitum*). God's 'motion' is identified with God's will in willing all things to be made (*quo uult omnia fieri*).[77]

He concludes that motion and rest are used metaphorically of God in a sentence which deserves to be quoted because of its methodological scope:

*Haec igitur nomina sicut et multa similia ex creatura per quandam diuinam metaphoram ad creatorem referuntur.*[78]

It is interesting to note that here in the first book of *Periphyseon,* Eriugena gives quite a long account of God as *quae creat et non creatur,* including the above treated methodological reflection on metaphorical predication of God, before this major work comes to the extended methodological account of apophatic and kataphatic theology and of the possibility of talking about God within the ten categories for which it is famous.[79]

---

[72] See too *Expositiones in ierarchiam coelestem,* I, 175–182, J. BARBET, (ed.), p. 5, (= PL 122 130D–131A).

[73] Jeauneau in his apparatus gives references to, among others, Macrobius *Saturnalia;* Gregory of Nyssa *Ad Ablabium quod non sint tres dei* and *In Canticum canticorum homiliae;* and Ps. Dionysius *De div. nom.*

[74] In his apparatus Jeauneau gives references among others to Plato's *Cratylus;* Macrobius, *Saturnalia;* Gregory of Nazianzus, *Orationes.*

[75] Eriugena says that most probably it is derived from both, since the meaning of both (when applied to God, that is), is one and the same. He goes on to expand on this: ΘEΩPΩ implies God sees; ΘEΩ implies God runs, for God runs through all things and never stays in the sense of Ps. 147:15 "*Velociter currit sermo eius*". It is not two things to say that God runs through all things and God sees all things: "*Non enim aliud est deo currere per omnia quam uidere omnia; sed sicut uidendo, ita et currendo fiunt omnia*", PP I, 451–453, p. 19, (= PL 122 452D). See too PP I, 754–762, p. 28, (= PL 122 460A).

[76] PP I, 458–459, p. 19, (= PL 122 453A).

[77] PP I, 460, p. 19, (= PL 122 453A).

[78] PP I, 468–469, p. 19, (= PL 122 453A–B).

[79] By the time he reaches that reflection, he has already dealt with the bible's most frequent name for the divine, has already made observations about proper and metaphorical talk about God. He has also considered to some extent the possibility of predicating the category of motion of God. His de facto theological and biblical interpretation of the nature of God, his academic *praxis* in this sense, precedes his *theory* in this important example. Certainly he is writing on the strength of the reflection on the divisions of nature and modes of interpretation of existence in the opening pas-

## 2.3 *The resolution of the puzzle of God being made: the manifestation of God*

Eriugena must now face a dilemma. He has spoken of God within two frames of reference. First, the scheme which divided nature into four species: within this scheme God is that which creates and is not created, (that which are created and create are the primordial causes). The second framework within which he has spoken about God is the patristic assertion that God not only makes but is also made. He must now explain the seeming contradiction between these two ways of speaking about God. His solution is to stress that the divine nature isn't created *by anything else,* hereby allowing a being created *by itself* in the sense of becoming manifest *in* all things.

He offers an illustration for this taken from the realm of cognition and communication. He draws attention to the way our intellect may be said to become when it comes to know and remember and be formed in fantasies and expressed in sounds and signs. He compares this to the way that the divine essence, itself of course existing in a manner which far exceeds our intellect, may be said to be created in the things which are made by itself and through itself and in itself and for itself, so that it comes to be known by others:

*Hac similitudine, quamuis a diuina natura remota sit, suaderi tamen posse arbitror quomodo ipsa, dum omnia creat et a nullo creari nesciat, in omnibus quae ab ea sunt mirabili modo creatur, ut, quemadmodum mentis intelligentia seu propositum seu consilium seu quoquo modo motus ille noster intimus et primus dici possit dum in cogitationem, ut diximus, uenerit quasdamque phantasiarum formas acceperit deindeque in signa uocum seu sensibilium motuum indicia processerit, non incongrue dicitur fieri – fit enim in phantasiis formatus qui per se omni sensibili caret forma – ita diuina essentia, quae per se subsistens omnem superat intellectum, in his quae a se et per se et in se et ad se facta sunt recte dicitur creari, ut in eis siue intellectu si solummodo intelligibilia sunt, siue sensu si sensibilia sint, ab his qui eam recto studio inquirunt cognoscatur.*[80]

The distinction between being created in, and being created by, the former applying to God, the latter applying in no way to the divine nature, is evident in this passage.

The ontological background to the notion of the divine nature being made is provided by the notion of the participation in the good and the specifically biblical notion of creation out of nothing: *"Creat ... omnia quae de nihilo adducit ut sint ex non esse in esse; ..."*[81]

He then goes on to explain how this creation is also a being created. The divine nature: *"creatur autem quia nihil essentialiter est praeter ipsam, est enim omnium*

---

sages of *Periphyseon.* But his presentation of the divine nature quickly goes beyond what is endorsed by that reflection. We thus witness a recurring pattern in Eriugena's writings: his interweaving two-step of the exercise of interpretation and reflection on those conditions which make possible that interpretation and attest to its legitimacy.

[80] PP I, 520–533, p. 21, (= PL 122 454C–D).
[81] PP I, 498–499, p. 20, (= PL 122 453D–454A).

*essentia.*"[82] Nothing, he claims, exists as an essence except it, for it is the essence of all things. Being the essence of all is explained in terms of participation in the good:

*Nam sicut nullum bonum naturale est, sed omne quod dicitur bonum esse ex participatione unius summi boni est, ita omne quod dicitur existere non in se ipso existit sed participatione uere existentis naturae existit.*[83]

He thus reintroduces the apparitional perspective which he has now grounded in an ontology of creational participation. "... *cum dicitur se ipsam creare, nil aliud recte intelligitur nisi naturas rerum condere. Ipsius nanque creatio, hoc est in aliquo manifestatio, omnium existentium profecto est substitutio.*"[84] Furthermore Eriugena presents this as a complementary position to the (also affirmed by him) birth of the Word of God in Christians through faith and hope and love (1 Cor. 1:30).[85]

Much of Eriugena's position on the divine becoming is held in common with Pseudo-Dionysius, however Eriugena's proper contribution to the issue is the heightening of the apparitional aspect of the analysis[86]. He can conclude on the divine nature: "... *diuina natura ... quia in omnibus quae sunt apparet quae per se ipsam inuisibilis est, non incongrue dicitur facta.*"[87] The divine 'creating-itself' is a founding of things and an appearing in others. The theophanic apparitional moment of God's relationship with God's Self and the world is stressed. This apparitional moment is central to Eriugena's understanding of the God-world relationship, more central than an ontology of causation which is clearly subordinated to the manifestational aspect.

### 2.4 A further biblical impulse: God one and three

Eriugena's account of 'that which creates and is not created' must be confronted with the trinitarian doctrine of the church. Now *what* God is cannot be grasped by a created intellect be it human or angelic. But from the things which exist as an essence we may conclude *that* God exists.[88] The theologians deduce (*recto mentis contuitu theologi scrutati sunt*) that God exists from the things that are; that God is wise from the divisions of existing things into essence, genera, species, differences and so on (that is from the fact that reality submits to an ordering); that God is liv-

---

[82] PP I, 499–500, p. 20, (= PL 122, 454A).

[83] PP I, 500–503, p. 20, (= PL 122 454A).

[84] PP I, 554–557, p. 22, (= PL 122 455A–B).

[85] See PP I, 503–510, p. 20, (= PL 122, 454A).

[86] See, É. Jeauneau, "Néant divin et théophanie", in: A. de Libera, (éd.), *Langages et philosophie. Hommage à Jean Jolivet,* Paris 1997, pp. 331–337.

[87] PP I, 505–510, p. 20, (= PL 122 454A–B).

[88] See PP I, 562–572, p. 22, (= PL 122 455B–C). This insight is vitally important in Cappadocian theology, see Gregory of Nazianzus, *Orationes,* XXVIII, 5, 10–18, Paul Gallay / Maurice Jourjon (ed.), SC 250, p. 110, (= PG 36, 32 B–C), here lines 16–18: Πλεῖστον γὰρ διαφέρει τοῦ εἶναί τι πεπεῖσθαι τὸ τί ποτέ ἐστι τοῦτο εἰδέναι. See too Maximus Confessor, *Ambigua ad Iohannem,* XI, 18–20, É. Jeauneau (ed.), CCSG 18, p. 117, (= PG 91, 1216B).

ing from the stable motion and moving rest of all things[89]. So the cause of all is and is wise and lives. He concludes that in this way the theologians discovered that the cause of all things is a three-fold substance (*ter subsistentem uerissime inuenerunt*)[90]. Eriugena then goes on to affirm this in trinitarian terms:

*Ac per hoc per essentiam patrem, per sapientiam filium, per uitam spiritum sanctum intelligi inquisitores ueritatis tradiderunt.*[91]

In his scriptural commentaries the trinitarian perspective is ever present. In *Periphyseon* too it surfaces and submerges alternatively[92]. In some passages, especially in PP II, Eriugena reflects on the *imaging* of the trinity in the human. In the opening book of *Periphyseon* however the account of the trinity as three and one has a different function[93]. It is part of an investigation of the possibility of predication of God, more precisely the possibility of predicating unity and trinity of God.

With the help of Dionysius, *De diuinis nominibus XIII, 3*[94] in part quoted, in part paraphrased, Eriugena offers a reflection on the limitation of all predication of attributes of God. "*Nulla uerborum seu nominum seu qualicunque articulatae uocis significatione summa omnium atque causalis essentia potest significari.*"[95] He applies this to the question at hand. It is not that unity or trinity which the human or angelic mind can understand which is here expressed. Why then do theologians still persist in trying to speak about God? This is said to take place in order that the ineffable and incomprehensible may to some extent be thought and spoken of by

---

[89] PP I, 566–572, p. 22, (= PL 122 455B–C). "God is Being, as Cause of Being in all that is (the Father); Wisdom, as the Cause of the rational disposition of all that is (the Son); Life, as the Cause in all that is of motion and life (the Holy Spirit)." I. P. SHELDON-WILLIAMS / L. BIELER, endnote 77, SLH, vol. VII, p. 229–230, here provide a lengthy account of the history of this triad in Plotinus, Proclus and the Christianising modification to the triad in the works of PSEUDO-DIONYSIUS. Important references to the Dionysian Corpus, almost certainly sources for Eriugena, De div. nom., V, I, B. SUCHLA (ed.), p. 180, 8 – p. 181, 6 (= PG 3, 816 B–C), for the triad, supplemented by De div. nom. VI, I, p. 190, 3 – p. 191, 8, (= PG 3, 856A–B) where life and motion are explicitly linked. The whole section De div. Nom. V–VII, p. 180, 8 – p. 200, 2, (= PG 3, 816B–873A) is also relevant.

[90] PP I, 572–573, pp. 22/3, (= PL 122 455C).

[91] PP I, 576–578, p. 23, (= PL 122 455C). For further examples of the uses of this triad in the church fathers see MAXIMUS CONFESSOR, *Ambigua ad Iohannem*, VI, 577–583, É. JEAUNEAU (ed.), CCSG 18, p. 63, (= PG 91, 1136B–C), (... *esse et sapiens esse et uiuens* ...); AUGUSTINUS, *De uera religione*, XXXI, 57, 1–4, K.-D. DAUR (ed.), CCSL 32, p. 224, (= PL 34, 147): "*Nec iam illud ambigendum est incommutabilem naturam, quae supra rationalem animam sit, deum esse et ibi esse primam uitam et primam essentiam, ubi est prima sapientia.*"

[92] For an account of Eriugena's trinitarian theology, see W. BEIERWALTES, "Einheit und Dreiheit", in: IDEM, Eriugena. Grundzüge, pp. 204–256.

[93] I thus interpret the emphasis in the passages PP I, somewhat differently to ANSORGE in Johannes Scottus Eriugena, pp. 108–110 which he entitles "Das Geschaffene als Abbild des dreieinigen Gottes". He too points out that Eriugena's most substantial treatment of the trinity is in *Periphyseon* Book II.

[94] Ps. DIONYSIUS, De div. nom., XIII, 3, B. SUCHLA (ed.), p. 229, 6–p. 230, 5, (= PG 3, 980D–981B).

[95] PP I, 587–589, p. 23, (= PL 122 456A).

pious minds. It is particularly for the sake of those who demand a rational account of the Christian religion from catholics, either (if they are of good will) in order to learn the truth, or (if they are ill disposed) in order to attack and criticise this religion, that theologians devised and handed on these religious expressions by which the faith is symbolised. Finally this proclamation is said to help all believers: so that we may believe in our hearts and confess with our lips[96] that the divine goodness is constituted in three substances of one essence (*in unius essentiae tribus substantiis esse constitutam* )[97].

Eriugena describes this discovery, only to be attained as the result of an investigation which is both rational and spiritual (*spiritualis intelligentiae rationabilisque inuestigationis*).[98] In a passage reminiscent of the Ps. Dionysius, he points out that the unity of the ineffable cause of all things is not a sterility or a singularity but a marvellous multiplicity and fertility[99]. The three 'substances' are the unbegotten, the begotten and the proceeding. The 'condition' ('*habitum*') of the Unbegotten substance to the begotten is called the father; the condition of the begotten to the unbegotten is called the Son and the condition of the substance proceeding to the unbegotten and to the begotten substance is called the Holy Spirit[100].

'Father' does not refer either to a nature nor to an operation but to a relation (*habitudo*) to the son. Gregory of Nazianzus (*diuina gratia illuminatus*) worked this out in defence of the trinity against the Eunomians[101]. The first possibility which he rules out (i.e. that Father refers to a nature) would involve him in affirming diverse natures of father and son, that the father and son are ETEPOYCIAC. The second (that father and son refer to operations) would lead to an affirmation that the son was created.

Nutritor reflects further on the way the names father and son involve relations and do not signify substances either in humans or in God. In this passage reminiscent of Augustine[102] he writes:

---

[96] See Rom. 10:10.

[97] PP I, 598–599, p. 23, (= PL 122 456B). Note that Eriugena uses the Greek trinitarian terminology here but will later explicitly say that the Greek and Latins do not differ doctrinally, but only in terms of terminology.

[98] PP I, 599–600, p. 23, (= PL 122 456B).

[99] See De div. nom., I, 4, p. 112, 14–p. 113, 2, (= PG 3, 589D–592A).

[100] See MAXIMUS CONFESSOR, *Ambigua ad Iohannem Marginalia ad XXI*, 32, É. JEAUNEAU (ed.), CCSG 18, p. 278, 70–72, (Marginalia not available in PG 91) "*De habitu siquidem ingenitae substantiae ad genitam Pater, de habitu genitae ad ingenitam Filius, de habitu procedentis ad mittentem Spiritus praedictur.*"

[101] See GREGORY OF NAZIANZUS, *Orationes*, XXIX, 16, P. GALLAY / M. JOURJON (ed.), p. 210–212 (= PG 36, 93C–96B). MAXIMUS CONFESSOR, *Ambigua ad Iohannem*, XXII, É. JEAUNEAU (ed.), CCSG 18, p. 153–154; (= PG 91, 1265C–1268B).

[102] See, AUGUSTINUS, *De trinitate* V, V, W. J. MOUNTAIN (ed.), FR. GLORIE (assistance), CCSL 50, Turnhout, 1968, p. 210–211; (= PL 42, 914), here 1–4. "*In deo autem nihil quidem secundum accidens dicitur quia nihil in eo mutabile est; nec tamen omne quod dicitur secundum substantiam dicitur. Dicitur enim ad aliquid sicut pater ad filium et filius ad patrem, quod non est accidens …*".

*Non enim potes negare talia nomina, id est patrem et filium, relatiua esse, non substantiua. Si ergo apud nos, hoc est in nostra natura, non substantialiter sed relatiue tales uoces praedicantur, quid de summa ac sancta dicturi sumus essentia, in qua substantiarum inter se inuicem relationis (id est habitudinis) talia nomina, pater uidelicet et filius et spiritus sanctus, sancta scriptura constituit?*[103]

The methodological standpoint of the *Periphyseon* demands that the author go into *how* God may be spoken of as three and one. This leads Eriugena into a further reflection on the scope and limitation of all predication of God. This is executed first by a reflection on kataphatic and apophatic theology. Then by a lengthy treatment of the question of the possibility of predicating the ten categories of God.

## 2.5 The possibility of talking about God: kataphatic and apophatic theology

One of the most important elements of the heritage which Eriugena inherited from the Pseudo-Dionysius is the distinction between apophatic and kataphatic theology latent in that author's work.

In his work *De mystica theologica* Ps. Dionysius refers explicitly to an affirmative theology[104]. In affirmative speech something is affirmed analogously of God; in negative speech a predication is negated of God. Thus it is possible to engage in 'towards speech' about God or 'away from speech' about God.[105] Even in Eriugena's day one could then speak of 'kataphatic' and 'apophatic' theology.

Eriugena broaches the matter as an apparent conflict between the scriptural affirmation of the inaccessibility of God[106] (1 Tim. 6:16) which seems to imply that a commitment to the simplicity of the faith in silence is the most appropriate reaction on the one hand, and the practise of academic theology on the other. Eriugena maintains that the discussion of the matters of faith necessarily involves one in a multitude of arguments and forms of argumentation. The aim of this argumentation is often the demonstration of the most probable truth. Eriugena in turn proposes that two principle forms of theology are employed, the affirmative (affirmativa) which is called by the Greeks ΚΑΤΑΦΑΤΙΚΗ (kataphatike) and the negative (abnegativa) which is called ΑΠΟΦΑΤΙΚΗ (apophatike)[107].

---

[103] PP I, 659–665, p. 25, (= PL 122 457C–D).

[104] "τὰ κυριώτατα τῆς καταφατικῆς θεολογίας ὑμνήσαμεν" *De mystica theologia,* III, A. M. RITTER (ed.), Berlin: de Gruyter, 1991, (= Patristische Texte und Studien, vol. 36), p. 146, 1–2, (= PG 3 1032D); "I have praised the main notions of affirmative theology". One may compare the translation of COLM LUIBHEID in: Pseudo-Dionysius. The Collected Works.

[105] See DEIRDRE CARABINE, *The Unknown God,* p. 2 and compare PAUL ROREM, *Pseudo-Dionysius. A Commentary on the Texts and an Introduction to Their Influence,* Oxford: Oxford University Press, 1993.

[106] Vulgata: "*qui solus habet immortalitatem et lucem habitans inaccessibilem quem videt nullus hominum sed nec videre potest.*" Quoted according to *Biblia Sacra iuxta vulgatam versionem,* Stuttgart: Deutsche Bibelgesellschaft, ³1983.

[107] See PP I, 674–682, p. 26, (= PL 122 458A).

Eriugena's explanation of these methods deserves to be quoted:

*Vna quidem, id est ΑΠΟΦΑΤΙΚΗ, diuinam essentiam seu substantiam esse aliquid eorum quae sunt, id est quae dici aut intelligi possunt, negat; altera uero, ΚΑΤΑΦΑΤΙΚΗ, omnia quae sunt de ea praedicat, et ideo affirmatiua dicitur, non ut confirmet aliquid esse eorum quae sunt, sed omnia quae ab ea sunt de ea posse praedicari suadeat.*[108]

It is clear that the notion of causality underlies the possibility of kataphatic predication. Eriugena continues "*Rationabiliter enim per causatiua causalis potest significari*": a cause may be expressed in terms of the things caused[109]. This idea with its lengthy history in Platonic thought is also to be found in Maximus[110]. The examples which Eriugena lists (truth, goodness, essence, light, justice, sun, star, spirit, water, lion, bear, worm) remind us of those treated by Ps. Dionysius in De div. nom.[111].

We may note that various categories are represented: those which apply to all beings as such, e. g. goodness; metaphors taken from the moral realm, e. g. justice; metaphors from the natural world i. e. the names of animals. Eriugena goes on to point out that even words which are contrary to nature are *de facto* predicated of God: being drunken, being mad[112]. Eriugena himself refers to the Ps. Dionysius as one who has handled these matters in great detail, referring to the *Symbolic Theology* for the names taken from the world to which the senses have access.[113] Although this work is not extant, we may trace the ideas treated in the passage just reported (PP I, 689–695, 26, PL 122 485B) to other writings of the pseudo Areopagite[114]. It is significant that we are here dealing with attributes which are *biblical* names for God: (*ueritatum:* Jn. 14:6; *bonitatem:* Ps. 118:1; *essentiam:* Exod. 3:14; *lucem:* Jn. 1:5; *iustitam:* Is. 45:8; *solem:* Dan. 7:5; Mal. 4:2; *stellam:* Rev. 22:16; *spiritum:* Jn. 4:24; *aquam:* Jn. 4:15; *leonem:* Hos. 5:14, *ursum:* Hos. 13:8, *uermem:* Ps. 22:7[115]). Here too Eriugena is greatly influenced by the pseudo Areopagite, who also takes as his starting point the different kinds of names which occur for God in the bible.

Eriugena uses the notion of opposites to approach the metaphorical nature of the predication of even "the most divine" attributes of God. The reflection on the

---

[108] PP I, 682–688, p. 26, (= PL 122, 458A–B).

[109] PP I 688–689, p. 26, (= PL 122 458B).

[110] Compare Maximus Confessor, *Ambigua ad Iohannem*, VI, 577–580, É. Jeauneau (ed.), CCSG 18, p. 63, (= PG 91, 1136B).

[111] PP I, 688–691, p. 26, (= PL 122 458B). See De div. nom. chapters four and following.

[112] Compare Ps. Dionysius, *De mystica theologia*, III and *Epistula* IX, 5–6 (ed.), G. Heil / A. M. Ritter, (ed.), Berlin: Walter de Gruyter, 1991, (= Patristische Texte und Studien, 36), p. 146–147, 204–207, (= PG 3, 1033AB, 1112B–1113C).

[113] This work is not however extant. Compare De div. nom. I, 8, B. Suchla (ed.), p. 121, 3, (= PG 3, 597B), where the Ps. Dionysius refers to this fictitious or lost work.

[114] Ps. Dionysius Areopagita, De coel. hier., II, G. Heil (ed.), pp. 9–17, (= PG 3, 136D–164C); De div. nom. I, 6, B. Suchla (ed.), p. 118–119, (= PG 3 596A–596C). And Ps. Dionysius, *De mystica theologia*, III, A. M. Ritter (ed.), p. 146–147, (= PG 3 1033D).

[115] This has been shown in detail for each of these names with the corresponding reference in the works of Dionysius by I. P. Sheldon-Williams / L. Bieler in their critical apparatus, SLH, vol. VII, p. 74.

notion of opposites is also important because through it the status of the apophatic and kataphatic theological methods may also be discussed, namely by considering whether they can respectively express opposites of God.

Eriugena avails of both the concept of opposition and the concept of co-intelligence. Neither is anything *opposed* to God, nor is anything which is ETEPOYCION conceived *alongside* God. This is relevant for the question of the metaphorical nature of the predication of even the highest attributes in question of God. For if even these names may be confronted with their opposites, (and thus the realities they express possess opposites) then Eriugena concludes, not even the exalted names which were introduced in the discussion may be *properly* predicated of God. (His reasoning is based on the premise that anything to which an opposite may be opposed is not properly predicable of God). Rather God is *more* than essence, *more* than goodness, *more* than truth, *more* than justice, *more* than wisdom and so on. He thus affirms the 'hyper' (ὑπερ-) prefixes so loved by the Ps. Dionysius[116].

The 'the more than word constructions' be they constructed in word combinations as is usual in the Latin language (*plus quam ueritas* etc., *superessentialis* being the exception) or through single words with prefixes as in the Greek (for example ΥΠΕΡΟΥCΙΟC) straddle the two forms of theology, but are said to belong more properly to apophatic theology than to kataphatic theology.[117] What is outwardly positively phrased, is really a negation. Thus the hyper-names belong better in the realm of apophatic or negative theology. For when we say for example that God is more than essence (*superessentialis*), we are outwardly making an affirmation, but the intellect supplies a negation. We are really saying what God is not.

---

[116] See De div. nom., II, 3–4, B. Suchla (ed.), p. 125–126; (= PG 3, 640B–641B), *De mystica theologia*, I,1, A. M. Ritter (ed.), p. 141–142, (= PG 3, 997A–1000A).

[117] Eriugena is aware of the history of the distinction between these two forms of predication. While he writes Cicero called them *intentio* and *repulsio,* he prefers to call them affirmation and negation. See M. Tullius Cicero, *De inuentione*, I, X, 13, Theodor Nüsslein (ed.), Düsseldorf: Artemis & Winkler Verlag, 1998, pp. 30–32. Compare I. P. Sheldon-Williams / L. Bieler, SLH, vol. VII, endnote nr. 95, p. 230–231, a long note on the history of the Greek and the here introduced Latin names for the various methods. Sheldon-Williams / Bieler write that the terms καταφατική (kataphatike) and αποφατική (apophatike) θεολογία (theologia), although no doubt according to him *derived* from distinctions within the 'status theory' of Hermagoras of Temnos (second century BC), do not seem to have occurred before Ps. Dionysius. Sheldon-Williams / Bieler go on to point out that in their opinion the casual way in which the Areopagite introduces the terms would indicate that his readership were familiar with them.

The status theory seems to have a rhetorical and logical / legal background. It was adopted by C. Julius Victor in the fourth century AD. Julius used *intentio / repulsio* (or *depulsio*) to translate *cataphasis* and *apophasis.* Cicero, write Sheldon-Williams / Bieler, was familiar with the theory of Hermagoras but that the Greek terms apophasis / kataphasis are not given by Cicero for *intentio / depulsio.* Sheldon-Williams and Bieler argue Eriugena's earlier studies in rhetoric could have occasioned an acquaintance with Julius Victor. This possibility seems plausible to me especially in the light of the explicit correlation of *intentio / depulsio* and apophasis / cataphasis (sic!) in C. Iulius Victor, Ars Rhetorica, Remo Giomini and Maria Silvana Celentano, (ed.), Leipzig: BSB B. G. Teubner Verlagsgesellschaft, 1980, pp. 4, line 26–p. 5, line 20.

*Nam quae dicit 'superessentialis est' non quid est dicit sed quid non est. Dicit enim essentiam non*
*esse sed plus quam essentiam, quid autem illud est quod plus quam essentia est non exprimit.*[118]

And Eriugena astutely points out that the hyper-predication does not reveal what
this 'more' in the '*plus quam*' predication is, or in 'definitional' terms reminiscent
of the start of the discussion of the divine nature: "*Dicit enim deum non esse aliquod*
*eorum quae sunt sed plus quam ea quae sunt esse, illud autem esse quid sit nullo modo*
*diffinit.*"[119]

Are affirmation and negation not at the first sight opposed to each other? For
example if one says that God is truth and God is not truth: are these statements not
opposed to each other? Eriugena however goes on to deny that the predicates are
opposed to each other when applied to the divine nature. Rather in this latter case
they are fully compatible with each other. He gives an illustration. It is compatible
to say that God is truth (not in the sense of a proper predication but rather by way
of metaphorical predication, in the sense that this term is transferred to the divine
essence from the things which it has created) and on the other hand, to say that
God is not truth. By the apophatic statement that God is not truth is meant that
the incomprehensible and ineffable divine essence is not properly called, nor is not
properly truth. So Eriugena concludes on the two ways: "*Vna igitur dicit 'hoc uocari*
*potest', sed non dicit 'hoc proprie est'; altera dicit 'hoc non est', quamuis et hoc appel-*
*lari potest*".[120] The two ways of doing theology are complementary: "*per omnia in*
*omnibus sibi inuicem consentiunt.*"[121]

### 2.6 The possibility of predicating the ten categories of God

Whereas an account of the Aristotelian categories belonged as a commonplace to
every learned account of reality composed in his day, Eriugena's treatment of the
categories in *Periphyseon* is more than simply a compulsory exercise[122]. His account

---

[118] PP I, 879–882, p. 32, (= PL 122 462C–D).

[119] PP I, 882–884, p. 32, (= PL 122 462D).

[120] PP I, 841–843, p. 31, (= PL 122 461D).

[121] PP I, 826–827, pp. 30/31, (= PL 122 461C). On the harmony of the two ways see MAXIMUS
CONFESSOR, *Ambigua ad Iohannem*, XXX, 17–25, É. JEAUNEAU (ed.), (CCSG 18), p. 167–168, (= PG
91, 1288C), and ERIUGENA, *Epistula praefixa Versioni Ambiguorum Maximi*, 42–45 (CCSG 18, p. 4):
"*Quam clare pulcreque aperit quomodo, cum inter se oppositae ualdeque contariae uideantur, ad unum*
*tamen consensum peruenient ut, dum una neget, alter confirmet, utrunque in utraque contineatur!*".

[122] See JOHN MARENBON, *From the circle of Alcuin to the School of Auxerre. Logic, theology and*
*philosophy in the Early Middle Ages*, Cambridge: Cambridge University Press, 1981, (= Cambridge
studies in medieval life and thought: third series; vol. 15), esp. pp. 72–73, 86–87, and pp. 141–142.
This book is substantially a study of the fate of Aristotle's theory of the categories in the Early
Middle Ages. In particular it focuses on the question of essence and the Universals. See too JOHN
MARENBON, "John Scottus and the 'Categoriae Decem'", in: W. BEIERWALTES (ed.), Eriugena.
Studien zu seinen Quellen, pp. 117–134. This article studies the influence on Eriugena of the
Latin paraphrase of, and commentary on, Aristotle's Categories, the 'Categoriae Decem'. In this

is highly significant both from the point of view of his method, and from the point of view of the theme of the divine manifestation.

Of interest with regard to his method is the fact that here we encounter a case where we may observe how his theological interests override a merely passive reception of the academic tradition on the categories as mediated through Augustine. Thus the account of the nature of apophatic theology had prepared the reader for *Eriugena's* conclusion that none of the categories, not even essence may be applied to God[123]. Even the way he structures his account in *Periphyseon* is revealing. He first gives an account of the first eight categories in their relationship to God. With open theological intent, this section (PP I, 885–1291, (= PL 122 462D–472B)) is an application of the theory of the two forms of theology to the question at hand. He then doubles back and deals with these same first eight categories, paying attention to the property of each (*in qua proprietate singula*)[124] not that which they have in common with each other (PP I, 1291–2635, (= PL 122 472B–503D)). While at first glance this section might not seem to be of theological import, in fact he introduces many insights here which are central to his theology of God and his theory of the appearing of God.[125] Finally he deals with the last two categories, with *agere* and *pati* which are extremely relevant to the biblical naming of God and the question of God's loving (PP I, 2636–3495, (= PL 122 503D–524B)). Here his perspective is once again that of the relation of the two categories to God. We may summarise that Eriugena's treatment of the categories is a learned treatment but it is above all the treatment of a biblically oriented theologian grappling with the biblically inspired issue of the question of naming God[126].

Aristotle, the most astute of the Greeks, is said to have divided created things into ten universal genera which he called the ten categories, that is, predicables. Eriugena gives the following Greek names for the categories: OYCIA; ΠΟCΟΤΗΤΑ; ΠΟΙΟΤΗΤΑ; ΠΡΟC ΤΙ; ΚΕΙCΘΑΙ; ΕΞΙC; ΤΟΠΟC; ΧΡΟΝΟC; ΠΡΑΤΤΕΙΝ;

---

earlier work Marenbon is also reticent on the coherence of the system which results in Eriugena's *Periphyseon,* see p. 130, and 133. See his comment on his own earlier work in: From the circle of Alcuin, p. 87, footnote 63.

[123] Marenbon tells us that in this point Eriugena modifies Augustine who is said to apply ousia to God, J. MARENBON, John Scottus and the 'Categoriae Decem', p. 123 with, in my opinion, a fitting reference to *De Trinitate,* V, 2, 3, W. J. MOUNTAIN / FR. GLORIE (ed.), pp. 207,1–p. 208, 17, (= PL 42 912). Marenbon argues that Eriugena uses several senses of the term 'ousia', see pp. 121–123.

[124] PP I, 1293–1294, p. 44, (= PL 122 472C).

[125] For example the infinity of God is a constant premise in his reasoning in these sections and the theory of the apparitional function of matter is important in his theological aesthetics.

[126] Compare MARENBON, "… the key to why Eriugena chose to treat a certain philosophical concept in a certain way will rarely be found by asking what philosophical question John sought to answer. Far more often, it is a wish to reconcile sources, and the demands of his imaginative theological system, which have shaped Eriugena's thoughts.", John Scottus and the 'Categoriae Decem', p. 133.

ΠΑΘΕΙΝ, and the Latin names, *essentia, quantitas, qualitas, ad aliud, situs, habitus, locus, tempus, agere, pati.*[127]

There are many good summaries of Eriugena's account of the ten categories. I do not intend to repeat the achievements of other authors here[128]. In the following I shall rather try to deal with salient aspects of Eriugena's *methodology* in this account and to highlight the material in this account of the ten categories which is relevant to the *thematic* of the appearing of God.

The hermeneutic with which we must approach Eriugena's presentation of the first eight categories is revealed in an exchange between the two speakers in the dialogue. The speaker known as Alumnus notes that in the first account of the first eight categories they have almost all been presented as so interrelated that they can scarcely be distinguished from each other[129]. This is a fitting observation that Eriugena first treats the categories in their enchainment (*inter se inuicem concatenatas*) and then approaches them more individually. Behind this lies the overriding intention to emphasise that which the categories have in common, namely that they may not be applied to God.

With a reference to Augustine's *De trinitate* Eriugena limits the scope of the categories and reports that the categories lose their power when confronted with theology, the investigation of the divine essence[130]. Eriugena however appeals to the fact that almost every thing which may be properly predicated of created reality may be metaphorically applied to God, so too the categories may be applied to the cause of all things, not in the sense that they properly signify what it is in itself, but in the transferred sense that they show us what we most probably may think about the divine essence.

Eriugena points out how useful the discussion on the two parts of theology has been. For therein was established that even the most noble of categories could not properly be predicated of the divine essence. Even those primordial causes such as essence, goodness, virtue, truth, wisdom which were created first, only metaphorically signify God. So therefore it shouldn't surprise us that the ten genera do not properly express something about the divine nature[131].

The principles of apophatic theology are applied rigorously to the category of οὐσία (*ousia*). God is not οὐσία because God is more than οὐσία, and yet the divine nature is called it because it is the creator of all οὐσίαι.

---

[127] Dialectic is introduced in this context as the part of philosophy which concerns itself with the divisions and collections of the myriad subdivisions of the categories.

[128] See for example the detailed summary of this section of *Periphyseon* in: DIRK ANSORGE, Johannes Scottus Eriugena, pp. 118–164, or the concentrated analysis of GANGOLF SCHRIMPF in: Das Werk des Johannes Scottus Eriugena, pp. 188.

[129] PP I, 1289–1292, p. 44, (= PL 122, 472 B–C).

[130] PP I, 903, p. 33, (= PL 122 463B). See AUGUSTINUS, *De trinitate,* V, II [3], W. J. MOUNTAIN / FR. GLORIE (ed.), p. 207–208, (= PL 42 912). Note however that as mentioned above, Eriugena denies that ousia may be predicated properly of God.

[131] PP I, 921–936, p. 33, (= PL 122 463C–464A).

Quantity and quality are denied of God. The category of relation requires some discussion for it seems to be predicable of God considered as trinity[132]. Yet Eriugena is forced to assert that even relation is predicated *translative,* that is analogously, of God[133]. Even in the context of the trinity, relation in God is more than relation: "*Nunquid ueris ratiocinationibus obsistit si dicamus patrem et filium ipsius habitudinis, quae dicitur 'ad aliquid', nomina esse et plus quam habitudinis?*"[134]

Eriugena says that the category ΚΕΙϹΘΑΙ which he says equals the Latin *iacere* is called *situs* by others. Bodies are said to lie or to stand, the mind may also be said to lie when it is at rest or to stand if it is alert. But God neither stands nor lies. For God is the cause of standing or lying. In God all things stand (that is they have their immutable reasons) and they lie, that is, they lie at rest, for God is the end of all things. Once again this predicate is only analogously *(translative)* predicated of the divine[135].

In the case of condition (*habitus* / ΕΞΙϹ) too Eriugena says that it cannot properly be predicated of God[136]. This would imply that the divine essence would not be of itself but of another (*nequaquam suimet sed alterius esset*)[137]. For *habitus* is always in some subject and habitus is always an accident of something. God is neither an accident to anything else nor does God have accidents. So once again we have a category which is not properly predicated of the divine nature although it may be predicated in another sense because the divine nature is its cause.

With regard to the categories of place (*locus*) and time (*tempus*) the pattern is again repeated: God is said to be neither place nor time and yet metaphorically (*translative*) God is called the place and time of all things because God causes all places and all times. Eriugena relates place to definition: all the definitions of things subsist in God as a sort of a place (*quasi quidam loci*)[138]. Unlike the things of this world which are defined in place and moved in time God is neither defined nor moved. God is not defined by anything but defines all things because God is the cause of all things. Similarly God is the cause of time. "*Est enim plus quam tempus et plus quam motus. Non est locus igitur neque tempus.*"[139]

---

[132] Here he refers to the discussion of Gregory of Nazianzus on this point, GREGORIUS NAZIANZENUS, *Orationes,* XXIX, 16, P. GALLAY / M. JOURJON (ed.), p. 210–212, (= PG 36, 93C–96B).

Eriugena's treatment is also of interest because, while dealing with what in Greek appears as ΠΡΟϹ ΤΙ, Eriugena alternates between the Latin terms *relatio* and *habitudo.* He will, however, also deal with *habitudo* as a category corresponding to the Greek ΕΞΙϹ see PP I, 1013–1014, p. 36, (= PL 122 466A). He does not adequately distinguish between these two categories.

[133] PP I, 978–979, p. 35, (= PL 122 465A).

[134] PP I, 981–983, p. 35, (= PL 122 465C).

[135] PP I, 1003–1005, p. 36, (= PL 122 465C–D).

[136] With regard to this category a major point which Eriugena makes is that condition is found in all the categories. Eriugena claims this explicitly for essence, quantity, and quality too, see, PP I, 1099–1108, pp. 38–39, (= PL 122 468A–B).

[137] PP I, 1116, p. 39, (= PL 122 468B).

[138] PP I, 1125, p. 39, (= PL 122 468C).

[139] PP I, 1142–1144, p. 40, (= PL 122 469A).

In what Sheldon-Williams and Bieler have called a "long digression" Eriugena next goes through the individual categories highlighting what is proper to each[140]. Whereas at first glance the first account is more theological and thus more relevant not only to the train of thought in Eriugena's *Periphyseon* but also to the subject matter of this study, we must observe that the somewhat encyclopaedic second run through the categories includes some details which are also relevant to the theme of the present investigation[141].

For example a comparison between the formlessness of God and the formlessness of matter yields a valuable insight into the apparitional function of matter. The context is a lengthy discussion on the nature of matter[142]. In particular it is unformed matter which is the centre of attention. There are two things which Eriugena reports the fathers said cannot be defined: God and matter. "*Deus siquidem infinitus informisque, quoniam a nullo formatur, dum sit forma omnium. Materia similiter informis infinita; aliunde enim formari indiget finirique, dum per se non forma sed formabilis sit.*"[143] This similarity is to be understood in a contrary sense *(e contrario intelligitur)*[144] for there is a world of difference between God the cause of all things, from whom and in whom and through whom and for whom all things exist,[145] and matter, which Eriugena calls the unformed cause, which is created to the end that those things which in themselves cannot be grasped by the senses, might by some means gain a sensible appearance in it "*quae ad hoc creata est ut ea quae per se sensibus attingi non possent quodam modo in ea sensibiliter apparerent ...*"[146]. This is a very interesting presentation of the function of matter in apparitional, manifestational terms. The appearing to the senses is presented as a further good. Thus within Eriugena's account of the individual categories we encounter an ontological reflection on God and matter which, far from being a minor 'aside' must rather be interpreted as an 'overture' which introduces the major aesthetic perspective of all Eriugena's writings.[147]

---

[140] See I. P. SHELDON-WILLIAMS / L. BIELER, SLH VII, p. 30. Sheldon-Williams / Bieler locate the start of the digression in PL 122 469A where a review of the ten categories is given. The digression is said by them to end in PL 122 504A whereafter *pati* and *agere* are dealt with in terms of their relationship to God, op. cit. p. 31.

[141] Two of the most important are the emergence of the theory of the infinity of God as a premise in all his accounts of the divine nature and, with respect to method, an account of the intertwining of anthropology and the seven arts. In line with the systematic structure of this study, the material relevant to these points will be introduced where relevant in later sections.

[142] PP I, 2445 and following, p. 79, (= PL 122 499B and following).

[143] PP I, 2466–2469, p. 80, (= PL 122 499D–500A).

[144] PP I, 2473–2474, p. 80, (= PL 122 500A).

[145] Rom. 11:36.

[146] PP I, 2472–2473, p. 80, (= PL 122 500A).

[147] The passage yields information on Eriugena's understanding of God. God as supreme cause is without limit and without form because of God's eminence above all that God forms and limits. For God is not only the principal form (*forma principalis*) of all things but God is more than form, forming everything that can receive form and everything that cannot (receive form). This formative

In a final section[148] Eriugena completes his analysis of the categories by considering the last two categories *agere* and *pati* in relation to God. That this high point of his analysis is steeped in the biblical tradition is clearly discernible. Already in PP I 2663, (= PL 122 504B) Eriugena turns from the discussion of *agere* and *pati* in general, to the privileged example of *amare* and *amari*. The biblical roots of the investigation are revealed when Eriugena quotes from Jn. 14:21. "*Qui deligit me deligetur a patre meo et ego deligam eum et manifestabo me ipsum illi*"[149]. This citation is then interpreted in trinitarian terms in dialogue with the theological tradition, especially with the works of Augustine. Thus at the close of the first book of *Periphyseon*, Eriugena carries through the apophatic and kataphatic ways of speaking of God on the basis of the trio that God is *amor, visio, motus*. That is, through an analysis of *motus* with its concomitant *agere* and *pati*, the especially interpersonal biblical terms of *amor* and *visio* are examined.

## 2.7 The biblical naming of God revisited: amor, visio, motus, facere

*Actio* and *passio* are said to be predicated metaphorically of God, not properly.[150] The cases of *mouere / moueri* and *amare / amari* are said to be similar. A possible objection is considered: if such words are only predicated '*translate*' that is, analogously, of God and in the sense that they do not say anything properly about God (*non re uera sed quodam modo de eo dicuntur*), then the multitude of scriptural predications of God seems to be called into question. "*Quotiens enim, ut nosti, sancta scriptura deum manifeste pronuntiat agere et pati, amare et amari, diligere et diligi, uidere et uideri, mouere et moueri caeteraque id genus!*"[151] The objection is presented as a theological one, one which has to do with finding an adequate hermeneutic for Scripture. An example from Augustine's *De Genesi ad litteram*, (referred to as his Hexaemeron by Eriugena) introduces the trinitarian perspective reflecting on the motion of the *spiritus creator*: "*Spiritus quidem creator mouet se ipsum sine tempore et loco, mouet conditum spiritum per tempus sine loco, mouet corpus per tempus et locum*"[152]. Further details on what God's loving seemingly involves are divulged: God's love involves both moving and being moved. God is moved by His love for the things He has made in loving them; God moves the things He has made to love God when they are

---

influence of God is described in terms of attraction. The to-be-formed either desire the cause or they are converted to it (*eam aut appetunt aut ad eam conuertuntur*).

[148] The section bounded by PP I, 2646, p. 85, (= PL 122 504A ) up to the closing of book one at PP I, 3495, p. 111, (= PL 122 524B).

[149] Quoted in PP I, 2679–2680, p. 86, (= PL 122 504C).

[150] PP I, 2657 and following, p. 86, (= PL 122, 504 A–B). The section is a dialogue between the two speakers.

[151] PP I, 2673–2676, p. 86, (= PL 122 504C). The Alumnus is speaking.

[152] PP I, 2681–2684, p. 87, (= PL 122 504C). See AUGUSTINUS, *De Genesi ad litteram*, VIII, 20, JOSEPH ZYCHA (ed.), p. 259, 22–25, (= PL 34, 388). The text of the critical edition is only slightly and insignificantly different to the citation given by Eriugena.

drawn by a love of God's beauty. "*At si amat deus quae fecit, profecto uidetur moueri; suo enim amore mouetur. Et si amatur ab his quae amare possunt, siue sciant quid amant siue nesciant, nonne apertum est quia mouet? Amor siquidem pulchritudinis ipsius ea mouet.*"[153] The problem remains: how can one maintain that God neither moves nor is moved, neither acts nor suffers?

The resolution of this apparent difficulty draws on the distinction between agent, ability to act, and the acting itself; between the person who suffers, the ability to suffer and the suffering itself.

Eriugena discusses the elements of this trio (*agens, posse agere, agere*).[154] For his argumentation Eriugena needs to stress that *agere, pati, mouere, moueri, amare, amari,* later on *facere* are, in the normal usage of these words, concerned with accidents. Since God does not have accidents, Eriugena can thus exclude the proper predication of these accidents of God.[155] To this end he brought in the trio, with its distinction between substance and accidents.[156]

A further difficulty is that of communicating this position on the status of biblical predication to simple people[157]. Thus Eriugena has occasion to present his theory of the mutual roles of reason, the truth of scripture, and scholarly authority. All these are handled within the context of a communication dynamic to persons of differing

---

[153] PP I, 2695–2698, p. 87, (= PL 122 505A). The Alumnus is expressing the problem. It is interesting how often the notion of God as end, eliciting the love of all beings occurs even in the early books of *Periphyseon*.

[154] He also discusses the relationship between this trio and the more fundamental trio οὐσία, δύναμις, ἐνέργεια, that is to use Eriugena's translation which he here repeats *essentia, uirtus, operatio*. The unity of the first trio and their inseparability had been stressed. How does this square with the distinction and the difference between the status of the three elements just affirmed and emphasised of the new trio? The three now introduced are not only distinct but they are also not homogenous. The agent is a substance; the ability to act and the acting are accidents.

The distinction of the two trios is upheld and so the differences between the relationships within the two sets of three elements may stand. The second trinity is said to follow from the first: "*Sequens uero trinitas ueluti praecedentis trinitatis effectus quidam intelligitur esse*" PP I, 2756–2757, p. 89, (= PL 122 506B). The universal trinity is said to consist in universal essence, universal power and universal virtue. The elements of the second trinity, the trinity which may be considered in individuals ("*haec tria quae in singulis considerantur*") are said to be a kind of accidents of the universal trinity ("*quasi quaedam accidentia praedictae uniuersalis trinitatis dicantur*"), PP I, 2769–2770, p. 89, (= PL 122 506C). The elements of the second trinity are also said to be the first manifestations of the first trinity, PP I, 2770–2771, p. 89, (= PL 122 506C).

[155] He does this with respect to *agere* and *pati* in PP I 2850–2855, p. 92 (= PL 122 508B–C).

[156] But was subsequently forced to show how it doesn't contradict statements which were made about the earlier one *ousia, dunamis, energeia*. Drawing on I. P. SHELDON-WILLIAMS / L. BIELER's endnote 144 on PL 122 486C, we may observe that the apparent contradiction may perhaps be based only on Eriugena's application of the first trio. For the note points out differences in Eriugena's, Ps. Dionysius' and Julian's understanding and application of that triad. The question is to be raised whether the unity and homogeneity of ousia, dynamis, and energeia are to be affirmed in the case of God alone, or in the case of all beings, or in both these cases. As the endnote astutely implies, it is in the case of the application of this trio to beings other than God that the problem of homogeneity and unity emerges.

[157] PP I, 2865–2868, p. 92, (= PL 122 508D).

abilities, but in all cases of limited ability, to grasp the infinite truth of who God is and God's dealings with us.

In a passage rich in nuance, Eriugena consoles the reader:

*Noli expauescere. Nunc enim nobis ratio sequenda est, quae rerum ueritatem inuestigat nullaque auctoritate opprimitur, nullo modo impeditur ne ea quae et studiose ratiocinationum ambitibus inquirit et laboriose inuenit publice aperiat atque pronuntiet. Sanctae siquidem scripturae in omnibus sequenda est auctoritas, quoniam in ea ueluti quibusdam suis secretis sedibus ueritas possidet. Non tamen ita credendum est ut ipsa semper propriis uerborum seu nominum signis fruatur diuinam nobis naturam insinuans, sed quibusdam similitudinibus uariisque translatorum uerborum seu nominum modis utitur infirmitati nostrae condescendens nostrosque adhuc rudes infantilesque sensus simplici doctrina erigens.*[158]

Do not be afraid he says: Reason is to be followed. Reason is said not to be over-thrown by any authority. This is a very clear and consistently held Eriugenian posi-tion. Yet lest we might be tempted to think that scripture and reason are in opposi-tion, we are told that precisely the *authority* of scripture must always be followed. Scripture must thus be understood as having no normal 'authority'. Furthermore this scriptural authority is not here justified in terms of its divine *origin,* but in terms of its *content:* Scripture is said to *possess truth* in a unique way. He then goes into the dynamics of how scripture communicates its truth: the verbs and nouns are often used analogously. The reason for this is the divine condescension to our weakness.

Eriugena introduces the scriptural citation 1 Cor. 3:2: "*Lac uobis potum dedi, non escam*". He applies this to the metaphorical way of speaking so evident in Scripture. The aim behind the divine accommodation is to enable some communication of the ineffability and incomprehensibility of the divine nature in order to foster our faith. He continues on Scripture and our obligation in the face of Scripture:

*Siquidem de deo nil aliud caste pieque uiuentibus studioseque ueritatem quaerentibus dicendum uel cogitandum, nisi quae in sancta scriptura reperiuntur; neque aliis nisi ipsius significationibus translationibusque utendum his qui de deo siue quid credant siue disputent. Quis enim de natura ineffabili quippiam a se ipso repertum dicere praesumat praeter quod illa ipsa de se ipsa in suis sanctis organis, theologis dico, modulata est?*[159]

Thus in Eriugena's understanding, Scripture represents the scope of the truth which we may express about God. Its meanings and metaphors and they only, are here said to be used for God.[160] They are thus our privileged, if not indeed normative, starting place for talking about God. Reason, he will later tell us, is assigned the role of discerning the limitations of our talk about God[161].

---

[158] PP I, 2869–2880, pp. 92–93, (= PL 122 508D–509A).

[159] PP I, 2883–2890, p. 93; (= PL 122 509B). Here, as in the writings of the Ps. Dionysius, *theologi* are those who composed the sacred scriptures.

[160] As was common in his day, Eriugena makes no distinction between the possibility of pursuing a discourse on the divine, that is talking about God, and the possibility of believing in God.

[161] PP I, 2932–2934, p. 94, (= PL 122 510B).

On the scriptures, as the well from which the concepts which are to be metaphorically predicated of God are to be drawn, Eriugena is following closely the line of argumentation of the Pseudo-Dionysius on the same theme in the first chapter of *De diuinis nominibus*. Eriugena comments that the Ps. Dionysius expresses himself in his usual way, that is *"perplexe yperbaticeque"* which is very difficult to understand[162]. Eriugena undertakes to mediate the Ps. Dionysius through a more simple word order to his readership. He 'quotes' extensively[163]. The first sentence he quotes is the gist of the argumentation: *"Uniuersaliter ... non audendum dicere neque intelligere quid de superessentiali diuinitate praeter diuinitus nobis ex sacris eloquiis expressa."*[164] It is reason's job to prove that nothing may be said properly of God: *"nil de deo proprie posse dici"*[165].

This position is objectively grounded in the incomprehensibility of God. Eriugena also presents this theocentric heart of his apophatic theology in terms of his theological sources. On the matter of the divine incomprehensibility he introduces the formula often used by himself and known to St. Augustine: God as *"qui melius nesciendo scitur"*[166]. Again drawing on the Ps. Dionysius, he speaks of God *"cuius ignorantia uera est sapientia"*[167].

Another presentation of apophatic theology is also found in *Periphyseon,* again in dialogue with Eriugena's sources, especially with the Ps. Dionysius. Eriugena adds that God is more truly negated in all things than affirmed *"uerius fideliusque negatur in omnibus quam firmatur."*[168] For whatever you negate of God is a true negation but not every affirmation about God is a true affirmation. God is not to be identified with any existing thing which can be spoken of or understood. No

---

[162] PP I, 2896–2900, p. 93, (= PL 122 509C).

[163] The I. P. SHELDON-WILLIAMS / L. BIELER edition has extensive notes on the rendering into Latin of the Dionysian Greek in these passages, see *Periphyseon,* Book I, SLH VII, endnotes 198 following, pp. 242 following. Eriugena's skill as a translator is assessed by PHILIP LEVINE, "Two early Latin versions of St. Gregory of Nyssa's περὶ κατασκευῆς ἀνθπώπου", in: *Harvard Studies in Classical Philology,* LXIII (1958) 473–492. He considers Eriugena's translation of Gregory of Nyssa's *De hominis opificio* and compares it with that of Dionysius Exiguus. Levine is singularly critical of Eriugena's rendering of Greek into Latin.

[164] PP I, 2900–2903, p. 93, (= PL 122 509C) and see DIONYSIUS ARIOPAGITA, De div. Nom., I, I, B. SUCHLA (ed.), pp. 108, 6–109, 2, (= PG 3, 588A; PL 122, 1113A–B), here p. 108, 6–8: Καθόλου τοιγαροῦν οὐτολμητέον εἰπεῖν οὔτε μὴν ἐννοῆσαί τι περὶ τῆς ὑπερουσίου καὶ κρυφίας θεότητος παρὰ τὰ θειωδῶς ἡμῖν ἐκ τῶν ἱερῶν λογίων ἐκπεφασμένα.

[165] PP I, 2934, p. 94, (= PL 122 510B).

[166] PP I, 2936, p. 94, (= PL 122 510B). See AUGUSTINUS, *De ordine,* II, XVI, 44, P. KNÖLL (ed.), CSEL 63, p. 177, 25–26, (= PL 32, 1015): *"qui scitur melius nesciendo".* See also ERIUGENA, Comm., I, XXV, 98, É. JEAUNEAU (ed.), p. 126; PL 122, 302B) where it is again quoted in the same form as in the first book of *Periphyseon.*

[167] PP I, 2936–2937, p. 94, (= PL 122, 510B). See: Ps. DIONYSIUS ARIOPAGITA, *Epistula* I, A. M. RITTER (ed.), p. 157, 3–5, (= PG 3, 1065A–B; PL 122, 1177B), here Καὶ ἡ κατὰ τὸ κρεῖττον παντελὴς ἀγνωσία γνῶσίς ἐστι τοῦ ὑπὲρ πάντα τὰ γινωσκόμενα. See too ERIUGENA, Comm., I, XXV, 98–99, É. JEAUNEAU (ed.), p. 126, (= PL 122, 302B) where the phrase is quoted in the same form as in the first book of *Periphyseon.*

[168] PP I, 2937–2938, pp. 94–95, (= PL 122 510B).

one may approach the divine essence without having first abandoned all the senses and intellectual operations and all 'sensibles' and all that is and is not *"sensus omnes deserat et intellectuales operationes et sensibilia et omne quod est et quod non est"*[169]. This is the God of Eriugena and Ps. Dionysius alike: the God of whom there is neither reason, nor understanding, who is neither spoken of nor understood, for whom there is neither a name nor a word[170].

Eriugena reports that God has created both things which are like God and things which are unlike God[171]. God is the cause of all, even of contraries[172]. Eriugena is ultimately working his readers towards the Ps. Dionysian insight that the *desimilia*, the things which are patently unlike God, are less likely to lead the soul into the error of taking them literally. On the scriptural terms for God which are taken from things said to be contrary to nature Eriugena tells us:

*Eoque mirabilius, non solum ex creatura ad creatorem artifex scriptura translationes fecit, uerum etiam ex naturae contrariis, ex insania uidelicet, ebrietate, crapula, obliuione, ira, furore, odio, concupiscentia caeterisque similibus, quibus minus simplicium animi falluntur quam superioribus transfigurationibus quae ex natura fiunt.*[173]

---

[169] Quoted in PP I, 2945–2946, p. 95, (= PL 122 510C ) from Ps. Dionysius Ariopagita, *De mystica theologia*, I, I, A. M. Ritter (ed.), p. 142, 6–7, (= PG 3, 997B).

[170] See PP I, 2944–2950, p. 95, (= PL 122 510C–D).

[171] On the predication of 'similars' and 'dissimilars' of God see, Ps. Dionysius Ariopagita, De coel. hier., II, 3, G. heil (ed.), pp. 12–13, (= PG 3, 140C–141C).

In a passage of great beauty both the divine simplicity and the way it upholds the harmony of the diverse elements of the universe are presented. God is the periphery (*ambitus*) of all things that are and are not. God gathers them together and composes them into a beautiful and ineffable harmony:

"*Fatetur enim deum infinitum esse plusque quam infinitum – infinitas enim infinitorum est – et simplicem et plus quam simplicem; omnium enim simplicium simplicitas est. Et cum ipso nihil esse credit uel intelligit, quoniam ipse est ambitus omnium quae sunt et quae non sunt et quae esse possunt et quae esse non possunt et quae ei seu contraria seu opposita uidentur esse, ut non dicam similia et dissimilia. Est enim ipse similium similitudo et dissimilium dissimilitudo, oppositorum oppositio, contrariorum contrarietas. Haec enim omnia pulchra ineffabilique armonia in unam concordiam colligit atque componit. Nam quae in partibus uniuersitatis opposita sibimet uidentur atque contraria et a se inuicem dissona, dum in generalissima ipsius uniuersitatis armonia considerantur, conuenientia consonaque sunt.*", PP I, 3224–3237, pp. 103–104, (= PL 122 517B–C). See too Eriugena, *De praedestinatione*, XVIII, 135–140, G. Madec (ed.), p. 115, (= PL 122 443D–434A), where Madec refers to places in Augustine's writings on the theology of order.

[172] Speaking of the contraries of goodness and wickedness he broaches the eschatology of 1 Cor. 15:54 *"absorbebitur mors in uictoria"* when only goodness will both appear and reign in all things, PP I, 2962–2974, pp. 95–96, (= PL 122 511A–B) and evil shall perish totally. Once again we witness the manifestative colouring of this eschatological scene. There appears a reference to a fuller discussion of these matters in book five: "*Sed de his in quinto latius disputabitur*", PP I, 2973, p. 96, (= PL 122 511B). É. Jeauneau in the corresponding footnote explains that Eriugena himself had written "*alibi disputabitur*" and that the scribe known to scholarship as "i2" wrote in "*in quinto latius*" when book five had been completed or at least had been started. See also É. Jeauneau / P. E. Dutton, *The Autograph of Eriugena.*.

[173] PP I, 2995–3001, p. 96, (= PL 122 512A).

Reason too is said to play a role in protecting the faithful from taking the names for God in the bible as proper predications of God.[174] This applies to the various kinds of names for God found in the scripture: the most exalted names such as life or virtue; the intermediate names taken from the higher regions of the visible world, such as sun or light; those taken from the lower motions of visible creatures such as breath or cloud.

No words taken from created reality are predicated properly of God. This Eriugena insists is true in the case of substantives and of verbs alike. Eriugena gives the example of God as love (substantive) and God loves (verb).

*Si deus per metaphoran amor dicitur, dum sit plus quam amor omnemque superat amorem, cur non eodem modo amare diceretur, dum omnem motum amoris exsuperat, quia nihil praeter se ipsum appetit, dum solus omnia in omnibus sit?*[175]

Another important verb from the point of view of the creation accounts of the Judaeo-Christian scriptures is that of making (*facere*). It is discussed in its relationship to suffering (*pati*) and motion (*motus*). Both maker (*faciens*) and made (*factum*) are said to suffer their own motions (*motus suos patiuntur*).[176] For that which makes, suffers its own motion towards making; that which is made suffers its own motion from that which is not into that which is, and sustains that of the maker.

Eriugena gives a lengthy account of motion and its different types: he draws on, and quotes extensively from the writings of Maximus Confessor[177]. Although Eriugena eventually reaches the negative conclusion that *agere* and *pati,* here *motus,* do not apply to God certain aspects of the argumentation are of additional interest. They reveal the senses in which God is the cause of all motion. Particularly prominent is the idea of God as the *end* of all motion.

No motion can lack a beginning or an end: every motion starts from a beginning and tends to some end, in which it rests when it arrives. The cause of all things is the same as the end of all things, for God is both the beginning (that is the cause) of all creatures and their end. From God they receive their being and begin to be and they are moved towards God in order that they may rest in God.

Quoting from Maximus, Eriugena goes on to say that all of the beings which have come into existence are moved and God is the motion of these things; whether the intellectual motion of intellectual things, or the sensible motion of the sensible things. Likewise only God is an end and perfection itself and impassibility, since only God is unchanging and fulfilled and impassible. The things which have been

---

[174] He speaks of reason functioning so that "… *simplices adhuc in cunabulis ecclesiae nutriti pie casteque corrigat, ne quid indignum de deo uel credant uel aestiment, ne omnia quae sanctae scripturae auctoritas de causa omnium praedicat proprie praedicari examinent,* …" PP I, 2982–2986, p. 96, (= PL 122 511C).

[175] PP I, 3029–3033, p. 97, (= PL 122 512D–513A).

[176] PP I, 3080, p. 99, (= PL 122 514A).

[177] Here Eriugena draws on the *Ambigua ad Iohannem,* see MAXIMUS CONFESSOR, *Ambigua ad Iohannem,* É. JEAUNEAU (ed.), CCSG 18, III, 20–22, p. 21, (= PG 91, 1069B).

made are moved towards an end. He quotes and translates Maximus "*Finis est pro quo omnia, ipse uero pro nullo.*"[178]

All things come from God and seek their end in God: "*Finis enim eorum quae mouentur motus, ipsum in eo quod semper est bene esse est, sicut et principium est ipsum esse quod quidem est deus, qui et esse dat et bene esse donat, iure principium et finis.*"[179] Further, Eriugena quoting Maximus and translating that author, shows how this might come about in *intellectual, loving* creatures (that is, to use modern terminology, in the conscious subject's attending to God):

*Si autem mouetur corrationabiliter sibimet intellectualiter intellectuale, omnino etiam intelligit. Si autem intelligit, omnino amat quod intelligit. Si amat, patitur omnino ad ipsum ut amabile excessum. Si autem patitur, profecto etiam festinat. Si festinat, omnino intendit ualidum motum. Si autem intendit ualidum motum, non stat quousque fiat totum in toto amato, et a toto comprehendatur libenter totum secundum uoluntatem salutarem accipiens circumscriptionem, ut totum toto afficiatur circumscribente, ut nihil omnino restet uelle ex se ipso, se ipsum totum cognoscere ualendo circumscriptum, sed ex circumscribente, sicut aer per totum illuminatur lumine, et igne ferum totum toto liquefactum.*[180]

I have quoted this at length because of its interest for the theme of the conscious attending of intelligent, loving being to God, a matter dealt with at length as a 'return' to God in books four and five of *Periphyseon*. The familiar images of light in air, iron and fire are quoted and the link to Maximus as source is clearly observable. Important for Eriugena's own argumentation is that he is leading up to the approving presentation of Maximus' teaching that there is no motion except in things with a beginning and end[181] therefore, Eriugena can introduce the conclusion, presented as his own, that there can be no motion in God:

*Deus autem anarchos (hoc est sine principio) est, quia nil eum praecedit nec eum efficit ut sit, nec finem habet quoniam infinitus est; nil enim post eum intelligitur, dum terminus omnium sit, ultra quem nihil progreditur. Nullum igitur motum recipit; non enim habet quo se moueat, dum plenitudo et locus et perfectio et statio et totum omnium sit, …*[182]

Eriugena can conclude that making (*facere*) and suffering (*pati*) are automatically excluded from God if motion is excluded. Giving an interesting definition of faith, he does however mention the particular case of God 'being made' in the souls of the faithful:

---

[178] PP I, 3118–3119, p. 100, (= PL 122 514D). See MAXIMUS CONFESSOR, Ambigua ad Iohannem, III, 70–71, É. JEAUNEAU (ed.) CCSG 18, p. 23: PG 91, 1072C. Jeauneau's apparatus in CCSG 18 gives references to Aristotle, the Ps. Dionysius Areopagita and others on this point.

[179] PP I, 3132–3135, p. 100, (= PL 122 515B). The distinction between *esse* and *bene esse* will be developed in Eriugena's eschatology.

[180] PP I, 3137–3148, pp. 100–101, (= PL 122 515B–515C).

[181] PP I, 3149–3151, p. 101, (= PL 122 515C).

[182] PP I, 3167–3172, p. 101, (= PL 122 516A).

*Dicitur etiam in animabus fidelium fieri, dum aut per fidem et uirtutem in eis concipitur, aut per fidem quodam modo inchoat intelligi. Nil enim aliud est fides, ut opinor, nisi principium quoddam, ex quo cognitio creatoris in natura rationabili fieri incipit.*[183]

The proposition that God does not make is an important one. This seems to contradict the Scriptures and what Eriugena calls the catholic faith (*fides catholica*). The solution lies in certain insights into the nature of God's 'making': into its timelessness and its inseparability from the divine essence. It is not correct to say that God existed before God made the world: this would imply that the making would have to be considered an accident. "*Aliud praeter eum et extra eum esse non crediderim; in ipso enim omnia sunt et extra ipsum nihil est. Nullumque ei accidens temere dederim ...*"[184]. God's making is coeternal with God and coessential with God. It is not one thing for God to be and another for God to make.

Eriugena may then conclude on God's relationship to created things that when we hear that God makes all things we should understand nothing other than that God is in all things, that God is the essence of all things. This passage presents Eriugena's adoption of the concept of participation:

*Cum ergo audimus deum omnia facere, nil aliud debemus intelligere quam deum in omnibus esse, hoc est essentiam omnium subsistere. Ipse enim solus per se uere est, et omne quod uere in his quae sunt dicitur esse ipse solus est. Nihil enim eorum quae sunt per se ipsum uere est; quodcunque autem in eo uere intelligitur participatione ipsius unius qui solus per se ipsum uere est accipit.*[185]

Eriugena concludes on the scriptural speech about God through *verbs*: All verbs are to be treated in the same way as that of 'to make.' They occur as terms referring to God's essence which in itself is ineffable, they are terms which are adapted to our nature (*connaturalibus nobis significationibus*). The reason for this divine condescension is not only the instruction of the faithful but also the refutation of heretics. Eriugena draws the threads of his argument together in terms of the unity of activity and essence in God:

*Non aliud itaque deo esse et uelle et facere et amare et diligere et uidere caeteraque huiusmodi quae de eo, ut diximus, possunt praedicari, sed haec omnia in ipso unum id ipsumque accipiendum suamque ineffabilem essentiam eo modo quo se significari sinit insinuant.*[186]

It is significant from the point of view of a biblical hermeneutic that the example of 'God loves' is treated in detail. First a definition of love (*amor*) is presented. Then a theology of God as loving is presented which draws on the Pseudo-Dionysius and finally on Maximus. The case of God's love is presented in terms of the principles of apophatic and kataphatic theology already outlined. Finally, Eriugena will reflect on the trinitarian God in terms of the verb 'to love'.

---

[183] PP I, 3191–3195, p. 102, (= PL 122 516C).
[184] PP I, 3218–3220, p. 103, (= PL 122 517A–B).
[185] PP I, 3258–3264, p. 104, (= PL 122 518A–B).
[186] PP I, 3284–3288, p. 105, (= PL 122 518 C–D).

We are offered the following definition of love:

*Amor est connexio ac uinculum, quo omnium rerum uniuersitas ineffabili amicitia insolubilique unitate copulatur. Potest et sic diffiniri: Amor est naturalis motus omnium rerum quae in motu sunt finis quietaque statio, ultra quam nullus creaturae progreditur motus.*[187]

Eriugena's account of love, including the definitions given above, is heavily indebted to the fourth chapter of *De diuinis nominibus* and quotes extensively from that chapter. Love is presented in a hierarchical setting. Love moves the higher things to provide for the lower, it moves things of equal status to a common reciprocity, and the lower things are moved to turn to these higher things. In hierarchical interaction, the loves of all existing things are directed to the cause of all love[188].

Eriugena weaves the information gleaned from the Ps. Dionysius into his own account of love. God is said to be rightly called love because God is the cause of all love, and is diffused through all things and gathers all things into one in an ineffable return, bringing to an end in God's Self the motions of love of the whole creature.[189] This diffusion is explained: it does not imply that God (who is completely without motion and who fills all things at once) is diffused, but that God diffuses the rational mind's viewing throughout all things. God is the cause of the motion and diffusion of the mind, causing it to seek and find, and as far as is possible, to understand God. Eriugena also stresses the unifying function of God with respect to all beings. God is the one who fills all things so that they might be and in the pacific embrace of universal love gathers all things together into an indivisible unity and holds them inseparably together. A possible misunderstanding of God's being loved is also ruled out: God is said to be loved by all the things which come from God, not in that sense that God suffers anything through them, but in the sense that all things seek God and are drawn to God by God's beauty.[190] God alone is said to be truly loveable because God alone is supreme and real goodness and beauty. Whatever in creatures is held to be really good, beautiful or loveable, that God is. God alone is essentially good and beautiful and loveable. Eriugena brings in the image of the magnet attracting iron to illustrate the attraction which the divine beauty exercises on all creatures without itself being moved.

Finally, Eriugena concludes on God and motion in terms of the theoretic account of apophatic and kataphatic theology which he has already outlined. He speaks of God:

---

[187] PP I, 3304–3308, p. 106, (= PL 122 519B).

[188] See PP I, 3310–3315, p. 106, (= PL 122 519 B–C).

[189] PP I, 3329–3332, p. 107, (= PL 122 519D). Although Eriugena has returned to his own words, these words must also be considered to be indebted to the Ps. DIONYSIUS. See, De div. nom., IV, 7, B. SUCHLA (ed.), p. 150, 15–p. 152, 9, (= PG 3, 701C–704B), especially p. 151, 18–p. 152, 9, (= PG 3, 704A–B).

[190] PP I, 3341–3343, p. 107, (= PL 122 520A–B). See AUGUSTINUS, *De uera religione*, LV, 113, K.-D. DAUR (ed.), CCSL 32, p. 260, 128–129, (= PL 34, 172): "*Unde apparet spiritualibus animis per hanc formam esse facta omnia, quae sola implet, quod appetunt omnia.*"

*Mouet se ipsum et mouetur a se ipso in se ipso et in nobis, non tamen mouet se ipsum nec mouetur a se ipso in se ipso et in nobis, quia plus quam mouet et mouetur in se ipso et in nobis. Et haec est cauta et salutaris et catholica de deo praedicanda professio: ut prius de eo iuxta catafaticam (id est affirmationem) omnia siue nominaliter siue uerbaliter praedicemus, non tamen proprie sed translatiue; deinde ut omnia quae de eo praedicantur per catafaticam eum esse negemus per apofaticam (id est negationem) non tamen translatiue sed proprie.*[191]

Once again it is pointed out that negation is *properly* said of God: "*Verius enim negatur deus quid eorum quae de eo praedicantur esse quam affirmatur esse.*"[192]

After this relative conclusion in his exposition of *agere / pati* and God, having dealt especially with the cases of *videre, movere, amare,* Eriugena then once more spirals in on his subject matter from a distinctly trinitarian level. From the notion of God moving in us Eriugena proceeds to the theological theme of the spirit speaking in us. He quotes from Mt. 10:20: "*Non uos estis qui loquimini, sed spiritus patris qui loquitur in uobis.*" He says that right reason compels us to believe and say and understand similarly of other similar things. Thus he gives a trinitarian account of God loving, moving and seeing in us[193]: "*Non uos estis qui amatis, qui uidetis, qui mouetis, sed spiritus patris, qui loquitur in uobis ueritatem de me et patre meo et se ipso, ipse amat et uidet me et patrem meum et se ipsum in uobis, et mouet se ipsum in uobis ut diligatis me et patrem meum.*"[194] The spirit moves himself in the faithful so that they might desire (*diligatis*) the father and the son. The divine incomprehensibility which underpinned the general conclusion on the impossibility of predicating motion properly of God is also reaffirmed in this trinitarian context. Eriugena now quotes from 1 Tim. 6:16 and Rom. 2:34:

*De ineffabili enim quis et quid potest fari? Cuius nec nomen proprium, nec uerbum, nec ulla uox propria inuenitur, nec est nec fieri potest, 'qui solus habet immortalitatem et lucem habitat inaccessibilem'; 'Quis enim cognouit intellectum domini?'*[195]

---

[191] PP I, 3415–4324, p. 109, (= PL 122 522A–B).

[192] PP I, 3424–3425, p. 109, (= PL 122 522A). See Ps. Dionysius Ariopagita, De coel. hier., II, 3, G. Heil (ed.), pp. 12–13, (= PG 3, 140C–141A).

[193] See Eriugena, Hom. XIII, 16–23, É. Jeauneau (ed.), p. 266, (= PL 122, 290D–291A): "*Audi ipsum uerbum: "Non uos, inquit, estis qui loquimini, sed spiritus patris uestri qui loquitur in uobis". Hac una sententia uoluit nos docere id ipsum in caeteris intelligere, ac semper in aure cordis nostri ineffabili modo sonare: Non uos estis qui lucetis, sed spiritus patris uestri qui lucet in uobis, hoc est, me in uobis lucere uobis manifestat, quia ego sum lux intelligibilis mundi, hoc est, rationalis et intellectualis naturae; ...*"

[194] PP I, 3431–3435, pp. 109–110, (= PL 122 522B–C).

[195] PP I, 3440–3444, p. 110, (= PL 122 522C).

# CHAPTER 3

# God appears in creation

The result of the reflection on the possibility of attaining knowledge about God, or indeed of speaking about God, was that we do not know what God is but merely that God is, and that we cannot predicate any category properly of God. The limited knowledge namely, that God exists, is given to us through created reality. God appears not as an abstract deity but as creator. God appears in created reality, in all that creation's variety. It is this divine appearing which must now be considered. In the present chapter the recurring characteristics of the appearing of God in reality in general will be considered. A following chapter will devote attention to the special case of the appearing of God in the human creature[1].

## 1. The primordial causes: nature as
### "*ea quae et creatur et creat*"

In the concept of the primordial causes Eriugena finds a notion which is of ontological and epistemological relevance alike[2]. From an ontological perspective the primordial causes represent the prototypes of all created or 'to-be-created' reality as these prototypes of reality subsist in God. From the epistemological perspective they represent the intrinsic intelligibility of all contingent being. Thus the primordial causes can play a pivotal role with a creational theology. They receive lengthy attention within Eriugena's system[3]. Gangolf Schrimpf sees in the concept of the *causae primordiales* the most central, the most suitable tool for approaching an understanding of reality as the appearing of God[4]. A further point of interest is

---

[1] In my opinion this is the best way to approach the special status of the human within the order of creation. In devoting a chapter to the appearing of God in the human, this study reflects an Eriugenian emphasis on the unique case which the human creature is.

[2] GANGOLF SCHRIMPF in Das Werk des Johannes Scottus Eriugena, speaks of a cosmological, eschatological, soteriological and, what he calls, a '*gnoseologische*' function, p. 256. I see the cosmological (I would prefer to call it 'ontological') and gnoseological functions as intrinsic to the concept of the primordial causes, and see these functions exercised within the eschatology and soteriology of Eriugena's system as a whole.

[3] This has led GANGOLF SCHRIMPF to present them as the thematic centre of *Periphyseon*. See Das Werk des Johannes Scottus Eriugena, pp. 256–292: "Der Begriff der Entstehungsgründe: primordiales causae".

[4] "*Der Begriff der Entstehungsgründe ist das geeignetste Instrument, um die gesamte Wirklichkeit als göttliche Erscheinung zu denken. ... Der Zweck der Schöpfung geht immer dann in Erfüllung, wenn*

that Eriugena openly acknowledges the debt which his thought on these primordial causes owes to other authors writing before him[5]. We must thus investigate not only the functions of this term and it's role within Eriugena's system, but also his sources for this term.

The world-God relationship is repeatedly approached in terms of creation and its expression through the four-fold division of nature. The second and the third forms of nature are particularly relevant. The second form of nature (that which is both created and creates) is understood to consist in the primordial causes of created things. The third form of nature (that which is created and does not create) consists in the effects of the primordial causes.

_____

*ein Mensch, gestützt auf Wissenschaft und Hl. Schrift, die konkrete Welt, die ihm begegnet, als Erschei-nung Gottes denkt. Das geschieht dadurch, daß er die Dinge nicht mehr nur in ihrer raumzeitlichen Erscheinungsform denkt, sondern darüber hinaus als einen jeweils individuellen Ausdruck bestimmter göttlicher Vollkommenheiten. ... Der oberste Zweck der Schöpfung besteht somit darin, es dem Menschen zu ermöglichen, jene Gedanken Gottes nachzuvollziehen, die in der sichtbaren und unsichtbaren Welt zum Ausdruck kommen.*", GANGOLF SCHRIMPF, Das Werk des Johannes Scottus Eriugena, p. 288. In this passage we see that Schrimpf's analysis concentrates on the *intellectual* aspect of the encounter between the human and God. The return in virtue to a loving God receives less analysis although, as I shall argue, this is an important aspect of Eriugena's system as a whole and of the later books of *Periphyseon* and of his Johannine commentaries in particular. On p. 290–295 Schrimpf does explicitly consider the return of all creation to the creator and the role of human knowledge of individual things in this. Here he does use the slightly more personalistic category of 'conversa-tion': "*Der Mensch jedoch, der über das Wissen verfügt, das in der Hl. Schrift enthalten ist, ist sich dabei der Tatsache bewußt, daß er in jenem Dingbegriff, der bis zu den Entstehungsgründen des Dings zurückgeht, jenen Gedanken nachvollzieht, den Gott ihm durch dieses Ding mitteilen wollte, er also vermittels dieses Dings eine Art Gespräch mit Gott führt.*" p. 292. I see, however, in the brevity of the treatment of *Periphyseon* books four and five in the closing pages of Schrimpf's study, an invitation to complement his analysis of the primordial causes through further studies of the material on the appearing of God precisely in the light of these academically relatively neglected, books. His hint at the importance of the human person as *creaturarum omnium officina* in the return, has in the meantime been expanded by Willemien Otten's study of the role of Eriugena's anthropology in *Periphyseon*. The return as *encounter* (where not only a cognitive element but also a meeting of the individual virtuous person with a loving God) which is a theme dealt with above all in *Periphyseon* book five, must, in my opinion, be more clearly elucidated than is the case in Schrimpf's study. This must be stated even in the light of his remarks on p. 294 where he speaks of the personal way that God is revealed to the human. Schrimpf's study with its exhaustive account of the role of the primordial causes retains a very strong intellectual emphasis in its analysis of (even the heavenly) encounter with God.

[5] Schrimpf emphasises the innovative in Eriugena's treatment of the primordial causes. See however the two articles of Robert D. Crouse on the debt of Eriugena to Augustine's theology of creation: see R. D. CROUSE, "The Meaning of Creation in Augustine and Eriugena", in: ELIZABETH A. LIVINGSTONE (ed.), *Studia Patristica XXII. Papers presented to the Tenth International Conference on Patristic Studies held in Oxford 1987*, Leuven: Peeters Press, 1989, pp. 229–234 and "*Primordiales Causae* in Eriugena's Interpretation of Genesis: Sources and Significance", in: G. VAN RIEL/C. STEEL/J. McEVOY,(ed.), Iohannes Scottus Eriugena. The Bible and Hermeneutics, pp. 209–220. While also praising the intensified systematic treatment which the theme receives in Eriugena's writings, Crouse emphasises the continuity of Eriugena's treatment of the primordial causes when compared with the writings of Augustine more than Schrimpf does. He emphasises the trinitarian context within which Augustine and Eriugena alike describe the function of the primordial causes in creation.

Eriugena initiates an account of the primordial causes in *Periphyseon* book two[6]. One characteristic of this account which deserves mention is the fact that it is carried through in terms of the dialectic methods of analytic collection (ἀναλυτική) and division (διαιρετική)[7]. Eriugena presents the discipline called α ναλυτική as that by which the oppositions and differences and similarities return and are collected. All rational divisions, be it of essence, or of genus into species, or of the whole into parts, or that of the universe into those divisions which reason contemplates therein may be brought back to the original unity from which they proceeded. He gives an etymology of the term ἀναλυτική: "*ANAΛΥTIKH a uerbo ANAΛΥΩ deriuatur, id est resoluo uel redeo …*"[8].

It is clear from Eriugena's text that ἀναλυτική is not merely the principle of the knowledge of the cosmos but also the principle of the cosmos itself. Speaking of ἀναλυτική he says "*Est igitur reditus et resolutio indiuiduorum in formas, formarum in genera, generum in OYCIA, OYCIArum in sapientiam et prudentiam, ex quibus omnis diuisio oritur in easque finitur.*"[9] The end in question is the perfection of the Christian plan of salvation in wisdom and prudence[10].

Eriugena applies this method to the divisions of nature. He carries out an exemplary collection of the four-fold division of nature. The first and the fourth divisions may be united in that both refer to God, namely as Creator and as end of all creation. "*Est enim principium omnium quae a se condita sunt et finis omnium quae eum appetunt ut in eo aeternaliter immutabiliterque quiescant.*"[11] Eriugena goes on to describe this being the beginning and being the end in terms of procession and return ("*ad eandem causam omnia quae ab ea procedunt dum ad finem peruenient reuersura sunt, …*")[12] All things are united in the primordial causes from the start and in the return to their divine Cause, they remain immutably and eternally united in the primordial causes. "*Nam quae in processionibus naturarum multipliciter diuisa atque partita esse uidentur, in primordialibus causis unita atque unum sunt, ad quam unitatem reuersura in ea aeternaliter atque immutabiliter manebunt.*"[13]

---

[6] PP II, 134, p. 8, (= PL 122 529A). On the principles with which É. Jeauneau edited book two of *Periphyseon,* see PP II, CCCM CLXII, Jeauneau, (ed.), Introduction, pp. VII–XII. The difference between his methods of editing in book one and book two result in "une légère asymétrie entre la présentation du livre I et celle du livre II", (Introduction to book two, p. XII).

[7] See PP II, 64–119, pp. 5–7, (= PL 122 5226C–528B). See Eriugena, *Expositiones in ierarchiam coelestem,* VII, 575–603, J. Barbet (ed.), p. 106–107, (= PL 122 184C–185B); XV, 35–41, pp. 187–188, (= PL 122 252 B–C).

[8] PP II, 49–50, (= PL 122 526B).

[9] PP II, 60–62, p. 5, (= PL 122 526B–C).

[10] See Prov. 3:19; Jer. 10:12 and 51:15. See too Maximus Confessor, *Ambigua ad Iohannem,* XXXVII, 181–195, CCSG 18, p. 186, (= PG 91, 1313A–B).

[11] PP II, 67–69, p. 5, (= PL 122 526C). See Ps. Dionysius Ariopagita, De div. nom., V, 10, B. Suchla (ed.), p. 189, 7–9, (= PG 3, 825B; PL 122, 1151A) and Maximus Confessor, *Ambigua ad Iohannem,* III, 111–114, É. Jeauneau (ed.), CCSG 18, p. 25, (= PG 91, 1073C).

[12] PP II, 73–75, p. 5, (= PL 122, 526D).

[13] PP II, 79–83, p. 6, (= PL 122, 527A).

He concludes that the first and the fourth forms of nature have been reduced to a unity.

In these passages on procession and return, following so closely on his account of 'analytike', and as an example of a collection, one sees the 'circumincession' of the principles of *knowing the cosmos* and the *ontological principles of the cosmos*.

He turns his attention to the second and the third forms. The second which is both created and creates is understood to consist in the primordial causes of created things, the third which is created and does not create consists in the effects of the primordial causes. This pair may not only be distinguished but also be reduced to a unity because both are contained within one and the same genus, namely that of created nature, and are one in it. Having reduced the four forms of nature to two unities, Eriugena's next step is to effect a further collection.

The creator and the creature are said to be one. Eriugena establishes this by showing that the existence of the creature and that of God are not of the same order. Rather only God may be said truly to exist. The creature exists by participation. In this sense one may say that there is nothing in the creature except God. Thus a unity is established between creator and creation.[14] This is however a far cry from pantheism. It is rather the affirmation of a way of viewing the God-world relationship, one in which the radical dependence of the world on God is emphasised. For Eriugena the collection (ἀναλυτική) and division (διαιρετική) of God and the world are simultaneously valid. It is therefore not legitimate to raise the charge of pantheism against him on the basis of a selective review of isolated sentences in Eriugena's presentation of this complex matter.

So Eriugena can use analytike to make a reduction of the four forms of the universe to a unit (*ad unum indiuiduum*) which is both principle and end of everything else[15].

It is within this context that Eriugena then turns his attention to the second form of nature.[16] The second form of universal nature, that which is both created and creates is equated with the primordial causes. In an introductory passage Eriugena gives an outline of the various names for the primordial causes with the nuances

---

[14] See PP II, 109–114, p. 7, (= PL 122 528B).

[15] PP II, 117–119, p. 7, (= PL 122 528B). In a textual addition the distinction is made between the status of the division between the first and the fourth forms, which is said to arise from our way of understanding God, and that between the second and the third forms, which is rooted in the real distinction between the primordial causes and the effects which proceed from them. The one distinction is due to our reason alone, the other is also rooted in reality, PP II, textual addition number 7, 35–49, p. 7, (= PL 122 527D–528A).

[16] PP II, 134 following, p. 8 following, (= PL 122 529A following.) In a textual addition it is explained that not only the procession of all things through the primordial essences but also the return of all things through them will be discussed. It is impossible to separate the procession from the return or collection, PP II, addition Nr. 9, 52–65, p. 8, (= PL 122 528C–529A).

involved in the various names. He also brings in immediately the trinitarian context within which creation through the primordial causes takes place.[17]

He elaborates the Greek origins of this concept: "*Ipsae autem primordiales rerum causae a graecis ΠΡΩΤΟΤΥΠΑ (hoc est primordialia exempla) uel ΠΡΟΟΡΙСΜΑΤΑ (hoc est praedestinationes uel praediffinitiones) uocantur.*"[18] Key aspects are that they are the exemplars, the predestinations and pre-existing definitions of created realities. The notion of *praedestinationes* has a volitional connotation. This aspect of the primordial causes is elaborated in the next sentence: "*Item ab eisdem ΘΕΙΑ ΘΕΛΗΜΑΤΑ (hoc est diuinae uoluntates) dicuntur.*"[19] Continuing his collection of connotations, he now draws on the Augustinian tradition and writes: "*ΙΔΕΑ quoque (id est species uel forma in qua omnium rerum faciendarum, priusquam essent, incommutabiles rationes conditae sunt) solet uocari.*"[20] The last sentence within this passage, a sentence which must indeed be viewed as its crowning point, gives the trinitarian frame of reference: The father, the principle of all things, is said to have pre-formed all things in the word, that is, the only begotten son, before all things came into being in their genera and species: "*... pater, hoc est principium omnium, in uerbo suo, unigenito uidelicet filio, omnium rerum rationes quas faciendas esse uoluit, priusquam ⟨procederent⟩ in genera et species numerosque atque differentias caeteraque quae in condita creatura aut considerari possunt et considerantur, aut considerari non possunt et non considerantur et tamen sunt, praeformauit.*"[21]

So the order of his exposition is: first the Greek patristic position (Dionysius and Maximus)[22] then the Latin position (indebted to Augustine), finally the trinitarian theological position.

## 2. The primordial causes and the biblical divine names

In a significant summary Eriugena recapitulates on the various nuances of meaning which attend the notion of the primordial causes.[23]

---

[17] PP II, 134–148, p. 8–9, (= PL 122 529A–529C).

[18] PP II, 136–139, p. 8, (= PL 122 529A–B).

[19] PP II, 139–140, p. 8, (= PL 122, 529B). This is because it brings up the controversial issue of a possible 'createdness' of divine volitions. This must, of course, be answered negatively.

[20] PP II, 140–142, p. 8–9, (= PL 122 529B). É. Jeauneau's apparatus refers to AUGUSTINUS, *De trinitate* IV, i, 3, W. J. MOUNTAIN / FR. GLORIE, pp. 162–163, (= PL 42 888), however Augustine does not speak of the divine ideas in this passage.

[21] PP II, 143–148, p. 9, (= PL 122 529B–C).

[22] PP II, lines 136–40, that is, with the terms ΠΡΩΤΟΤΥΠΑ; ΠΡΟΟΡΙСΜΑΤΑ; ΘΕΙΑ ΘΕΛΗΜΑΤΑ, are indebted to Ps. DIONYSIUS, *De div. nom.*, V, 8, B. SUCHLA (ed.), p. 188, 6–10, (= PG 3, 824C; PL 122, 1150C–D). Maximus Confessor in turn refers to the passage in De div. nom. MAXIMUS CONFESSOR, *Ambigua ad Iohannem*, III, 318–322, p. 31, É. JEAUNEAU (ed.), CCSG 18, (= PG 91 1085A).

[23] PP II, 3142–3191, pp. 124–125, (= PL 122, 615D–617A).

- They are the immutable reasons in which the world is both formed and governed. Here both the moments of formation and ongoing providence are present. In this context he associates the primordial causes with the Greek term, ἰδέαι and the Latin terms *species, formae, rationes*.[24]
- They are also called πρωτότυπα that is, he explains, principal exemplars. Here he provides a trinitarian perspective. He says that the Father made them in the Son and divides and multiplies them into their effects through the Spirit.[25]
- They are also called προορίσματα predestinations. Here the moment of predestination is emphasised and the instantaneous nature (*simul et semel*) of a divine providence active in the past, present and future[26].
- The volitional aspect of the primordial causes is even more strongly apparent in the reported use of the expression θεῖα θελήματα for them by certain philosophers[27].
- These volitions are presented as participations in the one cause of all things precisely as the most high trinity[28].
- They are immediately caused by God, but they in turn cause other causes which come after them. This is precisely the function which made them so interesting from the point of view of the four-fold division of nature.

The roots of this theory emerge explicitly, roots grounded in a Dionysian account of the possibility of speaking about God and knowing God. Eriugena says that in case people should think that his account of the primordial causes has all been said without any authority, he will add quotations from Dionysius' work, *On the Divine Names*. This he does. The following quotation (Eriugena's translation) shows how closely Eriugena's theory is related to his understanding of the pseudo Areopagite. Here we can observe three of the key nuances of meaning which accrue to the notion of the primordial causes:

*Paradigmata autem dicimus esse ipsas in deo existentium substantificas et uniformiter praetextas rationes, quas theologia praedestinationes uocat et diuinas et optimas uoluntates, existentium discretiuas et factiuas, secundum quas ipse superessentialis existentia omnia et praedestinauit et adduxit.*[29]

---

[24] PP II, 3142–3145, p. 124, (= PL 122 615D–616A).

[25] See PP II 3145–3148, p. 124 (= PL 122 616A).

[26] PP II, 3148–3151, p. 124, (= PL 122, 616A).

[27] PP II, 3151–3157, p. 124, (= PL 122 616A–B). The expression is used by the Ps. DIONYSIUS *De div. nom.*, V, 8, B. SUCHLA (ed.), p. 188, 6–10, (= PG 3, 824C; PL 122, 1150C–D and reported by MAXIMUS in: *Ambigua ad Iohannem* 3, 318–322, É. JEAUNEAU (ed.), CCSG 18, p. 31, (= PG 91, 1085A) where (in Eriugena's translation) it is given as "*diuinas uoluntates*".

[28] PP II, 3160–3161, p. 124, (= PL 122 616B).

[29] PP II, 3276–3280, p. 128, (= PL 122 619A–620A) translating from Ps. DIONYSIUS AREOPAGITA, *De div. nom.*, V, 8, B. SUCHLA (ed.), p. 188, 6–10, (= PG 3, 824C; PL 122, 1150C–D).

Eriugena brings the primordial causes into close relationship with what the Pseudo-Dionysius had called the most exalted names for God which have been considered in *De div. nom.*, pointing out their role in bringing order into the web of creation:

*Sunt igitur primordiales causae, quas rerum omnium principia diuini sapientes appellant, per se ipsam bonitas, per se ipsam essentia, per se ipsam uita, per se ipsam sapientia, per se ipsam ueritas, per se ipsum intellectus, per se ipsam ratio, per se ipsam uirtus, … per se ipsam pax, et omnes uirtutes et rationes, quas semel et simul pater fecit in filio, et secundum quas ordo omnium rerum a summo usque deorsum texitur …*[30]

From the point of view of assessing Eriugena's academic method, it is interesting to observe what the dialogue partner Alumnus says as a reaction to the proposition to quote from the Pseudo-Dionysius: "*Nil aptius, nil ueris rationibus conuenientius subiungitur, quam sanctorum patrum inconcussa probabilisque auctoritas.*"[31] Usually the qualification '*inconcussa*' is used by Eriugena for the authority of Scripture.[32] It would be false to oppose Dionysius and Scripture in Eriugena's thinking: for one thing, the supposed 'Areopagite' enjoyed a respect almost comparable to that of the biblical authors, and secondly *De div. nom.* deals with the biblical naming of God.

## 3. The creator God as "triune"

Accordingly it does not surprise us that the further consideration of the primordial causes is imbedded within a 'hexaemeron', an interpretation of the first six days of creation.

Eriugena's reasoning takes its rise from scripture "*Ratiocinationis exordium ex diuinis eloquiis assumendum esse aestimo.*"[33] In particular three biblical quotations give structure to his account of the primordial causes:

*(1)*
"*In principio fecit deus caelum et terram*": (Gen. 1: 1).[34]
After a brief survey of various interpretations[35] of what heaven and earth might be in this sentence, Eriugena quickly introduces his own opinion:

*Mihi autem multorum sensus consideranti nil probabilius nil uerisimilius occurrit quam ut in praedictis sanctae scripturae uerbis, significatione uidelicet caeli et terrae, primordiales totius creaturae causas, quas pater in unigenito suo filio qui principii appellatione nominatur ante omnia quae condita sunt creauerat, intelligamus, et caeli nomine rerum intelligibilium caelestiumque*

---

[30] PP II, 3168–3176, p. 125, (= PL 122 616C).
[31] PP II, 3192–3193, p. 125, (= PL 122 617A).
[32] See PP III, 2176–2177, p. 76, (= PL 122 672C).
[33] PP II, 578–579, p. 27, (= PL 122 545B).
[34] See PP II, 583, p. 28, (= PL 122 545B–C).
[35] Interestingly he speaks of the various interpretations of what the prophet, or rather the Holy Spirit through the prophet, wished to have signified by the words heaven and earth.

*essentiarum, terrae uero appellatione sensibilium rerum, quibus uniuersitas huius mundi corporalis completur, principales causas significatas esse accipiamus.*[36]

Eriugena is at the heart of a theology of the primordial causes: not only is scripture the chosen starting point, but even in interpreting a text from the Old Testament Eriugena has adopted a trinitarian perspective. This short passage represents a synopsis of book two of *Periphyseon*. In the term 'beginning' (*principio*) Eriugena sees a reference to creation in the Son. It would not be accurate to speak of a trinitarian digression in book two. Rather Eriugena sees the trinitarian perspective as one intrinsic to the biblical text he is interpreting and to the matter at hand, i. e. the primordial causes. 'Heaven' and 'earth' signify the primordial causes, through the term 'heaven' the principle causes[37] of intelligible and celestial essences, through the term 'earth' those of sensible things.

Eriugena has occasion to reflect on the relationship between the primordial causes and matter in all its formlessness. Being and non-being are opposites of each other. The primordial causes are most near to being, the formless is next to nothing. This suggests the huge difference between the causes and unformed matter. Unformed matter is itself created through the primordial causes[38]. In lines indebted to Augustine, *De uera religione,* the speaker known as the Alumnus reminds readers that the forms are turned towards the one form of things, the form which all forms desire, the Word of the Father[39].

## (2)

The next section of a verse of Genesis (Gen. 1:2) which Eriugena expounds is "*Terra autem erat inanis et uacua et tenebrae super faciem abyssi*"[40].

In his long commentary on this verse Eriugena once starts with the opinions of others[41]. Subsequently his own opinion is presented.

*Sed si quis dixerit praedicta prophetae uerba non aliud quam primordiales rerum causas innuere, non uidebitur ex ueritate deuiare.*[42]

Eriugena once again elaborates on the πρωτότυπον. This, he says, is the principle exemplar of bodily reality which is signified by the word 'earth' and which was cre-

---

[36] PP II, 606–614, pp. 28–29, (= PL 122 546A–B).

[37] In the above given quote both expressions, primordial causes and principal causes, occur.

[38] The Alumnus makes this suggestion. See PP II, 664–668, p. 30, (= PL 122 548A).

[39] In PP II, 648–651, p. 30, (= PL 122 547B–C).

[40] Eriugena himself points out the variant of the Septuaginta which he translates as "*inuisibilis et incomposita*" instead of "*inanis et uacua*". See Gen. 1:2; Septuaginta, J. W. WEVERS (ed.), p. 75; Vetus latina, B. FISCHER (ed.), Freiburg, 1951–1954, pp. 3–6: "*invisibilis et inconposita*".

[41] He adds a comment on how this diversity of opinions is to be approached: "*Non enim nostrum est de intellectibus sanctorum patrum diiudicare, sed eos pie ac uenerabiliter suscipere. Non tamem prohibemur eligere quod magis uidetur eloquiis rationis consideratione conuenire.*" PP II, 700–703, p. 32, (PL 122, 548D–549A). The 'others' whose opinions are presented are AUGUSTINE in *De Genesi ad litteram,* and BASIL OF CAESAREA in *Homiliae in Hexaemeron.*

[42] PP II, 703–705, p. 32, (= PL 122, 549A).

ated by God in the beginning, that is by the Father in the Son, before the sensible world. This πρωτότυπον may be called void and waste. Void because before it issued forth into the genera and species of sensible nature in time and space, it was free from every sensible aspect such as accrue to its effects. It may be called waste because it involves no quality or quantity, nothing filled out by corporeal matter, nothing extended in place or moving in time. Thus Eriugena presents the attributes 'waste' and 'void' as positive attributes in this context, signifying the perfection of the primordial nature.

Eriugena also interprets the alternative version of the verse (*Septuaginta*) which says that the earth was 'invisible' and 'incomposite' and shows that an interpretation of these terms which is compatible with the first interpretation of 'waste' and 'void' is possible.[43] The 'invisibility' of the mystical earth ('*mystica terra*') refers to the profundity of the primordial causes; the 'lack of composition' to their simplicity.

Next he proceeds to the primordial causes of the so-called intellectual essence (*intellectualis essentia*). These are signified by the words 'dark abyss'. The term 'abyss' is said to be suitable because of their depth and the fact that they are diffused through all things; the term 'dark' because of the excellence of their purity. Before the primordial causes entered into the plurality of celestial essences no created intellect could know them.

In the things of which they are the causes, be these things intelligible or sensible, the causes are said to appear, but in themselves they remain (even after the procession of things through them) incomprehensible. They do not depart from their principle which is the wisdom of God the Father[44]. Again an Augustinian influence is detectable[45].

*(3)*

The next section of a verse of Scripture which Eriugena comments on is "*Et spiritus dei superferebatur super aquas*" (Gen. 1: 2).[46]

This marks a decision to progress further with the exposition of Genesis rather than to concentrate on a systematic exposition of the primordial causes organised according to other principles such as the opening passages of book two (and indeed the initial four fold division) might have led us to expect.

---

[43] PP II, 754ff, p. 34, (= PL 122, 550B). Interposed between the interpretations of the two text versions is the cosmological passage, PP II, 723–743, p. 32–33, (= PL 122 549B–550 A).

[44] PP II, 803–804, p. 35, (= PL 122 551C).

[45] I think lines 798–9, (= PL 122 551B) ("… *in secretissimis dico diuinae sapientiae sinibus* …") are more specifically indebted to Augustine than lines 800–807 which É. Jeauneau in his critical apparatus links to AUGUSTINUS, *De trinitate,* IV, i, 3 W. J. MOUNTAIN / FR. GLORIE (ed.), pp. 162–163, (= PL 42 888). This foregoing passage is interesting because here he speaks of the secret folds, not of nature or of human nature, but of the divine wisdom. See É. JEAUNEAU's note on Eriugena's use of *sinus* (singular and plural), on his debt to Augustine, and on the influence of 1 Jn 1:18 on Eriugena in his note on Hom., XVII, 5, p. 282.

[46] PP II, 842–843, p. 36, (= PL 122, 552C). Gen. 1: 2; Vetus Latina, B. FISCHER (ed.), pp. 6–7.

Eriugena first interprets this verse in terms of the divine *knowledge* of the primordial causes: the primordial causes are not so infinite and incomprehensible that the God who made them cannot comprehend them. That God's Spirit was borne over the waters signifies the eminence of the Spirit's knowledge of the primordial causes.

Further, he points out, the primordial causes are themselves caused by a higher principle. They are caused out of, through, in and for (*ex qua et per quam in qua et ad quam*) God[47]. Things proceed from God through the plan of divine *providence,* some things proceed through intermediary causes, some through no intermediary cause. (This is not meant in a temporary sense but in the sense of an order of the dignity of creation). This is all part of the plan of the divine providence and is an alternative interpretation of the expression that the Spirit 'was borne' above the waters.

Eriugena proceeds to summarise this twofold interpretation of the scriptural words:

*Spiritus ergo dei super tenebrosam abyssum causarum omnium primordialiter factarum superfertur, quia solus conditor spiritus conditas causas cognitionis excellentia supereminet, omniumque causarum quas creauerat una ac sola praecedens et superexcellens causa est et principalissimus fons omnium quae a se in infinitum profluunt et in se recurrunt et a nullo alio, si de spiritu sancto proprie intelligitur, nisi a patre manat.*[48]

Also of interest is the use of *profluunt / recurrunt.* It is interesting that these terms have been introduced by Eriugena although up to this, another terminology (that of ordered causation) had been predominant in *Periphyseon*[49].

Eriugena develops the trinitarian context of creation. The Son is said to be from the Father through an ineffable generation. Everything is made in the Son as in the Beginning. From the Father in procession is the Holy Spirit. For the Father wills, the Son makes, the Spirit perfects. The identity of willing and making in the Father is affirmed[50]. It is also pointed out that there are not three wills but one willing, one love in the trinity. The trinity is said, to be, to be wise, and to be living[51].

Next the translation of the verse Gen. 1:2 which reads "*Et spiritus dei fouebat aquas*" is interpreted. This translation is reported by Basil of Caesarea in his *Homi-*

---

[47] PP II, 859–860, p. 37, (= PL 122 553A–B), speaking of the cause of all things.

[48] PP II, 875–881, pp. 37–38, (= PL 122, 553C).

[49] We note the 'Greek' position on the procession of the Holy Spirit, i.e. procession from the Father alone.

[50] PP II, textual addition number 75, 323–338, p. 38, (= PL 122, 553D–554B).

[51] "*Est igitur, et sapit, et uiuit.*", PP II, textual addition number 75, 338, p. 38, (= PL 122 554B). I. P. Sheldon-Williams has a lengthy endnote (his number 235) on this trio and on its history. Of interest is that whatever its roots in Plotinus, Proclus, Neoplatonism, Ps. Dionysius and so on, Eriugena doesn't merely adopt the trio, he adapts it. More precisely he changes the usual order of the trio to fit in with the biblical Christian doctrine of the trinity. "Eriugena alters the traditional and logical order of the triad under the influence of his doctrine of the Trinity, ..." I. P. Sheldon-Williams, note 235, p. 229.

*liae in Hexaemeron* and ascribed to a certain Syrian[52]. "*Spiritus enim sanctus causas primordiales, quas pater in principio (in filio uidelicet suo) fecerat, ut in ea quorum causae sunt procederent fouebat, hoc est diuini amoris fotu nutribat.*"[53] The key word '*fouebat*' is explained in terms of the divine love: nourished in the fermentation / quickening of the divine love.

One corner-stone of Eriugena's trinitarian theology is the tenet that the Word proceeds all things causally but not temporally. A medley of verses from the Psalms is woven into the argumentation supporting this, including verses from Ps. 103[54], Ps. 44 and Ps. 109. An interpretation of Ps. 109:3 plays a singular role in his presentation of the inherence of all created realities in the Word[55]. In the Vulgate the text reads: "*tecum principium in die uirtutis tuae in splendoribus sanctorum ex utero ante luciferum genui te*"[56].

Eriugena, speaking through the Alumnus, uses the phrase '*tecum principium*' to underline that the Word was never without the things of which it is the beginning[57].

Eriugena's Alumnus then interprets '*in die uirtutis tuae*'. The power of the Father is the wisdom of the Father in which he made everything. He thus interprets the day here as the coming-to-be-known of the divine wisdom. In particular the coming-to-be-known of the generation of the Son from the Father and the creation of all things in the Son, (in Wisdom).

A textual addition qualifies this becoming known. Here the theophanies are said to be the means of access (insofar as it is possible to possess some knowledge of the in-itself-unknowable). The theophanies are said to be divine manifestations which are instilled into, and implanted in, pure intellects.

---

[52] See BASILIUS CAESARIENSIS, *Homiliae in Hexaemeron,* II, 6, S. GIET (ed.), SC 26 bis, Paris: CERF, 1968, pp. 166–170; PG 29, 44A–B); AMBROSIUS, *Exameron,* I, viii, 29, K. SCHENKL (ed.), CSEL 32, 1, Vienna: Tempsky, 1897, pp. 28–29; AUGUSTINUS, *De Genesi ad litteram,* I, XVIII, 36, JOSEPH ZYCHA (ed.), pp. 26–27, (= PL 34, 260).

[53] PP II, 889–892, p. 38, (= PL 122 554B).

[54] "*Omnia in sapientia fecisti*" (Ps. 103:24). At same time / in the one act (Latin = simul) the father is said to have brought forth wisdom (his son) and made all things in this wisdom.

It is interesting that with this Alumnus section (PP II, 981, p. 42 and following, (= PL 122, 556C ff), Alumnus' role seems to change. Alumnus is not just the secondary figure who questions, but the speaker giving the exposition. It is also of interest that in the section which follows (PP II, 1071, p. 46, (= PL 122 560A)) the Migne and I. P. Sheldon-Williams / L. Bieler assignment of passages to Nutritor and Alumnus differs from that of the Jeauneau edition. In their endnote 263, p. 232, I. P. SHELDON-WILLIAMS / L. BIELER show that they are aware both of the Alumnus taking the initiative in the discussion at the point mentioned above and the alternative assignment of the passages. From this point in PP II on, it becomes less important for an interpreter to distinguish between which speaker is speaking, as both communicate Eriugena's own position.

[55] PP II, 995 following; p. 42, (= PL 122, 557A following).

[56] Ps. 109:3, Vulgate.

[57] See PP II, 998–999, p. 42, (= PL 122 557B): "*nunquam erat et principium non erat, sed semper principium erat.*"

*Quantum datur creaturae intelligere quod superat omnem intellectum et ad lucem inaccessibilem conceditur accessus per theophanias (hoc est diuinas apparitiones), quas theologia puris intellectibus ingerit et ineffabili modo nullique cognito infigit, ut de omnino per se ipsum incognito habitum quendam uerae cognitionis in semet ipsis possideant.*[58]

The knowledge of the generation of the Son from the Father is realised in the human through faith, in the angel through a special form (*per speciem*). Yet in neither case is this a knowledge of the trinitarian generation as this really is. Only the Father and the Son are said to know what generation really is. A textual addition confirms that this is an interpretation of Mt. 11: 27[59]. Eriugena then mentions the rules for the application of such words as 'who' and 'what' (implying person and substance) to God, rules established in the first book of *Periphyseon*. Of interest is the order in which Eriugena has operated: first he emphasised the limitation of the knowableness of the trinity (even in the light of the Bible), then he reiterates the methodological reflections on the application of attributes to God as established by him in book one. Thus the context of the incomprehensibility of God remains the dominant one in his thought.

It is also of interest that Eriugena doesn't just handle the question of whether the Word existed temporally before creation on its own but immediately considers it within the context of the becoming known of the trinity, and of the becoming known of the generation of the Son on the part of humans. His theology of God operates from the perspective of the self-revelation of God to us. The Son is considered as the Wisdom of God. This is a wisdom in which things are created. Creatures then come to return to this God, that is, to approach this God through knowledge.

The generation of the Son from the Father is interpreted in terms of the words "*In splendoribus sanctorum ex utero ante luciferum genui te*". Eriugena interprets this non-temporally: "*Vterum hic intellige secretos paternae essentiae sinus, ex quibus unigenitus filius qui est uerbum patris natus est, et de quibus semper nascitur, et in quibus dum semper nascitur semper manet.*"[60] Again it is interpreted not only in inner trinitarian terms, but also in terms of the *appearing* of this generation to us through Jesus Christ. Eriugena introduces Jn. 1: 18 "*Deum nemo uidit unquam. Vnigenitus autem filius qui est in sinibus patris ipse narrabit*". Then he interprets the being born "*in splendoribus sanctorum*" in terms both of the coming to be known of this generation on the part of the faithful (*cognitiones*)[61], and of the precognition (*praedestinationes*)

---

[58] PP II, textual addition number 78, 346–352, p. 42, (= PL 122, 557B–557C).

[59] PP II, textual addition number 83, 356–361, p. 43, (= PL 122, 557A–558A): "*Si enim 'nemo nouit patrem nisi filius et cui uult filius reuelare', nonne consequens est dicere: Nemo nouit filium nisi pater et cui uult pater reuelare? Ita ut intelligamus: reuelare per theophanias. Nam essentiam patris et filii et spiritus sancti atque substantiam per se ipsas immediate creaturae reuelari impossibile est. Similiter de modo et qualitate diuinae generationis intelligendum.*"

[60] PP II, 1026–1029, pp. 43–44, (= PL 122 558B).

[61] But see I. P. SHELDON-WILLIAMS endnote 253, where *cognitiones* is explained as the being known of the elect by God. I do not regard this as the only way of reading the phrase. An active sense (*cognitiones* on the part of the elect) fits with what has gone before and thus the sentence forms

on God's part of all creation in the son: "*Nascente enim filio ex patre splendores fiunt sanctorum, hoc est cognitiones electorum et praedestinationes, …*"

Eriugena develops the notion of '*praedestinationes*' and creation using a series of biblical texts. The notion of the divine creative foreknowledge is linked to the motive of 'life'. Eriugena quotes Jn. 1:3–4: "*Quod factum est in ipso uita erat*"[62] and introduces the biblical notion that not only are we initiated through the divine life but that we live and move and are in God: "*In ipso enim uiuimus et mouemur et sumus*" (Acts 17:28)[63]. Eriugena does not use this to claim a pantheistic relationship between God and the world. Rather it is the biblical crowning to a differentiated presentation of the theological *scenario* in which the divine knowing and loving both initiate and permeate creation and in which creatures approach God through their cognition.

This encounter takes place within the life fostering wisdom of God: "*Sanctorum enim in sapientia patris cognitio, eorum est creatio.*"[64]

Eriugena relies heavily on Augustine on the matter of the divine foreknowledge of all things[65]. He quotes from *De trinitate*: "*Verbum dei per quod facta sunt omnia, ubi incommutabiliter uiuunt omnia, non solum quae fuerunt, sed etiam quae futura sunt; nec tamen in illo fuerunt nec futura sunt, sed tantummodo sunt, et omnia unum sunt, et magis unum est*".[66] Eriugena also handles the theme of the inherence of all things in the divine foreknowledge in his homily on John's Gospel[67]. Here too the debt to *De trinitate* as just quoted is evident. Moreover the influence of Augustine's *De Genesi ad litteram* is also present as is evident in Eriugena's lines: "*Omnia … in ipso uiuunt et uita sunt, et aeternaliter subsistunt.*"[68]

In *Periphyseon* book two Eriugena concludes that the whole of reality inheres in the divine wisdom: "*Nil enim est aliud omnium essentia, nisi omnium in diuina sapi-*

---

a hinge between two important ideas. The French translation of Bertin gives "les préconseptions et les prédestinations substantielles des élus", *Jean Scot Érigène, De la division de la nature (Periphyseon), Livre I–IV*, FRANCIS BERTIN (trans.), Paris: Presses Universitaires de France, 1995–2000. Nonetheless I still think my version is possible and supported by the Latin which distinguishes "*cognitiones electorum et praedestinationes*", PP II, 1035–1036, p. 44, (= PL 122 558B).

[62] PP II, 1050–1051, p. 45, (= PL 122 559A). In his Homily on John's Gospel ERIUGENA considers the various ways of rendering the Greek into Latin. See Hom. IX, 16–30, JEAUNEAU (ed.), pp. 242–243, and his compromise translation in X,1–2, p. 246: "*Omnia itaque quae per uerbum facta sunt, in ipso uiuunt incommutabiliter et uita sunt.*"

[63] In textual edition 87 in PP II, the unity of knowing and making in God is affirmed: PP II, textual addition number 87, 371–375, p. 45, (= PL 122, 559B).

[64] PP II, 1053–1054, p. 45, (= PL 122 559A).

[65] The passage PP II, 1041–1058, pp. 44–45, (= PL 122, 558D -559B) is heavily indebted to Augustine.

[66] AUGUSTINUS, *De trinitate*, IV, i, 3, W. J. MOUNTAIN / FR. GLORIE (ed.), p. 1162, (= PL 42, 888). Quoted in PP II, 1046–1049, p. 45, (= PL 122 559A).

[67] See ERIUGENA, Hom., X, 1–37, É. JEAUNEAU (ed.), pp. 246–252, (= PL 122 288C–289B).

[68] Hom., X, 1–8, É. JEAUNEAU (ed.), p. 246, (= PL 122 288C–D), compare AUGUSTINE, *De Genesi ad litteram*, V, XV, (= PL 34, 333) "*Apud illum erant eo modo nota quo sempiterne atque incommutabiliter uiuunt et uita sunt.*"

*entia cognitio.*"[69] In the Homily chapter ten, a quotation from the Pseudo-Dionysius provides his conclusion: "*Et ut ait magnus Dionisius ariopagita, 'esse omnium est superessentialis diuinitas'.*"[70]

Eriugena's emphasis is that the Son is generated from the Father 'before' this world was generated and it was through this Son that the Father created the primordial causes of all natures:

*Prius igitur quam mundus iste uisibilis in genera et species omnesque numeros sensibiles per generationem procederet, ante tempora saecularia deus pater uerbum suum genuit, in quo et per quem omnium naturarum primordiales causas perfectissimas creauit.*[71]

The meaning of this priority of the generation of the Son from the Father has to be clarified.

While God the Father, and the Word, and the principal causes of things which are made in it are coeternal, Eriugena's Alumnus goes on to distinguish between the coeternity of the Father and Son (*omnino coaeternus*) and that of the primordial causes and the Son (*non omnino coaeterna*)[72]. There is a sense in which the maker precedes the things made and this applies to the relationship between the Word and the primordial causes made in the Word. The primordial causes are not coeternal with the Son in the sense that the Son cannot exist without them. The primordial causes receive their being, not from themselves, but from the creator.

Eriugena returns to his starting point, the movement of the Holy Spirit over the waters: "*Spiritus ergo sanctus mysticas aquas, quas fouet et foecundat, in se ipso aeternaliter aeternitatis suae uirtute et superat et praecedit.*"[73]

Eriugena considers the economic roles of the three persons of the trinity. While the three divine substances are said to have one operation, he does however affirm certain distinctions and properties[74]. The presentation of the trinitarian roles is openly biblical. Theology is said to assign the creation of natures to the Father[75]. '*Theologia*' in this context indicates the Holy Scriptures. Scriptural quotations on each of the persons of the trinity are listed suggesting their functions. Thus the Father creates, but *in* the Son, the Word and the wisdom of God. Eriugena devotes remarkable attention to the role of the Holy Spirit[76]. His argumentation is that just as the Spirit distributes the gifts of grace, so too is the Spirit responsible for the 'division' of the primordial causes. Eriugena relies on 1 Cor. 12:8–11 on the spirit as gift

---

[69] PP II, 1058–1059, p. 45, (= PL 122 559B).

[70] Hom., X, 35–37, É. Jeauneau (ed.), p. 252, (= PL 122 289B), quoting from Ier. coel, IV, I, 15, p. 20, (= PG 3, 177D; PL 122 1046B–C).

[71] PP II, 1076–1080, p. 47, (= PL 122, 560 A–B).

[72] See PP II, 1116–1117, p. 48, (= PL 122 561C).

[73] PP II 1144–1145, p. 49, (= PL 122 562 B).

[74] In textual addition number 96, PP II, 410–417, p. 49, (= PL 122 562C) the examples given are all scriptural showing that Eriugena's treatment of the properties of the divine persons is an attempt to interpret biblical truth.

[75] PP II, 1157–1158, p. 50, (= PL 122 563A).

[76] See too PP II, 2624–2627, p. 108, (= PL 122 603D).

giver, gift distributor[77], and quickly[78] spirals back to Gen. 1:2 saying that this activity of the Spirit can also be gleaned from the words of Genesis where it is written that the Spirit "*fouebat aquas*". He justifies this interpretation of the Old Testament by asking what is to be understood by the Spirit of God, fertilising or nourishing ('*fouebat*') the waters of the primordial causes except the distribution and ordering of those things which are made simply in the Word, into the differences of genera and forms and wholes and parts and numbers.[79] We thus witness the harmonious circumincession of a reasoned scheme of analysing reality (the primordial causes), and the interpretation of both the Old and the New Testaments, a circumincession which is typical of Eriugena's method.

In a textual edition the speaker develops this in terms of the role of the Spirit and of Christ (as head of the church) in the distribution of both the gifts of grace (*dona gratiae*) and the gifts of nature (*dona naturae*)[80]. The gifts include the gift of essence, life, sense, reason, and intelligence. We may note that even in what appears to be an account of the proper role of the Holy Spirit, the trinitarian context is not abandoned. In the example at hand we can observe the explicit rebinding within the trinity (through the Christological perspective) of what is substantially an account of the proper role of the Spirit.

The trinitarian dispensing of the gifts is presented by Eriugena in explicitly manifestational terms[81]. Eriugena uses an image taken from Zach. 4:2 (with a reference to Ex. 25:31), the biblical image being that of a golden lamp-stand, with seven lamps. Eriugena speaks of the lamp as singular. The lamp with its light from above is said to be the light of the Father, namely the Son who appears in the world. The light shines down on the candle-stand, the church. The role of the Spirit in distributing the so called seven gifts is once more presented. The Spirit of God rests on him, the Son[82]. First Jesus Christ, the head of the church, receives the seven gifts (wisdom, understanding, counsel, strength, knowledge, piety, and fear of the lord) in his humanity and mediates these through his Spirit to church. We can observe the trinitarian movement: from Spirit to Son, back to Spirit and to church. These gifts are not only the gifts of the Spirit alone, but those of the Son and Father too. In this rich Eriugenian passage the roles and indeed the relationships of the trinitarian persons

---

[77] Introduced at PP II, 1175–1181, pp. 50–51, (= PL 122 563C).

[78] PP II, 1182 and following, p. 51, (= PL 122 563D).

[79] See PP II, 1183–1188, p. 51, (= PL 122 563C–D).

[80] "*Et si nemo sane credentium recteque intelligentium haesitat affirmare spiritualia dona, quae propheta Isaias super caput ecclesiae (quod est Christus) requietura prophetauit, non per alium nisi per spiritum sanctum deo uerbo incarnato distributa esse, quid mirum si ecclesiae (quae est corpus eius) non solum dona gratiae per Christum sed etiam dona naturae per eundum Christum idem spiritus diuidat et det?*", PP II, textual addition number 99, 423–429, p. 51 (= PL 122 564A).

[81] In the main text a long section (heavily indebted to MAXIMUS CONFESSOR, *Quaestiones ad Thalassium una cum latina interpretatione Ioannis Scotti Eriugenae*, LXIII, 133–155, C. LAGA und C. STEEL (ed.), p. 153–155, (= PG 90 672)) begins at PP II, 1188 and runs to 1222, (= PL 122 564B–565A).

[82] See Is. 11:2.

in an economy of grace centring on Jesus Christ and his church are very apparent. Eriugena has adopted a Maximian scriptural interpretation with its trinitarian and ecclesiological emphases and worked it into his own system.

Once again it is stressed that not only the gifts of grace by which the church is cleansed, edified and illuminated and perfected come from the trinity, but also all good things: "*ex patre dico ex quo omnia, per filium in quo sunt omnia, nec eorum per alium nisi per spiritum sanctum esse distributionem, qui diuidit omnia omnibus prout uult.*"[83]

In an important passage which despite its length, deserves to be quoted, Eriugena summarises:[84]

*'Omne', inquit theologus, 'datum optimum et omne donum perfectum desursum est descendens a patre luminum.' Quid apertius, quid clarius? Non aliunde, ait, nisi a patre luminum, hoc est a patre omnium bonorum, quae sunt secundum naturam et quae sunt secundum gratiam. Pulchre siquidem lumina dicuntur omnia dona, quae ex ingenito lumine per genitum lumen descendunt, et per procedens lumen singulis prout est capacitas ⟨107⟩ uniuscuiusque siue generalis siue specialis siue indiuiduae essentiae substantiae diuiduntur. ... Si igitur nil in natura rerum creatarum esse cognoscitur praeter quod a creatore donatur, sequitur nil aliud esse creaturam siue essentialiter siue secundum accidens nisi creatoris dona. Donorum autem distributionem quasi quandam proprietatem spiritui sancto theologia dedicat. Omnia igitur, quae pater in filiio facit, spiritus sanctus distribuit et unicuique propria prout uult diuidit.*

Eriugena quotes the scriptural text which subsumes what he has just expounded: "*Omne datum optimum et omne donum perfectum desursum est descendens a patre luminum*"[85]. He then interprets these gifts as light, the light of the Father and the Son. Again we observe the Eriugenian emphasis on the bestowal through the divine bounty and the presentation of the given in terms of the possibility of knowledge of God. This is the aspect of the return of creation to the creator as 'encounter-in-knowledge'. All being is received being, received sensing, received intelligence, received reason, received life. All is gift. The notion of the divine generosity is a central one in Eriugena's system and this notion colours all his treatments not only of creation but also, as here, of the economy of encounter with God in knowledge. Every human approach to God in knowledge is the result of an endowment of God, the result of a generous condescending on God's part.

Further we may comment that here we have the authentic Eriugena himself presenting themes and ideas which he previously approached through quotes and paraphrases of Maximus. Other Eriugenian writings confirm that this doctrine is consistently held and taught by the author[86].

Eriugena's basic position on the common and proper action of the three persons of the trinity is as follows. Their operation is not divided (*non segregata operatio*):

---

[83] PP II, 1233–1236, p. 53, (= PL 122 565B). See 1 Cor. 12:11.
[84] PP II, 1237–1258, pp. 53–54, (= PL 122 565C–566A).
[85] Jas. 1:17.
[86] See Comm. III, IX, 51–74, É. Jeauneau (ed.), pp. 252–256, (= PL 122 325C–326A).

what the Father does, the Son does too and the Holy Spirit as well. Nevertheless scripture (*diuina theologia*) appears to assign them different properties[87]. The proper roles of the divine persons in distributing the gifts of the divine bounty are summarised:

*Videsne igitur quomodo theologia singulis diuinae bonitatis substantiis seu personis suas ueluti proprietates dare intelligitur? Patri enim dat omnia facere. Verbo dat omnes in ipso uniuersaliter, essentialiter, simpliciter primordiales rerum causas aeternaliter fieri. Spiritui ‹109› dat ipsas primordiales causas in uerbo factas in effectus suos foecundatas distribuere, ...*[88]

The discussion of the economic roles of the persons of the trinity in *Periphyseon* book two is an exercise in biblical interpretation and this is confirmed by the Alumnus' concluding comment on what has been said on the trinity: "*Video plane, et mihi uidetur esse uerisimile ac diuinis eloquiis conuenire.*"[89]

Returning to the universal cause from which and in which the primordial causes both exist and were established, Eriugena must broach the question of how this one universal cause may cause as trinity and unity.[90] Pursuing his investigation of causation and the trinity he investigates the Eastern and Western theological accounts of procession. The 'roman' theologians speak of one substance in three persons. The Greek usage is said to be one essence in three substances[91]. Eriugena in his speaker Nutritor proposes that the possibility of speaking of one essential cause in three subsistent causes be investigated. So the Nutritor embarks on the task of showing how the cause of all things (as he now calls the divinity) is one essential cause in three substantial causes. In trying to accommodate the notion of the one essential cause and that of the trinity, Eriugena is attempting to give a philosophically tenable account of what the faith tells us i. e. God the creator is one in three, whereby we must reiterate that Eriugena never separated the two disciplines we now call philosophy and theology. Belief and understanding, and indeed the dissemination of what one holds in faith and knowledge, form a unity for Eriugena[92].

The Alumnus insists that what we affirm by faith may be investigated in philosophical terms.

*Nam si unum deum per se existentem in tribus substantiis per se subsistentibus fides fatetur catholica, quid obstat ne similiter dicamus unam causam per se existentem in tribus causis per se subsistentibus?*[93]

---

[87] See PP II, 1270–1274, p. 55, (= PL 122 566C).

[88] PP II, 1259–1264, p. 54, (= PL 122 566A–B).

[89] PP II, 1275–1276, p. 55, (= PL 122 566D).

[90] PP II, 2411, p. 100 and following, (= PL 122 598C and following).

[91] Eriugena discusses the matter of the '*filioque*' in PP II, 2521 and following, p. 104 and following, (= PL 601B following). Here he mentions how difficult a matter this is: "*Vere uere densissima caligo est.*", here 2531.

[92] See PP II, 2427–2428, p. 101, (= PL 122 599A): "*... et credere et quantum datur intelligere et praedicare ...*".

[93] See PP II, 2431–2439, p. 101 (= PL 122 599 A–B), here PP II, 2436–2439, p. 101, (= PL 122 559B).

We are however not alone in our search for the truth about the divine trinity. Operating on the strength of the promise 'seek and you will find' the human subject can seek to understand something of the God it believes in and to whom it raises a hymn of praise, the God whose trinitarian character is, according to Eriugena, intimated by the very structure of created things:

*Vnde ergo diuinae bonitatis trinitatem in unitate et unitatem in trinitate quaerere et inuestigare possumus ut aliquid de ea quo eam laudemus uerisimile credamus et, quantum datur, intelligamus, nisi prius, quasi quibusdam gradibus, exemplis naturae ab ea conditae ad eam ascendamus, ea duce atque praecipiente: 'Quaerite et inuenietis'? Praesertim diuino Paulo testante: 'Inuisibilia enim eius' (id est patris), inquit, 'a creatura mundi per ea quae facta sunt intellecta conspiciuntur; sempiterna quoque eius uirtus' (hoc est filius) 'et aeternitas' (hoc est spiritus sanctus).*[94]

Eriugena claims here to be relying on a Maximian interpretation of Rom. 1:20 on the traces of the trinity in the created world[95]. He sometimes draws on images taken from physical reality, for example following the Pseudo-Dionysius he illustrates the trinity through the image of fire, it's ray and it's brightness[96]. However, Eriugena stands firmly within the tradition of writers who see in a psychological analogy the clearest aid to understanding how the Christian God is one and three: "*Et ut mihi uidetur, interioris nostrae naturae trinitatis similitudine hoc ipsum possumus approbare. Mens etenim et notitiam sui gignit, et a se ipsa amor sui et notitiae suae procedit, quo et ipsa et notitia sui coniunguntur.*"[97]

It is significant that Eriugena in his speaker Alumnus can write that the most perfect image of God is achieved when the triad of *mens, notitia, amor* is directed through self-knowledge and self-love towards the knowledge and love of its Creator. It is the human spirit in operation and concerned with God which provides the clearest imaging: "*Ac per hoc, rationis uiribus nil aliud appetit, nisi ut cognoscat qualiter et quantum se ipsam nouit, et se ipsam et notitiam sui amat; et dum hoc totum ad cognitionem et amorem creatoris sui conuertit, perfectissima imago eius efficitur.*"[98]

Again, claiming to rely on Maximus he proposes that the knowledge gained through introspection is necessary in order to most profitably approach God in knowledge. The next sentence reads:

---

[94] PP II, 2783–2792, p. 113, (= PL 122 607B–C).

[95] É. JEAUNEAU notes that he has not found a corresponding place in Maximus' oeuvre, see his comment on PP II, 1330–1334, p. 58, (= PL 122 568B–C).

[96] PP II, 2824, p. 114–2910, p. 116. (= PL 608B–610B). See Ps. DIONYSIUS, De coel. hier., Xv, 2, G. HEIL (ed.), pp. 51–53, (= PG 3, 328C–329C).

[97] PP II, 2916–2919, p. 117, (= PL 122 610 B–C). In PP II, the psychological analogy is discussed in order to learn something about God. In later books the Christian doctrine of the trinity will be called upon to shed light on the mental processes of the human. Eriugena is explicitly aware of the two directions of argumentation. His account of the psychological analogy relies heavily on Augustine's *De trinitate*, see for example *De trinitate*, X, W. J. MOUNTAIN / FR. GLORIE (ed.), pp. 311–332, (= PL 42 971–984).

[98] PP II, 2933–2937, p. 117, (= PL 122 610D).

*Et hic est maximus, ac paene solus, gradus est ad cognitionem ueritatis, id est humanam naturam se ipsam prius cognoscere et amare, ac deinde totam cognitionem suam totumque amorem ad laudem creatoris et cognitionem et dilectionem referre. Si enim quod in se ipsa agitur nescit, quomodo ea quae supra se sunt nosse desiderat?*[99]

The contrast between the emphasis here on the possibility of knowing God, and the former sections of *Periphyseon* and the other writings of Eriugena which express the limitation of the possibility of our knowledge, is indeed extreme, yet it can and must be accommodated within his theory of the two ways of doing theology. In the analogy and ascent at hand we are firmly within the sphere of kataphatic theology.

Eriugena's treatment of the controversy involved in the '*filioque*' credal addition is interesting both from the point of view of his trinitarian doctrine and from the point of view of his method. He recognises the legitimacy of the Greek and the Latin options[100], he displays however a theological preference for the formulation of those Greek theologians who say that the Spirit proceeds from the Father through the Son. Further he suggests a practical reason why the Creed originally omitted the '*filioque*' addition. He suggests that when the (as he sees it) Nicene synod said that the Spirit proceeds from the Father without the reference to the Son, this was to prevent public discussion of the matter (*ne talis quaestio uentilaretur*)[101]. In *Periphyseon* however he, as a scholar, is prepared to consider some of the thorny questions concerning the trinity and the inner-trinitarian processions.

If we say that the Spirit proceeds from the Father through the Son, we are not however forced to say that the Son is born of the Father through the Spirit. Eriugena explains that the scriptural texts which might seem to support this last, refer not to the eternal procession of the Son, but to the Word being conceived from the Holy Spirit in the incarnation or may be accounted for within a theory of baptism as the conception and birth of the Son in the hearts of faithful through the Spirit.[102]

The next technical question is whether it is from the essence or the substance of the Father that the Son is born and the Spirit proceeds[103]. Whether this matter is approached through the Eastern or the Western terminologies for the divine three in one, Eriugena concludes that the procession takes place from the proper substance or person of the Father.

Of interest to this study is not so much the intricacies of Eriugena's trinitarian doctrine so much as his appraisal of how, and to what extent, this trinity is revealed. The Nutritor reflects on the depth of trinitarian truth in a very rich passage. Once

---

[99] PP II, 2937–2942, p. 117, (= PL 122 611A).

[100] See PP II, 3012–3017, p. 120, (= PL 122 612D–613A) where the Alumnus says "*Quoquo enim modo quis ecclesiasticum symbolum pronuntiauerit, sine naufragio sanae fidei recipio, hoc est, siue spiritum sanctum a patre solummodo procedere dixerit, siue a patre et filio, salua illa ratione qua et credimus et intelligimus eundem spiritum ex una causa, id est ex patre, substantialiter procedere.*"

[101] PP II, 2982, p. 119, (= PL 122, 612A).

[102] PP II, 2967, p. 118–2980, p. 119, (= PL 122 611C–D).

[103] PP II, 3012, p. 120–3080, p. 122, (= PL 122 612D–614B).

again it is the limitation of our knowledge of God which is the focus of attention. It assigns our knowledge of these matters to theophanies. In this context theophanies are to be understood as limited glimpses of a truth not fully attainable in this life. The language of the passage is that of a prayer: it extols the transcendence of God and invites us to rejoice that we know something about the trinity at all!

*Sed haec altius ac uerius cogitantur quam sermone proferuntur, et altius ac uerius intelliguntur quam cogitantur, altius autem ac uerius sunt quam intelliguntur; omnem siquidem intellectum superant. Nam quaecunque de simplicissimae bonitatis trinitate dicuntur seu cogitantur seu intelliguntur uestigia quaedam sunt atque theophaniae ueritatis, non autem ipsa ueritas, quae superat omnem theoriam non solum rationalis uerum etiam intellectualis creaturae. ... Iubemur tamen aliquid de ea [the trinity – HM]dicere et cogitare et intelligere, quantum intellectus eam attingit, sancta theologia duce atque magistra, ut quodam modo materiam habeamus laudandi eam atque benedicendi.*[104]

The Dionysian tones of his elegy on the trinitarian transcendence are apparent: "*Neque enim talis unitas est seu trinitas, qualis ab ulla creatura potest excogitari seu intelligi, seu aliqua phantasia, quamuis lucidissima et uerisimillima, formari. ... Siquidem plus quam unitas est et plus quam trinitas.*"[105] Behind this incomprehensibility lies the infinity of God:

"*Est enim infinitum quod quaerunt, et incomprehensibile quod appetunt, et super omnem intellectum quod concupiscunt, et ab omni creatura exaltatum.*"[106]

## 4. The creator God as "good"

Eriugena's whole system of thought is concerned to reflect in manifold manner on the relationship between the creator and created reality. "*Natura*" has indeed been chosen because it is a term which embraces not only created reality but also the creator within its divisions[107].

One form of reflection on the relationship of God and creation is in terms of a participation in the divine, where the divine is understood as absolute goodness. Eriugena thus elucidates the first division of universal goodness, bringing in the link to the other good – good by participation – which stems from it: "*Nam uniuersalis boni prima sectio est in illud unum ac summum incommutabile per se et substantiale bonum, ex quo omne bonum manat, et in illud bonum quod participatione summi et*

---

[104] PP II, 3081–3095, p. 122, (= PL 122 614C–614D).

[105] PP II, 3088–3092, p. 122, (= PL 122 614C).

[106] PP II, 3109–3111, p. 123, (= PL 122 615A). See H. A. MOONEY, "*Infinitus enim infinite, etiam in purgatissimis mentibus, formatur. Die Struktur der Begegnung mit dem unendlichen Gott nach Johannes Scottus Eriugena*", in: *History and Eschatology in John Scottus Eriugena and his Time. Proceedings of the Tenth International Conference of the Society for the Promotion of Eriugenian Studies*, Maynooth and Dublin, August 16–20, 2000, Leuven: Leuven University Press, 2002, pp. 463–486.

[107] "*Eo nanque nomine quod est natura non solum creata uniuersitas, uerum etiam ipsius creatrix solet significari.*" PP III, 77–79, p. 5, (= PL 122 621A).

*incommutabilis boni bonum est.*"[108] Other divine attributes can also be described as a source of participation. He thus for example speaks of the divine essence, life, wisdom, and power as being subject to participation[109].

The primordial causes are presented by Eriugena in terms of participation: "*Et haec regula in omnibus primordialibus causis uniformiter obseruatur, hoc est, quod per se ipsas participationes principales sunt unius omnium causae, quae deus est.*"[110]

In his account of participation Eriugena assigns a certain priority to the notion of the participation of all beings in the divine goodness. This is evident in his account of an order of the primordial causes.[111] He presents an order in the primordial causes, an order which he says is presented by Dionysius the pseudo Areopagite: goodness (*bonitas*), essence (*essentia*), life (*vita*), reason (*ratio*), intellect (*intelligentia*), wisdom (*sapientia*), power (*uirtus*), blessedness (*beatitudo*), truth (*ueritas*), eternity (*aeternitas*) and then mentions magnitude, love, peace, unity, perfection.[112] He says that this order is an order established by the mind. In themselves the primordial causes are one and simple.[113]

He concludes that all the principles of all things can be presented in this way, whether these principles can be named or not: "*Praedicta siquidem theoria uniformiter in omnibus rerum omnium principiis in infinitum progredientibus mentis obtutibus deiformiter arridet ubique, siue in his quae et intelligi et nominari possunt, siue in his quae solo intellectu percipiuntur significationibus tamen deficiunt, ...*"[114] In this sense then, the primordial causes extend to infinity, just as the first cause is infinite. Only God's will sets a limit to the primordial causes: "*Vt enim prima omnium causa ex qua et in qua et per quam et ad quam conditae sunt infinita est, ita et ipsae finem nesciunt quo claudantur, praeter creatoris sui uoluntatem.*"[115]

The authority of the Pseudo-Dionysius is not, however, his only argument. Eriugena presents intrinsic arguments for the order he had presented, in particular for the primacy of the good. He says that it is the property of the divine goodness to call the things that were not into existence. Goodness is the key to why things exist at all: "*Omnia siquidem quae sunt in tantum sunt, in quantum bona sunt;*"[116] In

---

[108] PP III, 83–86, p. 5, (= PL 122 621A–B).

[109] See PP III, 86–93, pp. 5–6, (= PL 122 621B).

[110] PP III, 142–145, p. 7, (= PL 122 622C).

[111] See PP III, 133–145, p. 7, (= PL 122 622B–C).

[112] See Ps. DIONYSIUS, De div. nom. XI, 6, B. SUCHLA (ed.), pp. 221–223, (= PG 3 953B–956B); II, 1, pp. 122–124, (= PG 3 636C–637C)

[113] "*Et notandum quod ordo iste primordialium causarum, quem a me exigis ad certum progrediendi modum inconfuse discerni, non in ipsis sed in theoria (hoc est in animi contuitu quaerentis eas earumque quantum datur notitiam in se ipso concipientis eamque quodam modo ordinantis) constitutus sit, ut de eis certum aliquid puraque intelligentia diffinitum pronuntiare possit. Ipsae siquidem primae causae in se ipsis unum sunt et simplices nullique cognito ordine diffinitae aut a se inuicem segregatae; hoc enim in effectibus suis patiuntur.*" PP III, 211–219, p. 9, (= PL 122 624A).

[114] PP III, 197–201, p. 9, (= PL 122 623C).

[115] PP III, 207–210, p. 9, (= PL 122 623D–624A).

[116] PP III, 389–390, p. 15, (= PL 122 628 A).

a discussion of the relationship of goodness and essence he can write: "*Non enim per essentiam introducta est bonitas, sed per bonitatem introducta est essentia.*"[117] All reality is grounded in this divine goodness. His argumentation is more differentiated than a simple affirmation of the coextension of good and essence: he counters the argument that one might just as well say "no good without essence" with the argument that there are things which are not, but which are good.

Eriugena is also familiar with the word which the Greek thinkers use for participation (ΜΕΤΟΧΗ or ΜΕΤΟΥϹΙΑ) and explains how fitting (*significantius expressiusque et ad intelligendum facilius*) this term is. He mentions two points: a connotation of 'having after' and a connotation of 'after-essence'. These support his understanding of participation as an essence 'after' or 'derived from' another higher essence.[118]

He then brings in examples from nature which illustrate this. The first image is that of a source and the river that flows from it.

*Siquidem ex fonte totum flumen principaliter manat et per eius alueum aqua quae primo surgit in fonte, in quantamcunque longitudinem protendatur, semper ac sine ulla intermissione diffunditur. Sic diuina bonitas et essentia et uita et sapientia et omnia quae in fonte omnium sunt primo in primordiales causas defluunt et eas esse faciunt, deinde per primordiales causas in earum effectus ineffabili modo per conuenientes sibi uniuersitatis ordines decurrunt, per superiora semper ad inferiora profluentia, iterumque per secretissimos naturae poros occultissimo meatu ad fontem suum redeunt.*[119]

Eriugena writes: "*Omne quod est aut participans, aut participatum, aut participatio est, aut participatum et participans.*"[120] The supreme principle, God, has a unique position: "*Participatum solummodo est, quod nullum superius se participat, quod de summo ac solo omnium principio, quod deus est, recte intelligitur.*"[121] We note the importance of having nothing superior to it. This participation in the divine can be mediate or immediate: "*Ipsum siquidem omnia quae ab eo sunt participant, quaedam quidem immediate per se ipsa, quaedam uero per medietates interpositas.*"[122]

Eriugena mentions two other types of being. First of all there are those which only participate. These are the sensible bodies: they participate in higher things but there is nothing below them which participates in them. Secondly, others both participate and are participated. In this case he is referring to the primordial causes and to all other orders of creation which find themselves between the primordial causes and sensible bodies.

---

[117] PP III, 384–385, p. 15, (= PL 122 627D).

[118] "*Hinc facillime datur intelligi nihil aliud esse participationem nisi ex superiori essentia secundae post eam essentiae deriuationem, et ab ea quae primum habet esse secundae, ut sit, distributio.*" PP III, 557–560, p. 21, (= PL 122 632A).

[119] PP III, 561–570, p. 21, (= PL 122 632B–C).

[120] PP III, 475–476, p. 18, (= PL 122 630A).

[121] PP III, 476–478, p. 18, (= PL 122 630A).

[122] PP III, 478–481, p. 18, (= PL 122 630A).

Eriugena makes a comparison between the proportionalities (collations of proportion) among the proportions of numbers and the harmonies between the participations of natural orders. In a passage in part dependant on Boethius he writes:

*Sicut enim numerorum concordia proportionis, proportionum uero collatio proportionalitatis, sic ordinum naturalium distributio participationis nomen, distributionum uero copulatio amoris generalis accepit, qui omnia ineffabili quadam amicitia in unum colligit.*[123]

We see here the emergence of a notion of a love and a friendship governing the orders of participation, notions embedded in Eriugena's presentation of the providential ordering of the universe through the divine Wisdom (*creatrix omnium sapientia*).[124] Here we can observe the interweaving of specifically biblical terms with an underlying Neoplatonic scheme.

Another factor further illustrates that Eriugena is offering a biblical theological interpretation of participation. For Eriugena participation is not an automatic emanation. The moving force which lies behind the diffusion of all things is the free giving of the generous Christian God. He thus approaches the distribution of all good things from a specifically theological perspective, namely according to the *donum / datum* distinction which he detects in James 1:17.[125] The abstract notion of a general diffusion of the absolute good is thus made more precise through an account of how the Christian God gives the goods of nature and the goods of grace. Pointing out that participation is not primarily about 'taking' but about the divine 'giving' Eriugena says: "*Est igitur participatio non cuiusdam partis assumptio, sed diuinarum dationum et donationum a summo usque deorsum per superiores ordines inferioribus distributio.*"[126] In one of the few texts where Eriugena does use '*assumptio*' to describe participation, he is in fact giving a translation of the Pseudo-Dionysius and he explains '*assumptio*' in terms which express the divine endowing as '*divinae sapientiae fusio.*'[127]

The *donationes / dationes* pattern, is applied to the whole mediatory ranks of participation (*datur esse, donatur bene esse*):

---

[123] PP III, 516–520, p. 19, (= PL 122 630D–631A). See BOETHIUS, *De institutione arithmetica*, II, XL, G. FRIEDLEIN (ed.), Leipzig: Minerva, first published 1867, reprint 1966, p. 137, 8–26.

[124] PP III, 513, p. 19, (= PL 122 630D).

[125] ERIUGENA also uses a *dationes / donationes* distinction. See PP III, 412–416, p. 16, (= PL 122 628C): "*Bonorum siquidem una species est in his quae sunt, altera in his quae non sunt. Ac per hoc, a generalioribus diuinae largitatis donationibus inchoans, et per specialiores progrediens ordinem quendam primordialium causarum, theologia duce, constitui.*"

[126] PP III, 520–523, p. 19, (= PL 122 631A).

[127] "*Audisti summi theologi Ariopagitae Dionysii praeclarissimi Athenarum episcopi de participatione diuinae essentiae sententiam, qua apertissime manifestat omnia quae sunt et quae non sunt nihil aliud intelligenda praeter diuinae essentiae participationem, ipsam uero participationem nihil aliud esse praeter eiusdem diuinae essentiae assumptionem. 'Non enim', inquit, 'fortassis essent, nisi eorum quae sunt essentiae et principii assumptione.' Est igitur participatio diuinae essentiae assumptio, assumptio uero est sapientiae diuinae fusio, quae est omnium substantia et essentia et quaecunque in eis naturaliter intelliguntur.*" PP III, 1061–1071, pp. 38–39, (= PL 122 644B–644C).

*Ac sic distributio essendi et bene essendi a summo omnium bonorum datorum uel donationum fonte gradatim per superiores in inferiores usque ad extremos ordines defluit.*[128]

Eriugena gives a definition of the difference between *dationes* and *donationes:*

*Inter dationes autem et donationes talis differentia est. Dationes quidem sunt et dicuntur proprie distributiones quibus omnis natura subsistit, donationes uero gratiae distributiones quibus omnis natura subsistens ornatur.*[129]

He draws the conclusion: "*Itaque natura datur, donatur gratia.*"[130] For Eriugena the perfect creature involves both.[131]

This consideration of the nature of participation leads to the consideration of the inherence of the created realities in God. The real subsistence of creatures is closely connected with their participation in God: "*ueritas ipsa in intellectibus pie quaerentium ac diligentium creatorem suum intelligibili uoce proclamet generaliter de omnibus quae sunt et quae non sunt ... nihil aliud subsistere, praeter unius solius omnium causae participationem.*"[132] He quotes repeatedly a sentence from Pseudo-Dionysius' *De cael. hier.* IV, I: "*Existentia igitur omnia esse eius participant; esse enim omnium est super esse diuinitas.*"[133]

Eriugena also quotes a significant passage from De div. nom. chapter four. The divine love, the divine loving goodness not only fosters all created things through its providence (*in bonitate et dilectione et amore fouet),* but also through an incredible condescension descends to 'become in all things'.

'*Audendum uero et hoc de ueritate dicere quia et ipse omnium causalis bono et optimo omnium amore per excellentiam amatoriae bonitatis extra se ipsum fit in omnia quae sunt prouidentiis, et ueluti in bonitate et dilectione et amore fouet et ex super omnia ab omnibus remoto ad hoc in omnibus deducitur secundum mente excedentem superessentialem potentiam inconuersibilemque suam.*'[134]

---

[128] PP III, 526–529, p. 19, (= PL 122 631A).

[129] PP III, 542–545, p. 20, (= PL 122 631C–D).

[130] PP III, 545–546, p. 20, (= PL 122 631D).

[131] Of interest is the content of a textual addition in Eriugena's text which, once again centring on the distinction between *donum* and *datum*, links grace and the becoming apparent of natural beauty: "*Vbi notandum duobus modis bene esse intelligi, uno quo omnia quae sunt bona dicuntur esse, quoniam a summo bono facta sunt et in tantum sunt in quantum participant bonitatem, altero autem quo omnia quae naturaliter bona subsistunt uirtutum donationibus, ut eorum naturalis bonitas plus appareat, exornantur. Quamuis enim maxime ac principaliter rationali et intellectuali creaturae dona gratiae (quae uirtutis uocabulo solent significari) distribuantur, nulla tamen naturarum etiam extremarum secundum suam proportionem diuinae gratiae participationis expers esse arbitranda est. Vt enim omnia participant bonitatem, ita participant et gratiam; bonitatem quidem ut sint, gratiam uero ut et bona et pulchra sint.*" PP III, textual addition number 1, 1–11, p. 19, (= PL 122 631A–B).

[132] PP III, 1037–1043, p. 38, (= PL 122 643D–644A).

[133] PP III, 1056–1057, p. 38, (= PL 122 644B). Here quoted according to the text of PP III.

[134] PP III, 1096–1102, pp. 39–40, (= PL 122 645B–C).

## 5. The creator God as "nothing"

The account of creation as participation in, and through the divine goodness must next be further informed by the biblical account of creation and reconciled with further details of the biblical account. The key theological statement on creation on which Eriugena focuses is that God created all things out of nothing[135]. This tenet, traditionally part of the theology of creation, is rooted in 2 Mc. 7:28 "*peto nate aspicias in caelum et terram et ad omnia quae in eis sunt et intellegas quia ex nihilo fecit illa Deus ...*"[136]

Thus the interpretation of the notion of *creatio ex nihilo* or the investigation of the *quaestio de nihilo* is, ultimately, a task for biblical theology.[137]

What, Eriugena asks is this "nothing" out of which the divine goodness creates?[138] A first possible answer is the traditional answer to the question: "*ex nihilo*" indicates the total absence of essence, or substance, or accident. The Alumnus reports: "*Eo igitur nomine, quod est nihilum, negatio atque absentia totius essentiae uel substantiae, immo etiam cunctorum quae in natura rerum creata sunt insinuatur.*"[139]

---

[135] Eriugena'a most substantial treatment of this question is given in PP III, 633–2942, pp. 23–101, (= PL 122 634A–690A).

[136] Quoted from the Septuaginta.

[137] GUSTAVO A. PIEMONTE's investigation "Notas sobre la 'Creatio de nihilo' en Juan Escoto Eriugena", part 1, *Sapientia*, 23 (Buenos Aires, 1968) 37–58, has influenced all subsequent studies. See too DONALD DUCLOW, "Divine Nothingness and Self-Creation in John Scottus Eriugena", in: *Journal of Religion* 57 (1977) 109–123; MARCIA L. COLISH, "Carolingian Debates over *Nihil* and *Tenebrae:* A Study in Theological Method", in: *Speculum* 59 (1984) 757–795; DEIRDRE CARABINE, *John Scottus Eriugena,* Oxford: Oxford University Press, 2000, pp. 46–48.

[138] Eriugena explicitly rejects the secular philosophical position which regards matter as coeternal with God. Implied in the latter position is that from matter, as though from something external to God, God took the material for God's works. This position asks how God could be the cause of something so dissimilar as matter. Eriugena says, however, that following scripture and its interpreters, and believing by faith, and understanding as far as we are allowed, we affirm that God made both the forms and the formlessness of all things. See PP III, 757–762, p. 28, (= PL 122 637B).

According to Eriugena, God does create dissimilar things, indeed this belongs to the divine perfection. "*Non enim uniuersitatis conditor omnipotens et in nullo deficiens et in infinitum tendens similia sibi solummodo, uerum etiam dissimilia creare potuit et creauit.*" PP III, 763–765, p. 28, (= PL 122 637B). He suggests that God might be judged to be less than perfect if God failed to create everything which reason teaches that it is possible to make: "*Nam si solummodo sui similia, ... condiderit, in dissimilium et oppositorum creatione deficisse uideretur, et non omnino cunctorum quae ratio innuenit posse fieri opifex iudicaretur.*" (PP III JEAUNEAU (ed.), 765–771; PL 122 637B–C). A further reason for this seems to be that the beauty and harmony of the universe is good and this requires diversity. "*Horum itaque omnium, similium dico et dissimilium, unus atque idem artifex est, cuius omnipotentia in nullius naturae deficit operatione. Proinde pulchritudo totius uniuersitatis conditae similium et dissimilium mirabili quadam armonia constituta est, ex diuersis generibus uariisque formis, differentibus quoque substantiarum et accidentium ordinibus in unitatem quandam ineffabilem compacta.*" PP III, 779–786, pp. 28–29, (= PL 122 637D–638A). There follows the famous comparison with harmony within the art of music which has given rise to a discussion on the sense of musical harmony in Eriugena. See W. WIORA, "Das vermeintliche Zeugnis des Johannes Eriugena für die Anfänge der abendländischen Mehrstimmigkeit", in: *Acta musicolica* 43 (1971) 33–43.

[139] PP III, 655–657, p. 24, (= PL 122, 634D–635A).

Eriugena recognises the problems involved in this interpretation. For example, if we conceive of creation out of nothing as a description of the fact that we may say of each and every creature that there was a time when it was not, that is, that the creatures did not exist before they started to become (*"De nihilo nanque facta sunt, quia non erant priusquam fierent"*[140]) then we have a problem of reconciling this with the biblical affirmation that all things subsisted eternally in the Word of God. This was the sense in which Gen. 1:1 *"In principio fecit deus caelum et terram"* and Ps. 103: 24 *"Omnia in sapienta fecisti"* had been interpreted by Eriugena[141]. In Eriugena's system the primordial causes were eternally made by the Father in His only begotten Word, that is in His Wisdom: *"Hinc conficitur in patris sapientia omnia aeterna esse, non tamen ei coaeterna"*[142]. Now this presents a problem when one interprets the 'out of nothing' of creation as the fact that all things *"non erant priusquam fierent"* for, as the Alumnus asks: *"Si omnia quae sunt in sapientia creatrice aeterna sunt, quomodo de nihilo sunt facta?"*[143] How, he continues, can that which exists eternally be identified with that which was not before it was made. The insufficiency of the category of privation as an explanation for the *creatio ex nihilo* is thus evident.

Eriugena's way out of this dilemma, a dilemma involved in finding an adequate explanation for all the biblical texts relevant to this subject matter, is to say that creation out of nothing is creation out of the superessentiality of God. The way to this conclusion had been prepared for by his reflection on the senses in which something is said to be or not to be. On this basis he is able to call the divine superessence 'nothing'. It is *"nihil per excellentiam"*[144]!

Furthermore he takes his argumentation a step further by making explicit the link between the becoming of creatures and the appearing of God. His solution is not only that all things appear out of God and thus are made out of the 'nothing' which the divine superessentiality is, but that God appears and is made in all things. He reiterates the daring application of both appearing and becoming to God! In terms which fit in with what he had said on the diffusion of the divine goodness as the moving force in creation he writes: *"Quae ineffabilis diffusio et facit omnia et fit in omnibus et omnia est."*[145]

---

[140] PP III, 653–654, p. 24, (= PL 122 634C).
[141] Eriugena himself is aware of the biblical issue, see PP III, 2490–2509, pp. 86–87, (= PL 122 679C–680A).
[142] PP III, 700–701, p. 26, (= PL 122 636A).
[143] PP III, 707–709, p. 26, (= PL 636A).
[144] See PP III, 2549–2550, p. 88, (= PL 122 681A).
[145] PP III, 624–625, p. 23, (= PL 122 634A).

## 6. The Creator God appears[146]

It has emerged that the central context within which Eriugena's mature treatment of '*creatio ex nihilo*' occurs (and indeed within which he situates the relationship between the world and God) is that of the appearing of the divine superessentiality. The Creator God appears.

How, he asks, can all things be made and eternal. The simplest answer is to consider creatures as eternal in the primordial causes and made in the effects of those causes. Eriugena's reasoning however goes beyond this. Through the voice of the Alumnus he reiterates that the problem is how all things are both eternal and made, not just eternal in the primordial causes but made insofar as they proceed into their effects in time. He asks "*non quomodo sunt aeterna et facta, sed qua ratione dicuntur et facta et aeterna.*"[147] A second important emphasis in his argumentation emerges through his use of the word 'all' in all causes and all effects of those causes. "*Non ergo dubitas omnes omnium causas causarumque omnes effectus in uerbo aeterna esse et facta, nec me aliter docere aestimas.*"[148] Even in the case of the primordial causes he professes that they are both eternal and made. Just as with regard to their effects he has to explain how they are not just made, but also eternal in the Word[149].

The primordial causes are the result of the will of God: they are eternally made by God[150]. The effects of the causes too may be considered as both eternal and made. That they are made is evident. How are they eternal? Eriugena argues that they are eternal in the sense that God is made in them. In them God appears. Thus in resolving the issue of how all things are both made and eternal Eriugena advances to a daring presentation of the inherence of all reality in the divine nature.[151] He distinguished God and creature but says that they can not be thought of separated from each other. There is nothing 'outside' of God; there is nothing that God has

---

[146] See É. JEAUNEAU, The Neoplatonic Themes of *Processio* and *Reditus* in Eriugena, in: *Dionysius* 15 (1991) 3–29.

[147] PP III, 2119–2120, p. 74, (= PL 122 670D).

[148] PP III, 2010–2012, p. 70, (= PL 122 667C).

[149] The creation of all things in the Word is explained in explicitly trinitarian terms. The one operation of the three persons is emphasised: "*pater enim facit, in filio fiunt, spiritu sancto distribuuntur – una tamen atque eadem summae sanctaeque trinitatis est operatio.*" PP III, 2188–2190, pp. 76–77, (= PL 122 672C–D).

[150] How does God 'see' what God makes? It is asserted that God's knowledge does not arise from things outside God. Eriugena through his dialogue partner Alumnus quotes from Maximus to provide the position that God knows the things made by means of God's volitions: "*igitur ut suas uoluntates deus cognoscit ea quae sunt, quoniam et uolens ea quae sunt fecit.*" PP III, 2216–2217, p. 77, (= PL 122 673B).

[151] "*Proinde non duo a se ipsis distantia debemus intelligere deum et creaturam, sed unum et id ipsum.*" PP III, 2443–2444, p. 85, (= PL 122 678B–C). The context is the manifestation of God in creation. See further "*Nunc uideo te perpure inspicere de quibus uidebaris dubitare, et nec ulterius titubabis, ut arbitror, fateri omnia et facta et aeterna esse, et omne quod in eis uere intelligitur subsistere nil aliud praeter ineffabilem diuinae bonitatis esse naturam.*" PP III, 2414–2417, p. 64, (= PL 122, 677D–678A).

to learn about from something other than God's superessentiality and God's own knowledge of what God wills to exist. "*Et extra se non cognouit omnia, quia extra eam nihil est, sed intra se. Ambit enim omnia et nihil intra se est, in quantum uere est, nisi ipsa, quia sola uere est. Caetera enim, quae dicuntur esse, ipsius theophaniae sunt, quae etiam in ipsa uere subsistunt.*"[152] [153]

Eriugena explicitly points out that he is not here talking about the incarnation alone but the condescension of the divine goodness in appearing in every creature.[154]

A divine self-sufficiency is important for his interpretation of the '*nihil*' of '*creatio ex nihilo*'. God does not need anything apart from God in order to make.

*Et de se ipsa se ipsam facit; non enim indiget alterius materiae, quae ipsa non sit, in qua se ipsam facit.*[155]

This divine self-sufficiency is also expressed not only on the levels of knowing and creating, but also on the level of appearing:

*A se igitur ipso deus accipit theophaniarum suarum (hoc est diuinarum apparitionum) occasiones, quoniam ex ipso et per ipsum et in ipso et ad ipsum sunt omnia.*[156]

Eriugena understands his method to consist, not only in an interpretation of the scripturally based tradition of the *creatio ex nihilo* but also in the interpretation of this tenet in the light of the verses of scripture as a whole.[157] "*In principio, enim, fecit deus caelum et terram.*" Gen. 1:1 and "*Omnia in sapientia fecisti*" Ps. 103: 24[158] evoke the trinitarian understanding of creation, the Father makes all things in the Son, in the Word[159]. Eriugena holds that when considered in trinitarian terms too, God does not make anything external to God. What is made in the Son that is not

---

[152] PP, III, 582–586, p. 22, (= PL 122 633A).

[153] See too PP III, 2444–2455, p. 85, (= PL 122 678C–678D): "*Nam et creatura in deo est subsistens, et deus in creatura mirabili et ineffabili modo creatur, se ipsum manifestans, inuisibilis uisibilem se faciens, et incomprehensibilis comprehensibilem, et occultus apertum, et incognitus cognitum, et forma ac specie carens formosum ac speciosum, et superessentialis essentialem, et supernaturalis naturalem, et simplex compositum, et accidentibus liber accidentibus subiectum et accidens, et infinitus finitum, et incircumscriptus circumscriptum, et supertemporalis temporalem, et superlocalis localem, et omnia creans in omnibus creatum, et factor omnium factus in omnibus, et aeternus coepit esse, et immobilis mouetur in omnia et fit in omnibus omnia.*"

[154] "*Neque hoc de incarnatione uerbi et inhumanatione dico, sed de summae bonitatis, quae unitas est et trinitas, ineffabili condescensione in ea quae sunt ut sint, immo ut ipsa in omnibus a summo usque deorsum sit, semper aeterna, semper facta, a se ipsa in se ipsa aeterna, a se ipsa in se ipsa facta. Et dum sit aeterna, non desinit esse facta; et facta, non desinit esse aeterna.*" PP III, 2455–2461, p. 85, (= PL 122 678D).

[155] PP III, 2461–2462, p. 85, (= PL 122 678D–679A).

[156] PP III, 2464–2467, p. 85, (= PL 122 679A ).

[157] The Alumnus can say to the Nutritor: "*Et auctoritas sanctae scripturae id ipsum, dum intentius consideratur, suadet et praedicat.*" PP III, 2490–2491, p. 86, (= PL 122 679C).

[158] Quoted according to Comm. III, XII, 40–42, É. JEAUNEAU, pp. 272–274; (= PL 122 330A–B).

[159] See PP II, 1045–1055, p. 45, (= PL 122 559A).

the Son himself?, asks the Alumnus:: *"Deus pater in deo filio uniuersitatem totius creaturae uisibilis et inuisibilis condidit. Et quid in principio suo, in uerbo suo, in filio suo unigenito pater conderet, quod ipse filius non esset? Alioqui non in ipso conderet, sed extra ipsum, quod aliunde accepit aut de nihilo fecit."*[160] This is an important renewed visitation of the scriptural texts, bringing to their interpretation the fruits of the foregoing philosophical reflection on the sense in which all things are eternal and made.

Eriugena can conclude that the divine superessence so condescends that it is in a real sense true to say that only this essence (i. e. nothing foreign to this essence) is found in all things which God creates:

*Ineffabilem et incomprehensibilem diuinae bonitatis inaccessibilemque claritatem omnibus intellectibus siue humanis siue angelicis incognitam – superessentialis est enim et supernaturalis – eo nomine significatam crediderim, quae, dum per se ipsam cogitatur, neque est, neque erat, neque erit. In nullo enim intelligitur existentium, quia superat omnia. Dum uero per condescensionem quandam ineffabilem in ea quae sunt mentis obtutibus inspicitur, ipsa sola inuenitur in omnibus esse, et est, et erat, et erit.*[161]

The motive of the divine condescension, ever recurring in Eriugena's account of creation, had earlier been emphasised in the writings of Maximus Confessor.[162]

It is important to point out that the transcendence of God is explicitly defended in Eriugena's scheme. In the passage quoted above the author emphasised that the divine essence is incomprehensible and transcends not only the individual creature but even creation as a whole: *"In nullo enim intelligitur existentium, quia superat omnia."*

The dialectic of the incomprehensibility, and yet willed appearing, of God is central to Eriugena's understanding of creation out of nothing and the ensuing theophany. All creatures are not only the fruit of the diffusion of the divine goodness, but, considered in their translucence to their source, may aptly be called theophanies.

*At uero in suis theophaniis incipiens apparere, ueluti ex nihilo in aliquid dicitur procedere; et quae proprie super omnem essentiam existimatur, proprie quoque in omni essentia cognoscitur. Ideoque omnis uisibilis et inuisibilis creatura theophania (id est diuina apparitio) potest appellari.*[163]

The sensual aspect is not excluded: rather the manifestational aspect of the divine appearing reaches a certain superlative degree in sensible things: *"In quantum uero*

---

[160] PP III, 2493–2497, p. 86, (= PL 122 679C).

[161] PP III, 2541–2549, p. 88, (= PL 122 680D–681A).

[162] See MAXIMUS CONFESSOR, *Ambigua ad Iohannem*, III, 303; XXIX; 24; LXVII, 63, É. JEAUNEAU (ed.), CCSG 18, pp. 31, 167, 257, (= PG 91, 1084C, 1288A, 1412A).

[163] PP III, 2550–2555, p. 88–89, (= PL 122 681A). The other side of the account of theophany is an account of the divine 'darkness': *"Omnis siquidem ordo naturarum a summo usque deorsum (hoc est ex caelestibus essentiis usque ad extrema mundi huius uisibilis corpora), in quantum occultius intelligitur, in tantum diuinae claritati appropinquare uidetur. Proinde a theologia caelestium uirtutum inaccessibilis claritas saepe nominatur tenebrositas."* PP III, 2555–2560, p. 89, (= PL 122 681A–B).

*longius ordo rerum deorsum descendit, in tantum contemplantium obtutibus manifestius se aperit. Ideoque formae ac species rerum sensibilium manifestissimarum theophaniarum nomen accipiunt.*"[164]

This aesthetic aspect of Eriugena's account of theophany is significant and shall be devoted more attention in later sections of this investigation.

Creation is the appearing of the divine in line with an apparitional interpretation of the 'Let there be light' of Gen. 1:3:

*Processio uero eius per principia in creaturas uisibiles et inuisibiles, suas dico theophanias, claritatis nomine meruit significari. In ipsis enim quodam modo patitur intelligi, qui omnem superat intellectum. 'Fiat', ergo, 'lux', inquit deus, hoc est, procedant primordiales causae ex incomprehensibilibus naturae suae secretis in formas ac species comprehensibiles intellectibusque contemplantium se manifestas. 'Et facta est lux': Deo uidelicet uolente et dicente, obscuritas primordialium causarum in formas ac species processit apertas.*[165]

We may conclude that the *creatio ex nihilo* is understood by Eriugena as a descent of the divine goodness out of nothing into something.[166] In explicitly apparitional terms he speaks of the appearing of God in the effects of the primordial causes as the end of the descent of the divine nature[167]. This descent culminates in the manifestation of God in theophanies.[168] Herewith Eriugena offers his interpretation of the traditional and biblically rooted notion of the *vestigiae diuinae: "Atque ideo omnis creatura corporalis atque uisibilis sensibusque succumbens extremum diuinae naturae uestigium non incongrue solet in scripturis appellari.*"[169] In Eriugena's terminology every intelligible and sensible creature is a theophany, that is, an intelligible or sensible appearance, of that which in itself is non-apparent.[170]

Thus Eriugena closes in on an understanding of theophany by means of paradoxical description. Not only is theophany said to involve the appearance of that which in itself is non-apparent but also "the manifestation of the hidden, the affirmation

---

[164] PP III, 2566–2569, p. 89, (= PL 122 681B).

[165] PP III, 3047–3055, pp. 105–106, (= PL 122 692C–D). See too PP III, 3029–3034, p. 105, (= PL 122 692A–B): "*Nos autem primordialium causarum conditionem, siue uisibilium siue inuisibilium, in factura caeli et terrae in principio, earumque in effectus suos processiones in his uerbis sanctae scripturae 'Fiat lux, et reliqua' uolentes intelligere, dicimus creatione lucis processionem primordialium causarum in suos effectus significari.*"

[166] "*Diuina igitur bonitas, quae propterea nihilum dicitur quoniam ultra omnia quae sunt et quae non sunt in nulla essentia inuenitur, ex negatione omnium essentiarum in affirmationem totius uniuersitatis essentiae a se ipsa in se ipsam descendit, ueluti ex nihilo in aliquid, ex inessentialitate in essentialitatem, ex informitate in formas innumerabiles et species.*" PP III, 2569–2575, p. 89, (= PL 122 681 B–C).

[167] "*... in ipsis finem descensionis suae (hoc est apparitionis suae) constituit.*" PP III, 2914–2915, p. 100, (= PL 122 689C).

[168] "*Deinde ex primordialibus causis, quae medietatem quandam inter deum et creaturam obtinent (hoc est inter illam ineffabilem superessentialitatem super omnem intellectum et manifestam substantialiter naturam puris animis conspicuam), descendens in effectibus ipsarum fit, et manifeste in theophaniis suis aperitur.*" PP III, 2643–2648, p. 91, (= PL 122 683A–B).

[169] PP III, 2916–2918, p. 100, (= PL 122 689C).

[170] PP III, 589–590, p. 22, (= PL 122 633A).

of the negated, the comprehension of the incomprehensible, the utterance of the unutterable, the access to the inaccessible, the understanding of the unintelligible, the body of the bodiless, the essence of the superessential, the form of the formless, the measure of the measureless, … the definition of the infinite, the circumscription of the uncircumscribed …"[171]

It is true that Eriugena builds on Neoplatonic schemes of analysis in his presentation of the appearing of God. It is nonetheless important to recognise that he integrates this material within a biblically centred theology of the appearing of God.[172]

We can observe this in his account of the incarnation. While Eriugena is at pains to stress that theophany applies to the revealing of God in every creature, he nonetheless does consider the special role played by the revealing of God in the incarnation of the Word. In the concrete order of fall and grace, that is in salvation history, the Word incarnate opens the mind's eyes, revealing himself in all things and leading humans back to the vision of God and of the primordial causes in God:

*Ad quam uisionem humanam naturam reducere dei uerbum incarnatum descendit, ipsam prius lapsam quam ad pristinum statum reuocaret accipiens, delictorum uulnera sanans, falsarum phantasiarum umbras extinguens, oculos mentis aperiens, se ipsum in omnibus his qui digni sunt tali uisione manifestans.*[173]

A trinitarian contextualisation too shows that we are dealing with a theology of the appearing of God. All things that have been made in, and all participate in the Word of God. He quotes from Basil of Caesarea to support this: "*diuinum uerbum natura*

---

[171] The complete passage reads: "*Omne enim quod intelligitur et sentitur nihil aliud est nisi non apparentis apparitio, occulti manifestatio, negati affirmatio, incomprehensibilis comprehensio, ineffabilis fatus, inaccessibilis accessus, inintelligibilis intellectus, incorporalis corpus, superessentialis essentia, informis forma, immensurabilis mensura, innumerabilis numerus, carentis pondere pondus, spiritualis incrassatio, inuisibilis uisibilitas, illocalis localitas, carentis tempore temporalitas, infiniti diffinitio, incircumscripti circumscriptio, et caetera quae puro intellectu et cogitantur et perspiciuntur et quae memoriae sinibus capi nesciunt et mentis aciem fugiunt.*" PP III, 589–598, p. 22, (= PL 122 633A–B). English translation from I. P. SHELDON-WILLIAMS / L. BIELER, SLH XI, p. 59.
[172] The return of all creation to God is handled and expressed in theological, biblical terms. In a passage commenting on the writings of the Ps. Dionysius, ERIUGENA offers a sentence which combines a presentation of the return of the causes, with the more biblically inspired 'God will be all in all': "*Et hoc manifestissime docet omnium reditus in causam, ex qua praecesserunt, quando omnia conuertentur in deum, sicut aer in lucem, quando erit deus omnia in omnibus.*" PP III, 2658–2660, p. 92, (= PL 122 683 B–C). Then there immediately follows a fuller biblical contextualisation which centres on the possibility of our knowing that God is all in all in this life: "*Non quod etiam nunc non sit deus omnia in omnibus, sed quod post praeuaricationem humanae naturae et expulsionem de sede paradisi (hoc est de altitudine spiritualis uitae) et ex cognitione clarissimae sapientiae in profundissimas ignorantiae tenebras detrusae, nemo nisi diuina gratia illuminatus et in diuinorum mysteriorum altitudinem cum Paulo raptus, quomodo deus omnia in omnibus est uerae intelligentiae contuitu potest perspicere, nube carnalium cogitationum uanarumque phantasiarum caligine interposita, mentisque acie irrationabilibus passionibus infirmata et ex splendoribus perspicuae ueritatis repercussa, consuetisque corporalibus umbris contenta.*" PP III, 2660–2671, p. 92, (= PL 122 683C–D). See too É. JEAUNEAU, "The Neoplatonic Themes of Processio and Reditus in Eriugena".
[173] PP III, 2677–2682, p. 92, (= PL 122 684A).

*est eorum quae facta sunt.*"[174] Eriugena himself comments that the Word of God is both the nature of all things and consubstantial with the Father before all things.[175]

Ever at pains to insist that theophany is a characteristic of all created reality considered in its translucence to the divine, the theologian Eriugena does nevertheless also consider the particular biblical scenes which the theological tradition has referred to as theophanies. For example he gives account of the appearing of God to Moses in the blazing thorn-bush and on the summit of the mountain (*Moyses in rubo et in montis cacumine*)[176] and of Abraham gazing at the stars of heaven.[177] He interprets these scenes as instances of privileged access to a knowledge of God through visible creatures. New Testament texts are also considered: for example the scene of the apostles at the transfiguration of the Lord.[178] Here Jesus' garments, in themselves creaturely reality, lead the apostles to an insight into mystery: "*per uisibilia symbola in diuina mysteria introducti sunt.*"[179] Eriugena situates such special privileged access to a knowledge of God through creaturely reality as a special case within the general access to a limited knowledge of God which all creatures provide. Further, the transformed garments of Jesus are a symbol for this general translucence of all reality. Eriugena refers to Rom. 1:20 in the context of God's invisible attributes being 'made visible' by means of created reality.[180]


## 7. Conclusion

Eriugena's theory of God as triune, good, superessential nothingness: a God who appears, informs his account of the relationship of God and world. It culminates in an account of all creatures as theophanic manifestations of the creator God. This theophanic manifestation is rooted in the divine goodness, indeed in the divine 'love'; it involves the free condescension of God; it extends even to sensible things, indeed here the process of manifestation achieves a certain extreme; it is a trinitarian revealing of God in God's Word, and the relationship to the incarnation, while not yet fully explicated, has been indicated in those texts which present the appearing of God in the context of salvation history.

---

[174] PP III, 2748–2749, p. 95, (= PL 122 685C). The text in BASIL is from *Homiliae in Hexaemeron*, VIII, I, S. GIET (ed.), pp. 428–430, (= PG 29 164 C–D).

[175] PP III, 2756–2757, p. 95, (= PL 122 658C).

[176] Ex. 3:2; 19:3. PP III, 2928–2929, p. 101, (= PL 122 689D).

[177] Gen. 15:5. PP III, 2926–2927, p. 101, (= PL 122 689D).

[178] Mt. 17:2.

[179] "*Apostoli deinde post legem sub gratia cum Christo in monte per uisibilia symbola in diuina mysteria introducti sunt. 'Vestimenta' enim 'eius candida sicut nix' uisibilem creaturam, in qua et per quam dei uerbum quod in omnibus subsistit intelligitur, significabant.*" PP III, 2929–2933, p. 101, (= PL 122 689D–690A).

[180] "*Audi Apostolum dicentem: 'Inuisibilia eius a creatura mundi per ea quae facta sunt intellecta conspiciuntur; sempiterna quoque eius uirtus et aeternitas.*'" PP III, 2933–2935, p. 101, (= PL 122 690A).

CHAPTER 4:

# God appears in manifold ways
# in the human creature

*"Nulla quippe alia uia est ad principalis exempli purissimam contemplationem, praeter proximae sibi suae imaginis certissimam notitiam."*[1]

In chapter four Eriugena's understanding of human nature is presented so that on the basis of this outline we may in turn to approach his understanding of the appearing of God in human nature.[2]

## 1. The divine trinity and the incarnation as defining parameters for understanding human nature

Eriugena's understanding of the human creature is radically theological. We observe this not only in his emphasis on the fact that as a creature the human is dependant on God, but also in the fact that the human is conceived within a creational and redemptive plan which centres on the Word becoming flesh. In the fourth book of *Periphyseon,* Eriugena takes up again his great opus after a lengthy interruption during which he seems to have studied some works of Epiphanius of Salamis (Cyprus) and imbued ideas taken from that author. Now calling the academic investigation, which we know as *Periphyseon,* '*physiologia*'[3] (discourse on nature), he quotes at length from Epiphanius' *Ancoratus* on the three in one of the trinity and uses Epiphanius' analogical teaching on the trinity to introduce the trinitarian and salvation context of the creation of the human.

---

[1] PP V, 3650–3652, p. 114, (= PL 122 941C). The speaker is the Alumnus.

[2] As we have already mentioned, an adequate treatment of human nature was so important to Eriugena that he revised his original plan to complete *Periphyseon* in four books, and decided to divide his remaining material into two books, book four and book five. See É. JEAUNEAU, PP IV, CCCM CLXIV, Introduction, pp. LVII–LVIII; PP IV, SLH XIII, p. 279, endnote 9; PP I, CCCM CLXI, Introduction, pp. XI–XV.

[3] "*Prima nostrae physeologiae intentio praecipuaque materia erat ΥΠΕΡΟΥϹΙΑΔΕϹ (hoc est superessentialis) natura, quod sit causa creatrix existentium et non existentium omnium, a nullo creata, unum principium, una origo, unus et uniuersalis uniuersorum fons, a nullo manans, dum ab eo manant omnia, trinitas coessentialis in tribus substantiis, ANAPXOC (hoc est sine principio), principium et finis, una bonitas, deus unus, OMOYϹΙΟϹ et ΥΠΕΡΟΥϹΙΟϹ (id est coessentialis et superessentialis).*" PP IV, CCCM CLXIV, 1–9, p. 3, (= PL 122 741C ). On the title 'Physiologia' see D. J. O'MEARA, The Concept of Natura in John Scottus Eriugena, esp. p. 142, note 39.

Important is that the trinitarian perspective of the third book of *Periphyseon* is not abandoned but rather reinforced by this quoting from Epiphanius.

Epiphanius emphasises the three in one nature of the sanctity, agency, designing, operation, and subsistence of the trinity, and the existence for one another of the Father, Son and Spirit. Epiphanius, noting that we may only know how the trinity is, to the extent that the trinity itself makes this known to us, presents an analogy for the trinity as ΦΩΣ, ΠΥΡ, and ΠΝΕΥΜΑ[4].

Eriugena relating this analogy with what he has already written about the trinity, points out that spirit has been named where heat might have been expected in the analogy. "*Et mihi uidetur spiritum pro calore posuisse, quasi dixisset in similitudine: Lux, ignis, calor.*"[5] Using the notion that each individual divine person may be called light and fire and heat, that all three illuminate and burn and heat, he links this to the biblical notions of wisdom (all three illuminate), of burning like a holocaust in the process of the deification of the human (all three burn), and of being warmed with the love of charity (all three warm). Epiphanius thus treats of the trinity in it's sanctification of the human and Eriugena's commentary on the quotation from Epiphanius develops this Christologically: it culminates in a citation of Eph. 4:13 in the context of the charity of the members of the trinity leading the human on to perfection in the era of Christ. Eriugena explains: "*Vir autem perfectus est Christus, in quo omnia consummata sunt, cuius aetatis plenitudo est consummatio salutis uniuersalis ecclesiae, quae in angelis et hominibus constituta est.*"[6]

Thus human perfection is understood Christologically, as the work of the trinity and is cast in the mould of salvation history.

Eriugena's theological reading of the creation of the human creature fits in well with his deeply trinitarian understanding of creation as a whole. He is ever alert to what he considers allusions to the trinity present in the first verses of Genesis[7]. In the verse "*Dixit deus: Fiat lux*" (Gen. 1:3): he sees in '*Deus*' an allusion to the Father and in "*Et uidit deus lucem quia bona est*" (Gen. 1:4) he reads an implication of the activity of the Holy Spirit making all things good[8]. He understands the unity and trinity of God to be expressed first in the combination of singular form, then plural

---

[4] EPIPHANIUS, *Ancoratus* 67, K. HOLL / P. WENDLAND (ed.), Leipzig: Hinrichs, 1915-1922, GCS 25, p. 82, 2-12, (= PG 43, 137C–140A).

[5] PP IV, CCCM CLXIV, 25–27, p. 3, (= PL 122, 743A). Eriugena had mentioned this trio: "*Quid dicam de igneo elemento quod, cum sit unum atque simplex in se ipso et per seipsum consideratum, caloris simul et lucis causa est?*" in PP II, 2572–2574, p. 106, (= PL 122 602C). Interestingly, here too, the context is that of a discussion of Epiphanius' teaching. In PP II the issue is the procession of the Spirit, the Filioque debate.

[6] PP IV, CCCM CLXIV, 39–42, p. 4; (= PL 122 743B).

[7] See the section PP IV, CCCM CLXIV, 1816–1844, pp. 64–65, (= PL 122 786A–786C).

[8] Both scriptural texts quoted according to PP IV, CCCM CLXIV, 1833–1839, p. 65 (= PL 122 786B).

form in "*Et dixit deus faciamus*" (Gen. 1:26) in the creation of the human in the image of God[9].

## 2. The human and the order of creation

### 2.1 Human nature: created nature

Eriugena's reflection on the status of the human among other creatures, more precisely among other animals, takes it's rise from the scriptural verse Gen. 1:24: "*Producat terra animam uiuentem in genere suo, iumenta et reptilia, et bestias terrae secundum species suas.*"[10]

He first of all concentrates on the words: "*Producat terra animam uiuentem*" and interprets this as a case of '*synecdoche*', or in the terminology of the Latin world, '*conceptio*' whereby the whole is implied in naming a part[11]. In this case the text may be interpreted as meaning: let the earth bring forth the whole living animal.[12] The word for earth '*terra*' is also considered to be in need of interpretation and Eriugena offers a minor theological treatise hung on the interpretation of the one word '*terra*' of Gen. 1:24.[13]

---

[9] On the three in one revealed in Gen. 1:26, see PP IV, CCCM CLXIV, 1839-1844, p. 65, (= PL 122 786B–C). Scriptural verse as given in *Periphyseon,* book IV where the alternative "*Et ait faciamus*" is also mentioned. "*Faciamus*" as a hint of the trinity has a long patristic tradition. One certain source is GREGORY OF NYSSA, *De Imagine* 6, CAPPUYNS (ed.), p. 215, (= PG 44 140B–C).

[10] PP IV, CCCM CLXIV, 90–92, pp. 5–6, (= PL 122, 744B–C).

[11] PP IV, CCCM CLXIV, 93–96, p. 6; (= PL 122, 744C). The Nutritor introduces a series of scriptural examples of synecdoche. One example: "*Spiritus quidem promptus est, caro uero infirma*" (Mt. 26:41; Mk. 14:38) leads on to an interesting Christological aside on the extent of suffering in Christ, important for a reconstruction of a Eriugenian Christology. In PP IV, CCCM CLXIV, 120–183, pp. 7–8, (= PL 122, 745A–746C), the Nutritor quotes extensively from Epiphanius, Ancoratus, 69 on Christological and pneumatological points. The Alumnus' response confirms that this passage is to be viewed as a digression. The justification offered for the digression is of methodological interest. The Alumnus says: "*Transitus iste, quamuis longius proposito uideatur recessisse, utilis tamen est uolentibus sanctam scripturam intelligere.*" PP IV, CCCM CLXIV, 184–185, p. 9, (= PL 122, 746C). For Eriugena the overriding task at hand is to grasp the fullest truth, the truth contained in Holy Scripture. This whole-truth is more important than the partial truth which a narrow line of argumentation would communicate. Eriugena rejoices in the possibility of digressing, of initiating his reader in the gems of scriptural interpretation which he has just gleaned from Epiphanius. Digression is seen positively, as a positive opportunity in the service of a truth which is greater than any narrow scheme. Digression is not viewed as a slip in style.

[12] He points out that of course the soul considered in itself is not from the earth.

[13] PP IV, CCCM CLXIV, 201–278, p. 9–12; (= PL 122, 747A–748C). This is not simply pointless amassing of information, or a display of one's scriptural knowledge. Nor is it an argument from authority (none was needed in order to explain Gen. 1:24). It is simply that what Eriugena himself called it: the presentation of a higher inquiry (*si quis altius hunc locum quaesierit*) into the text, we might say a fuller inquiry, resulting in the embracing perspective within which the text (and ultimately human nature) is to be understood.

Of interest to the theme at hand is a gradual change in the very referent of the word '*terra*'[14]. In book two of *Periphyseon,* '*terra*' in the exegesis of Gen. 1:1 was taken by Eriugena as referring to the primordial causes. Here in book four 'terra' develops from the more general meaning of the mass of totality of substantial nature[15] to later taking on the meaning of *human* nature in its God-willed, pre-fall condition, the condition to which it shall return in the resurrection[16].

Eriugena presents us with a Christological and a pneumatological context for this creation and return of human nature mediated by various scriptural references to '*terra*'. He carries this through on the basis of a medley of biblical texts. For example Eriugena offers us a double interpretation of the verse of Ps. 103,30 "*Emittes spiritum tuum, et renouabis faciem terrae*" both referring to the restitution of the integrity of human nature, the first Christological, the second pneumatological. In the first interpretation the spirit is Christ's soul and the context is thus the return of Christ to glory taking all human nature with him. In the second interpretation it is a return of the Holy Spirit to human nature. Using the verse Ps. 145:4 Eriugena constructs the passage: "... *et 'reuertetur in terram suam', hoc est in illam naturam quam propter peccatum primi hominis deseruerat.*"[17] In this interpretation the earth is called 'his' earth, indicating not the possession established by God through creation alone, but the possession brought about by love and election, and ultimately, by the pneumatological renewal of human nature at the end of time.

## 2.2  *The human: creation within the genus of animal*

The creation of the human can be viewed from two non-exclusive viewpoints: as included within the genus of animal and as a unique species of animal.

The relationship between the human and the genus of animal is reflected upon at length by Eriugena. Through an interpretation of Gen. 1:24 Eriugena will argue that the division into genus and species is not just the invention of the human mind but a discovery rooted in the nature of things. The Nutritor quotes this verse

---

[14] Nutritor commences his discussion of the meaning of '*terra*': "*Terrae siquidem uocabulo totius naturae substantialis uisibilium et inuisibilium incommutabilis soliditas solet insinuari, ...*" (PP IV, CCCM CLXIV, 202–203, p. 9, (= PL 122, 747A.) '*Terra*' here is that produced on the third day of creation. Using a quote from Col. 3:5 he goes on to represent *terra* as nature in abstraction from the fall and sin: "*Mortificate membra uestra quae sunt super terram.*" These members are those which stem from human wickedness alone and may not be said to have been made by God. Through Ps. 103: 35 he introduces the eschatological aspect: *Deficient peccatores a terra et iniqui ita ut non sint.* He here interprets the 'sinners' who disappear to stand for the sin which causes them to be called sinners; and as a result this text interpreted as speaking of the eschatological disappearance of all sin and iniquity from the earth. Here earth is then the eschatologically purged nature where sin has lost its appearance of being and is thus said to return to the nothingness which it always really was.

[15] PP IV, CCCM CLXIV, 202–204, p. 9, (= PL 122 747A).

[16] From PP IV, CCCM CLXIV, 265–271, p. 12, (= PL 122 748C). Compare É. Jeauneau, PP IV SLH XIII, footnote 24, p. 284.

[17] PP IV, CCCM CLXIV, 265–267, p. 12, (= PL 122 748C).

in the version in which it appears in the Vulgate, namely: *"producat terra animam uiuentem in genere suo iumenta et reptilia et bestias terrae secundum species suas"*.[18] Now the words meaning 'after their species' do not appear in the Septuagint[19]. Instead of '*in genere suo*'/'*secundum species suas*' it repeats κατὰ γένος. Eriugena has carefully chosen the version of Scripture which fits his argumentation. He draws the conclusion that dialectic is not merely a human invention but has been instilled in all things by the Creator.

*Ac per hoc intelligitur quod ars illa, quae diuidit genera in species, et species in genera resoluit, quaeque ΔΙΑΛΕΚΤΙΚΗ dicitur, non ab humanis machinationibus sit facta, sed in natura rerum ab auctore omnium artium, quae uere artes sunt, condita, et a sapientibus inuenta, et ad utilitatem sollertis rerum indagis usitata.*[20]

Eriugena explains how all animals are created *"causaliter et primordialiter"*. This he says takes place through the creation as body and soul in the earth (*terra*). In a textual addition we read that this is because all were made in the human (*"nam in homine omnia facta sunt"*).[21]

That these words, namely, 'for all things were made in the human' are a manuscript addition in the hand of the writer known as i¹ has been pointed out by Jeauneau[22]. If i¹ is indeed the autograph of Eriugena as Jeauneau has elsewhere argued, then the emphasis on this newly emerging point implied through the addition seems to be important. The statement that all things were created in the human has consequences not only as an indication of the eidetic inherence of all created things in the human creature within the plan of creation in the divine intellect, but also for the subsequent understanding of created reality as a whole *on the part of* created intellects. In other words, it reveals something of the central role of the human creature in the plan of creation, and it indicates that *any* created intellect which tries to understand creation must grasp the plurality of facets of the human in order to intellectually approach the possible and actual order of creation as a whole. Thus the *knowledge* of all things was created in the human. The bridge from the level of the providential plan of God to the possibility of a created *cognition* of all things is made in the second part of the long Latin sentence: *"quid mirum si diuino praecepto iubeatur animam uiuentem (hoc est animal uiuens) producere, ut quod causaliter oc-*

---

[18] Here quoted from Vulgata, Gen.1:24. Eriugena quotes the verse in two parts in PP IV, CCCM CLXIV, 278–283, p. 12, (= PL 122 748D).

[19] See É. JEAUNEAU endnote 21 in, PP IV SLH XIII, p. 283. É. Jeauneau says the theme is to be found in Eriugena's Greek sources and mentions Maximus Confessor.

[20] PP IV, CCCM CLXIV, 283–288, p. 12, (= PL 122 749A).

[21] PP IV, CCCM CLXIV, 272–277, p. 12, (= PL 122 748C) with textual addition number 3: *"quoniam in homine omnia facta sunt"*.

[22] See É. JEAUNEAU, PP IV SLH XIII, footnote 20, pp. 282/3. "By adding these words, Eriugena announces the thesis he is about to demonstrate, namely, that the knowledge of all things had been created in man causaliter et primordialiter. Just as the primordial causes are contained in the Word of God, so the concepts (notiones) of all things are contained in human nature. In this way, too, man, created according to the image of God, mirrors the divine model.", p. 283.

*culte in causis et rationibus habebat, hoc in genera et species aperte produceret?*"[23] The transition is already present in the connotation of the hidden reasons (*rationibus*) of things and it is made even more explicit in the mention of species and genera, categories which on the first hearing remind us of the human logical ordering of reality but which for Eriugena have been introduced into the order of reality in the act of creation.

When we consider his account of the human created in the genus of animal together with the concomitant insight that all things are created in the human, we witness how closely interwoven the ontological and the cognitional levels are for Eriugena. We see how in his opinion the very plan of creation holds within it the promise of a cognitional return of all created reality to God through the knowledge *of* the human creature (that is, the recognition of what the human creature is according to its genus and species), a knowledge to be achieved *by* the human as a thinking creature[24].

A further indication that all things are created in the human is signified by the fact that the human was created on the sixth day, a number which is equal to the sum of its factors (3, 2, and 1). In the fourth book of *Periphyseon*, having dealt with the fifth day of creation and reached the creation of the human on the sixth day, Eriugena asserts:

*Ipse itaque homo, cuius conditio in praedictis diuinae operationis contemplationibus per singula latenter insinuatur, quoniam in ipso et cum ipso praedicta omnia condita sunt, non per moras temporum, sed ordinatione causarum in effectus suos manantium, in fine totius uniuersitatis manifeste formatur, senaria repetitione propheticae theoriae peracta, ...*[25].

### 2.3  The human: a unique species of animal

The earth was commanded to bring forth the living soul in its genus. The words 'in its genus' are important, for the human is said to be of the genus animal although it is a special species of animal, superior to the other animals by virtue of reason and intelligence. It is said only to be placed with the other species of animal because the writer of Holy Scripture intended to deal with the human as made in the image and likeness of God further on in the biblical text.

The Nutritor must explain to the Alumnus how the human can be said to have been brought forth with cattle, reptiles and beasts of the field. These are creatures over which the human will be said to have dominion. This time Eriugena answers in allegorical terms. In his speaker Nutritor he allegorises the cattle (or quadrupeds), the beasts that resist reason, and the reptiles. Aspects of an anthropology emerge, an

---

[23] PP IV, CCCM CLXIV, 274–277, p. 12, (= PL 122 748C).

[24] The knowledge of the human creature in both subjective and objective sense of this genitive are thus pivotal.

[25] PP IV, CCCM CLXIV, 1808–1814, p. 64, (= PL 122 785D).

anthropology which lays the basis for Eriugena's account of the appearing of God in the human.

The animal, Eriugena explains, is the nexus of soul and body ("*est enim animal corporis et animae connexio*")[26]. The genus of animal, he explains, falls into three groups: cattle, reptiles, and beasts of the field. He argues that all of these three may be taken to stand for three kinds of motion of the soul with respect to the body and thus are inherent allegorically in the human person[27]. His argument is that the *three*-fold motion may be understood of the human only, the only rational animal ("*quidem ternarius ille motus in homine solo, qui solus est rationabile animal, intel-ligitur, …*"[28]). 'Cattle' is taken to signify the motions which are subjected to reason, for example the use made of sensation by reason. Eriugena gives an etymological explanation of '*iumenta*' linking it to the verb '*iuuare*', to help. The alternative expression for this group, 'quadrupeds,' is linked to the fact that sensation has to do with sensing of corporeal reality which is formed out of the four elements. The beasts that resist reason are taken to signify irrational motions arising from the lower nature, such as rage or inordinate desire. 'Reptiles' is taken to signify motions in the augmentative and nutritive part of the soul. Now, only the human is said to partake of all three of these kinds of motions. So Eriugena argues that the human is in all animals and all animals are in the human, and yet the human transcends all animals[29].

An allegorical biblical interpretation is also central to Eriugena's presentation of human sensation.

On the fourth day, the second light is said to have been created. Whereas the first light created on the first day is interpreted as the principal part of the human, that is, intellect and reason, the creation of the secondary light is interpreted as the creation of exterior sense. On this basis there follows an account of human sensation corresponding to the creation of the sun, the moon and the stars 'in' the human:

*Quod enim sol est in mundo, hoc est clarissimus et non fallens sensus in homine; et quod luna, hoc est ambigua phantasia ac ueluti dubia lux animi sentientis; et quod stellae, hoc sunt incomprehensibiles et minutissimi phantasiarum numeri, ex innumerabilibus et incomprehensibilibus corporalium rerum speciebus procreati.*[30]

A key aspect of Eriugena's anthropology is the respect which he maintains for the dignity of the human creature. He is of the opinion that one human alone is greater than the whole visible world, not of course physically larger but greater in dignity[31].

---

[26] PP IV, CCCM CLXIV, 401–402, p. 16, (= PL 122 751C).

[27] He quotes Gen. 1: 24 according to both the Vulgate and a Latin translation of the Septuaginta. This shows that he was familiar with both, used both where this suited him, but was also willing to choose between the versions of scripture where one version fits his argument more than the other.

[28] PP IV, CCCM CLXIV, 403–404, p. 16, (= PL 122 751C).

[29] PP IV, CCCM CLXIV, textual addition number 4, 7, (= PL 122 752C).

[30] PP IV, CCCM CLXIV, 1753–1758, p. 62, (= PL 122 784C).

[31] See, PP IV, CCCM CLXIV, 1761–1764, (= PL 122 784 C–D).

Eriugena establishes the superiority of human sensation over the bodies of the world
with arguments such as the affirmation that the sensible objects were created for the
sense and not the sense for the sensibles[32]. This is a radical affirmation of the value
of aesthetic perception. Eriugena concludes that just as the intelligible principles
of created nature, insofar as they may be understood, are created in the human
intellect, so too the sensible species, insofar as they may be sensed, find the causes
of their creation in the human sense and subsist in it. This is an argument from the
fact that sensation is the final cause of the sensibles.

Eriugena draws attention to the paradox that the human both has the form of
an animal and transcends this form. We may say that the human is an animal, and
the human is not an animal.[33] This logical observation is backed up by 'scriptural
corroboration' (*etiam ex auctoritate diuinae scripturae possumus corroborare*) using
three New Testament passages which in his opinion indicate a duality which at-
tends the human creature.[34] Thus we should not be surprised if the human creation
displays a certain duality since the human itself is in a way 'double' or 'two-fold':
"*Quid ergo mirum, si duplex hominis conditio intelligatur, cum ipse quodammodo
duplex sit; …*"[35]

How is this duality to be understood? Eriugena denies that the human has more
than one soul: "*Unam uero eandemque rationabilem animam humano corpori ineffabili modo adiunctam hominem esse assero …*"[36] He also denies that this soul may
be considered to have 'parts'. He tolerates the formulation that the *human* has two
parts, the one in the human is created in the image of God, and the other produced
out of earth and linking the human to the animal: "*ipsumque hominem mirabili
quadem et intelligibili diuisione, ea parte qua ad imaginem et similitudinem creatoris
factus est, nullius animalitatis participem esse et ab ea omnino absolutum, ea uero qua
animalitati communicat, in uniuersali animalium genere de terra (hoc est de communi
omnium natura) productum.*"[37] The simplicity of the human soul is something which
he holds most firmly. It is, as he says, whole in itself and pervades the whole of its
nature: "*Tota enim in seipsa ubique est per totum.*"[38] He says that it is as a whole
that the soul undertakes each of its several types of motion, ending his list of such
motions with the intelligible motion in which the purified soul revolves about its
creator ("*circa suum creatorem intelligibile motu atque aeterno, dum omnibus uitiis*

---

[32] PP IV, CCCM CLXIV, 1771–1772, p. 63, (= PL 122 784D–785A).
[33] Note in the text the words '*mirabilem ac penitus ineffabilem*' are used for the constitution of the human condition. Later mirabilis will recur in the context of the human as created as imago dei.
[34] PP IV, CCCM CLXIV, 447–448, p. 18, (= PL 122 753A). In the verses which follow the texts 1 Cor. 2:14–15; 2 Cor. 4:16 and Rom. 7:25 are implemented to support his argumentation. The notions utilised are: *animalis homo / spiritualis homo* (Vulgata: *spiritalis*); *exterior homo / interior homo* (Vulgata: *is qui foris est … is qui intus est*); *mente / carne*.
[35] PP IV, CCCM CLXIV, 473–475, p. 18, (= PL 122 753C).
[36] PP IV, CCCM CLXIV, 500–502, p. 19, (= PL 122 754A–B).
[37] PP IV, CCCM CLXIV, 502–507, p. 19, (= PL 122 754B)
[38] PP IV, CCCM CLXIV, 514, p. 20, (= PL 122 754B–C).

*phantasiisque purgatur, circumuoluitur.*"[39]). The plurality of the human soul's motions (mentioned here are intellect, discursive reason, sense, vital motion) is given
as the reason for its (albeit apparent) division. But in each of these motions the soul
is not divided but present as a whole.

The consequence is drawn by the Alumnus: the whole soul is produced by the
earth and the whole soul is created in the image of God.

Eriugena has argued from the abstract level of genus and species. The definition
of the human includes its rationality; the human is the rational animal. Yet the other
animals are irrational animals. How can the mutually opposed species, rational and
irrational, be embraced within one genus? His answer on this level was that the
predication of 'rational' and in turn of 'irrational' must not be considered a problem
as the predicates represent the differences between the species within the genus
animal. He has however a series of further arguments which explain the apparent
paradox from various perspectives. Eriugena delves deeper into the nature of the
human and its pivotal role with respect to the rest of reality in order once again to
show that the paradox is only apparent. *"Constat enim inter sapientes in homine un-
iuersam creaturam contineri: Intelligit enim et ratiocinatur ut angelus, sentit et corpus
administrat ut animal, ac per hoc omnis creatura in eo intelligitur."*[40] The sentence
quoted above presents the human as straddling the extremes of created living reality.
Eriugena offers a complementary argument from inclusiveness: created nature may
be divided into five kinds of being (i.e. a creature may be a body, a living being,
a sensitive being, a rational being or an intellectual being); the human nature is
said to be a creature in all five senses. Further, he speaks of parts of human nature.
Considered from the perspective of what it has in common with the other animals,
human nature is truly animal nature. But insofar as it participates in the divine and
celestial essence, it is not animal. It is because of this higher part of human nature
that it is said to be created in the image of God.[41] Eriugena also turns from the
abstract consideration of contradictories and mutually opposed predicates to the
concrete situation of the human within the world of sin and grace.

*Et notandum quod etiam in hac uita, priusquam totum quod in homine animale est uertatur in
spirituale, et omne quod in eo compositum est in ineffabilem adunetur simplicitatem, potest totus
homo et animalis fieri et spiritualis, sed animalis sola libertate arbitrii, spiritualis uero et libero
arbitrio simul et gratia, sine qua naturalis potentia uoluntatis mouere hominem in spiritum nullo
modo sufficit.*[42]

---

[39] PP IV, CCCM CLXIV, 520–522, p. 20, (= PL 122 754C).

[40] PP IV, CCCM CLXIV, 548–551, p. 21, (= PL 122 755B).

[41] Eriugena introduces a quote from Augustine saying that it is only with this part of the human
that God speaks. The quote is from Augustinus, *De ciuitate dei* XI, ii, 14–20, B. Dombart / A.
Kalb (ed.), p. 322; (= PL 41, 318), quoted in PP IV, CCCM CLXIV, textual addition number 5,
23–27, p. 21, (= PL 122 755C–D).

[42] PP IV, CCCM CLXIV, 565–571, p. 22, (= PL 122 755D–756A).

Of significance in this passage is not only the ease with which Eriugena changes key to a biblical interpretation of the human duality (the *homo animalis / homo spiritualis* of 1 Cor. 2:14–15) but the importance which human freedom plays within his interpretation. Freedom is not considered abstractly but within the concrete order of fall and redemptive grace. Eriugena does not oppose an abstract human freedom and a bestial determinism. Rather he opposes an isolated free will to that free will which cooperates with grace. That free will which refuses to cooperate with grace is then linked to the bestial in the human (*homo animalis*). *Homo spiritualis* is the human being cooperating in freedom with grace[43].

## 3. The human: created in the image of God

The human 'animal' is unique. Eriugena repeatedly implements the biblical notion of the creation of the human in the image of God to express this uniqueness. Only the human 'animal' is said to be created in the image of God[44]. It is now opportune to examine the various ways in which Eriugena understands the human imaging of God.

### 3.1 The human participates in the perfection of God: a basic presupposition of the divine imaging

The basic scheme of reference within which Eriugena approaches the human mirroring of God is through the notion of human participation in divine perfection, that is human participation in that one divine perfection which is appropriated by the human through individual virtues. In this bold analysis the human is said to become 'God' according to grace ('theosis').[45] Perfection is said to be predicated of God essentially, the analogous perfection of the image, by participation.

All participation in the divine perfection may be the occasion for knowing that God, as cause of this perfection, exists. Certain participations in this perfection are however of a remarkable apparitional quality. Because of their high degree of translucence of the divine they make possible the proposition that the human is said to be created in the image of God. However, the fundamental difference between creature and Creator is always simultaneously emphasised by Eriugena. It is expressed by

---

[43] This however says nothing about Eriugena's opinion on abstract freedom (if he had one!) as a special characteristic of the human. This observation is important when we consider the importance of freedom as a constituent of the person as created in the image of God. For Gregory of Nyssa the greatest generosity of God implied the gift of human freedom. In *Periphyseon* however Eriugena felt the need to stress that only graced freedom belongs to the dignified side of the human.

[44] See the discussion which starts in PP IV, CCCM CLXIV, 638, p. 24, (= PL 122 757C).

[45] PP V, 853–878, pp. 29/30, (= PL 122 879C–880A). ERIUGENA quotes MAXIMUS CONFESSOR, *Ambigua ad Iohannem* III, É. JEANNEAU (ed.), CCSG 18, 358–384, p. 33, (= PG 91, 1088A–C) on this theosis.

the distinction which lies in the respective subjects, the one (God) possessing the perfection essentially, the other (the human) by participation alone:

*Nam quomodo imago esset, si in aliquo ab eo cuius imago est distaret, excepta subiecti ratione? De qua in superioribus libris diximus, dum de prototypo (hoc est de principali exemplo) eiusque imagine disputabamus, dicentes ipsum deum principale exemplum esse per se ipsum, a se ipso, in se ipso, et a nullo creatum uel formatum uel conuersum subsistens, imaginem uero eius (quae est homo, ab ipso creata) nec per se ipsam esse, nec a se ipsa, nec in se ipsa subsistere, sed ab eo cuius imago est accepit esse secundum naturam, et deus esse secundum gratiam, caetera quoque omnia quae de deo praedicantur, de imagine eius praedicari posse, sed de deo essentialitate, de imagine uero participatione.*[46]

Eriugena's theology is rich in complementary ideas and schemes of analysis. He offers us several approaches to the human imaging of the divine.

## 3.2 God and the human as carriers of mutually exclusive predication: a first approach to creation in the image of God

In passages in the fourth book of *Periphyseon* Eriugena discusses the possibility of contrary predication in the case of predication of God. The way Eriugena does this is of interest from the point of view of his method. He does not plunge into a theoretical account of positive and negative theology (although he has clearly established this theoretical level of reflection in earlier books of *Periphyseon*). Rather he deals with a concrete case. He discusses the apparent contradiction between the words of Christ in Jn. 14:6 and the words of the Ps. Dionysius in *De mystica theologia.*[47] In the Johannine passage we read: 'I am the way, the truth, and the life'. In the Ps. Dionysius we read: 'neither is he knowledge or truth' (referring to God)[48]. A theoretical

---

[46] PP IV, CCCM CLXIV, 1473–1484, p. 54, (= PL 122 778A–B). See PP II, CCCM CLXII, 1900–1902, p. 81, (= PL 122 585A). The expression *"excepta subiecti ratione"* is influenced by a notion with which Eriugena was familiar from the *De hominis opificio* of GREGORY OF Nyssa. See PP IV, CCCM CLXIV, 2277–2284, p. 78, (= PL 122 796C): *"Ac sicut in aere charactera Caesaris imaginem euangelium dicit, per quod discimus iuxta quidem figuram similitudinem esse formati ad Caesarem, in subiecto uero differentiam habere, sic etiam secundum praesentem rationem imaginationum quae considerantur in diuina nature in humana etiam cogitantes, in his in quibus similitudo est, in subiecto differentiam inuenimis, quae in non creato et creato consideratur."* [Emphasis H. Mooney] Here Eriugena is quoting from the *De hominis opificio* in translation which uses the image of the coin in chapter 16 (17) to explain the difference between the image and the prototype. In that chapter GREGORY OF NYSSA explains the difference between image and prototype in terms of the one being created, the other not, with the ensuing consequences for mutability and immutability: *De hominis opificio,* GEORGE H. FORBES, (ed.), in: IDEM, *Sancti Patris Nostri Gregorii Nysseni Basilii Magni fratris quae supersunt omnia,* Vol.I, Burntsiland: Pitsligo, 1855, p. 102–318, here p. 204, (= PG 44 184 C). A critical edition of *De hominis opificio* is being prepared by H. Hörner for the *Gregorii Nysseni Opera* series. Since this edition is not yet available, the edition of G. H. FORBES has been used.

[47] PPV, PL 122, 1176B4–7, (= PG 3, 1048A3–6).

[48] It is interesting that Eriugena, like many other early writers, seems to regard the Ps Dionysius as a biblical authority as if we were here dealing with a clash in scriptural testimony.

resolution is later given through the speaker Alumnus in an account synopsising what had been established about positive and negative theology elsewhere[49].

Of interest is the application of the possibility of contrary predication to the case of the human as paradoxically animal and yet not animal.

*Quid igitur mirum si de homine, qui solus inter caetera animalia ad imaginem dei factus est, uere simul possit praedicari 'Homo animal est', 'Non est animal homo', ut per hoc saltem intelligamus ad imaginem dei illud animal specialiter esse conditum, de quo pugnantia sibimet in aliis animantibus proloquia uere simul praedicantur? Porro si propterea diuinae essentiae affirmationes et negationes conueniunt quoniam superat omnia quae ab ea facta sunt et quorum causa est, cui non liceat perspicere negationes et affirmationes imagini et similitudini eius, quae in homine est, unanimiter conuenire, quandoquidem superat caetera animalia, inter quae sub uno genere conditus est, et cuius causa condita sunt? Quis enim recte sapientum ignorarit hunc mundum uisibilem, cum omnibus suis partibus, a summo usque deorsum, propter hominem esse factum, ut ei praeesset, et dominaretur omnium rerum uisibilium ...*[50]

There is much worthy of comment in this passage. The attempt to present a parallel reason for the possibility of mutually exclusive predicates in the case of predication of God and that of the predication of the human is only convincing when one understands that God transcends the created realities which are metaphorically predicated of God. In comparison, the human transcends not only other individual animals, but the category of animal at all. Yet Eriugena's argumentation does not confine itself to this implicit comparison. The transcendence of God is also compared with the general transcendence of the human beyond all creation *as the final cause of that creation*. Further the passage also serves as a bridge to the next section of Eriugena's text where he will paraphrase Gregory of Nyssa's *De hominis opificio (De imagine)* on Gen. 1:26. "*Dixit enim deus: Faciamus hominem ad imaginem nostram et similitudinem, et dominetur piscium maris et bestiarum terrae et uolatilium caeli et pecorum et omnis terrae*"[51]. In Eriugena's as in Gregory's interpretation of this text the imaging of the divine is presented in terms of 'having dominion over others'. The passage which was quoted at length thus illustrates how multifaceted Eriugena's thinking can be, and indeed how the various strands of his thought are intertwined in his writing.

### 3.2 God and the human: in all things and beyond all things: a second approach to creation in the image of God

A further parallel between God and the human as created in the image of God is the observation that just as God is in all things and yet beyond all things, so too the human nature is its own world and yet it exceeds its own world[52]. This transcendence

---

[49] PP IV, CCCM CLXIV, 654–666, p. 25, (= PL 122 757D–758A).

[50] PP IV, CCCM CLXIV, 667–681, p. 25, (= PL 122 758A–B).

[51] See PP IV, CCCM CLXIV, textual addition number 8, pp. 25–25, (= PL 122 758C).

[52] "*Ut enim deus et super omnia et in omnibus est ..., ita humana natura in mundo suo (in subsistentia sua), in uniuersitate sua, in partibus suis uisibilibus et inuisibilibus, tota in seipsa est, et in toto*

of the human nature is the prerequisite for communion with God (*"Non enim aliter conditori suo adhaerere posset, si omnia quae sub ipso sunt et seipsam non excederet"*[53]). Note that this approach to the theme of the inherence of all things in the human, is already oriented to the cognitive level, to knowledge of God. Eriugena integrates the Johannine text, Jn. 12:26 *"Ubi ego sum, illic et minister meus"*, where even the idea of minister goes back to the domination of the human over the animal[54]. The master God is above all things and so thus the human clinging to God must also be above all things, even above him- or herself in so far as he or she is in all things: *"Est autem ille super omnia. Est igitur illi adhaerens homo super omnia et super seipsum, quantum in omnibus est."*[55] Eriugena is not attempting an abstract metaphysics in this passage but quickly adds the eschatological and salvation history perspectives. *"Et quamuis humana natura, dum in hac uita mortali uersatur, adhaerere deo re ipsa non possit, ueruntamen, quoniam possibile est ei et naturale creatori suo adhaerere eius gratia cui adhaeret, adhaerere non incongrui dicitur."*[56]

The train of thought takes its rise from the human created as animal and in the image of God. It quickly attained a preliminary endpoint in the knowledge of God. And yet we can observe the way in which the divine is held to be revealed in the human: not immediately (in the sense that the divine and the human are simply to be identified without any qualification). Rather the human is created in the image of the divine (this means the human reveals the divine to thinking creatures itself and to others); further its transcendence is the condition for communication with the divine.

The next step in Eriugena's argumentation is to affirm that the human's own world, (*'in mundo suo, in uniuersitate sua'*) is not only its body, but the world of created reality (*'in uniuerso mundo uisibili et inuisibili'*)[57]. He explains: *"Humana siquidem natura in uniuersitate totius conditae naturae tota est, quoniam in ipsa omnis creatura constituta est, et in ipsa copulata, et in ipsam reuersura, et per ipsam saluanda."*[58] All creation is established in the human and linked together, into it shall all return, and through it is all to be saved. The salvation history perspective of this sentence is striking. Eriugena is not presenting a purely philosophical notion of the inherence of all levels of being in the human, (the widespread notion of 'mi-

---

suo est, et in partibus suis tota, partesque eius in seipsis totae, et in toto totae. Nam et extrema pars eius et uilissima, corpus dico, secundum rationes suas tota est in toto homine, quoniam corpus, in quantum uere corpus est, in rationibus suis subsistit, quae in prima conditione factae sunt. Et cum in seipsa ita sit, humana uidelicet natura, totum suum excedit." PP IV, CCCM CLXIV, 696–708, pp. 26–27, (= PL 122 759A–B).

[53] PP IV, CCCM CLXIV, 709–710, p. 27, (= PL 122 759C).

[54] Quoted from PP IV, CCCM CLXIV, 713–714, p. 27, (= PL 122 759C–D).

[55] PP IV, CCCM CLXIV, 714–716, p. 27, (= PL 122 759D).

[56] PP IV, CCCM CLXIV, 716–719, p. 27, (= PL 122 759D).

[57] PP IV, CCCM CLXIV, 720 and following; pp. 27–28, (= PL 122, 760A).

[58] PP IV, SLH XIII, p. 42, 28–31; PL 122 760A.

crocosm'[59]), rather he is arguing that the creation of all things, and further, not just the eschatological perspective of a return of all things, but the *salvation* of all things happens through the human creature. He immediately introduces a scriptural quotation which gives him the chance to expand on this. He quotes Mk. 16:15–"*Praedicate euangelium omni creaturae*" and interprets this as meaning, preach the Gospel to all creatures in the human[60]. For he explains, in the human, intellect, reason, sense, seminal life and body are to be found. He then points out that he means the spiritual body, not the corruptible body which is the result of sin. Eriugena quotes 1 Cor. 15:43–44: "*Seminatur in contumelia, surget in gloria; seminatur corpus animale, surget corpus spirituale*" (it is sown in derision, it will rise in glory; it is sown an animal body, it will rise a spiritual body).[61] And unfolds the eschatology which he finds latent in these verses: an optimistic anthropological eschatology based on the conserving justice of God: "*Omne siquidem quod naturaliter in homine est creatum, necessario aeternaliter manet integrum atque incorruptum. Non enim diuinae iustitiae est uisum ex eo quod fecit quicquam perire, praesertim cum non ipsa natura peccauerit, sed peruersa uoluntas, quae contra naturam rationabilem irrationabiliter mouetur.*"[62] This is an eschatological principle which will recur and be explained in greater detail in book five: nothing of that which God has made shall perish.

Eriugena discusses the image in the animal and claims that the context within which this must be understood is that of the pre-fall / post-fall dynamic and the consequences this has for humanity, (especially for the corporeality of the human)[63]. He presents the fall as a case of deception: human nature did not wish to sin, but it was able to be deceived. The rational and intellectual nature was especially capable of deception when one considers that it was not yet in the state of perfection (*theosis*) which it would have attained had it shown obedience. He insists that the image of God is not ultimately damaged by inhering in an animal in the fallen state of sin. "*Non te igitur moueat quod de humana natura dictum est totam in seipsa ubique esse, et imaginem in animali totam, et animal in imagine totum. Omne siquidem quod in ea conditor suus primordialiter creauit, totum integrumque manet, adhuc tamen latet, reuelationem filiorum dei expectans.*"[64] He displays his understanding of the salvation in which fallen human nature is brought back to the revelation of God's children (Rom. 8:19). Speaking of human nature he holds before his readers' eyes the consoling perspective brought about by the hypostatic union: "*Sed dei sapientia, quae*

---

[59] Eriugena distances himself from this word and points out the danger it entails of reducing the human to what the human has in common with the rest of creation. In this he agrees with GREGORY OF NYSSA in *De hominis opificio*, chapter 11.

[60] Here PP IV, CCCM CLXIV, 727, p. 28, (= PL 122, 760A).

[61] As quoted in PP IV, CCCM CLXIV, 741–742, p. 28, (= PL 122 760B). English translation according to I. P. SHELDON-WILLIAMS / J. J. O'MEARA, SLH XIII. The Latin text of the scriptural quotation is not identical with the Vulgate.

[62] PP IV, CCCM CLXIV, 742–746, p. 28, (= PL 122 760 B–C).

[63] PP IV, CCCM CLXIV, 748–781, pp. 28–29, (= PL 122, 760C–761B).

[64] PP IV, CCCM CLXIV, 776–781, p. 29, (= PL 122 761B). Emphasis from Hilary Mooney.

*eam creauit, eamque in unitatem sibi substantiae accepit ut sic eam saluaret, cuncta liberauit miseria.*"[65]

The human was created an animal. Even before the fall the human was an animal: a spiritual and wise animal[66]. The Alumnus asks: The angels are not animals, why was the human created an animal? Thus a really systematic exposition (as opposed to an at times defensive exegesis of Genesis) of the creation of the human is required. The answer will involve a theological aesthetic in the true sense of this expression: a vision of a God who in freedom deems that it is good to appear, not only in an intellectual other (as would be the case if a hypostatic union with angelic nature had occurred) but in an other who includes a sensual aspect and who in its five-fold attributes spans the whole of created reality.

Eriugena's first short answer to the question is given by his speaker Nutritor: "*Quia ita uoluit eum condere, ut quoddam animal esset, in quo imaginem suam expressam manifestaret.*"[67] We immediately note the manifestative context of this answer. God wills to be imaged in an animal. The mirroring of God is given as a final cause for the creation of the human. A further key notion, the notion of the freedom of God, is further emphasised. He quotes from Rom. 11: 34 "*Quis enim cognouit sensum domini?*" and points out that we can never fathom why God chooses to act as God does.[68] Eriugena makes the distinction between relating *why* God has done what God has done (the knowledge of which is not in itself accessible to us) and, relating *what God has told us about what* God does. The fact that we are limited to what God has told us is a significant qualification of our knowledge of God. He proposes to expound this received information despite its limitation, and tells us: "*Omnem quidem creaturam uisibilem et inuisibilem in homine fecit, quoniam ipsi uniuersitas conditae naturae inesse intelligitur.*"[69] This inherence of all things in the human is a central point in the rationale of the imaging of God. The human creature is more suitable than the angelic creature for the function of imaging God because while there is nothing in the angel which is not also in the human[70] (i.e. intelligence, reason, spiritual body), the angel lacks the sensual body which relates the human to the creatures which are lower than it.

Having expressed the manifestational reason for creating the human being as an animal, Eriugena next turns to the ontological aspect. "*Propterea deus hominem in genere animalium uoluit substituere, quoniam in ipso omnem creaturam uoluit*

---

[65] PP IV, CCCM CLXIV, 774–776, p. 29, (= PL 122, 761A–B).

[66] PP IV, CCCM CLXIV, 782–817, pp. 29–30, (= PL 761B–762B). In this discussion both the Alumnus and the Nutritor speak.

[67] PP IV, CCCM CLXIV, 863–864, p. 32, (= PL 122 763C).

[68] Quoted from PP IV, CCCM CLXIV, 867, p. 32, (= PL 122 763C), see PP IV, 865–871, pp. 32–33, (= PL 122 763C–D).

[69] PP IV, 872–874, p. 33, (= PL 122 763D).

[70] Although this fact is, he claims, more easily understood of the risen human being.

*creare.*"[71] Yet the ontological and the manifestational levels are never to be separated in Eriugena.

In reply to the Alumnus' questioning on how all things were created in the human, and on how they subsist in the human,[72] Eriugena's speaker Nutritor steers the discussion to a consideration of how all things are in the human because the human has knowledge of all things[73]. In reason, intellect and indeed in imagination, the things are in a certain way created within the subject. These concepts (*notiones*) exist in the soul as something different to the things which they represent, indeed they are superior to the things of which they are the concepts[74].

If we summarise, albeit in the language of today, we can conclude that Eriugena understands the inherence of all things in the human creature in several related but distinct senses:

– all are in the human ontologically because human creature displays all of the five levels of activity;
– all are in the human in the sense that the human acts as an image of all things for other observers;
– all are in the human because the human subject itself understands all things.
– A further differentiation is added through considering the substantial definition of the human, and the question of the inherence of all things in the human is raised anew within this further context.

The Nutritor then reports the definition of the human as: "*Homo est notio quaedam intellectualis in mente diuina aeternaliter facta.*"[75] The concept of the human in the mind of God, and the substance realised in the existing human form a certain identity. The Alumnus says "*... intelligo non aliam esse substantiam totius hominis, nisi suam notionem in mente artificis, qui omnia priusquam fierent in seipso cognouit, ...*"[76] A similar 'definition' may of course be asserted of the notion of *any* thing, so in his speaker Alumnus, Eriugena goes on to report a more specific definition of the human: "*Homo est animal rationale, mortale, sensus et disciplinae capax.*" In a passage which is vitally important because it introduces much on Eriugena's understanding of the scope of substantial definition in general and that of the human in particular, the Nutritor denies however that this last definition is a substantial

---

[71] PP IV, CCCM CLXIV, 888–890, p. 33, (= PL 122 764B). In verses 30 to 32 Nutritor adds that just as the primary exemplar excels all by the excellence of God's essence, so its image excels all created things in dignity and grace.

[72] PP IV, CCCM CLXIV, 900–901, p. 34, (= PL 122 764C).

[73] PP IV, CCCM CLXIV, 941–943, p. 35, (= PL 122 765C).

[74] See the Nutritor's question in PP IV, CCCM CLXIV, 967–970, p. 36, (= PL 122 766A).

[75] PP IV, CCCM CLXIV, 1072–1073, p. 40, (= PL 122 768B).

[76] PP IV, CCCM CLXIV, 1066–1068, p. 40, (= PL 122 768B). See too PP IV, CCCM CLXIV, 1142–1143, p. 43, (= PL 122 770A). ("*... consequens ut et ipsa notio, qua seipsum homo cognoscit, sua substantia credatur.*")

definition. Rather it is a definition which concerns the specific accidents of the human nature.

*Nec uereor eos quo diffiniunt hominem non secundum quod intelligitur esse, sed ex his quae circa eum intelliguntur, dicentes: 'Homo est animal rationale, mortale, sensus et disciplinae capax', et quod est mirabilius, hanc diffinitionem oysiadem uocant, dum non sit substantialis, sed circa substantiam, ex his quae per generationem substantiae accidunt extrinsecus assumpta.*[77]

The substantial definition is the approximation of the limited intellect to the simple, comprehensive intuition of the nature of a thing which the divine intellect alone can attain. The passage just quoted continues:

*Notio nanque hominis in mente diuina nihil horum est. Ibi siquidem simplex est, nec hoc nec illud dici potest, omnem diffinitionem et collectionem partium superans, dum de ea esse tantum praedicatur, non autem quid sit. Sola etenim ac uera oysiades diffinitio est, quae solummodo affirmat esse, et negat quid esse.*[78]

Important is the denial that we humans can understand any substantial definition as to what a thing is, only that it is. The question can then arise is the human special in not being able to understand itself as to what it is? No thinking thing (besides God) can know what the substantial definitions of things are! All essences exhibit a certain unfathomableness. The uniqueness in the case of the human understanding (and ignorance) of what it is lies on the side of the subject. Unlike unthinking creatures the human can *realise* that it only knows that it is and cannot comprehend itself as God comprehends it. In Eriugena's thought this privileged ignorance will play a significant role in imaging the divine. All creatures demonstrate a unfathomableness with regard to their essences. This is a position which Eriugena found in Gregory of Nyssa. In his writings, as in Eriugena's, it bears witness to a creational ontology where each and every creatures carries within it the depths of its infinite creator. Only the thinking creature, in reflecting on this ignorance, can grasp something of the absolute incomprehensibility of the infinite divine essence.

A further point is that there is in the human a concept (*notio*) of all the sensible and intelligible things that the human mind can understand. Indeed this distinguishes the human from other creatures: "… *quod cunctorum, quae siue aequaliter sibi creata sunt siue quibus dominari praecipitur, datum est ei habere notionem.*"[79] This insight is offered in the context of an interpretation of Gen. 2:19: the task given to the human of naming all the animals would not have been possible without such a concept.

---

[77] PP IV, CCCM CLXIV, Textual addition number19, 88–93, p. 40, (= PL 122 768 B–C).

[78] PP IV, CCCM CLXIV, Textual addition number19, 93–97, p. 40, (= PL 122 768C). This definition of the human has a long history and belonged to the standard content of learning in Eriugena's circles. É. JEAUNEAU (ed.) / M. A. ZIER (assistance) Iohannis Scotti Periphyseon (De Diuisione Naturae), Liber Quartus, has a detailed endnote nr. 73, page 293–4 on the history of this definition of the human and Eriugena's objection that it is not a substantial definition.

[79] PP IV, CCCM CLXIV, 1081–1082, p. 41, (= PL 122 768C–D).

The consideration of the way that the *notio* or intelligible substance is said to be created in the human leads on to a renewed consideration of the human imaging of the divine. The intelligible substance of all things is said by the Nutritor to be created in the human. This 'being-created-in' is not merely ontological but Eriugena seems to be referring to an actual or potential knowledge of all things. This knowledge establishes a likeness to the divine mind of God (*ad similitudinem uidelicet mentis diuinae*)[80].

The history of the fall and the promise of salvation are however relevant factors influencing the possession of this knowledge. "*Quorum omnium uera cognitio humanae naturae insita est, quamuis adhuc inesse ei lateat seipsam, donec ad pristinam integritatem restituatur, in qua magnitudinem et pulchritudinem imaginis in se conditae purissime intellectura est, et nihil eam latebit ex his quae in se condita sunt, diuino lumine ambita et in deum conuersa, in quo omnia perspicue contemplabitur.*"[81] We may observe that *the restoration to the image of God* means here the realisation oneself of the knowledge of all things. This then, with a concomitant subjective perception thereof, is a human functioning in the image of God.

### 3.3 Ignorance and the imaging of the divine: a third approach to the human created in the image of God

Perhaps the most original way in which Eriugena presents the mirroring of the divine in the creation of the human is in terms, not of a latent conception of all things, but in terms of ignorance. In the following his understanding of the phenomenon of ignorance, his account of its relevance for the mirroring of God, and his analysis of its roots will be presented.

### 3.3.1 The extent of human ignorance of what the human is

Eriugena distinguishes between the substance as it exists in the primordial causes and the substance as the effect of these causes, that is, between the substance as an intelligible and the substance as a really existing reality[82]. He applies this distinction to the human. In so doing he does not say that the human has two substances, but rather one substance which may be conceived under two aspects (*unam dupliciter intellectam*)[83].

---

[80] See PP IV, CCCM CLXIV, 1095, p. 41 (= PL 122 769A). According to ERIUGENA not only the substances of things are in the human this way but also the differences and properties and accidents.

[81] PP IV, CCCM CLXIV, 1111 -1117, p. 41–42, (= PL 122 769B–769C).

[82] "*Et illa quidem substantia in sapientia dei constituta aeterna et incommutabilis est, ista uero temporalis et commutabilis; illa praecedit, ista sequitur; illa primordialis et causalis, ista procedens et causatiua; ...*", PP IV, CCCM CLXIV, 1164–1167, p. 43–44, (= PL 122 770C).

[83] PP IV, CCCM CLXIV, 1178, p. 44, (= PL 122 771A).

In a very interesting sentence Eriugena reflects on the cognitive accessibility and inaccessibility of the human substance when considered under the second aspect, that is, as a really existing effect of its primordial counterpart. "... *cognitio uero, qua seipsam in seipsa intelligit intellectualis et rationalis creatura, ueluti secunda quaedam substantia eius est, qua se nouit solummodo se nosse et esse.*"[84] We can observe that here it is again implied that the human does not know what it is. Yet, from a contemporary perspective we may observe that Eriugena does indeed assign the human quite a degree of knowledge of itself: it knows that it knows, it knows that it is! For some behaviourally oriented modern philosophers this would indeed be considered to be a knowledge of just what a thing the human is. Eriugena however explicitly rules out that the essence of the human is to be grasped either in the first way that the substance may be considered or in the second way.

*Vna itaque eademque ueluti duplex dicitur propter duplicem sui speculationem, ubique tamen suam incomprehensibilitatem custodit, in causis dico et in effectibus, hoc est, siue nuda in sua simplicitate siue accidentibus induta. In his enim omnibus nulli intellectui creato, neque sensui succumbit, nec a seipsa intelligitur quid sit.*[85]

The contemporary reader asks what importance the (residual) human ignorance of itself should have? Eriugena will use it to develop his most daring account of the human imaging of the divine.[86]

### 3.3.2 The imaging of the divine mind in the human experience of ignorance

A key passage which presents the knowing and not knowing on the part of the human mind occurs in *Periphyseon* book four and reads as follows:

*Humana siquidem mens et seipsam nouit et seipsam non nouit. Nouit quidem quia est, non autem nouit quid est.*[87]

Eriugena then claims that it is above all in this knowing that it is, but not knowing what it is, that the imaging of God is established in the human.

---

[84] PP IV, CCCM CLXIV, 1161–1164, p. 43, (= PL 122 770C).

[85] PP IV, CCCM CLXIV, 1186–1191, p. 44, (= PL 122 771A–B).

[86] The human is just as ignorant of the essences / substantial definitions of other creatures so the ignorance, which is due to the ontological depth of all created reality, is not something proper to its self-knowledge. The experience of ignorance is however proper on the part of human creature. Other creatures, non-thinking creatures do not grasp the extent and limitation of their self-knowledge / ignorance. God's ignorance of God's self is of a different calibre: it rests on the absolute infinity of God. Eriugena's system will also have to account for angelic self-knowledge. He proceeds as if the experience of self-ignorance is something special to the human and God. Yet the case of angels also seems to be a case where they know not what but that they are. Yet classically angels are not said to be created in the image of God. The answer to this problem in Eriugena's system seems to me to lie in an inadequate distinction between angelic nature and human nature in ERIUGENA's writings. See for example the Alumnus in PP IV, CCCM CLXIV, 1243–1247, p. 46, (= PL 122 772B–C) and the following discussion.

[87] PP IV, CCCM CLXIV, 1196–1197, p. 44, (= PL 122 771B).

*Ac per hoc, ut in prioribus libris docuimus, maxime imago dei esse in homine docetur.*[88]

Eriugena proceeds to explain how the imaging takes place and expands on the incomprehensibility of God of whom it can only be known that God exists:

*Ut enim deus comprehensibilis est dum ex creatura colligitur quia est, et incomprehensibilis est quia a nullo intellectu humano uel angelico comprehendi potest quid sit, nec a seipso, quia non est quid, quippe superessentialis, ita humanae menti hoc solum datur nosse se esse, quid autem sit nullo modo ei conceditur.*[89]

We observe that Eriugena makes the daring proposition that not even God (*nec a seipso*) knows 'what' God is.[90]

Eriugena also offers corroboration from some of his immediate sources for this position:

*Et quod est mirabilius, et considerantibus seipsos et deum suum pulchrius, plus laudatur mens humana in sua ignorantia, quam in sua scientia. Laudabilius nanque in ea est se nescire quid sit, quam scire quia sit, sicut plus et conuenientius pertinet ad diuinae naturae laudem negatio eius quam affirmatio, et sapientius est ignorare illam quam nosse, 'cuius ignorantia uera est sapientia', 'quae melius nesciendo scitur'.*[91]

The first quotation is from the Pseudo-Dionysius Areopagite, the second from Augustine.[92]

This imaging has of course limits:

---

[88] PP IV, CCCM CLXIV, 1197–1199, p. 44, (= PL 122 771B). ERIUGENA quotes the similar argumentation in the second half of chapter 11 of GREGORY OF NYSSA's *De hominis opificio*, in PP IV, CCCM CLXIV, 1918–1954, p. (= PL 122 788B–789A). For the heart of Gregory's argumentation that the mind in its incomprehensibility images the divine incomprehensibility, see *De hominis opificio*, G. FORBES, (ed.), p. 158, (= PG 44 156A–B):

οὐκοῦν ἐπειδὴ ἕν τῶν περὶ τὴν θείαν φύσιν θεωρουμένων ἐστὶ τὸ ἀκατάληπτον τῆς οὐσίας. ἀνάγκη πᾶσα καὶ τούτῳ τὴν εἰκόνα πρὸς τὸ ἀρχέτυπον ἔχειν τὴν μίμησιν ...

ἐπειδὴ δὲ διαφεύγει τὴν γνῶσιν ἡ κατὰ τὸν νοῦν τὸν ἡμέτερον φύσις, ὅς ἐστι κατ' εἰκόνα τοῦ Κτίσαντος, ἀκριβῆ πρὸς τὸ ὑπερκείμενον ἔχει τὴν ὁμοιότητα, τῷ καθ' ἑαυτὸν ἀγνώστῳ χαρακηρίζων τὴν ἀκατάληπτον φύσιν.

[89] PP IV, CCCM CLXIV, 1199–1204, pp. 44–45, (= PL 122 771B–C).

[90] Eriugena's immediate sources and the development which this notion undergoes in Eriugena's system is treated in detail in: H. MOONEY, "Johannes Scottus Eriugena. Kreativer Umgang mit dem Erbe der Tradition", in: *Freiburger Universitätsblätter* Heft 146 (1999) 39–51, esp. pp. 45–49; for a broader discussion see, Thomas BÖHM, "Unbegreiflichkeit (lat. *incomprehensibilitas*)", in: *Historisches Wörterbuch der Philosophie*, JOACHIM RITTER, KARLFRIED GRÜNDER und GOTTFRIED GABRIEL (ed.), völlig neubearbeitete Ausgabe des "*Wörterbuchs der Philosophischen Begriffe*" von RUDOLF EISLER, Bd. 11, U–V, Basel: Schwabe & Co., 112–115, for example p. 113: "*Mit Philon von Alexandrien setzt die Tradition der U. in der Gottteslehre ein.*"

[91] PP IV, CCCM CLXIV, 1205–1211, p. 45, (= PL 122 771C).

[92] See PSEUDO DIONYSIUS AREOPAGITA, *Epistula* 1, A. M. RITTER (ed.), p. 157, 3–5, (= PG 3 1065A–B; see PL 122 1177B)); AUGUSTINUS, *De ordine*, II, xvi, 44, WILLIAM M. GREEN (ed.), CCSL 29, Turnhout: Brepols, 1970, p. 131, 15–16, (= PL 32, 1015). The context in Augustine is however human ignorance before God.

*Apertissime ergo diuina similitudo in humana mente dinoscitur, dum solummodo esse scitur, quid autem est nescitur et, ut ita dicam, negatur in ea quid esse, affirmatur solummodo esse. Nec hoc ratione uacat. Si enim cognosceretur quiddam esse, circumscripta profecto in aliquo esset, ac per hoc, imaginem sui creatoris non omnino in se exprimeret, qui omnino incircumscriptus est et in nullo intelligitur, quia infinitus est, super omne quod dicitur et intelligitur superessentialis.*[93]

In my opinion the word '*omnino*' in the phrase '*omnino incircumscriptus est*' is important. It communicates the uniqueness of the divine nature. The human nature cannot be circumscribed by something else either, but it is not wholly unlimited. This important point must be explained in the coming paragraphs.

### 3.3.3 *Ignorance and its ontological root in infinity*

In his analysis of the roots of ignorance which Eriugena presents the limited similarities and the differences between the human situation, the situation of creatures in general, and the divine situation emerge. We can observe that the indefinability of God, the human and other creatures are explained in slightly different if related ways.

In the first place, Eriugena's position rests on the premise that no creature is able to be defined with respect to what it is, but only with respect to its accidents.[94] Secondly, when the Alumnus speaks of the concept of the human he says that because of its superior nature it is circumscribed by no finite substance. Further, of God is argued that of that which is the substance of all things we cannot have a definition[95].

Of the creature as such it is argued that since its very subsistence is rooted in the '*ratio*' by which it subsists in the primordial causes, it cannot be grasped as to what it is. Thus a theocentric reason for the unfathomableness of the creature as such clearly emerges[96]. But we may ask, what is the special situation of the human creature which is implicitly asserted in the mention of being made in the image of God?

---

[93] PP IV, CCCM CLXIV, 1211–1219, p. 45, (= PL 122 771C–D).

[94] "*Atque hinc datur intelligi nullius creaturae aliam subsistentiam esse, praeter illam rationem, secundum quam in primordialibus causis in dei uerbo substituta est, ac per hoc diffinire non posse quid sit, quia superat omnem substantialem diffinitionem; diffinitur autem per suas circumstantias, quae sibi accidunt, in speciem propriam per generationem seu intelligibilem seu sensibilem proueniens.*" PP IV, CCCM CLXIV, 1236–1242, (= PL 122 772B).

[95] And on unknowableness of God: RENÉ ROQUES, "'Valde artificialiter'. Le sens d'un contresens", in: *Libres sentiers vers l'Érigènisme*, Rome: 1975, 45–98.

[96] This aspect of all created reality has been well highlighted in the DIRK ANSORGE's study: *Johannes Scottus Eriugena. Wahrheit als Prozeß*. Compare BERNARD J. McGINN, "The Negative Element in the Anthropology of John the Scot", in: RENÉ ROQUES (ed.), *Jean Scot Érigène et l'histoire de la philosophie*, 315–326. McGinn writes: "What is original in John's doctrine of the unknowability of essence, is as M. Cristiani has pointed out …, the fact that it is not treated within the context of the intellect's return to God, but is rather a deduction from basic premisses about the ontological structure of the universe.", footnote nr. 4, p. 321. However when one considers Gregory of Nyssa as Eriugena's source for the unknowability of essence, then this ontological context seems not to be original but rather to be something that he inherited. McGinn refers here

Light on the unique foundation for the human as alone being created in the image of God is shed by Eriugena's reflection on limitation and lack of limitation.[97] He distinguishes between the '*omnino incircumscriptus*' of the Creator and the relative lack of limitation, the *nulla finita substantia circumcluditur* of the human[98]. Here we receive a clue to the uniqueness of the human creature. The case of the human is not unique in not being able to be substantially defined (this applies to all creatures), but the case of the human is unique in not being circumscribed by a finite substance, in not being defined *in something else*.

Thus the inherence of all other creatures in the human nature seems to be an intrinsic part of the unique incomprehensibility of the human creature in Eriugena's system. Human nature is not only incomprehensible because of its causation by an infinite God; it is also incomprehensible because of the inherence of all other creatures notionally and finally in it. This may be said of no other creature[99]. Not even of the angels[100]. Thus the point which explains the uniqueness of the human

---

to M. CRISTIANI, "Lo Spazio e il Tempo nell'Opera dell'Eriugena",in: *Studi medievali,* 3rd series, 14 (1973), 39–136, esp. pp. 40–54.

See also on the unknowableness of essence: TULLIO GREGORY, Note sulla dottrina delle 'teofanie', note 38.

[97] In his article, Pseudo-Dionysius, John Scotus Eriugena, Nicholas of Cusa, D. F. DUCLOW reflects on the unlimited, the limit and the limited.

[98] PP IV, CCCM CLXIV, 1211–1219, p. 45, (= PL 122 771C–D).

[99] "*Proinde non irrationabiliter iubemur credere et intelligere omnem uisibilem et inuisibilem creaturam in solo homine esse conditam, cum nulla substantia sit creata, quae in eo non intelligatur esse, nulla species, seu differentia, seu proprium, seu accidens naturale in natura rerum reperiatur, quae uel ei naturaliter non insit, uel cuius notitia in eo esse non possit;*" PP IV, CCCM CLXIV, 1286–1291, p. 48, (= PL 122 773D).

[100] ERIUGENA's theology of the angels is influenced by the angelology of Dionysius and by the ideas of Gregory of Nyssa on Paradise, the Fall and the last things. His theology is however ultimately his own. It is characterised by an incomplete distinguishing between the angelic and the human natures.

According to Eriugena the angelic and the human nature enjoy a mutuality (*reciprocam copulationem et unitatem*) which allows us to say that the angelic nature is created in the human and the human in the angelic, PP IV, CCCM CLXIV, 1565–1566, p. 56, (= PL 122 780A). If the human had not sinned this unity (*societas*) would have been even greater: "*Tanta quippe humanae naturae et angelicae societas fuerat – et fieret, si primus homo non peccaret – ut utraque unum efficeretur.*"PP IV, CCCM CLXIV, 1569–1571, p. 57, (= PL 122 780B). Further on he expresses this even more strongly: if the human had not sinned and not been hampered with the earthly body then, ERIUGENA says, the human would have been coessential ("*coessentialis (hoc est cointellectualis et corrationalis*))" PP IV, Jeauneau (ed.), CCCM CMLXIV, 1688–16889, (= PL 783A) with the angel. Even now, this union persists in eschatological promise: this is beginning to happen in what he calls the greatest of humans (*in summis hominibus*), whose first fruits are among the celestial natures: PP IV, CCCM CMLXIV, textual addition number 24, (= PL 780B). Underlying Eriugena's argumentation is the premise that if the human had not sinned it would have a different kind of body to the one we see today.

The 'being made in' is expressed in cognitive terms: the angel is made in the human through the understanding of the angel which is in the human and the human is in the angel through the knowledge of the human which is in the angel, PP IV, CCCM CLXIV, 1571–1574, p. 57, (= PL 122 780B). It is the mutual (*ratione reciprocae intelligentiae*) understanding which grounds the relation-

creature in it's imaging of God is best grasped when we simultaneously consider what I have called Eriugena's second argument for the human created as *imago dei* (the human in all things, beyond all things; a conception of all things in the human) and what I have called Eriugena's third argument for this imaging (the human is not defined in anything else; the human does not know what it is). It seems that the imaging of God exists in the event of not knowing what human nature is, but in being simultaneously aware that it is, or in Eriugena's own terminology knowing that but not what human nature is[101]. Expressed psychologically we may interpret this as the combination of being aware that one exists as a human, and not comprehending all the implications and presuppositions that this implies. On this subjective side it is not just a bare knowing that and not what. It is rather a becoming aware of something of what the human is, but not all that it is. To the positively intuited belongs the insight that all things are created in the human[102]. It is an experience of wonder at the ontological richness and giftedness and depth of human nature!

---

ship of being created in each other, PP IV, CCCM CLXIV, 1596–1597, p. 57, (= PL 780D); see too PP IV, CCCM CLXIV, 1691–1694, p. 60, (= PL 122 783A) (*"per mutuam cognitionem sibi inuicem inseruntur, ita ut et angelus in homine ueluti homo, et homo in angelo ueluti angelus, reciproco intellectu adunati simpliciqua ueritatis contemplatione formati, procreatur."*)

This incomplete distinguishing has consequences for his presentation of the human *alone* as created in the image of God. This position is more plausibly argued by him in certain approaches to the imaging of the divine than in others. In terms of the third approach, in terms of an imaging through ignorance, the unique position of the human is *not* clear for ERIUGENA implies that the intellectual nature (the angel) too knows that but not what it is: *"Nulla natura siue rationalis siue intellectualis est, quae ignoret se esse, quamuis nesciat quid sit."* PP I, CCCM CLXI, 2050–2052, p. 67, (= PL 122 490B).

[101] See B. MCGINN's reflection on the difference between 'being aware of' and 'knowing' a distinction which he finds implicit in Eriugena and which McGinn skilfully compares with similar distinctions in other theologians including some contemporary theologians, see "The Negative Element in the Anthropology of John the Scot", in: RENÉ ROQUES (ed.), Jean Scot Érigène et l'histoire de la philosophie, 315–326, esp. pp. 316, 322–325. "Knowing 'that it is' means being present to itself in consciousness, as is shown by John's many analyses of the structure of self-consciousness. … The Irishman's notion of *quia est* knowledge then is not as bare as might be thought. … Knowing *that* it is, namely, the conscious appropriation of the subject's self-presence, is essential to the constitution of created spirit.", pp. 322–323. McGinn compares Eriugena's thought to that of Rahner on the issue of human consciousness. A comparison with the epistemology of Bernard Lonergan might also be fruitful. McGinn only mentions Lonergan's historical work (BERNARD J. LONERGAN, *Verbum. Word and Idea in Aquinas*, FREDERICK E. CROWE (ed.), Toronto: University of Toronto Press, 1997, (= Collected Works of Bernard Lonergan; 2) not his systematic account of human knowing (BERNARD J. LONERGAN, *Insight. A Study of Human Understanding*, FREDERICK E. CROWE (ed.), 5. ed., revised and augmented, Toronto: Toronto University Press, 1992, (Collected Works of Bernard Lonergan; 3).

[102] This point is not developed by B. MCGINN who as the title suggests, concentrates in the article, "The Negative Element in the Anthropology of John the Scot" on the negative aspect of Eriugena's anthropology.

### 3.3.4 Human knowledge of the self in Eriugena

Self-knowledge is not a tidy chapter in any one book of Eriugena. Rather just what form of self-knowledge is possible according to the writings of Eriugena is something which academics must reconstruct through those hints which are dispersed throughout his writings. On the basis of a dialogue passage we may reconstruct what, from a contemporary perspective, might be called Eriugena's account of the *cogito*.[103] The Nutritor asks *Non eras ergo, priusquam scires uel nescires te esse?*[104] and with this question, he, in apprehension of an affirmative answer, asserts the concomitance of human being and knowing. The Alumnus' answer is clear: at one and the same time he received his being, and the knowledge that he was, and the understanding that he did not know what he was[105].

### 3.3.5 Human and divine knowledge of all things

Eriugena presents us with an extended account of what, in his opinion, the human being in its concrete reality in this sinful world knows. We see once again the theologically interested Eriugena tackling a question within the context suggested by his biblical faith. The human gets its knowledge in a general manner and secretly in the causes, that is in the creation in which all humans were made in their primordial causes[106]; secondly the human is said to receive knowledge of itself, in a special manner and manifestly in the effects, that is, when the individual humans proceed into the world. Yet in the concrete case, the case of fallen humanity, the human does not possess this perfect knowledge actually from birth onwards, but only potentially (*sola possibilitate*)[107].

And yet according to Eriugena this possibility is of significance. Once again he compares the human and divine situations. More precisely he compares the *sapientia creatrix* of God (that is the word of God) and *creata sapientia*. The divine vision and the human knowledge of all things before creation is said to be the very essence of the things. The essence of all things in the Word and the essence of all things in the human are not two things but one essence under two aspects. The divine

---

[103] See É. Jeauneau, "Le Cogito érigénien", in: *Traditio. Studies in Ancient and Medieval History, Thought, and Religion*, 50 (1995) 95–100. This excellent article reviews the textual basis in various manuscripts for the comparison between Eriugena and Descartes on the 'cogito'. It draws attention to the striking difference between the positions of the two authors: Descartes' *cogito* does not only discover *that* it is but *what* it is; Eriugena insists that the human cannot know what it is (pp. 103–4). Jeauneau also traces the triadic form of human knowledge that it exists which results in an imaging of the trinitarian God (pp. 106–110). Older literature includes: Brian Stock, "'Intelligo me esse'. Eriugena's 'Cogito'", in: René Roques (ed.), Jean Scot Érigène et l'histoire de la philosophie, pp. 327–334; B. Stock, The Philosophical Anthropology of Johannes Scottus Eriugena.

[104] PP IV, CCCM CLXIV, 1415, p. 52, (= PL 122, 776C).

[105] See PP IV, CCCM CLXIV, 1416–1417, p. 52, (= PL 122, 776C).

[106] PP IV, CCCM CLXIV, 1424–1424, p. 52, (= PL 122 776D). The Alumnus is speaking in the passage.

[107] Compare PP IV, CCCM CLXIV, 1502–1503, p. 54, (= PL 122 778C).

wisdom is the cause of the things that are. The human wisdom is itself caused by the divine wisdom. "*Et quemadmodum diuinus intellectus praecedit omnia et omnia est, ita cognitio intellectualis animae praecedit omnia quae cognoscit, et omnia quae praecognoscit est, ut in diuino intellectu omnia causaliter, in humana uero cognitione effectualiter subsistant.*"[108]

The next point is that the creation of no creature preceded the creation of the human, neither in time nor in space, nor in dignity nor in origin, nor in eternity nor in any order of precedence[109]. When one considers the creation of the human and that of all creatures which were created with it, or in it, or below it then one can say that in rank and honour the creation of the human has precedence though not in time and space. But the creation of man is simultaneous (*concreata est*) in knowledge and rank with the creation of those creatures which are the human's equals, the celestial essences.

*3.4 How the soul images the divine: a fourth approach to the imaging of God*

Eriugena raises the question, with respect to which part, or parts of the human the creation in the image of God takes place[110]. The Alumnus points out that it is not in respect of the body that the human is created in the image of God, but in respect of the soul. The historical debate whether in all parts or in its (i. e. the soul's) highest parts is referred to, and the conclusion said to have been reached in this scholarly controverse, namely, that the image lies in the highest part of the soul is reported[111]. This 'part' has already been presented in *Periphyseon* as the root of intelligence with its threefold structure of intelligence, reason and interior sense. However, Eriugena through the Alumnus, points out that it is not accurate to speak of various 'parts' of the human soul. Rather the one soul has a variety of functions: intellect, reason, interior sense, exterior sense and vital motion[112]. The Alumnus says of the soul "… *non illius partium diuersitas (si tamen partes in ea esse dicendum est), sed administrationum ac motuum uarietas (motus quippe eius partes eius sunt) diuersas intelligentias in anima faciunt.*"[113]. The whole soul is accordingly present wherever one of these functions is exercised.[114]

Eriugena thus concludes that the whole soul is created in the image of God:

*Hinc datur intelligi totam animam humanam ad imaginem dei factam, quia tota intellectus est intelligens, tota ratio disputans, tota sensus et sentiens, tota uita et uiuificans.*[115]

---

[108] PP IV, CCCM CLXIV, 1531–1535, p. 55, (= PL 122 779 B–C).

[109] PP IV, CCCM CLXIV, 1550–1556, p. 56, (= PL 122 779D).

[110] Alumnus' exposition commences in PP IV, CCCM CLXIV, 1854, p. 66, (= PL 122 786D).

[111] PP IV, CCCM CLXIV, 1858–1862, p. 66, (= PL 122 786D–787A).

[112] PP IV, CCCM CLXIV, 1886–1892, p. 67, (= PL 122 787C–787D).

[113] PP IV, CCCM CLXIV, 1881–1884, p. 67, (= PL 122 787B).

[114] PP IV, CCCM CLXIV, 1903–1904, p. 67, (= PL 122 788A). ERIUGENA makes a reference to GREGORY OF NYSSA's *De imagine*, whose influence on him in this point is noteworthy.

[115] PP IV, CCCM CLXIV, 1905–1907, pp. 67/68, (= PL 122 788A).

The consideration of the imaging of the divine and the parts of the human (Eriugena, as we have already pointed out, distances himself from the possibility of speaking of 'parts' of the soul, is less reluctant to speak of 'parts' of the human)[116] leads Eriugena to speak of the role of the soul in the imaging of the divine.

Through the Alumnus he recapitulates the two ways in which human *soul* may be especially said to be made in the image of God. Just as God is said to be diffused through all things but may not be comprehended by any of them, so too the soul is said to be diffused through the body but not contained by it. The second way is through the already familiar phenomenon of knowing that but not what it is:

*Primo quidem quod, sicut deus per omnia quae sunt diffunditur et a nullo eorum potest comprehendi, ita anima totum sui corporis organum penetrat, ab eo tamen concludi non ualet; secundo uero quod, quemadmodum de deo praedicatur solummodo esse, nullo modo autem diffinitur quid sit, ita humana anima tantummodo intelligitur esse, quid autem sit, nec illa ipsa nec alia creatura intelligit …*[117]

### 3.5 Human willing: a fifth approach to the imaging of the divine

In his early work *De diuina praedestinatione liber* Eriugena speaks of the gift of human freedom as something particularly praiseworthy, a gift given to no other animal:

*Cui debemus ineffabiles gratias reddere, non solum quod naturam nostrae mentis bonitatis suae copia condiderit rationalem, liberam, uoluntariam, mobilem, sed quod nobis largitatis suae munere concessit, proprio nostro nutu rationabiliter, libere, uoluntarie posse non mouere. Qui motus nulli animalium praeter hominem concessus est.*[118]

Furthermore, in that work Eriugena explicitly speaks of the gift of free will in the context of the imaging of the divine:

*Non enim aliter debuit fieri rationalis uita nisi uoluntaria, cum ab ea uoluntate quae est causa omnium creata sit ad imaginem et similitudinem sui. Aut quomodo eam diuina uoluntas, summa uidelicet uniuersitatis ratio, quae nulla necessitate stringitur, quoniam sua liberrima potentia potitur, imaginem sui similem faceret, si non eius substantiam crearet uoluntatem liberam rationalem?*[119]

A human free rational will is here presented as a prerequisite for the human imaging of the free God.

However, in *Periphyseon* this unique function of human freedom falls into the background. It is mentioned in passing in book five but it does not receive the same

---

[116] PP IV, CCCM CLXIV, p. 18446–1847, p. 66, (= PL 122 786C): "… *homo, dum sit unus, ueluti ex multis partibus compositus est …*".

[117] PP IV, CCCM CLXIV, 1909–1915, p. 68, (= PL 122 788A).

[118] *De diuina praedestinatione liber,* chapter 8, 159–165, G. MADEC (ed.), p. 53, (= PL 122 388 B–C).

[119] *De diuina praedestinatione liber,* chapter four, 157–164, G. MADEC (ed.), p. 31, (= PL 122 373 A–B).

attention as other approaches to the human as created in the image of God[120]. How are we to explain this apparent neglect of a very privileged human capacity?

One possible explanation may be the concrete perspective of *Periphyseon*. An abstract freedom is not here the focus of attention, but rather willed activity on the part of the human is viewed as the capacity to cooperate with grace, to fall in with God's plans.

In book four of *Periphyseon* there occurs a very interesting presentation of the willed activity of the human[121]. The context is that of human participation in the divine omnipotence, something which Eriugena holds to have been possible if the human had not sinned[122]. The focus falls on an adherence and conformation to the divine will as normative voluntary activity. The moment of 'freedom', so highly valued in *De diuina praedestinatione liber* and in *De hominis opificio* of Gregory of Nyssa is played down here[123]. Eriugena speaks of the human being turned to (*conuersa*) the divine omnipotence and of the ideal case of adhering completely to the creator (*ei omnino adhaereret*). If it had not sinned the human would have willed as God willed in all situation. It would thus participate in the divine omnipotence, and in doing so effect an imaging of the divine.

*Quicquid enim in natura rerum fieri uellet, necessario fieret, quippe dum nil aliud fieri uellet, praeter quod creatorem sui fieri uelle intelligeret; creatoris autem sui uoluntatem omnipotentem incommutabilem omnino intelligeret, si ei omnino adhaereret eumque non desereret, ne sibi dissimilis esset – et caetera quae recta ratione de deo eiusque imagine intelligi uel cogitari uel praedicari possunt.*[124]

In *Periphyseon* it is not the moment of freedom, but of the realisation of that freedom in conformity to the will of a higher being, of God, is emphasised. Now 'conformity to the will of God' is a notion which names an imaging of the divine, only mediately, that is through a consideration of the participation in the divine omnipotence it entails. Thus concrete right willing is a rather complicated candidate for effecting an imaging of God. It was, in my opinion, above all, the concrete perspective adopted in the fourth book of *Periphyseon,* which deterred Eriugena from considering an abstract notion of freedom or an extensive consideration of human willing within his analysis of the human created in the image of God in that work.

---

[120] In *Periphyseon* book V, 4835–4838, p. 149, (= PL 122 966D), we read: "*Si enim libertas naturae rationabilis ad imaginem dei conditae a deo data est – non enim imago dei ullis legibus detineri debuit coacta – …*"

[121] PP IV, CCCM CLXIV, 1473–1497, p. 54, (= PL 122 778A–778C).

[122] PP IV, CCCM CLXIV, 1489–1491, p. 54, (= PL 122 778B).

[123] See H. A. Mooney, The Notion of the Liberality of God in Gregory of Nyssa and Johannes Scottus Eriugena. Compare Gregory of Nyssa, *De hominis opificio*, G. Forbes (ed.), chapter 17, p. 202, ἕν δὲ τῶν πάντων καὶ τὸ ἐλεύθερον ἀνάγκης εἶναι …

[124] PP IV, CCCM CLXIV, 1491–1497, p. 54, (= PL 122 778B–C).

## 3.6 Imaging in terms of triads in the mind: a sixth approach to the imaging of the divine

In addition, the creation of the human in the image of God is presented by Eriugena in trinitarian terms. The imaging of the trinity in various triads to be found in the human has already been commented on by many writers in the theological and philosophical traditions before him. Thus this approach to the imaging of the divine is not Eriugena's most original contribution to the issue. Accordingly it is only treated briefly here.

Eriugena calls on several triads as an analogy for the blessed trinity. Thus in the fourth book of *Periphyseon* we are lead into a reflection on the case of the liberal arts and the assertion that the mind (*mens*) and its skill (*peritia*) and its discipline (*disciplina*) are of the same substance. This triad too is said to form a kind of a trinity. Further, "*Mens itaque et peritiam et disciplinam suam intelligit, et a sua peritia suaque disciplina intelligitur, non quid, sed quia est; aliter enim coessentialis et coaequalis trinitas non erit.*"[125] In an endnote Édouard Jeauneau has pointed out that the words meaning 'though not as to what it is, but as to that it is', so important for the issue of the extent of the analogy, are likely a textual addition[126]. This trinity is said to be created by a higher nature, by God. Only God has the true concept (*notitia uera*) of the trinity (*mens, peritia, disciplina*) in the human, for this trinity was formed by God and for God[127].

One particularly clear presentation of imaging of the trinitarian God in the human is presented in the second book of *Periphyseon*.[128] Here he states that the divine trinity is revealed in three motions of the human soul[129]. The likeness of the Father is reflected by the intellect (*intellectus*) or mind (*animus*), that of the Son in the reason (*ratio*) and that of the Spirit in sense (*sensus*).[130] Eriugena explicitly

---

[125] PP IV, CCCM CLXIV, 1047–1049, p. 39, (= PL 122 767D).

[126] PP IV, SLH XIII, endnote 71, p. 292.

[127] PP IV, CCCM CLXIV, 1060–1062, p. 39, (= PL 122 768A).

[128] PP II, 1670–1714, pp. 72–73, (= PL 122 579A–580A).

[129] PP II, CCCM CLXII, 1678–1679, p. 71 (= PL 122 579B). Here Eriugena speaks of a likeness (*similitudo*): "*Patris siquidem in animo, filii in ratione, sancti spiritus in sensu apertissima lucescit similitudo.*"

[130] Édouard Jeauneau has a lengthy endnote on this triad in PP IV, SLH XIII, endnote nr. 4, p. 278–279. He points out that the words 'in mind, reason and sense' have been added in the hand of i¹ in the manuscript of Rheims (f. 264 v). This marginal addition emphasises that the human has been created in the image of the *triune* God. Jeauneau gives an account of various triads in the philosophical and theological tradition before Eriugena and points out that for Eriugena they coincide. "The three terms of the Augustinian triad, *esse, uelle, scire,* correspond to those of the Neoplatonic triad, *essentia, uirtus, operatio: Periphyseon* V, 942A–B. In its turn, this last triad coincides with that of the faculties of knowledge. Mind (νοῦς, *mens*) corresponds to being (οὐσία, *essentia*), Reason (λόγος, *ratio*) corresponds to power (δύναμις, *uirtus*), Interior Sense (διάνοια) corresponds to operation (ἐνέργεια, *operatio*): *Periphyseon* II, 570 A–C. These three faculties of knowledge are in man a created image of the Creating Trinity. The Creating Trinity is Father, Son, Holy Spirit; the created trinity is Mind, Reason, Sense: *Periphyseon* II, 567A–580A."

refers to the revealing of God through this triad as the image of God in mind and reason and sense.[131] In his account of the imaging in book two through his speaker the Alumnus, Eriugena is, however, careful to point out, that the trinity in human nature is not itself the image of God, but is made in the image of God: "... *quae non imago dei est sed ad imaginem dei condita – sola enim uera imago inuisibilis dei est et in nullo dissimilis unigenitum dei uerbum patri et spiritui coessentiale – ...*"[132]

Eriugena draws on differing triads[133]. Édouard Jeauneau has pointed out that the various triads "coincide" in Eriugena's understanding and lists the places in *Periphyseon* where the corresponding elements in each triad are identified with each[134]. More important than the choice of the elements in the triad is the fact that the imaging of the divinity is conceived of in trinitarian terms at all and a recurring moment of condescension and divine initiative in the imaging which recurs independently of which triad is currently being employed. Thus in book two the *way* in which the appearing of God is presented in the passage at hand is more important than which three aspects of the human to which the imaging is assigned. The infinite divine goodness, itself beyond all creatures and unknowable to them, is said to descend through its image and likeness and to become known and 'comprehensible' and present and to appear in human nature. The divine initiative in this appearing is highlighted through the foregoing emphasis on the fact that God is in God'sself unknowable and through the metaphors Eriugena uses for the condescension to becoming known. He uses the images of cleaning the mirror, or to change the metaphor, of God impressing God's traces upon the image, thereby emphasising both the divine initiative and the processual nature of appearing[135].

### 3.7 *The imaging of God within the economy of salvation*

Certain aspects of the theme of the appearing of God in the human, the creature created in the image of God, change in Eriugena's hands when he considers the dynamic of the fall and the return of creation to God. We see this in Eriugena's interpretations of the biblical accounts of original paradise. The biblical paradise

---

[131] At the start of book four of *Periphyseon* he reviews his treatment of this triad in book three and says he has given an account of "*deque deo eiusque imagine*" PP IV, CCCM CLXIV, 54, p. 4 and in textual addition number 1 on the same page, he continues "*in animo et ratione et sensu*" (= PL 122 743C).

[132] PP II, CCCM CLXII, 1718–1721, pp. 73–74, (= PL 122 580A–B).

[133] See É. JEAUNEAU, Le Cogito érigénien, esp. pp. 107–110 where Jeauneau deals with the imaging of the trinity. Jeauneau points out that only the human creature has the three fold structure in its knowing faculties which mirrors the trinitarian God: "Car si l'on ne peut nier que l'ange porte en lui-même une divine similitude, l'Écriture ne dit pas qu'il a été créé à l'image de Dieu ... L'ange possède les deux facultés supérieures, intellect et raison, mais il lui manque la troisième, à savoir la sensibilité. La nature angélique n'a donc pas été dotée de cette trinité des facultés de connaisance qui, en la nature humaine, est l'image de la Trinité créatrice." p. 109.

[134] PP IV, SLH XIII, endnote nr. 4, p. 278, quoted above.

[135] PP II, CCCM CLXII, textual addition number 145, 589–593, (= PL 122 579A–B).

is identified with the human nature created in the image of God. The human according to Eriugena never fully loses this imaging. Eriugena illustrates this by the enduring presence of God to the human expressed in the Genesis sentence that the Lord walked in the garden. The Lord's walking in Paradise is presented as God's presence in the human made in God's image. Eriugena invites us to hear Ambrose' account:

> *Audi etiam eundem de domini dei deambulatione in paradiso, humana uidelicet natura, quam ad imaginem suam condidit, quam nunquam deseruit neque perire permisit, in qua semper deambulat occulte ac spiritualiter, scrutans corda singulorum et renes, intelligibilique uoce causas praeuaricationis interrogans, et plus misericorditer increpans et corrigens, quam iuste ulciscens.*[136]

The fall did however, in his opinion, occasion changes and these ensuing changes are most noticeable in the case of the third approach to the human imaging of the divine, that is, in the matter of human knowledge and ignorance.

Eriugena argues that as a result of the fall, the human imaging of the divine is severely impaired. The human lacks the knowledge it would have possessed if it had not sinned. The Alumnus explains that the knowledge which remained in the human after the fall is presented as a desire for happiness: *'appetitus beatitudinis'*[137]. If the human had not sinned he and she would not have fallen into such a depth of ignorance. Our saviour was born without sin and is said to have knowledge of himself and of all things from the very beginning of the incarnation event. This wisdom, and indeed the whole humanity of the Word incarnate, is said to possess a redemptive function.

> *Ipse siquidem qui solus absque peccato natus est in mundo, redemptor uidelicet mundi, nusquam nunquam talem ignorantiam perpessus est, sed confestim ut conceptus et natus est, et seipsum et omnia intellexit, ac loqui et docere potuit, non solum quia sapientia patris erat, quam nil latet, uerum etiam quia incontaminatam humanitatem acceperat, ut contaminatam purgaret, non quia aliam acceperit praeter eam quam restituit, sed quia ipse incontaminatus in ea remansit, et ad medicamentum uulneris uitiatae naturae in secretissimis ipsius rationibus reseruatus. Tota quippe in totus perit, praeter illum in quo solo incorruptibilis permansit.*[138]

Through what he calls the general return, the human can be restored to the level of imaging of God which was originally planned for it. In addition to this, through the deification which is involved in what he calls the special return, it can attain to a level of blessedness which is way beyond anything which it could expect as a creature. The human imaging of the divine is thus embedded within a dynamic which in the final consummation, not only of a general, but in particular of the special return, leads human nature on to unexpected heights. Here Eriugena will eventually cease

[136] Quoted from PP IV, CCCM CLXIV, 4276–4282, p. 140, (= PL 122 840B); see AMBROSIUS, *De paradiso*, XIV, 68, (CSEL 32, 1, pp. 325–326).
[137] See PP IV, CCCM CLXIV, 1467–1468, p. 53, (= PL 122 777D).
[138] PP IV, CCCM CLXIV, 1446–1456, p. 53, (= PL 122 777B–C).

to speak the language of imaging. Among the expression he implements instead are the notion of deification or that of receiving the highest theophanies.

All return to their first principle, be that sensible or intelligible. The human nature returns to its principle which he calls the Word of God in which it was created and immutably subsists and lives. Eriugena points out that God is the principle of all things, not just the human, but of all sensible and intelligible things. We should not doubt that the human returns to God, especially because the human never issued forth in such a way as to abandon the Principle from which it came. He quotes "in Him we live and move and have our being"[139]. He immediately proceeds into a theology of our relationship to this first principle, to God. Leaving God is not just the case of being created but the losing of a degree of likeness through sin *"sed quod quadam dissimilitudine propter peccatum decolorata est, dicitur recessisse."*[140] He brings in the case of the creation in the image of God, of the fall, of the return with the help of grace in concrete salvation-history terms. Drawing nearer and pulling away are represented, not in creational terms, nor (as he explicitly excludes) in local terms, but in the spiritual terms of knowledge and virtue *"Non enim gressibus corporis, sed affectibus mentis elongatur a deo, aut ei appropinquatur."*[141] He then introduces the simile of leprosy. He uses this to point out that like the physical illness, the spiritual illness may be healed, (by grace) and that the image of God is never completely lost through sin. The form created by God cannot be lost, it remains immutable although it is possible for it to acquire corruptible qualities through sin. In support he then quotes from Gregory of Nyssa's *De hominis opificio* chapter 27 on the human returning where the story of the ten lepers is used. He claims that the quote demonstrates that the natural form of the body is incorruptible and immutable *"... Nyseus astruit quod non solum forma animae ad imaginem Dei facta, verum etiam naturalis forma corporis, quae imaginem animae imitatur, semper incorruptibilis et incommutabilis permaneat."*[142] He then harvests all that he can on the human return from the metaphor of leprosy as it occurs in the biblical story. The Syrian is said to stand for human nature, Syria for the heavenly contemplation which would have been the human lot if it had not sinned. Our Elijah is said to be Jesus Christ. The ten lepers bear the characteristics of our nature which is being daily redeemed in individuals. We can observe the processual, step-by-step tone in the following quotation. *"Quid dicam de decem leprosis? Num et ipsi eiusdem nostrae naturae charactera gessere, quae a suo redemptore redempta est, et cotidie in singulis redimitur, et in consummatione mundi uniuersaliter in omnibus et redimetur et liberabitur?"*[143] The body is said to consist of the four material elements and the form which 'informs' them. The soul is said to have a five-fold nature: mind, reason, the two-fold sense and vital motion.

---

[139] PP V, 492–493, p. 18, (= PL 122 871D), quoting from Acts 17: 28.
[140] PP V, 494–495, p. 18, (= PL 122 871D).
[141] PP V, 496–498, p. 18, (= PL 12 871D).
[142] PP V, 537–541, pp. 19–20, (= PL 122 872D).
[143] PP V, 589–593, p. 21, (= PL 122 873D–874A).

This decad will be reduced to a monad, to mind alone. "*Tota siquidem humana natura in solum intellectum refundetur, ut nil in ea remaneat praeter illum solum intellectum, quo creatorem suum contemplabitur.*"[144] This is his interpretation of the return of one leper alone to give thanks.

In the case both of good humans and of evil humans their human nature is said to remain essentially undamaged both in the fall and in their fate after death.[145] No one will be excluded from the participation in the gifts of the Father of lights which flow from the plenitude of the divine Goodness[146]. He distinguishes, however, between that return which accrues to the creature as such, the general return, and the special return. In the case of the human creature he accordingly distinguishes between its restoration to a state of imaging God "... *eandem humanam naturam in suam gratiam quam peccando perdiderat (diuinae uidelicet imaginis dignitatem) restitui ...*" and, on the other hand, the deification of the blessed "... *super omnem humanitatis uirtutem deificari, eoque modo semper ac beate uiuere et super omnia quae sunt exaltari.*"[147]

Eriugena's biblical eschatology received an important impetus from Gregory of Nyssa. In his reading and translation of *De hominis opificio* Eriugena encountered an account of the creation, fall and eschatological hope of the human creature. The creation of the human in the image of God was presented within Gregory's understanding of salvation history. This salvation history perspective is one which Eriugena made his own. This perspective has consequences for the imaging of the divine in the creation of the human. If the human had not sinned the imaging of God would have been more perfectly realised in the human: the knowledge of all things in the human would, for example, not only be potentially but actually. One significant difference which receives much attention is the question of sexual division, the division into man and woman.

Eriugena approaches this theme first by extensive quotation of *De hominis opificio* chapter 16 and 17 on the matter through his speaker Alumnus, secondly by the ratification of what has been quoted by his speaker Nutritor[148]. If the human had not sinned he / she would have been like the angels. The eschatological return is also to an angel like life. Had humankind not sinned, human multiplication would have been similar to that of the angels.

Gregory's theory of the two-fold creation is presented. This theory rests on an interpretation of the words of scripture: Gen. 1:27: *fecit deus hominem; secundum*

---

[144] PP V, 610–612, p. 22, (= PL 122 874B).

[145] On their fate after death see PP V, 3860–3862, p. 120, (= PL 122 946A).

[146] PP V, 3866–3870, p. 120, (= PL 122 946 A–B).

[147] PP V, 3987–3993, pp. 123–124, (= PL 122 948D–949A).

[148] The Alumnus quotes extensively from chapter 16 and 17 as numbered in the edition of G. FORBES, ERIUGENA calls them chapter 17 and 18, PP IV, CCCM CLXIV, 2141–2384, p. 74–81, (= PL 122 794C–799A); Nutritor appropriates the teaching as Eriugena's own, PP IV, CCCM CLXIV, 2385–2413, p. 81–82, (= PL 122 799A–C).

*imaginem dei fecit eum, masculinum et feminam fecit eos*[149]. Gregory distinguishes between what is said to be the state of being created in the image of God and the so called unhappy state in which human nature now exists, that is, divided into the sexes. A further scriptural basis for this theory is given in the text Gal. 3:28: *In Christo Iesu neque masculus neque femina est.* (For in Christ there is no man or woman). Sexual differentiation is clearly said to be outside of the principle image. Gregory speaks of a double fashioning of the human nature, one by which we are assimilated to God, the other by which we are divided by the sexual differentiation. Sexual division is alien to God[150]. The fact that the sexual differentiation is mentioned second shows, according to Gregory, that it is something added to the human.

The Nutritor confirms in his own words what Alumnus has presented in Gregory of Nyssa's words. He reports as Gregory's the position that the human is created in the image of God with respect to the mind and its innate powers only (*solo*).[151] All humans were created at once and together (*semel et simul*) in the one (first) human and in whom all sinned. All were driven out of paradise in the first human. Sexual differentiation is the consequence of sin. Had the human not sinned, its form of multiplication would be that of the angels. But because God foresaw the sin of the first human, God therefore added another form of multiplication to the human nature. Eriugena through the Nutritor, mentions that this form of multiplication is also a penalty; in Gregory's writings its remedial aspect is more strongly emphasised. Eriugena clearly states as his own opinion that sexual differentiation does not pertain to the image of God: "*Quae diuisio omnino diuinae naturae imaginis et similitudinis expers est; et nullo modo esset, si homo non peccaret, …*"[152] After the general resurrection it will not persist.

## 3.8 The liberality of God: why is the human created in the image of God?

The divine initiative in appearing in the creation of the human in the image of God is rooted in the divine goodness and generosity[153]. According to Eriugena God, 'the more than fullness and perfection', grants gifts which descend from above from the Father of Lights, and flow out through all things from the widely flowing fullness of the divine goodness[154]. In the context of the divine 'motivation' for the creation of the human in the image of God, the question of Eriugena's inspiration through

---

[149] Quoted from PP IV, 2191–2192, p. 76, (= PL 122 794C).

[150] PP IV, CCCM CLXIV, 2218, p. 76, (= PL 122 795B).

[151] PP IV, CCCM CLXIV, 2385–2388, p. 81, (= PL 122 799A).

[152] PP IV, CCCM CLXIV, 2396–2397, p. 82, (= PL 122 779B).

[153] See H. A. MOONEY, The Notion of the Liberality of God in Gregory of Nyssa and Johannes Scottus Eriugena.

[154] In the context of the eschatological return of all creatures to God ERIUGENA writes that the goods which human nature shall share "*sola diuinae bonitatis largiflua plenitudine omnibus per omnia uniuersaliter inexhausta effusione manant.*" PP V, 3873–3874, p. 120, (= PL 122 946B).

earlier sources arises. The source which immediately suggests itself is the *De hominis opificio* of Gregory of Nyssa. In addition to the translation of this work by Eriugena we witness his quotation (in Latin) from *De hominis opificio* within the *Periphyseon*. Jeauneau has pointed out that about 25% of the text is quoted in *Periphyseon*[155]. Cappuyns has pointed out that in addition to quoting from *De hominis opificio* Eriugena often paraphrases passages from the work.[156] When we take Jeauneau's observation that more than 76% of this quoting takes place within book four of *Periphyseon* into account we can see why his use of the text is of importance in his anthropology[157]. The influence of *De hominis opificio* on Eriugena is thus handled within our account of his understanding of the appearing of God in the human person. Now the influence of the work of the Cappadocian on six approaches to the mirroring of the divine in the human creature has already been mentioned within my account of these approaches. I shall however argue that the greatest debt that Eriugena owes to Gregory of Nyssa in the issue of the human created as *imago dei* is not his influence on a particular approach (for example, imaging through ignorance, or imaging and various triads) but rather his provision of a theological context within which this imaging occurs at all. I argue that Eriugena is heir to a presentation of the creation of the human in the image of God *within a theology of the divine goodness and generosity*. Let us look at the key passages:

θεὸς τῇ ἑαυτοῦ φύσει πᾶν ὅτι πέρ ἐστι κατ᾿ ἔννοιαν λαβεῖν ἀγαθὸν, ἐκεῖνό ἐστι – μᾶλλον δὲ, παντὸς ἀγαθοῦ τοῦ νοουμένου τε καὶ καταλαμβανομένου ἐπέκεινα ὤν, οὐ δι᾿ ἄλλό τι κτίζει τὴν ἀνθρωπίνην ζωὴν ἢ διὰ τὸ ἀγαθὸς εἶναι· τοιοῦτος δὲ ὤν, καὶ διὰ τοῦτο πρὸς τὴν δημιουγίαν τῆς ἡμετέρας φύσεως ὁρμήσας, οὐκ ἂν ἡμιτελῆ τὴν τῆς ἀγαθότητος ἐνεδείξατο δύναμιν, τὸ μέν τι δοὺς ἐκ τῶν προσόντων αὐτῷ, τοῦ δὲ φθονήσας τῆς μετουσίας· ἀλλὰ τὸ τέλειον τῆς ἀγαθότητος εἶδος ἐν τούτῳ ἐστὶν, ἐκ τοῦ καὶ παραγαγεῖν τὸν ἄνθρωπον ἐκ τοῦ μὴ ὄντος εἰς γένεσιν, καὶ ἀνενδεᾶ τῶν ἀγαθῶν ἀπεργάσασθαι·[158]

God is in His own nature all that which our mind can conceive of good; – rather, transcending all that we can conceive or comprehend of good, God creates human life for no other reason than that He is good; and being such, and having this as His reason for entering upon the creation of our nature, God would not exhibit the power of His goodness in a half-perfect form, giving our nature some one of the things at His disposal, and grudging it a share in another: but the perfect form

---

[155] "On constate d'abord que, sur les 2663 lignes que comporte cette édition, 537 sont citées textuellement dans le Periphyseon. En d'autres termes, un quart environ du De imagine est passé, mot pour mot, dans le dialogue érigénien.", Édouard JEAUNEAU, "La division des sexes chez Grégoire de Nysse et chez Jean Scot Érigène", in: WERNER BEIERWALTES (ed.), Eriugena. Studien zu seinen Quellen, p. 33–54, p. 35. (Reprint in ÉDOUARD JEAUNEAU, Études Érigéniennes, p. 343–364.)
[156] MAÏEUL CAPPUYNS (ed.), Le 'De Imagine' de Grégoire de Nysse traduit par Jean Scot Érigène, pp. 207–8.
[157] É. JEAUNEAU, La division des sexes, in: WERNER BEIERWALTES (ed.), Eriugena. Studien zu seinen Quellen, pp. 33–54, p. 36.
[158] *De hominis opificio*, chapter 17, G. FORBES (ed.), p. 202.

of goodness is here to be seen by His both bringing the human into being from nothing, and fully supplying him with all good gifts: ...[159].

Eriugena's Latin translation of this passage as it appears in *Periphyseon*, Book IV, is as follows.

*Deus in sua natura omne quodcunque est per notitiam accipiendum bonum, illud est, magis autem, omnis boni intellecti et comprehensi summitas existens, non ob aliud aliquid humanam uitam creat, quam quod bene esse talem oportet. Ac per hoc ad conditionem nostrae naturae motus, non nisi imperfectam bonitatis ostenderet uirtutem, aliquod quidem dans ex his quae sibi insunt, in aliquo autem inuidens suae participationi. Ast perfecta bonitatis species in hoc est, et adducere hominem ex non existente in generationem, et non indigentem bonorum perficere.*[160]

The divine generosity creates the human out of nothing and bestows on the human all good gifts. This is the context within which the various human attributes and capabilities which mirror the divine are to be considered.[161] This is the context within which the creation of the human in the image of God is to be understood. Although Eriugena's translation does not focus on *God's* goodness as the sole reason for creation (he has instead '*quam quod bene esse talem oportet*' referring to the well-being of the created reality) his translation does capture Gregory's position that God does not hold anything back, does not begrudge but generously gives (*non ... in aliquo ... inuidens suae participtioni*). Eriugena's translation of the passage and the fact that it is quoted in *Periphyseon* show his agreement. This is the theological background to the creation of the human in the image of God, a background which Eriugena appropriates and combines with his own opening scheme, the division of nature.[162]

---

[159] GREGORY OF NYSSA, *De hominis opificio*, chapter 17, G. FORBES (ed.), p. 202. I have strongly relied on the translation of REV. H. A. WILSON in *Gregory of Nyssa: Dogmatic treatises, etc.*, Nicene and Post-Nicene Fathers, second series, vol. 5, (Peabody, Massachusetts: 1995, first published in 1893), pp. 386–427, here p. 405 but have made adjustments to it.

[160] PP IV, CCCM CLXIV, 2239–2248, p. 77, (= PL 122 795C–796A).

[161] GREGORY OF NYSSA points out that it is not the mathematical multiplication of gifts which is important but the fullness itself. Within this received pléroma human freedom plays a pivotal role. *De hominis opificio*, ch. 17, p. 202.

[162] Finally, it is of interest to note that Eriugena uses the notion of the creation of the human in the image of God for two distinct, but related, purposes. In book two of *Periphyseon*, on the one hand, the emphasis falls on what we can analogously affirm, or indeed deny, of God on the basis of the scripturally revealed fact that the human is created in the image of God. In book four, on the other hand, the emphasis falls on discerning all we can about human nature on the basis of the same scriptural assertion *and* on the basis of what the Christian Scriptures have told us about the trinitarian God.

# CHAPTER 5

# God appears in Jesus Christ

*"Tolle a me Christum, nullum bonum mihi remanebit ..."* wrote Eriugena[1]. His devotion to Christ is beyond question, the contours of his understanding of Christ and, of Christ's revelatory function within the human search for God, are, however, more difficult to ascertain. Eriugena's Christology is not neatly assigned to one book or even one chapter within that book. Rather the references to Jesus Christ are scattered throughout all his works and must be assembled by scholars seeking to interpret them[2]. In this fifth chapter Eriugena's texts which speak of Christ will be

---

[1] PP V, 3863–3864, p. 180, (= PL 122 989A).

[2] Past studies include RENÉ ROQUES' monumental investigation, *Libres sentiers vers l'Erigènisme*, Rome: 1975, (= Lessico intellettuale europeo 9). It devotes attention to this theme and the insight of this great Dionysian scholar is, as always, insightful and balanced in its assessment of the philosophical and theological impeti integrated within Eriugena's synthesis. (See too, RENÉ ROQUES, "Jean Scot Erigène", in: MARCEL VILLER et al. (ed.), *Dictionnaire de spiritualité. Ascétique et mystique. Doctrine et histoire*, Paris: Beauchesne, 1937–1995, vol. 8, col. 754–755. Here Roques briefly compares Eriugena's and Dionysius Areopagita's respective Christologies.)
The work of later scholars has given rise to more controversy. Thus in 1981 M.L. Colish could write "John the Scot's Christology and soteriology are actually much more metahistorical and Neoplatonic that those of either Dionysius or Maximus. He certainly relies on these thinkers as sources of Neoplatonism as well as revering them as theological authorities. What he seems to have done was to extract the Neoplatonism from them, making it the basis of his own speculation on these topics, while ignoring or misinterpreting their other ideas. " (MARCIA L. COLISH, "John the Scot's Christology and Soteriology in Relation to his Greek Sources", in: *Downside Revue* 100 (1982) 138–51, p. 148/149). While there is some truth in Eriguena's selective use of his Greek sources I cannot agree with the list of concrete consequences of this for his position with which Colish continues: "This technique accounts for John's conspicuous depreciation of the reality of the physical world, his departure from the idea of a divine economy that operates in time, his elimination of the principle of synergy, and his lack of interest in the ecclesiastical and sacramental dimensions of Christ's saving action.", p. 149. In my opinion, the aesthetic in Eriugena's theory of the appearing of God with the strong affirmation that it is good that God appears in sensible things (that is his sacramentality of even physical reality) combined with his insistence that in the general return no creatures even sensible creatures perish utterly, shows that he does take the reality of the physical world very seriously. I believe that it is his opinion that the divine economy, a trinitarian economy operates through time influencing temporal realities. Eriugena's ecclesiology is handled in HILARY A. MOONEY, "*Der goldene Leuchter. Die ekklesiale Vermittlung der Offenbarung nach Johannes Scottus Eriugena*", in: JOHANNES ARNOLD; RAINER BERNDT; RALF M.W. STAMMBERGER (ed.): *Väter der Kirche. Ekklesiales Denken von den Anfängen bis zur Gegenwart. Festgabe zum siebzigsten Geburtstag von Hermann-Josef Sieben*, Paderborn: Schöningh, 2004, pp. 49–67. In this article the ecclesiastical aspects of Christ's revelatory action is outlined.
A different version of Colish's paper delivered in 1978 inspired the replique of Donald Duclow (DONALD DUCLOW, "Dialectic and Christology in Eriugena's *Periphyseon*", in: *Dionysius* 4

analysed. However, it is not the details of that author's theory of the metaphysics of the incarnation, (his understanding of the hypostatic union for example), which is directly of interest[3]. In line with the interest of this investigation the focus of my attention falls on texts in which the *appearing of God in Christ* is the matter at hand.

---

(1980) 99–118). Duclow's article has the advantage of having a scholar with detailed knowledge of Eriugena's writings as its author. Duclow skillfully situates Eriugena's Christology within the latter's dialectic. In my opinion, however, his treatment of Eriugena's Christology as it emerges in book five of *Periphyseon* needs to be supplemented by an account of the Christ of the parables for which book five is our source. Duclow does indeed treat Eriugena's interpretation of the parable of the ten virgins elsewhere albeit in the context of eschatology, see DONALD F. DUCLOW, "Virgins in paradise. Deification and Eschatology in 'Periphyseon' V", in: G.-H. ALLARD (Ed), *Jean Scot ecrivain*, pp. 30–49.

In the nineties Eriugena's christology once again merited the attention of an article ERIC D. PERL, "Metaphysics and Christology in Maximus Confessor and Eriugena", in: *Eriugena. East and West*, S. 253–279. Similarly to Colish, Perl seeks to assess and cast judgement on Eriugena's use of Maximus Confessor's christology. The article deals much more thoroughly with Maximus' Christology than it does with Eriugena's Christology. Perl argues that for Eriugena, the incarnation remains relatively extrinsic to the process of return. Furthermore, he seems to criticise Eriugena for distinguishing between 'types' of incarnation. "Thus, while Maximus overcomes the apparent distinction among the "types" of incarnation, that is, creation, historical incarnation, and deification, by understanding them all as the same ontological process, Eriugena clearly differentiates them" p. 263. It is true that Eriguena makes these dictinctions. It is interesting that Perl does not mention any texts in the biblical commentaries of Eriugena. For example in the context of various understandings of 'incarnation' a key Eriugenian text is found in his commentary on John's Gospel: Comm. I, 29, 58–71, É. JEAUNEAU (ed.), p. 156, (= PL 122 307B). It is not clear to me that this distinguishing must be considered a ground for criticism and not rather viewed as an analytic achievement. While dealing extensively with both, Eriugena clearly distinguishes between the role, for example of the eternal Word in creation, and of the role of the word incarnate in the salvific event of the special return. Perhaps this does render him more 'latin' than a Maximus (see PERL pp. 266/7). Does this have to be a point of criticism? Perl seems to imply that only through an incarnational theology along the lines of Maximus can the role of Jesus Christ in the return be adequately expressed. This seems to be a premiss running through the whole of his article. And yet when we consider the span of Christologies with which the history of the first ten centuries presents us, we must remark that Christologies can be different without necessarily being inferior. Maximus had one theory of the role of Jesus Christ. Gregory of Nyssa, for example, had another theory of the significance of Jesus Christ, namely as 'pleroma'. Perl does not mention the use which Eriugena makes of Gregory of Nyssa in order to come to a different (but not for this reason automatically less adequate) account of the role of Christ in the return. Perl wrote "Eriugena … is limited by the Christology available to him and lacks the resources needed to develop it into an all-embracing metaphysics.", p. 267. In my opinion Eriguena drew on further sources, other than and in addition to Maximus and Dionysius, most importantly on Gregory of Nyssa, in order to deal with Jesus Christ as the key intelligibility of the world, and as a key to theophany understood as encounter with Christ and in Christ with God. While this investigation shies away from competitive comparisons, it is the thesis of this book that this Eriugenian understanding of the revealing of God as theophany, represents a considerable systematic achievement.

[3] Studies on the hypostatic union of Eriugena cannot be handled in detail and are of direct interest mainly because of their treatment of the consequences of the hypostatic union for knowledge of God. To the examples mentioned in the last footnote must be added: THOMAS BÖHM, "Adnotationes zu Maximus Confessor und Johannes Scottus Eriugena," in: WALTER HAUG und WOLFRAM SCHNEIDER-LASTIN, (ed.), *Deutsche Mystik im abendländischen Zusammenhang. Neu*

I suggest that the appearing of God in Christ according to Eriugena is best approached in two major ways. Firstly, by considering the way that Jesus Christ is the key intelligibility of the whole of created reality and, of human nature in particular. The second approach to how God appears in Christ which we may trace in Eriugena's writings is his account of the interpersonal encounter of the believer with Christ. Each of these approaches is devoted attention within this chapter.[4]

In order to facilitate the exposition of the theme of the appearing of God in Christ this chapter proceeds in three steps. In a preliminary step Eriugena's use of Scripture in developing his Christology will be briefly presented (5.1). In a second step Christ as key to the intelligibility of all reality will be presented (5.2). The context within which Eriugena devotes this the most attention is that of the return of all reality to God. For this reason the general and special returns of reality to God and the role of Christ therein are treated. Within this second step the theme of the human created in the image of God will once more be approached, this time from a Christological perspective. In a third step, the encounter with Christ according to Eriugena will be presented (5.3). Here the theme of theophany will be revisited and examined in its Christological context.

## 1. Scriptural impulses for Eriugena's Christology

According to Eriugena his beloved Lord is to be sought and found in His words, that is, in the words of Holy Scripture: "... *non alibi aptius quaereris quam in uerbis tuis, ita non alibi apertius inueniris quam in eis.*"[5]

---

*erschlossene Texte, neue methodische Ansätze, neue theoretische Konzepte. Kolloquium Kloster Fischingen 1998,* Tübingen: Max Niemeyer Verlag, 2000, 51–60.

[4] The decision to structure the material in this way is innovative. Interpretations in the past opposed "the metaphysical, cosmic Christ" to a historical one; on these interpetations see for example MARCIA L. COLISH, John the Scot's Christology, p. 138. I observe that a metaphysics of the incarnation is not the direct focus of this study. For this reason the opposition between a 'metaphysical Christ' and an historical one is not demanded by this investigation. Secondly this division has been suggested by a consideration of the theological environment within which Eriugena's Greek sources found themselves, namely developments in theology after Chalcedon and its contemporary attempts to understand how Jesus Christ is both man and God. My investigation is not primarily historical and not directly concerned with a metaphysics of the incarnation according to Eriugena. Nor is it my concern to assess his orthodoxy in terms of Chalcedonian theology and its development in the fifth, sixth and seventh centuries. For these reasons I prefer to work with a structure which I suggest emerges from Eriugena's writings themselves. In his works there are accounts of encounter of believers with the risen Christ in prayer; these texts have been neglected in past investigations of his Christology. I suggest that they are vital to a balanced account of his Christology which takes its rise from Eriugena's *own* writing, and which considers *all* that he has to say about Jesus Christ. These are the intrinsic grounds for adopting this structure. There is also an additional, extrinsic reason for the structure. This is suggested by the topic of the investigation at hand: on the basis of this structure one can best investigate the issue of the appearing of God in Jesus Christ.

[5] PP V, 6824–6826, p. 210, (= PL 122 1010C).

Which books and indeed verses of Scripture are the pillars on which Eriugena's Christology is erected? Obviously the preoccupation with the Johannine writings witnessed to by the extant commentaries is of significance here. When we turn to these biblical commentaries to glean information on his Christology we notice that the incarnation of the Word is devoted a lot of attention. We only have to think of the *Homily on the Prologue*. This may be partially relativised by the fact that the Commentary has not survived in its entirety. A commenting on the chapters dealing with, for example, the death of Jesus is not at our disposal. However, the emphasis on the incarnation and on the trinitarian backdrop to Jesus Christ is also maintained in *Periphyseon*, a systematic work not in itself limited to any sequence of verses or sections of an individual book of Scripture.

I suggest that the conglomerate of Johannine trinitarian texts including the Prologue to John's Gospel is one important pillar of Eriugena's Christology. It is the first of three complexes of biblical texts which provide the main biblical support for Eriugena's Christology.

A second pillar which deserves explicit attention is provided by 'Pauline' texts on the inherence of all reality and human reality in particular in Christ. He relies for example in PP V, 994C–995A on the first and fourth chapter of the letter to the Ephesians. The Church is presented as the body of Christ. Eschatologically, Christ shall appear as the perfect human with, and in, the whole of His body.

A third pillar is provided by two parables of Jesus: the parable of the prodigal son, and the parable of the ten virgins[6]. We have already observed that the incarnation of the Word was devoted more attention than any historical deed of the Word incarnate. A further observation is that the words of Jesus Christ are devoted more attention than his deeds. Thus in *Periphyseon* it is two parables (the parable of the prodigal son and the parable of the ten prudent virgins) and indeed the nature of parabolic speech itself, which are devoted attention. It is in Eriugena's interpretation of these parables that we can trace a theology of encounter with Christ.

The recurrence of these three complexes will emerge in the systematic sections (5.2 and 5.3). Here (in 5.1) my aim is merely to identify these influences, not to expound them exhaustively. The emphasis is on the fact that Eriugena uses these biblical texts, not on whether his use of them is in line with the results of modern exegesis[7]. The issue at hand is whether his Christology is biblically informed and, if this is the case, through which texts.

---

[6] Lk. 15:11–32; Mt. 25:1–13.

[7] See KAVANAGH, CATHERINE. "Eriugenian developments of Ciceronian topical theory", in: STEPHEN GERSH and BERT ROEST (ed.), *Medieval and Renaissance Humanism*, pp. 1–30, pp. 8, esp. 28–30, for a discussion of the influence of Cicero and Boethius on his exegetical methods.

## 2. Christ as key to the intelligibility of all

In his accounts of creation Eriugena ever emphasised that the Father created the world in the Word. His Christology takes up the theme that this Word was made flesh or, as Eriugena often writes, made human ('*inhumanatus*'). Just as the trinitarian perspective through which the Word of the Father was the key to the intelligibility of the created universe had been emphasised in Eriugena's accounts of creation, so this is complimented by a Christological perspective through which the incarnation in it's consequences for the intelligibility of both creation in general and of the human creature in particular are examined.

### 2.1 *The Word was made flesh*

In a passage reflecting on the relevance of the incarnation for the endurance of the effects of the primordial causes Eriugena informs us of his understanding of how the Word became flesh and came into the visible world[8]. Eriugena, through his speaker the Alumnus, introduces the words of the Incarnate Word: 'I went forth from the Father and I came into the world, and now I leave the world again and go unto the Father' and interprets this with allusions to further biblical texts (emptying, taking on the form of a servant), spelling out the consequences of the incarnation not only for the salvation of humans but for the perfection of creation as a whole:

*hoc est exinaniui me ipsum, formam serui accipiens, caro uidelicet factus sum, totamque humanam naturam accepi. 'Et iterum relinquo mundum et uado ad patrem', hoc est, seruilem formam totamque humanam naturam, corpus uidelicet et animam et intellectum, et uniuersaliter omne, quod ex ipsa creatura (quae constat ex uisibili et intelligibili existentia) sumpsi, ultra omnem mundum in deitatem meam conuertens, salua naturarum ex quibus subsisto ratione manente, super omnia, quae sunt et quae non sunt exalto.[9]*

He holds that the reason for the fact that not only human nature is saved through the incarnation, lies in the fact that there is nothing in the world which does not subsist in human nature.

*Exiuit igitur a Patre et uenit in mundum, humanam uidelicet naturam accepit, in qua totus mundus subsistit. Nihil enim in mundo est quod non in humana natura comprehendatur.[10]*

---

[8] The passage begins at PP V, 2276, p. 71, (= PL 122 910C).

[9] PP V, 2298–2307, p. 72, (= PL 122 911A).

[10] PP V, 2307–2310, p. 72, (= PL 122 911A). Shortly after this quotation we meet sentences which reveal his understanding of the hypostatic union and its uniqueness:

"*Quanquam enim totam humanam naturam, quam totam accepit, totam in seipso et in toto humano genere totam saluauit, quosdam quidem in pristinum naturae statum restituens, quosdam uero per excellentiam ultra naturam deificans: in nullo tamen nisi in ipso solo humanitas deitati in unitatem substantiae adunata est et, in ipsam deitatem mutata, omnia transcendit*". PP V, 2314–2320, pp. 72–73, (= PL 122 911B).

Eriugena addresses the question why the Word descended *(quare descendit?)*. The answer is given in terms of the goal of the unification of the effects[11]. The Word descended not only to save the effects, but to save the causes too. These are mutually related so that if one were to pass away the other would too. The Alumnus summarises "*Totus itaque mundus in uerbo dei unigenito, incarnato, inhumanato adhuc specialiter restitutus est, in fine uero mundi generaliter et uniuersaliter in eodem restaurabitur.*"[12] Although we here witness the double naming *(incarnato/ inhumanato)* which is typical for Eriugena and which at first glance might suggest an anthropological concentration, Eriugena explicitly states that the inhumanation perfects not only all humans but all sensible things too: "*Quod enim specialiter in se ipso perfecit, generaliter in omnibus perficiet, non dico in omnibus hominibus solummodo, sed in omni sensibili creatura.*"[13]

### 2.2 Jesus Christ as perfect human

Nevertheless, the perfecting of the human creature does receive explicit and extended attention in Eriugena's writings. Christ is the perfect human into whom we shall all come together. The scriptural text which provides inspiration is Eph. 4:13. Thus in *Periphyseon* Eriugena relies on the biblical images firstly of the building, secondly, that of Christ as head of a body and writes:

*Vide initium aedificationis, unitatem quidem fidei; aedificationis perfectionem cognosce, unitatem uidelicet cognitionis filii dei. Hic igitur incrementa corporis Christi incipiunt; illic perficientur, quando Christus cum toto et in toto suo corpore quidam perfectus et unus uir, caput in membris et membra in capite, apparebit, quando mensura et plenitudo aetatis Christi non corporalibus oculis, sed uirtute contemplationis in omnibus sanctis suo capiti adunatis clarissime uidebitur, quando spiritualis aetas, hoc est uirtutem plenitudo, quae in Christo et ecclesia sua constituta est, consummabitur, et caetera quae de aeterna felicitate et perfectione beatitudinis in dei filio intelligi possunt.*[14]

In Christ everything is perfected, and this through Him. He is the end and consummation of our human nature.[15]

---

[11] See PP V, 2358–2360, p. 74, (= PL 122, 912A–B): "*inque suas causas reuocaret, ut in ipsis ineffabili quadam adunatione, sicut et ipsae causae, saluarentur.*"

[12] PP V, 2361–2363, p. 74, (= PL 122 912B).

[13] PP V, 2364–2366, p. 74, (= PL 122 912B–C). Donald Duclow has pointed to the significance of a sentence in Eriugena's commentary on John's Gospel where Eriugena speaks of the Word as though incarnate, that is to say made corporeal, in Scripture on the one hand, and in the forms and ordered ranks of visible things on the other. In my opinion Duclow's (in many other ways very helpful) article does not emphasise sufficiently that Eriugena says explicitly that this 'quasi incarnation' is a secondary sense of incarnation in addition to the hypostatic union. See Comm., 307B, É. JEANNEAU (ed.), p. 156; see DONALD F. DUCLOW in: "Dialectic and Christology in Eriugena's *Periphyseon*", p. 103.

[14] PP V, 6107–6118, p. 188, (= PL 122, 995A–B).

[15] See PP V, 5925–5927, pp. 181–182, (= PL 122, 990B): "*Et hoc totum in Christo et per Christum perficietur, qui finis est nostrae naturae et consummatio.*"

Another biblical image which Eriugena uses to illustrate how Jesus Christ is the perfect human is evident in his interpretation of the references in Gen. 2 to the tree of life, which in itself is said to contain all trees. He develops its significance by pointing out that the tree of life is said to be in the middle of paradise: (*in medio paradisi*): this, in his interpretation, indicates the very depths of human nature and is simultaneously Christologically interpreted:[16]

> ... *ut uocabulo paradisi totam humanam naturam quam omnes homines et boni et mali participant intelligas, medii uero eius significatione secretissimos intimosque eiusdem naturae sinus, in quibus imago et similitudo dei expressa est, ubi lignum uitae (hoc est dominus noster Iesus Christus) plantatum, cuius contemplatione nemo nisi purgatissimus fide et actione, et illuminatissimus scientia, et perfectissimus sapientia et diuinorum mysteriorum intelligentia frui sinitur.*[17]

Here the Christological context of the human imaging of the divine emerges. Not only ontologically but pedagogically too, Christ is the presupposition of our final imaging of God. Elsewhere Eriugena speaks of Christ as giving us an example of the return.[18]

## 2.3 Return in Christ

De facto Scripture tells about Christ, the key to the intelligibility of the world, in the concrete context of salvation history. It is a scenario of fall and, through the mediation of Christ, of return to a rightly ordered relationship with God.

Quoting the verse that no one has ascended into heaven but He who came down from heaven, the Christocentric of the return is developed. Eriugena emphasises that even when he descends the Son doesn't leave the Father. The Son and the father are ever one. It is within this trinitarian context that the unique position of Christ, a position which enables the return of others to God is emphasised.

---

Eriugena tells us that the Greeks call the two trees in Gen. 2 'gnoston' and 'PAN': "*lignum scientiae boni et mali gnoston graeci uocant, lignum uero uitae* ΠΑΝ", PP IV, CCCM CLXIV, 3344–3345, p. 112, (= PL 122 820B). See PP IV, CCCM CLXIV, 3458 and following, p. 115 and following; (= PL 122 823A and following). On the interpretation of the tree of knowledge of good and evil and the tree of life in Eriugena and in his patristic sources see Carlos Steel "The Tree of the Knowledge of Good and Evil", in: G. van Riel / C. Steel / J. McEvoy (ed.), Iohannes Scottus Eriugena. The Bible and Hermeneutics, pp. 239–255.

[16] In Eriugena's opinion the 'All-tree' of Paradise is the Word and Wisdom of the Father, Our Lord Jesus Christ. This occurs in two ways, first through His divinity by which he creates our nature, and secondly through taking the human nature upon him. "*Primo quidem secundum suam diuinitatem, qua nostram naturam et creat, et continet, et nutrit, et uiuificat, et illuminat, et deificat, et mouet, et esse facit: 'In ipso enim uiuimus, et mouemur, et sumus'. Secundo uero, quo nostram naturam, ut saluaret eam et in statum pristinum reuocaret, in unitatem substantiae sibi adiunxit, ut in duabus naturis subsisteret, diuina uidelicet atque humana.*" PP IV, CCCM CLXIV, 3485–3492, p. 116, (= PL 122 823B–C).

[17] PP V, 5496–5503, p. 169, (= PL 122 981 A).

[18] PP V, 1546–1548, p. 49, (= PL 122 894 A).

*In quam unitatem solus ille suam humanitatem subuexit, caeteros autem, quos deificat, sola participatione suae deitatis, unumquemque secundum altitudinem propriae contemplationis, post se constituit, ordinans in seipso, ueluti in quadam domu, omnes quos conformes suos fieri elegit.*[19]

Return is thus for Eriugena one of the main organising categories within which the relationship of the human to God is expressed. It is inspired by such biblical passages as the fourteenth chapter of John's Gospel as a whole and the verses 2 ("[i] n my Father's house are many rooms) and 6 ("I am the way, the truth, and the life; no one comes to the Father, but by me") of that chapter in particular.[20] Return as a biblically inspired notion is one of the most important hermeneutics for Eriugena's interpretation of further verses of the bible. Whereas the notion of return was also common in neo-Platonic analyses, it is in my opinion legitimate to point out these are not the only schemes of analysis influencing Eriugena.[21]

Further confirmation of the biblical colouring of Eriugena's notion of return is gleaned from his repeated use of the verse Gen. 3:22: "*Nunc ergo ne forte mittat manum suam, et sumat etiam de ligno uitae, et comedat, et uiuat in aeternum?*"[22]. These words are taken as containing the promise of the return of human nature to the happiness which it lost through sinning. Eriugena interprets the participle '*ne*' in the quotation not in a negative (prohibitive) sense but rather in a (positive) interrogative sense.

His argumentation is, however, not based on grammar alone. According to his systematic insight neither within a spiritual interpretation, nor within a historical interpretation of the event would it be logical for God to expel the first humans from the whole garden. Again he stresses that the spiritual meaning is the true one[23]. He embarks on his exposition of this return, intending according to his speaker Nutritor to give a scripturally oriented account[24]. This account is something which his speaker Alumnus regards as relatively new ground (*a paucis, ut opinor, tractata*)[25].

Eriugena gives a lyrical account of the depth of divine compassion and condescension (he writes of God *misericorditerque condescendens*) hidden in the words "now therefore" (*nunc ergo*)[26]. The end is described as the human passing wholly into God and being one in God ("*totus in deum transiturus et unum in illo futurus*")[27].

---

[19] PP V, 2331–2335, p. 73, (= PL 122 911C–D).
[20] Scripture verses here according to the R.S.V. of the Bible.
[21] Compare É. JEAUNEAU, "Le thème du retour", in: É. JEAUNEAU, (ed..), *Études Érigéniennes*, 365–394.
[22] Quoted according to PP V, 1–2, p. 3, (= PL 122 859D).
[23] PP V, 58–62, p. 4, (= PL 122 862A).
[24] "*Veni igitur, diuinorumque uerborum uirtute diligentius intuere.*" PP V, 62–63, p. 4, (= PL 122, 862A).
[25] PP V, 65–66, p. 5, (= PL 122 862A).
[26] PP V, 75–94, p. 5, (= PL 122 862B–C).
[27] PP V, 104, p. 6, (= PL 122 863A).

Eriugena gives a highly contoured interpretation of the biblical account of paradise. According to Eriugena, the paradise from which the human was expelled was human nature itself. The human did not, however, lose it completely, for being made in the image of God, it was incorruptible. But the happiness which would have accrued to human nature if it had been obedient was lost.

Now the word 'cherubim' which occurs in the story of paradise is (in reliance on the Pseudo-Dionysius) translated as *'multitudo scientiae'* or *'fusio sapientiae'*, or inspired by Epiphanius, *'cognitionem plenam'* or *'cognitionem multorum'*[28]. Eriugena interprets the verse at hand as saying that God placed the variety of knowledge or the pouring forth of wisdom before the garden of pleasure, that is, in front of the eyes of expelled rational human nature. This is said to be so that the human nature might have a means of regaining its knowledge of itself and return to its former happiness.[29] The word cherubim is then said to have an even deeper meaning, namely, the Word of God itself. *"Sed si quis altius uelit conspicere, cherubim uocabulo ipsum dei uerbum significari non incongrue intelliget."*[30] The flaming sword in Gen. 3:24 is also identified with the Word of God.[31] And guarding the path of the tree of life means ensuring that its memory and the memory of the way which leads to it are not forgotten. He quotes John's Gospel *"Ego sum uia, ueritas et uita"* identifying the way with the Son of God[32].

According to Eriugena all things return to their beginning (*principium*), even sensible things. All humans[33] whether perfect or imperfect, whether renewed in Christ through knowledge or still in the darkness of ignorance, desire the one and the same threefold fulfilment: 'being' and 'well-being' and 'being forever'. For this is a natural motion and every natural motion does not cease to seek nor rest until it arrives at the end which it seeks. No creature seeks non-being. The creature which is created in the image of God, even if it has strayed from this likeness, nonetheless always tries to return to its beginning, in order to attain the likeness again. 'Being' and 'living' and 'immortality' will be common to all humans, but 'well-being' and 'blessed being' will be, according to Eriugena, the special lot of those who are perfect in action and knowledge. *"Esse enim et uiuere et aeternaliter esse commune erit omnibus, et bonis et malis; bene autem et beate esse solis actione et scientia perfectis proprium et speciale erit."*[34]

---

[28] PP V, 131–135, p. 7, (= PL 122 863C).

[29] PP V, 156–164, pp. 7–8, (= PL 122 864 A–B).

[30] PP V, 171–172, p. 8, (= PL 122 864C).

[31] PP V, 183–184, p. 8, (= PL 122 864D).

[32] PP V, 205–207, p. 9, (= PL 122 865 B).

[33] Eriugena uses the expression *'Generaliter in omnibus hominibus'*, PP V, 307–308, p. 12, (= PL 122 867C).

[34] PP V, 335–338, p. 13, (= PL 122 868 B). Differences between a related distinction, that which Eriugena makes between a so-called general return and a so-called special return, and how this distinction applies to the return of humans to God shall be explained in what follows.

There are then various levels of return in what we must consider to be Eriugena's eschatology. These emerge in a significant speech of the Alumnus[35]. On the one level there is return to unity which applies to all creatures. Secondly, there is the element of overcoming sin (implied by terms such as '*saluauit*' and '*restaurauit*').[36] On a third level there is the epistemological element, the return through knowing to God. It is within the context of this epistemological element that Eriugena claims that the incarnation aided not just humans but the angels too. It is significant that according to him sensible theophanies of God are always a bonus, even the intellectually functioning angels benefit from them. This is once again evidence of Eriugena's radically aesthetic position which will be treated further on under the topic of theophany.

Eriugena uses several scriptural complexes in order firstly, to defend the differences between the situations of various individuals in paradise and, secondly, to allow the unique position of Christ in leading others in the return to emerge. One of the most significant is that of the building of the temple of Solomon[37]. Here again Eriugena's point is that different people are differently situated in paradise and that entering the holy of holies is only possible through, and in Christ. The allegory for Christ is worked out in great detail. Christ is the altar because of His strength; He is moreover an altar of incense, and his fragrance is His praise and glory; He is the ark containing all the treasures of wisdom and knowledge; He is the rod because He rules; He is the manna because He feeds all humans; He is the altar of sacrifice because He offers the father the universal sacrifice and the world's ransom, namely His humanity which He sacrificed and surrendered for the purification and redemption of the whole human race without exception. The two cherubim near the ark are interpreted as the intellectual nature of angels and the rational nature of human.

This image for the central role of Christ culminates in an incarnational understanding of the return in Christ:

*Nam quemadmodum in nullo inuenit (absque peccato) quod non acceperit, ita in nullo reliquit quod non redemerit et redimendo saluauit et sanctificauit, quoniam ipse est redemptio et salus, purgatio et illuminatio et perfectio uniuersae humanitatis in omnibus et singulis.*[38]

Christ took on all that is in our nature, remaining without sin, and saved all that He received.

Eriugena expresses this in terms not only of redemption, as in the last quotation, but also explicitly in terms of return:

---

[35] Starting at PP V, 2361, p. 74, (= PL 122 912 B).

[36] PP V, 2370, p. 74, (= PL 122 912 C).

[37] His use of the image begins at PP V, 5504, p. 169, (= PL 122 981 A). Another biblical text he uses is the already mentioned Jn. 14:2 "In my Father's house are many rooms".

[38] PP V, 5532–5536, p. 170, (= PL 122 981 D).

*Tota itaque humanitas in ipso, qui eam totam assumpsit, in pristinum reuersura est statum, in uerbo dei uidelicet incarnato.*[39]

### 2.3.1 Basic scheme of analysing return: the general return and the special return

Eriugena claims that the return must be examined under two aspects: the first considers the restoration of the whole of created reality; the second considers the beatification and deification of those who ascend into God[40]. In the general return all things are brought back to the principle of their creation. Of the special return he says: *"specialis uero in his qui non solum ad primordia naturae reuocabuntur, sed etiam ultra omnem naturalem dignitatem in causam omnium (quae deus est) reditus sui finem constituent."*[41] He illustrates this by the Genesis account of paradise and says that it is one thing to return into Paradise it is another to eat of the Tree of Life[42]. The tree of life is Christ and its fruit is the blessed life and eternal peace in the contemplation of the truth, which according to Eriugena, is properly called deification.[43] He offers the text "For we shall all rise again, but we shall not all be changed" as further scriptural support for his theory.[44] The fact that his system uses this distinction and specifically treats the special return explicitly shows that Eriugena's thinking embraces a specifically Judeo-Christian eschatology. The special return, a return which is more than just the fulfilment of a finality inherent in each creature, is an eschatological event whose description is necessary for an adequate interpretation of the Judaeo-Christian Scriptures. The notion of a special return is demanded by those scriptural texts which speak of a final encounter between the blessed creature and the creator. The notion of a general return is demanded by

---

[39] PP V, 5393–5395, p. 165, (= PL 122 978 D).

[40] For a detailed account of the reditus specialis / reditus generalis distinction see É. JEAUNEAU, "Le thème du retour," in the same author's *Études Erigéniennes*, pp. 367–394.
On p. 371 Jeauneau presents the distinction as an attempt to reconcile the position which reason suggests, namely that *all* humans return to God and the scriptural description of a last judgement in which the sheep are separated from the goats (Mt. 25: 31–46).
Jeauneau finds a similar distinction in MAXIMUS CONFESSOR. In his footnote number 49 on p. 375, JEAUNEAU gives references to *Quaestiones ad Thalassium*, LIV, scholion 18 (22). See C. LAGA (ed.), Turnhout: Brepols, 1980, CCSG 7, p. 474–475, (= PG 90, 532 C 11–15).
GUSTAVO A. PIEMONTE sees a similar distinction between kinds of grace occurring in the so called "C1–C2" homilies in the *Opus Imperfectum in Matthaeum*, PG 56, 756–798; 897–946, see "Some distinctive theses of Eriugena's Eschatology in his Exegesis of the Gospel according to St. Matthew", in: J. McEVOY / M. DUNNE, (ed.), History and Eschatology in John Scottus Eriugena and his Time, pp. 227–242, p. 228.

[41] PP V, 6392–6395, p. 197, (= PL 122 1001B). Under the second aspect, the return of the blessed, return is more than a restoration of the previously possessed position. As Stephen Gersh has pointed out the notion of return is really transcended in this case, see STEPHEN GERSH, "The Structure of the Return in Eriugena's *Periphyseon*", in: W. BEIERWALTES, *Begriff und Metaphor*, pp. 108–125, p. 110.

[42] PP V, 5400–5401, pp. 165–166, (= PL 122 979A).

[43] PP V, 5413–5416, p. 166, (= PL 122 979B).

[44] PP V, 5418–5419, p. 166, (= PL 122 979B). ERIUGENA writes: *"Omnes quidem resurgemus, sed non omnes immutabimur."* relying on the Vulgata translation of 1 Cor. 15:51.

those scriptural texts which speak of the infinite goodness of God. In Eriugena's account of the general return we see him pit scriptural text against scriptural text in order to defend God's goodness and the possibility of hell, both realities which in his opinion are asserted by Scripture. Both aspects of the return, general and special, are illustrated through biblical stories. Further, more than mere illustration is at hand: even in his account of the general return he is at pains to present the Christological context of this return, a context only accessible to those thinkers who draw on the Christian Scriptures.

### 2.3.1.1 The general return: Christ revealed in the return of all creation

The general return is a return whose main outlines Eriugena could have chosen to present in philosophical terms. However, Eriugena rather chooses to interpret it from a biblical-theological perspective[45]. He illustrates it by the biblical Exodus story. It is interpreted Christologically with Moses standing for Christ. It is interesting that the role of Christ is so strongly emphasised although Eriugena is interpreting a general return. He speaks of the help of grace *"diuina gratia adiuta"*.[46] The salient detail in the exodus story which makes the transfer to the general return possible is the detail that no single Israelite is said to have remained in Egypt. The story can therefore be implemented to prefigure that return in which all partake, the general return. He can accordingly speak of a baptism of all in the cloud, a baptism which is said to prefigure the baptism of all in the return. All vice shall be overwhelmed by the waters of the Red Sea, by the infinite effusion of grace which is poured upon human nature in payment for the blood of Christ *"profundissima copiosissimaque atque infinita effusione gratiae, quae in pretium sanguinis Christi humanae naturae diffusa est …"*[47] Nothing shall be seen in any human except the simplicity of that nature which Christ took upon Himself and purified. Further, the flooding of the red sea is identified with the shedding of the Lord's blood. Once again it is worth commenting, that this general return is presented, not only in terms of an intrinsic enduring value in created reality, but in explicitly Christological terms expounded through the pre-figuration of the biblical exodus story.

Eriugena sees what he calls the salvation of the human race in Christ *"salutem humani generis … in Christo"* also in Isaiah's words *"Terra Zabulon et terra Neptalim, uia maris trans Iordanen Galileae gentium. Populus qui sedebat in tenebris lucem uidit magnam, et sedentibus in regione umbrae mortis lux orta est eis."*[48] Eriugena offers his

---

[45] Édouard Jeauneau writes that the general return "satisfait non seulement aux exigences dialectiques du schéma néoplatonicien *processio – reditus,* mais aussi au dogme de l'universalité de l'oeuvre salvatrice accompli par le Christ", JEAUNEAU, Le thème du retour, p. 375.

[46] PP V, 6417, p. 198, (= PL 122 1001D).

[47] PP V, 6440–6442, p. 198–199, (= PL 122 1002 B).

[48] PP V, 6457–6461, p. 199, (= PL 122 1002C). "In the former time he brought into contempt the land of Zebulon and the land of Naphtali, but in the latter time he will make glorious the way of the sea, the land beyond the Jordan, Galilee of the nations. The people who walked in darkness

readers an interpretation of this text. The people is interpreted as the multitude of the human race, infinite in number. The people are in darkness because they left the light of paradise; they fell into the darkness of ignorance and shadows of death. Here he mentions the double death of sin and physical death. By light is meant the light which saves the whole human race from the double death.

Eriugena interprets the words 'Zabulon' and 'Nephthali' in order to demonstrate the fact that the salvation of the human nature is already effected in Christ. Zabulon is said to mean "the habitation of virtue". The Word is the virtue and wisdom of the Father. The habitation is identified with our nature which was taken on by the Word in His incarnation. Eriugena quotes the Scriptural text "*Et uerbum caro factum est, et habitauit in nobis*" and then himself writes "*Proinde spiritualis Zabulon humanitas Christi est, in qua nos omnes salui facti sumus et saluati habitamus et in aeternum habitabimus.*"[49]. Nephthali, he tells us, means "breadth", Christ is presented as our breadth, Christ who laid down his life for *all* of us ("*Cuius caritas et clementia totum genus amplectitur humanum …*")[50]. Once again Eriugena takes this as an occasion to work out the notion of universality: Christ dies for all humans.

Eriugena presents us with another way in which the word 'Nephthali' may be interpreted as breadth. "*Latitudo quippe est apparitio et superficies, ideoque graia significatione epiphania dicitur.*"[51] Christ is our *epiphania*. He presents in an objective sense: Christ is our epiphany in the sense that one divine person appears to us in Christ and addresses our senses: "*… nobis apparuit sensibusque corporeis comprehensibilem se fecit.*"[52] This last sentence with its emphasis on the appearing of a member of the trinity to our senses in Christ is one more indication of how radically aesthetic Eriugena's position is.

Eriugena presents other illustrations of the general return[53]. Here too he draws on the Scriptures, drawing on both testaments. He uses the parable of the Prodigal son, the parable of the lost hundredth sheep, and the parable of the lost drachma. In each case the matter illustrated is the so-called general return of the human race, that is, its return to its creator as such. In the two first cases this return is described in explicitly Christological terms: the fatted calf stands for Christ, filled with the sevenfold grace of the Spirit and made thick with the fatness of the letter and visible nature[54]. In the search for the lost sheep, the good shepherd represents Christ. In leading the hundredth sheep home Christ is said to restore human nature to the perfection represented by this number. Here we once again witness Eriugena's

---

have seen a great light; those who dwelt in a land of deep darkness, on them has light shined" Is. 9:1–2. Isaiah here quoted in English according to R. S. V. edition.

[49] PP V, 6489–6492, p. 200, (= PL 122 1003B); Jn. 1:14.

[50] PP V, 6494–6495, p. 200, (= PL 122 1003B).

[51] PP V, 6504–6506, pp. 200–201, (= PL 122 1003C).

[52] PP V, 6509–6510, p. 201, (= PL 122 1003D).

[53] PP V, 6512–6619, pp. 201–205, (= PL 122 1003D–1006A).

[54] PP V, 6576–6578, p. 203, (= PL 122 1005B): "*septena sancti spiritus gratia plenus, uel certe pinguedine litterae uisibilisque naturae incrassatus*".

strong affirmation of the role of Christ in the general return of human nature. In the case of the author's interpretation of the parable of the lost drachma the woman is said to stand for the Wisdom of God. Here the role of the divine Wisdom in leading human nature back to its creator is presented[55].

### 2.3.1.2 *The special return: Christ revealed to the elect*

Details of the special return, a return which applies not to humans as such (who all return to a state of imaging God) but to the elect (who not only return to this imaging but who also transcend this through a form of deification) emerge more clearly in Eriugena's complementary schemes of analysing return. In addition the special return involves a particularly intense encounter with Christ and it is therefore also dealt with in section (5.3) below.

### 2.3.2 *Complementary schemes of analysing return*

The distinction between the general return and the special return is one way that Eriugena organises his material on the return of all created reality to its creator. In this study it is treated as the most significant organising factor. This distinction is important from the point of view of the issue investigated in this study: It provides us with a distinction, intrinsic to Eriugena's system itself, on the basis of which we can investigate nuances in his understanding of the appearing of God. In the special return we are provided with an opportunity of observing the special relationship of the blessed with Christ, a relationship well described by the albeit contemporary category of encounter.

Furthermore, this study argues that through observing Eriugena's distinguishing between general and special return, one can draw conclusions on his method. Here one can best see Eriugena operating as a scriptural thinker, ever concerned to do justice to the full context, the context of graced deification, revealed by Scripture. Even the general return, a return which could also be described within a neo-Platonic scheme of analysing the end of all things, is described in explicitly Christological terms. Eriugena himself would not of course make a distinction between theology and philosophy. He was a thinker who operates with a sapiential understanding of truth which embraces all the wisdom at its disposal, even that truth accessible to

---

[55] Jeauneau has pointed out that the three parables from Luke chapter 15, the parable of the prodigal son, the parable of the lost drachma and the parable of the lost sheep are also all commented on by Maximus in his *Ambigua ad Iohannem* XXVII, 41–84, Jeauneau (ed.), CCSG 18, pp. 160–161, (= PG 91, 1276–1280A), see Jeauneau, Le thème du retour, p. 383. Jeauneau states that the interpretation of Maximus certainly exerted an influence on Eriugena (loc. cit.). In my opinion however, it is important to note that while the section in the *Ambigua* devotes nearly equal attention to each of the three parables, *Periphyseon* book V gives a much more extensive interpretation of the parable of the prodigal son than of the other parables in Luke chapter 15. Both Maximus and Eriugena however emphasise the role of Christ in leading the human to the salvation illustrated by the three parables.

non-Christian thinkers. He's is thus at pains to explain what he sees as an ultimately Christological eschatological event as fully as he can, and in so doing draws on the terminology of creatural reality and on Scripture. Because of the insight it allows into Eriugena's theological method, his distinguishing between general and special return has been devoted specific attention within this study.[56]

He also implements other schemes. These schemes of describing the return of creation to the Creator are of interest in this investigation insofar as they divulge Eriugena's understanding of the appearing of God, or more particularly, of God in Christ.

### 2.3.2.1 First complementary scheme (PP V, 685–694, p. 24)

Eriugena presents five steps in the return to original integrity. It is obvious that he is here primarily considering the return of the human creature, in which case all five steps may apply.

1.) The first step is the dissolution of the body into the four elements of the sensible world from which it was composed.

2.) The second step occurs at the resurrection when each person receives back his / her own body from the common fund of the four elements.

3.) The third step is when body is said to be turned into soul.

4.) The fourth is when spirit (and the whole of human nature) reverts to its primordial causes, which abide forever unchangingly in God.

5.) The fifth is when that nature with its causes is absorbed into God (*movebitur in Deum*) as air is absorbed into light (*sicut aer movetur in lucem*).[57]

---

[56] STEPHEN GERSH's paper "The Structure of the Return in Eriugena's *Periphyseon*" bears testimony to the various schemes of analysis within which the return is presented. His article first concentrates on the metaphysical assumptions which underlie the doctrine of return in *Periphyseon*. Here he deals with such topics as: unity, multiplicity and the Return; space, time and the Return. He then outlines what he calls two horizontal schemes and two vertical schemes. He comments "the horizontal articulation has connotations of temporality or quasi-temporality (cf. p. 118ff.), the vertical articulation connotations of spatiality or quasi-spatiality (cf. p. 119ff.)", footnote 71, pp. 117/8. Gersh's analysis of the schemes of return builds then on the metaphysical categories which he investigates in the first part of his paper, see p. 117: "These metaphysical ideas regarding levels of being, unity and multiplicity, and spatiotemporality are not the subjects of special excursus in the text of *Periphyseon* but rather assumptions underlying the discussion on the return in general." Gersh's excellent paper investigates these schemes of return according to the philosophical ideas which he sees associated with Eriugena's expositions. He is aware that there are certain ambiguities in Eriugena's writings on return and does not claim that his own analysis has eliminated all these ambiguities (see p. 124).

In my opinion my analysis of the return in Eriugena's writings does not challenge Gersh's work but complements it. It is significant that Gersh barely mentions Eriugena's distinction between the general / special aspects of return (see his p. 120). This axis is, however, of intense interest to scholars concerned with Eriugena's use of Scripture and his attempts to adequately account for the details of eschatology with which the Judaeo-Christian scriptures present us.

[57] PP V, 693–694, p 24, (= PL 122 876A–B). Here I. P. SHELDON-WILLIAMS / J. J. O'MEARA's translation ('is absorbed') is followed since the idea of absorption seems best to fit in with the

He also discusses the extent to which the five steps represent a consensus of academic opinion[58].

Eriugena gives some very important qualifications explaining what he himself means by these steps[59]. These are important in discerning whether the accusation of pantheism which has been raised against Eriugena in the past is legitimate or not. In my opinion it is not a *metaphysical* identity ("*Nec per hoc conamur astruere substantiam rerum perituram, sed in melius per gradus praedictos redituram*"[60]), but rather a *cognitive* unity which is proposed between the human substance and God: "*Mutatio itaque humanae naturae in deum non substantiae interitus aestimanda est, sed in pristinum statum, quem praeuaricando perdiderat, mirabilis atque ineffabilis reversio. Si enim omne quod pure intelligit efficitur unum cum eo quod intelligitur, quid mirum si nostra natura, quando deum facie ad faciem contemplatura sit in his, quo digni sunt – quantum ei datur contemplari – in nubibus theoriae ascensura, unum cum ipso et in ipso fieri possit?*"[61] It is clear that becoming one with God in this context may not be identified with pantheism. This is an important observation on Eriugena's eschatological schemes and one which may be made with respect to all his various analyses of return.[62]

---

image of the way air seems to disappear in a flood of light. See *Eriugena Periphyseon (The Division of Nature)*, Translation by I. P. SHELDON-WILLIAMS, revised by J. O'MEARA, Montréal: Bellarmin / Washington: Dumbarton Oaks, 1987, p. 541.

[58] Eriugena was well aware that scholarly opinion on these matters diverge. Some, he says, dispute the conversions of body into soul, and soul into cause, and the causes into God, and these, even in the case of the humanity of Christ.

[59] PP V, 695 and following, p. 24 ff., (= PL 122 876B and following).

[60] PP V, 695–697, p. 24, (= PL 122 876B).

[61] PP V, 698–706, p. 24, (= PL 122 876B).

[62] Eriugena gives a clear account of just what the unification of substances is and is not (PP V, 822–845, pp. 28–29, (= PL 122 878D–879B) using the famous metaphors of the way air and light seem to be one, and the way metal and the fire in which it glows seem to form a unity. Eriugena offers many explanations or illustrations of the unification of natures without the endangering of the individual properties. One example is the inseparable unity of essence, potency and natural act (*Essentia, uirtus, et naturalis operatio*, PP V, 922–940, p. 31, = PL 122 881A–B) and their enduring distinction. Another example of the unification of natures without confusion, mixture or composition "*sine confusione uel mixtura uel compositione*" is that of essence, genera, species, and individuals (PP V, 941–952, pp. 31–32, = PL 122 881B–C). Yet another illustration is that of numbers subsisting in the Monad (PP V, 952–975, p. 32, = PL 122 881C–882A). Another is lines joining at the centre in a point (PP V, 975–977, p. 32, = PL 122 882A–B). Another example is that of the sight of countless persons being directed to the one object, his example, a little golden ball. "*Si ergo tot radii in unum confluunt, et nullus alteri confunditur uel miscetur uel componitur, quoniam singuli intuentium quique proprietatem suam obtinent, dum circa unam eandemque rem mirabili quadam adunatione uersantur, quid mirum si tota humana natura in unitatem quandam ineffabilem redigatur, proprietatibus et corporis et animae et intellectus incommutabiliter permanentibus?*" (PP V, 1026–1033, p. 34, = PL 122 883B) The example is interesting because it is an example of unity in the *intention* of a common object. A further example is openly indebted to the Ps. Dionysius: the light coming from many lamps is one (PP V, 1033–1048, p. 34, = PL 122 883B–C). ERIUGENA then himself adds the illustration formed by the human voice and musical instruments and the production of harmony (PP V, 1049–1061, = PL 122 883C–884A).

*2.3.2.2 Second complementary scheme (PP V, 1507, p. 48–1545, p. 49;*
*PP V, 1622–1638, p. 52)*

Eriugena also implements another scheme of division (and unification) of nature further on in book V of *Periphyseon*. He presents this five fold division in its entirety twice.[63]

*Prima siquidem omnium naturarum divisio est, quae creatam a non creata, quae est Deus, segregat. Secunda creatam dividit in sensibilem et intelligibilem. Tertia sensibilem in caelum discernit et terram. Quarta separat paradisum et orbem terrarum. Quinta omniumque ultima divisio est hominis in masculum et feminam.*

In the first instance quoted above, Eriugena indicates his debt to the 37th chapter of Maximus' *Ambigua ad Iohannem.*[64]

The five-fold division ends in a division within the human, namely, that of the sexes. Commenting on this division Eriugena notes that the biblical account of creation introduces the human at the end and as the culmination of the totality of creation. The return is said to start in the overcoming of the division into the sexes. Eriugena's account centres on the human as the pivot of the return. It is of interest that in book four of *Periphyseon* the pivotal role of the human creature in the return was asserted because of its deliberate appropriation of this possibility, that is, in reaching out its 'hand' to paradise. Here in book five of *Periphyseon,* the pivotal

---

Stephen Gersh's observation that there may be a difference between the contexts in which Eriugena uses the image of the diffusion of light and that of the merging of light and air seems plausible: "To the simile of light's diffusion is added one of light blending with air which, although not an idea found only in Maximus (79), is developed by Eriugena after the manner of the Greek writer. ... one might ask if the similes of light's diffusion and of light blending with air together with their respective elaborations should really be viewed as comparable. It is true that both involve the notion of omnipresence, but do they not apply it to different contexts, the simile of light's diffusion explaining God's relation to the present world, that of light blending with air God's relation to the world that is to come? The texts discussed seem often to support such a distinction.", STEPHEN GERSH, "Omnipresence in Eriugena. Some Reflections on Augustino-Maximian Elements in Periphyseon", in: W. BEIERWALTES (ed.), Eriugena. Studien zu seinen Quellen, pp. 55–74, p. 73.

[63] First at PP V, 1507–1545, pp. 48–49, (= PL 122 893B–894A), then at PP V, 1622–1638, p. 52, (= PL 122 895C–896A).

[64] PP V, 1508–1509, p. 48, (= PL 122 893B). This scheme of division has its roots not in logic but in the Scriptures. It leads up to an affirmation of the pivotal role of the human creature in the return of all things to the God: "*In quo (uidelicet homine) omnis creatura uisibilis et inuisibilis condita est. Ideoque officina omnium dicitur, quoniam in eo omnia quae post deum sunt continentur. Hinc etiam medietas solet appellari. Extrema siquidem longeque a se distantia (spiritualia scilicet et corporalia) in se comprehendit et in unitatem colligit, corpore et anima consistens. ... Proinde ex adunatione diuisionis hominis in duplicem sexum praedictarum diuisionum incipit ascensus et adunatio*" PP V, 1517–1528, p. 49, (= PL 122 893B–C). See MAXIMUS CONFESSOR, *Ambigua ad Iohannem*, XXXVII, 3–32, CCSG 18, É. JEAUNEAU (ed.), pp. 179–180, (= PG 91, 1304D–1305B). Compare PP II, 209–490, (= PL 122, 531D–542C). Maximus is in turn indebted to GREGORY OF NYSSA, *De hominis opificio* 2, G. FORBES (ed.), (= PG 44, 132D–133B). See É. JEAUNEAU, La division des sexes chez Grégoire de Nysse et chez Jean Scot Érigène.

role of the human in the return is described in terms of the first consequence of the in-breaking return: in the resurrection the division of the sexes is done away with.

In this account of division and return too, the unique role of Christ emerges as well. Eriugena states that the whole process was both perfected by Jesus Christ in his rising from the dead, and shown to us as an example of what is to come "*Et hoc totum Dominus et saluator noster Iesus Christus resurgendo a mortuis in seipso et perfecit et exemplum omnium quae futura sunt praemonstrauit.*"[65]

Everything which Christ took upon himself from the terrestrial globe, (Eriugena mentions the material flesh and his masculine sex) Christ changed in Himself into a spiritual nature. "*Totum namque quod de orbe terrarum acceperat (materialem ui-delicet carnem cum suis accidentibus absque peccato et uirilem habitum) in spiritualem in seipso mutauit naturam.*"[66] Eriugena points out that human nature will be made higher than the angels and that what Christ achieves in himself particularly, he will bring about generally in the whole of human nature.

After this theological exposition of the return of Christ and of all humanity in the risen Christ Eriugena tells us not to be surprised that he has here treated topics which he had already treated in earlier books. He says that this recapitulation is necessary. It is of interest that he does not point out that the just given account of the return is intrinsically more biblical and Christological than what has gone before. Again we see how he thinks that 'philosophical' and 'theological' specula-tion belong radically together. He then says that he must give a further account of the return depending on Maximus which is more detailed than that which is to be gleaned from the fragments of Maximus quoted up to this. He thus then turns to Maximus' account of the return as it appears not in the *Ambigua* but in the *Scholia* chapter 48. Eriugena then quotes[67] a passage where the five steps in the return are presented (PP V, 1625–1638, p. 52, = PL 122 895D–896A).

### 2.3.2.3 *Third complementary scheme (PP V, 7276–7302, p. 224)*

Eriugena provides us with yet another scheme. Here he once again takes the return of the entirety of creation as his starting point. He considers the return of all effects into their causes. He says he found that the nature of the return is threefold: "*Cuius iterum reditus triplex occurrebat modus.*"[68]

Here he relates three aspects of the return. In this account he distinguishes two aspects of the general return, differentiating the human return from the return of nature which occurs in sensible reality.

In the human general return he emphasises the Christological context. It is a return to the dignity of the image of God and that it is through the blood of Christ,

---

[65] PP V, 1546–1548, p. 49, (= PL 122 894 A).
[66] PP V, 1596–1599, p. 51, (= PL 122 895 A–B).
[67] Note here he quotes whereas he formerly paraphrased the steps.
[68] PP V, 7276, p. 224, (= PL 122 1020A).

and that no human is deprived of the natural goods in which they were created. This return occurs independently of whether an individual lived morally well or badly in this life:

*Secundus uero modus suae speculationis obtinet sedem in reditu generali totius humanae naturae in Christo saluatae in pristinum suae conditionis statum ac (ueluti in quendam paradisum) in diuinae imaginis dignitatem, merito unius, cuius sanguis communiter pro salute totius humanitatis fusus est, ita ut nemo hominum naturalibus bonis in quibus conditus est, priuetur, siue bene siue male in hac uita uixerit.*[69]

He adds the theocentric reason for the universality of this aspect of the return too, i. e. the goodness of God. "*Ac sic diuinae bonitatis et largitatis ineffabilis et incomprehensibilis diffusio in omnem humanam naturam apparebit, dum in nullo punitur quod a summo bono manat.*"[70]

He then turns to the third aspect of return, an aspect applying to the special return of the elect (that is of those of whom he elsewhere has spoken of as being deified). According to Eriugena the elect ascend through and in Christ beyond all laws of nature and are transformed into God.[71]

This scheme of analysing return must not be considered as challenging the distinction between the general and the special return. Rather it amplifies this distinction by highlighting details of the return of the human creature in the case of the general return and special return respectively. The case of the humans who are among elect, who accomplish the special return, is then yet further amplified by Eriugena.

### 2.3.2.4 Fourth complementary scheme (PP V, 7302, p. 224–7318, p. 225)

Stephen Gersh has claimed that in the account of the seven stages in the path to deification, the author seems to be offering a 'recursion' through the last three steps of return as outlined in (PP V, PL 122 876A–876B).[72] I prefer to consider the passage on the seven stages as an amplification of the special return of humans to God[73]. My interpretation is not only based on the content of the account of the seven stages but also on the *ductus* of *Periphyseon*. The account of the seven stages of deification

---

[69] PP V, 7287–7293, p. 224, (= PL 122 1020B).

[70] PP V, 7293–7296, p. 224, (= PL 122 1020B–C).

[71] See PP V, 7297–7302, p. 224, (= PL 122, 1020C): "*… qui non solum in sublimitatem naturae in eis substitutae ascensuri, uerum etiam per abundantiam diuinae gratiae, quae per Christum et in Christo electis suis tradetur, supra omnes naturae leges ac terminos superessentialiter in ipsum deum transituri sunt unumque in ipso et cum ipso futuri.*"

[72] See PP V, 7302–7318, pp. 224–225, (= PL 122 1020C–1021A) and STEPHEN GERSH, "The Structure of the Return in Eriugena's Periphyseon", p. 119: "A second horizontal articulation of the return is inserted towards the end of *Periphyseon* at V. 1020 C–D. This consists of a 'recursion' (*recursio*) through seven 'stages' (*gradus*) corresponding to a more detailed analysis of the third to fifth phases in the previous horizontal scheme."

[73] In my opinion the passage runs to 1021A.

(PP V, PL 122,1020C–1021A) follows directly on Eriugena's renewed account of the special return in PP V, PL 122 1020 A–C.

Eriugena introduces seven grades which according to him represent stages in the path to deification: The earthly body (*corpus terrenum*) is said to be transformed into vital motion (*motus uitalis*). This vital motion in turn is said to be transformed into sensation (*sensus*). Sensation is turned into reason (*ratio*), and reason into mind (*animus*) or intellect (*intellectus*)[74]. In this context of these first four grades of transformation Eriugena speaks of the unification of the parts of our nature. Once again this unification is described as not endangering the existence of the lower nature. In the case of each stage the lower part is absorbed into the higher in such a way as not to lose its existence but to become one with the higher nature:

> ... *hanc quinque ueluti partium nostrae naturae adunationem (corporis uidelicet et uitalis motus sensusque rationisque intellectusque) ita ut non quinque sed unum sint. Inferioribus semper a superioribus consummatis, non ut non sint sed ut unum sint,* ...[75]

He then relates the transformation of mind into the knowledge of all things (*scientia omnium*), the knowledge of all things into wisdom (*sapientia*), and finally the transformation of the highest, most purified into God "*purgatissimorum animorum in ipsum deum*": here too the resulting unification is a cognitive one: "*secretissima diuina mysteria beatis et illuminatis intellectibus ineffabili quodam modo aperientur*".[76]

In this account of return too the identity of the human creature and the distinct identity of God are preserved. The cognitive unification with God does not obliterate the human as a creature distinct from its Creator.

### 2.3.2.5 Conclusion

Speaking of the various schemes of division of the return Bernard McGinn has claimed that "[p]erhaps the mechanics of the divisions are less important than the inner significance of the whole system ..."[77] The various schemes are certainly to be viewed as complementary not as corrective of one another. The recurring patterns within the schemes are more important than variations in detail. In conclusion, we may make the following observations: The use of Maximus' scheme supports the increasingly biblical orientation which occurs within the fifth book of *Periphyseon* with respect to Eriugena's interpretation of the phenomenon of return. In the case of the return of the human creature there is a concurrent emphasis on Christ as perfect human and initiator and example of the return for humans. The Christological context is evident for the human creature within the special and within the general

---

[74] PP V, 7303–7310, pp. 224–5, (= PL 122 1020C).

[75] PP V, 7307–7311, p. 225, (= PL 122 1020C–D).

[76] These three transformations are related in PP V, 7312–7320, p. 225, (= PL 122, 1020D–1021A).

[77] B. McGinn, "Eriugena Mysticus", in: C. Leonardi and E. Menestò (ed.), *Giovanni Scoto nel suo tempo*, pp. 235–260, p. 256.

return. In all the schemes for analysing return, the final unification with God is to be understood primarily in cognitive terms and human autonomy and individuality are always preserved.

## 3. God revealed in Jesus Christ: theophanic Christology

In a passage in his commentary on John's Gospel Eriugena describes the scene where God reveals God's very self in theophanies to those who love and seek God. Through these theophanies they are carried up to meet Christ.

*Item uirtutes purgatissimarum animarum ¦ et intellectuum theophaniae sunt, et in eis quaerentibus et diligentibus se deus ⟨seipsum⟩ manifestat, in quibus, ueluti quibusdam nubibus, rapiuntur sancti obuiam christo, ...*[78]

Theophany is presented as encounter with Christ (*rapiuntur ... obuiam christo*). This encounter is said to be granted to those who not only seek God (which could be a purely intellectual enterprise devoid of all attempts to live a moral life) but who in addition love God (*quaerentibus et diligentibus*).

This former text describes an encounter which happens to particular human individuals. In the complementary narrative level of the story of the ten virgins (where the characters are figures of a human situation rather than particular human individuals) we read in *Periphyseon* of the virgins who '... took up their lamps ... and went out to meet ... Christ' ("*accipientes lampades suas ... exierunt obuiam sponso*").[79] Here the wise virgins represent a class of humans, the elect, who experience the special return to God.

Such texts which depict the relationship between the Christian and Christ as an interpersonal encounter have been neglected in many academic interpretations of Eriugena's writings. I argue they should not be regarded as pious padding but rather as intrinsic parts of Eriugena's understanding of the appearing of God. Furthermore, it is the thesis of this section (5.3) that through these texts the concept of theophany, (the term occurs in the example taken from the commentary on John's Gospel mentioned above) is 'sublated' to a higher level, namely, that of endowed encounter with Christ[80]. The texts confirm and 'sublate' Eriugena's notion of theophany as a structure repeatedly occurring within his accounts of the appearing of God.

---

[78] Comm., I, XXV, 88–91, É. Jeauneau (ed.), p. 124, (= PL 122 302B).

[79] The full sentence in PP V, 6852–6855, p. 211, (= PL 122 1011A) reads '*Quae accipientes lampades suas (hoc est capacitatem aeternae lucis cognoscendae)exierunt obuiam sponso et sponsae', Christo uidelicet et ecclesiae ...*".

[80] By this I mean that it loses none of it's key characteristics but retains these, albeit on a new level. A similar thesis has been presented in the context of my study of the infinity of God according to Eriugena and its consequences for his eschatology: H. A. Mooney, Infinitus enim infinite, esp. 478–482.

## *3.1 Stories of encounter*

### *3.1.1 The ten virgins*

Eriugena was well familiar with the parable of the ten virgins which is to be found in the twenty fifth chapter of the Gospel according to Matthew (Mt. 25: 1–13). This Gospel, as we have already noted, was the Gospel which received the most attention from Irish commentators in the period from the fifth to the ninth centuries.[81] He interprets this parable within the eschatological context of the distinction between the general and the special return[82]. Here the significance of the numbers ten and five play a role. The ten virgins represent the general return, that is, the movement towards perfection which applies to the whole of humankind. Each virgin has the same desire for the eternal light, which is signified by the lamps. Yet, according to Eriugena, the situation of all ten virgins is not identical. They do not share in the reception of the light to the same extent. Eriugena proceeds to explain the situation of the five foolish and five wise virgins respectively. The one group (of foolish virgins) has the capacity to receive the light; and it actually experiences the natural goods which subsist in Christ, but the members of this group do not attain to deification in Him. The oil, which only the wise possess sufficiently, stands for possessing the light (as opposed the mere capacity to receive it). The wise virgins' oil is simultaneously said to stand for their merits. They themselves, in modesty, consider these to be few. Therefore it is not out of begrudging that they send the foolish virgins off to get oil from those who sell, that is, from those who, in the opinion of the wise but modest virgins, have enough merits to help others too.

Eriugena states that not all receive the light to the same degree. Eriugena is concerned to defend the divine generosity in this context. He points out that this is not due to an unwillingness of the light to communicate itself. "*Nec hoc in culpa ipsius luminis aut inuidia aut inopia constituitur, quoniam omnibus praesens est omnibusque aequaliter superfulgens et inexhausta effusione omnibus aequaliter profluens.*"[83]

Eriugena repeatedly insists on the role of virtue and grace in the special return[84]. In terms of the parable of the ten virgins he uses the image of the festivities. The marriage feast is said to stand for deification. '*Deificatio*' he notes, is hardly used by the Latin writers. However, he considers the reality to be implied in the writ-

---

[81] See JOSEPH F. KELLY, Hiberno-Latin Theology, esp. p. 560.

[82] PP V, 6848 p. 211, and following, (= PL 122 1011A following).

[83] PP V, 6904–6907, p. 213, (= PL 122 1012B).

[84] "*ad quas nemo intromittitur nisi sapientiae luce refulgens diuinique amoris inflammationibus ardens. Quae duo (sapientiam dico et caritatem) pinguedine scientiae et actionis nutriuntur. Et ad eas nuptias nullus scientiae et actionis expers, quamuis naturalibus bonis integerrime et pulcherrime floruerit, sinitur ascendere, sed omnino ab eis secluditur. Non enim illuc natura humanam mentem subleuat, sed gratia et mandatis dei oboedientiae purissimaeque (quantum in hac uita datur) dei per litteram et creaturam cognitionis meritum subuehit.*" PP V, 7013–7022, p. 216, (= PL 122 1014 C–D).

ings of Ambrose[85]. In the writings of the Greek fathers, Eriugena says, the word *theosis* stands for "*... sanctorum transitum in deum, non solum anima sed etiam et corpore, ut unum in ipso et cum ipso sint, quando in eis nil animale, nil corporeum remanebit, ...*"[86]. We may observe that in Eriugena's own system *theosis* consists in an intimate cognitive union with God.

The scene of encounter between Christ, his church and the holy souls longing for happiness is movingly presented[87]. The virgins take up their lamps (these are said to represent the ability to know the eternal light) and go out to meet Christ and the church: "*Quae accipientes lampades suas (hoc est capacitatem aeternae lucis cognoscendae) exierunt obuiam sponso et sponsae, Christo uidelicet et ecclesiae ...*"[88] There follows the question ("*quare obuiam?*") through which the moment of encounter is emphasised[89]. The driving force behind the encounter is subsequently disclosed: "*Quia uidelicet redemptor et sponsus rationalis naturae ineffabili clementiae suae condescensione et sollertia semper ad recipiendos nos spiritualiter uenit, caelestibus uirtutibus et animabus sanctis ei commeantibus affectione salutis nostra commotis.*"[90] God is in a permanent state of spiritually approaching.

### 3.1.2 *The parable of the prodigal son*

A second parable of Jesus which Eriugena relates at length is the parable of the prodigal son. This time, it is not initially the general and the special return which are compared by means of an interpretation of a parable, but the return of human nature and the return of angelic nature. The older son is interpreted as those angels

---

[85] PP V, 7055–7057, p. 217. In his apparatus JEAUNEAU makes the fitting reference to AMBROSIUS, *Expositio euangelii secundum Lucam*, VII, 192–194, (CCSL 14, pp. 281–282). The word *deificatio* does not appear in this passage.

[86] PP V, 7059–7062, p. 217, (= PL 122, 1015C).

[87] Eriugena's interpretation of the delay of the bridegroom, his sleep and the virgin's sleep reveal interesting Christological details, albeit details which are directly concerned with his understanding of the hypostatic union and not directly with the appearing of God in Christ. The delay in the coming of the bridegroom is the interval between the beginning and the end of the world. Throughout this period the virgins, that is those whose humanity while defiled but not destroyed, seeks to ascend to meet the bridegroom. Some (those who have died) are said to be sleepers, others (those who are alive when this world comes to an end) are called dozers. The middle of the night stands for the end of the world. One interpretation of the cry of the foolish virgins "Lord, Lord, open unto us" is that it entails a reference to two supposed substances of Christ (as opposed to the correct position of two natures) to which the uninstructed Christians call out. Eriugena makes clear that he does not agree with this widely held opinion, see PP V, 7190–7196, p. 221–222, (= PL 122 1018B). Christ's divinity and humanity are inseparably one. His Christology is loyally Chacedonian:
"*Verbum itaque adunatum carni et caro adunata uerbo in unitatem inseparabilem unius eiusdemque substantiae ex duabus naturis (diuina uidelict et humana) non alios recipit, nisi eos qui simplici perfectae contemplationis oculo unitatem substantiae suae intuentur, ita ut et homo in uerbo uere filius dei, et uerbum in homine uere filius hominis, absque ulla naturarum transmutatione, unus idemque filius dei et hominis, dominus noster Iesus Christus intelligatur.*" PP V, 7209–7217, p. 222, (= PL 122, 1018C–D).

[88] PP V, 6852–6855, p. 211, (= PL 122 1011 A).

[89] PP V, 6859, p. 211, (= PL 122 1011B).

[90] PP V, 6859–5863, p. 211, (= PL 122 1011B).

who never abandoned the creator. The younger son, the prodigal son, is interpreted as human nature. God is said to have created two natures capable of knowing God, the human and the angelic.[91] Aspects of the story are taken as symbols for aspects of the return; thus the garment is the former condition of human nature; the ring symbolises the virtues.

The fatted calf is said to represent the man Christ heavy with the letter (of the law of God and scripture in general) and with the visible nature (as partaking in created corporeal reality) *"pinguedine litterae uisibilisque naturae incrassatus …".*[92] In these two things, Eriugena tells us, the 'corporeality' of Christ becomes visible. *"His enim duobus, littera uidelicet et uisibili creatura, ueluti quaedam corpulentia Christi apparet, quoniam in eis et per eas intelligitur, quantum intelligi potest."*[93] Christ is said to be the spirit of the law. It is implied that Christ is thus said to inhere in all the words of scripture, not only in the words of the New Testament. In addition Christ is said to appear in and through all things, that is, to provide the ultimate intelligibility of all created things.

In this interpretation Eriugena is making use of a theology of the incarnation which he found in the writings of Maximus Confessor. He attributes the notion of the 'thickened' *(incrassatus)* Christ to that writer, quoting him to the extent that the Word 'was made thick' *(Verbum crassatur),* or to use the translation of Sheldon-Williams and O'Meara, 'was materialised'. That the Word *"incrassari dignatum est"* is translated by Sheldon-Williams / O'Meara as 'deigned to take on material substance'.[94]

On the matter of the Word becoming visible in scripture and in visible created reality Eriugena has however added the important *caveat:* in as far as this is possible. The question of the becoming visible of God in human nature is one which he must devote quite some attention. Thus Eriugena's exposition of the parable at hand provides him with an opportunity to reflect on the scope, but also on the limits, of the revealing of God to us in Christ's humanity.

Specifically he faces the question whether the humanity of the Word of God is, like his divinity, incomprehensible to every creature. He admits that this issue has been the subject matter for a controversy. While subscribing to the position that each person should be let hold the opinion he / she prefers *(unusquisque prout vult suam sententiam proferat),* he does however also give his own opinion. The unity between the two natures in the Word incarnate is said to be so perfect that not only the divinity, but also the humanity of Christ is said to possess an incomprehensibility:

---

[91] PP V, 6561–6563, p. 202, (= PL 122 1005A).

[92] PP V, 6577–6578, p. 203, (= PL 112 1005B).

[93] PP V, 6578–6581, p. 203, (= PL 122 1005B).

[94] PP V, 6588–6589, p. 203, (= PL 122, 1005B–C). The translation of SHELDON-WILLIAMS / O'MEARA is taken from, Eriugena Periphyseon (The Division of Nature), Translation by I. P. SHELDON-WILLIAMS, revised by J. O'MEARA, p. 694. O'Meara translated book five.

*Ego autem incunctanter uestigia eorum sequor, qui non temere praedicant humanitatem domini nostri Iesu Christi suae diuinitati unitam, ita ut unum, salua naturarum ratione, in ipsa et cum ipsa sit, quoniam una substantia est et, ut usitatius dicam, una persona humanitas Christi et diuinitas. Et quemadmodum diuinitas eius omnem superat intellectum, ita et humanitas, quae super uniuersalitatem uisibilis et intelligibilis creaturae, … super omne quod dicitur et intelligitur, super omne quod post deum est exaltata est et superessentialis facta est, omni creaturae incomprehensibilis et inuestigabilis.*[95]

The disputed point seems to be whether the humanity of the Word incarnate is *confined* within the limits of the created universe, that is within the number of things which can known.[96] It is not that Eriugena denies a certain important accessibility of the humanity of Christ to the human intellect. This indeed is an important part of his aesthetic approach to the appearing of God. But he is very concerned to defend the hypostatic union. His position on the incomprehensibility of the humanity of Christ is a consequence of this.

### 3.1.3  Conclusion on the stories of encounter

Eriugena is no naïve story teller. He does not only see one level of truth in the parables of the Lord which he relates. In his interpretation of the parables he himself, moves from one level of interpretation to another and holds that there are many ways in which a story may, and should, be interpreted.

What are the most important contents of his interpretation of the two parables at hand? One important point is the affirmation of difference and plurality in the possibility of knowing God. In the story of the wise and foolish virgins this plurality is rooted in the difference between a general and a special return. These two returns involve two radically different possibilities of knowing God. In the story of the prodigal son, the two natures angelic and human are the carriers of the difference. Here details also emerge on the consequences of the 'inhumanation' of the Word for the appearing of God. Both stories facilitate the presentation of the role of virtue in an increase in knowledge of God. Finally, the stories of encounter with Christ open up the issue of what is the object of this final knowledge: Christ, or the Godhead in general, or the trinitarian God? Furthermore the concept of theophany emerges as one instrument which Eriugena utilised to investigate the issues emerging through his accounts of the biblical stories.

In the following sections of this study we too move from the level of story to that of detailed analysis. We shall first of all investigate some of the technical details which Eriugena offers us with respect to the issues of role of the aesthetic in coming to a knowledge of God; secondly we shall consider the hierarchic progression and diversity in the knowledge of God; thirdly, the object of the knowledge of God is

---

[95] PP V, 2736–2748, p. 86, (= PL 122 921 A–B).

[96] See PP V, 2732–2735, p. 86, PL 122, 921A: "*an intra terminos uniuersitatis conditae rationabili et intelligibili naturae cognoscibilis circumscribitur (hoc est intra numeros qui cognosci possunt detinetur) …*".

further investigated. Finally, we shall turn to the function of Eriugena's key term theophany within the context of his account of the structured knowledge of God in Christ (5.3.3).

### 3.2 Appropriation of the appearing of God in Christ

### 3.2.1 Aesthetic appropriation of the knowledge of God

Eriugena presents us with the intriguing suggestion that the incarnation of the Word of God is of benefit to humans with regard to their redemption, and of benefit to the angels with regard to their knowledge.

*Hinc non incassum credimus et intelligimus incarnationem uerbi dei non minus angelis quam hominibus profuisse. Profuit namque hominibus ad suam redemptionem suaeque naturae restaurationem, profuit angelis ad cognitionem.*[97]

In what way does the incarnation of the Word make possible a different knowledge of God, a knowledge of God which the angels would not have possessed if the Word had not become flesh? How does the incarnation help angels to know God?

The Alumnus explains this cognitive moment:

*Incomprehensibile quippe erat uerbum omni creaturae uisibili et inuisibili, hoc est intellectuali et rationali, angelis uidelicet et hominibus, priusquam incarnaretur, quoniam remotum et secretum super omne quod est et quod non est, super omne quod dicitur et intelligitur. Incarnatum uero quodammodo descendens mirabili quadam theophania et ineffabili et multiplici sine fine in cognitionem angelicae humanaeque naturae processit; et super omnia incognitum ex omnibus naturam in qua cognosceretur assumpsit, mundum sensibilem et intelligibilem in se ipso incomprehensibili armonia adunans ...*[98]

The incarnation not only makes possible that God should appear in Jesus Christ, but according to Eriugena, the incarnation also determines how God appears in all creatures. Here we have a concept of theophany, the knowledge of God through creatures, which asserts that all theophany is qualitatively different because of the incarnation, more precisely because of the 'inhumanation'. Jesus Christ took on human nature and all creatures are contained in human nature. Eriugena claims that Jesus Christ in assuming the human accepted all creation: "... *uerbum assumens hominem omnem creaturam uisibilem et inuisibilem accepit* ..."[99] While Eriugena here uses the participle *assumens* taken from one verb *assumo* to describe the relation of human nature to the Word and a form of a different verb, *accipio*, to describe the Word's accepting of creation as a whole (*accepit*) this is not always the case. Elsewhere, he can write: *Accipiens igitur humanam naturam, omnem creaturam accepit.*[100]

---

[97] PP V, 2373–2376, p. 75, (= PL 122, 912C).
[98] PP V, 2376–2386, p. 75, (= PL 122 912C–D).
[99] PP V, 2415–2416, p. 76, (= PL 122, 913 C).
[100] PP V, 2368–2369, p. 74, (= PL 122 912 C).

The context however shows that he clearly distinguishes the levels of acceptance. This distinction is important. Similarly it is important to note that the redemptive context of the incarnation is maintained by Eriugena (there is no explicit suggestion that the word would have become incarnate if humans had not sinned) but the cognitive advance of the incarnation is strongly upheld[101].

It is significant that this knowledge of God in all things is represented as something which is of benefit to angels. He does not say that the knowledge of God as God which appears in creation is superfluous for these intellectual creatures. Rather he represents the situation of incarnation and its consequences as inspiring a liturgy of praise: "*Hinc est quod communiter angelicam ymnologiam uniuersalis ecclesia in caelo et in terra intelligibili et sensibili uoce cantare non desinit: 'Gloria in excelsis deo, et in terra pax hominibus bonae uoluntatis.*'"[102]

Once again Eriugena's radically aesthetic position emerges: even for intellectual creatures, it is of cognitive advantage to know God as God appears in all created (even material) reality.

### 3.2.2 *Hierarchic appropriation of the knowledge of God*

One of the most strongly recurring themes in Eriugena's presentation of the revealing of God in and through Jesus Christ is the assertion that this revealing is perceived to a different extent by different individuals. He highlights the difference between angelic and human perception of the theophanies:

*'In theophaniis' autem dixi pluraliter, quoniam nec intellectuales nec rationales naturae eodem modo ueritatem contemplaturae sunt, sed unicuique earum (hoc dicit de angelica et humana natura, quae sublimissimum uniuersitatis conditae obtinent locum) secundum propriam analogiam altitudo theoriae distribuitur atque definitur.*[103]

However, most of his discussions of this point do not focus on the difference between angels and humans but the differing situations of virtuous humans and of less virtuous humans. Thus even within the human perception of the theophanies there is said to be a wide spectrum of possibilities of reception.

He uses various scriptural metaphors to explain this situation. Thus he uses an extended understanding of the notion of place, the '*ubi*' in "*Ubi ego fuero, illic et minister meus*" (Where I am, there shall my servant be) to present the degrees of theophanies. Paradoxically, he draws on this quote not to establish the equality of location of all with the Lord in heaven but the higher place of Christ and the varying places of the blessed and the others.

---

[101] This is in my opinion an example where the position of Maximus and Eriugena on the centrality of the incarnation may be profitably compared and contrasted.

[102] PP V, 2388–2391, p. 75, (= PL 122 913A).

[103] PP V, textual addition number 3, 14–19, p. 65, (= PL 122 905B).

*Ministri igitur ipsius super omnia sunt. ... Caeteri uero, qui uirtutem purae contemplationis non attingunt, inferiores ordines obtinent ...*[104]

Further, Eriugena reflects on the house of the Lord and its many mansions. Here scriptural texts which speak of the house of the Lord provide inspiration. He quotes: "*Venite, ascendamus ad montem domini et ad domum dei Jacob*" and states "*Non enim alibi habitat deus, nisi in humana et angelica natura, quibus solis donatur contemplatio ueritatis.*"[105]

In particular he develops the biblical notion of the mansions within God's house: He quotes Jn.14:2: "*in domo patris mei mansiones multae sunt*".[106] He interprets this in the sense not just of many mansions but of many, different mansions and highlights the aesthetic advantage of this harmonious interplay of contraries and opposites: "*Nulla enim pulchritudo efficitur, nisi ex compaginatione similium et dissimilium, contrariorum et oppositorum ...*"[107]. He applies the architectural imagery to the variety of 'positions' in heaven:

*In paradiso itaque humanae naturae unusquisque locum suum secundum proportionem conuersationis suae in hac uita possidebit, alii exterius ueluti in extremis porticibus, alii interius tanquam in propinquioribus atriis diuinae contemplationi, alii in amplissimis diuinorum mysteriorum templis, alii in intimis super omnem naturam in ipso et cum ipso qui superessentialis et supernaturalis est theophaniis.*[108]

He also gives a Christological interpretation of the architectural imagery: blessed are they who enter into the shrine of wisdom which is Christ:[109] "*Domus illa Christus est, qui omnia et ambit uirtute, disponit prouidentia, regit iustitia, ornat gratia, continet aeternitate, implet sapientia, perficit deificatione, 'quoniam ex ipso et per ipsum et in ipso et ad ipsum sunt omnia'.*"[110]

A human is said to draw near to Christ or to be separated from Christ not in a local sense but by merit: "*non locorum interualla, sed meritorum qualitates faciunt hominem appropinquare Christo*"[111].

In the state of the universe established by God, there are many mansions which are to be understood as the degrees of merit and grace.[112]

Eriugena not only affirms this diversity and identifies its root in merit, but he expands on the diverse situations of individuals. He distinguishes between the just and the unjust, both being permitted differing contemplations of the truth: "*Quamuis enim non eodem modo, sed multiplicibus in infinitum diuinarum uisionum*

---

[104] PP V, 2069–2071, pp. 64–65, (= PL 122 905B).
[105] PP V, 5564–5567, p. 171, (= PL 122 982B–C).
[106] PP V, 5570–5571, p. 171, (= PL 122 982C).
[107] PP V, 5580–5582, p. 171, (= PL 122 982D).
[108] PP V, 5593–5599, p. 172, (= PL 122 983A).
[109] PP V, 5599–5602, p. 172, (= PL 122 983A).
[110] PP V, 5648–5652, p. 174, (= PL 122 984B).
[111] PP V, 5634–5636, p. 173, (= PL 122 984A).
[112] See PP V, 5646–5648, pp. 173–174, (= PL 122 984B).

*ascensionibus et descensionibus iustis et iniustis apparebit, omnibus tamen apparebit, ...*"[113] What the just accepted in faith in this life, in heaven they then grasp face to face (*per speciem*). They see this heavenly vision in individual ways: "*Sed qualis ipsa species sit, unusquisque in seipso uidebit experimento.*"[114] The blessed are confronted with phantasies or appearances which are representations of the divine contemplations: "*Vtrisque tamen erunt phantasiae ueluti facies quaedam expressae, iustis quidem diuinarum contemplationum ...*"[115]. Just as the situations of the just are diverse in heaven, so too those who are far from God experience different grades of ignorance: "*Et quemadmodum deificati per innumerabiles diuinae contemplationis gradus ascendent, sicut scriptum est: 'Ibunt sancti ac uirtute in uirtutem (in nubibus uisionis rapti) uidebuntque deum deorum in Sion', hoc est, non per se ipsum sed in specula diuinae phantasiae, ita a Deo elongati semper descendent per diuersos uitiorum suorum descensus in profundum ignorantiae inque tenebras exteriores, in quibus 'erit fletus et stridor dentium'.*"[116]

### 3.2.3 Christocentric appropriation of the knowledge of God

In what way is our final knowledge of God Christocentric? Granted that the eschatological vision of God is mediated by Christ, can we find evidence in Eriugena's writings for the position that this mediation is not just a means to an end but that the eschatological fulfilment is itself Christologically, or indeed trinitarianly, structured?

Eriugena quotes the scriptural text "*Rapiemur in nubibus obuiam Christo*" – we shall be swept up in clouds going to meet Christ.[117]. Here Christ seems more than just the means to a cognitive encounter with the deity as such. Here Christ emerges quasi as end of the elevation. There is a further allusion to the biblical text in the passage PP V, PL 122, 998D–999A where Enoch, Elijah, Abraham, Moses, Peter and Paul are all represented as being swept up into the presence of Christ, and said explicitly to be both with Him and in Him[118].

---

[113] PP V, 4704–4707, p. 1145, (= PL 122 964A).

[114] PP V, 3839–3840, p. 119, (= PL 122 945C). Here again the inspiring scriptural text is "in my father's house are many mansions".

[115] PP V, 3842–3843, p. 119, (= PL 122, 945C). I here rely heavily on the translation of I. P. SHELDON-WILLIAMS / J. O'MEARA, Eriugena. Periphyseon (The Division of Nature), p. 624.

[116] PP V, 3852–3859, p. 120, (= PL 122 945D–946A).

[117] PP V, 3847, p. 120, (= PL 122 945D). Compare the translation of Sheldon-Williams / O'Meara "We shall be snatched up into the clouds going before Christ", I. P. SHELDON-WILLIAMS / J. O'MEARA, Eriugena. Periphyseon (The Division of Nature), p. 624. Here too the meeting with Christ appears not just as means but as end.

[118] "*Nonne omnes isti eorumque similes obuiam Christo iuxta uniuscuiusque propriam communemue theoriam rapti cum illo sunt et in illo in spirituali aere uirtutum et contemplationum?*", PP V, 6287–6290, p. 194, (= PL 122 999A). Here I. P. SHELDON-WILLIAMS / J. O'MEARA translate *obviam Christo* as 'into the presence of Christ' which in my opinion, fits well into the context of the text where it is repeatedly asked whither (*quo*) the individuals are swept up.

In an account of the ascension of the Lord Eriugena speaks of the sensible clouds in which the Lord in his ascension was carried out of the sight of the disciples.[119] Eriugena tells us that although he needed no cloud to ascend, the Lord wished to show his disciples how he might ascend in the hearts of those who ascend to him: "*uoluit suis discipulis uisibiliter ostendere modum, quo inuisibiliter ipse in cordibus diligentium sequentiumque se ascendit.*"[120] Christ himself is said to ascend in the contemplations of those who ascend to him: "*Ipse siquidem ascendit in contemplationibus ascendentium ad se.*"[121] Here we see both an ascending in Christ and an ascending to Christ.[122] Thus we see here both aspects of the Christocentric appropriation of the knowledge of God. Christ does not only make the ascent possible but once ascended, the believing Christian contemplates Christ.

Eriugena indicates that the faithful ascend, not just to Christ, but to the Father. In this connection he quotes "No one ascends into heaven except him that came down from heaven." According to Eriugena whenever we read in the Gospel that the Lord turned his eyes to heaven we should understand to the Father[123]. "Heaven" in the Gospel can stand for the Father. Eriugena can thus interpret the ascent or return trinitarianly, as a return to the Father. Here the final vision is presented as a resting in the vision of the Father.

## 3.3 Theophany: provisional observations

This section focuses on Eriugena's use of the notion of theophany in the context of the appearing of God in Jesus Christ. It draws together aspects of this usage which have emerged in the foregoing sections of chapter five. Here we may present some provisional observations on Eriugena's usage of the notion of theophany in the context of the appearing of God in Christ.

Firstly we observe that his use of 'theophany' embraces both his concern to describe the ability of all creatures as such 'objectively' to reveal God (this is to be observed above all in his accounts of creation) and the use he makes of 'theophany' in an analysis of the differing 'subjective' capacities of knowing creatures hierarchically to receive knowledge of God. In the Christological context the second sense emerges strongly. In a short repetition of a position Eriugena ascribes to Maximus we can recognise the understanding of theophany which has emerged in this Christological context:

---

[119] PP V, 6290–6311, p. 194, (= PL 122 999A–B).

[120] PP V, 6299–6301, p. 194, (= PL 122, 999B).

[121] PP V, 6301–6302, p. 194, (= PL 122 999B). Compare: "*in sanctis intellectibus eos secum subleuans ad se ipsum ascendit.*" PP V, 6304–6305, p. 194, (= PL 122 999B).

[122] Indirect support may also be gleaned from the 'Christocentricity' of Eriugena's account of the transfiguration. The saints are said to be both in and with Christ in pure contemplation in three ways: "*Tribus autem modis sancti in puritate contemplationis cum Christi et in Christo fieri intelliguntur.*" PP V, 6312–6313, p. 194, (= PL 122, 999C).

[123] PP V, 6308–6310, p. 194, (= PL 122 999C).

*Unusquisque igitur sanctorum, … suam habebit nubem, propriam uidelicet suae contemplationis uirtutem et altitudinem. In quantum quippe quisque cognitioni ueritatis appropinquabit, in tantum rapietur obuiam Christo in aera, hoc est in purissimae intelligentiae altitudinem et claritatem, ac sic semper in nube contemplationis suae (in diuinis theophaniis) et erit et gaudebit.*[124]

Secondly we may observe that Eriugena presents to us God, the "*incomprehensibilem et inintelligibilem uniuersalitatis causam*".[125] This divine incomprehensibility implies that knowledge thereof can only be received as 'gift'. Eriugena uses theophany to express this reception of endowed knowledge. The grounding context of the divine generosity is one which is foundational for his use of the notion of theophany in the context of creation and the subjective conversion of the creature to God in knowledge alike:

*Propterea siquidem, inquis, omnia de nihilo facta sunt, ut diuinae bonitatis amplitudo et largitas per ea quae fecit et ostenderetur et laudaretur. … Si enim sola intra semet ipsam diuina bonitas quieta absque ulla operatione perseueraret, non fortassis laudis suae occasionem faceret. Iam uero in omnia uisibilia et inuisibilia se ipsam diffundens, et in omnibus omnia existens, rationabilem intellectualemque creaturam ad se ipsam cognoscendam conuertens, caeterarum uero rerum pulchras et innumerabiles species rationabili et intellectuali creaturae in materiem suae laudis praestans ita omnia fecit, ut nulla creatura sit quae non, aut per se ipsam et in se ipsa aut per aliud, summum bonum non laudet.*[126]

Thirdly we may observe that the notion of theophany, when linked to his accounts of the human body of the Word made human, is used to highlight the aesthetic mediation of this revealing of God.

Our observations remain, however, at this point of the investigation, of preliminary nature. There are still open questions. Here's one significant example: As we have seen, Eriugena uses the notion of theophany, less often that of apparition, to account for the appearing of God, be this in creation as a whole or in Jesus Christ. He can write that God is not known in God'sself but in apparitions: "… *nam non per se ipsum sed per quasdam suas apparitiones secundum altitudinem uniuscuiusque sanctorum contemplationis uidebitur deus …*"[127]. Even the happiness of the blessed will be provided in theophanies: "… *in phantasiis, quas propter differentiam aliarum phantasiarum theologi theophanias appellant, administrabitur.*"[128] Again and again Eriugena seems to insist that the divinity itself is inaccessible to human knowledge and that God can 'only' be known in theophanies. Only the humanity of the Word may be said to transcend all theophanies or attain to God without an intervening theophany.

---

[124] PP V, 6259–6266, p. 193, (= PL 122 998B–C).
[125] PP V, 2992–2993, pp. 94–95, (= PL 122 926C).
[126] PP V, 4126–4144, p. 128, (= PL 122 951D–952B).
[127] PP V, 3843–3846, pp. 119–120, (= PL 122 945C).
[128] PP V, 4689–4693, p. 145, (= PL 122 963C).

*Hoc autem dicimus, non quod ulla creatura praeter uerbi humanitatem ultra omnes theophanias possit ascendere, eumque 'qui solus habet immortalitatem et lucem habitat inaccessibilem', nulla theophania interposita, attingere, sed quod theophaniarum quaedam tantae altitudinis sint, ut supra omnem creaturam proxima deo contemplatione intelligantur exaltari, ac uelut theophaniarum theophaniae creduntur esse.*[129]

How are such sentences to be interpreted? In this last quotation we notice a sentence where Eriugena claims that only Jesus Christ ascends to a knowledge of God '*nulla theophania interposita*'[130]. Here our questioning becomes even more pointed. Does this negative case suggest the possibility of a positive counterpart? Are theophanies to be understood as 'interpositions', as intermediaries between the knower and God? Statements of Eriugena on anthropology seem to rule this out. The Alumnus asserted that humanity was created in order to contemplate God without the intervention of any creature: "*Ad creatoris sui siquidem contemplationem, nulla alia interposita creatura, humanitas creata est.*"[131] We may not simply identify theophany with creatural intervention between the human in its cognitive search for God. Thus we are presented with a series of affirmations: that we cannot know the divinity in itself; that we know it in theophanies; and that no creature intervenes between God and the human. The context within which each and all of these sentences may be affirmed must be outlined. It is the thesis of this investigation that it is to be sought in an analysis of the systematic function of the notion of theophany in Eriugena's writings. This shall be offered within the last chapter of our investigation.

---

[129] PP V, textual addition number 2, 4–10, pp. 64–65, (= PL 122 905C).
[130] PP V, textual addition number 2, 7, p. 65, (= PL 122, 905C).
[131] PP V, 3658–3660, p. 114, (= PL 122, 941D).

# Reflection
## on Eriugena's understanding
## of the appearing of God

*"Ex ipsa igitur sapientiae dei condescensione
ad humanam naturam per gratiam et
exaltatione eiusdem naturae ad ipsam
sapientiam per dilectionem fit theophania".*

PP I, 303–306, p. 13, (= PL 122 449B)

# Chapter 6

# Reflection on Eriugena's understanding
of the appearing of God

In this final chapter a three-fold reflection is undertaken. First, Eriugena's appropriation of the rich patristic tradition is reviewed (6.1). Neither the influence of past theologians on Eriugena's thought in general, nor their influence on other limited issues other than the revealing of God, is at the centre of investigation[1]. Rather this section focuses on the influence which his reading of earlier theological sources has had on his own interpretation of the issue of the appearing of God. In this section it is the content of his inheritance from former thinkers that is of interest. A complementary consideration of the hermeneutic with which Eriugena justifies and recommends the use of the ideas of others is one of the topics handled in the reflection on Eriugena's method which follows (6.2). In this section the author's use of scriptural ideas and his understanding of scriptural authority will also be reviewed. Finally there follows a systematic reflection on the issue investigated by this study: Eriugena's understanding of the appearing of God (6.3). Here the various facets of Eriugena's theology of the disclosure of God are reviewed and the questions of the coherence, consistence, and comprehensiveness of his theological position are raised.

## 1. Historical reflection: Eriugena's appropriation
of the theological tradition

### 1.1 Augustine

Augustine was the most widely read theological authority for Carolingian theology. The theological controversy within which Eriugena's *De pradestinatione* was com-

---

[1] General studies of Eriugena's sources range from the early work of JOHANNES DRÄSEKE, *Johannes Scotus Erigena und dessen Gewährsmänner in seinem Werke De Divisione Naturae libri V,* Leipzig: Dieterich'sche Verlags-Buchhandlung, 1902, (= Studien zur Geschichte der Theologie und der Kirche, IX/2), to the recent study, WILLEMIEN OTTEN, "The Texture of Tradition. The Role of the Church Fathers in Carolingian Theology", in: IRENA BACKUS, *The Reception of the Church Fathers in the West.*, 2 vols., vol. 1 From the Carolingians to the Maurists, Leiden: Brill, 1997, pp. 3–50. See also ÉDOUARD JEAUNEAU, "Pseudo-Dionysius, Gregory of Nyssa, and Maximus the Confessor in the Works of John Scottus Eriugena", in: U.-R. BLUMENTHAL (ed.), *Carolingian Essays,* pp. 137–149; GOULVEN MADEC, Jean Scot et ses auteurs; DEIRDRE CARABINE, The Unknown God. Studies of Eriugena's debt to individual fathers with respect to individual themes are also numerous.

posed bears witness to the importance which Carolingian bishops and theologians assigned to an adequate interpretation of Augustine[2]. In what sense was he an important source for Johannes Scottus Eriugena?[3] The ideas which Eriugena holds in common with Augustine represent the more widely held (and in this sense the more 'conservative') elements within the Irishman's system. They solicit much respect from his intellectual contemporaries and they represent a point of departure from which Eriugena may only remove himself with extensive apology[4].

The commonly held theological insights of Carolingian Augustinianism most relevant to the theme of the appearing of God will now be briefly mentioned. In the past chapters Eriugena's understanding of the appearing of God in the creation of the world, in the human creature and in Jesus Christ have been considered. Augustine's bequeathal to Eriugena on each of these matters deserves attention.

Eriugena and Augustine alike emphasise that the world was created in the Word, in the second person of the blessed trinity[5]. The agreement on the rationality of the world, a rationality whose foundation is the rootedness of the world in the intelligibility of the Word, is more important than the minor differences which do occur between the two thinkers' respective accounts of the *causae primordiales*[6].

---

[2] Compare ROBERT CROUSE, "Predestination, Human Freedom and the Augustinian Theology of History in Eriugena's De divina praedestinatione", in: J. McEvoy and M. DUNNE (ed.), History and Eschatology, pp. 303–311, p. 303.

[3] See AVITAL WOHLMAN, "John Scottus Eriugena, a Christian philosopher", in: *American Catholic Philosophical Quarterly* 79 (2005) 635–651.

[4] In at least one case Eriugena seems to 'bend' Augustine's theology so as to eliminate contradictions between that theology and his own. See John J. O'MEARA, "Magnorum Virorum Quendam Consensum Velimus Machinari" (804B). Eriugena's use of Augustine's De Genesi ad litteram in the Periphyseon", in: WERNER BEIERWALTES (ed.), Eriugena. Studien zu seinen Quellen, pp. 105–116.

[5] One only has to consider the influence of Augustine's *In Iohannis euangelium tractatus* on Eriugena's homily and commentary on John's Gospel. Compare É. JEAUNEAU in his introduction to Comm., p. 25–27.

[6] This complex of themes has been the subject of several careful essays written by Crouse: R. D. CROUSE, The Meaning of Creation in Augustine and Eriugena; IDEM, *Primordiales Causae* in Eriugena's Interpretation of Genesis: Sources and Significance: "Central to Eriugena's metaphysic of Genesis is the concept of primordial causes … I think it is clear that at least the term, 'primordialis causa', comes from St Augustine's De Genesi ad litteram, both directly and by way of Bede.", p. 210. See "*Sed haec aliter in uerbo Dei, ubi isti non facta, sed aeterna sunt, aliter in elementis mundi, ubi omnia simul facta futura sunt, aliter in rebus, quae secundum causas simul creatas non iam simul, sed suo quaeque tempore creantur: in quibus Adam iam formatus ex limo et dei flatu animatus, sicut fenum exortum, aliter in seminibus, in quibus rursus quasi primordiales causae repetuntur de rebus ductae, quae secundum causas, quas primum condidit, extiterunt, uelut herba ex terra, semen ex herba.*" AUGUSTINE, *De Genesis ad litteram*, VI, 10, JOSEPH ZYCHA (ed.), p. 182, 17–p. 183, 1. Other authors stress the innovation in Eriugena's development of the notion of the *causae primordiales:* GANGOLF SCHRIMPF points out that Eriugena himself assigns the term to Augustine, but in his own analysis Schrimpf emphasises the innovative aspects of Eriugena's use of the notion: "Sodann ist dieser Begriff eine originäre Reflexionsleistung Eriugenas.", GANGOLF SCHRIMPF, Das Werk des Johannes Scottus Eriugena, pp. 256–295, here p. 256. Kapriew has recently pointed out the theory of the causae primordiales, as it is developed by Eriugena belongs firmly in the realm of Latin theology and differs in its content to theories of the Greek theologians on the divine ener-

This theology provides a context for Eriugena's own theology of the appearing of God in the world. Eriugena's most innovative notions do not however stem from this Augustinian heritage. Even some cases where there is a verbal agreement, there must not be an identical meaning intended. Thus when Eriugena uses the key term 'theophany' he does not necessarily intend the same meaning as Augustine, still less is he indebted to the Bishop of Hippo for the meaning which he does intend.

In sections of *Periphyseon* on the human as created in the image of God Eriugena relies on Augustine's *De Trinitate* where the psychological analogy for the trinity is worked out in detail and indeed its limitations are made explicit. It is however interesting that in those passages of *Periphyseon* where Eriugena makes an innovative contribution to the theology of the human created in the image of God, that is in those passages where he focuses in on human ignorance as mirroring the divine ignorance, Augustine can only be of limited help. Eriugena values Augustine as an ally, quoting from him. He subtly changed the context (from human ignorance of God to 'divine ignorance' of God) to suit his systematic position.

If we turn to the Augustinian influence on Eriugena's theology of the appearing of God in, and through Jesus Christ, we reach similar conclusions. The Commentary on John's Gospel and the Homily on the Prologue to John's Gospel demonstrate a familiarity with Augustine's *Tractatus in Iohannis Evangelium*. However, it is the opinion of the present writer that Eriugena's most original ideas on the appearing of God in Christ are best understood not as a development of Augustinian ideas but rather of Maximian ideas and ideas which are inspired by the writings of Gregory of Nyssa[7].

We may conclude that Eriugena, in common with his contemporaries, owed a great debt to Augustine. His biblical hermeneutic is strongly Augustinian. The emphasis on the contribution of biblical truth to building up a community of those who love is common to both authors[8]. This is certainly relevant to the question of the mediation of the appearing of God through the scriptures. However, beyond this, with respect to the theme of this investigation, the appearing of God, Augustine of Hippo was not the particular author whose thought kindled new fires of speculation in the furnace of Eriugena's theology. However, much we may hear the existential tones of the direct prayers of *Confessiones* echoing in Eriugena's own

---

gies: GORGI KAPRIEV, "Eodem sensu utentes? Die Energienlehre der 'Griechen' und die causae primordiales Eriugenas," in: *Theologische Quartalschrift* 180 (2000) 289–307.

[7] Augustine's vast *oeuvre* is not, however, homogenous. Kari Kloos has carefully examined a development in what she calls Augustine's 'theophany narrative exegesis', see: KARI KLOOS, "Seeing the Invisible God: Augustine's Reconfiguration of Theophany Narrative Exegesis," in: *Augustinian Studies* 36 (2005) 397–420, esp. pp. 418–420.

[8] See PP V, 7357–7362, p. 237, (= PL 122 1022A); AUGUSTINUS, *De doctrina christiana,* book I, XXIX, 30, 1–28, J. MARTIN (ed.), p. 23. See HERMANN JOSEF SIEBEN, "Die 'res' der Bibel. Eine Analyse von Augustinus, De doctrina christian I–III", in: *"Manna in deserto": Studien zum Schriftgebrauch der Kirchenväter,* Köln: Koinonia-Oriens, 2002, (= Edition Cardo; 92), pp. 267–294.

prayer to his Lord Jesus, the theory of the appearing of this Lord is significantly refined through Eriugena's reading of the Greek authors[9].

### *1.2 Pseudo-Dionysius*

The most important methodological distinction within Eriugena's writings is that between the kataphatic and apophatic ways of talking about God. This distinction is implicit in the writings of Dionysius the pseudo-Areopagite. Eriugena's theory of the possibility of talking about God and the limitations of this possibility are heavily influenced by his predecessor[10]. From the pseudo Areopagite Eriugena learned to describe the limitation of the power of the probing mind and to appreciate that those insights into God which we are granted, we receive as gift.

Thus in the sphere of the appearing of God in creation Johannes Scottus Eriugena is heavily indebted to Dionysius. What can we summarise on the matters of the appearing of God in the human and in Christ?

Eriugena's theory of the human created in the image of God draws on the Dionysian understanding both of human and of divine ignorance. The combination of the two within a theology of the human created in the image of God, and the development of the Dionysian concept of divine incomprehensibility into an incomprehensibility on God's part of God's very self are, however, Eriugenian contributions.

According to Eriugena, the encounter of the blessed with God, in and through Christ, is characterised by a thoroughgoing individuality. This is not rooted in any lack of generosity on God's part; rather, theosis or deification, with its concomitant, received knowledge of God, is differently appropriated according to the different standards of virtue attained by the blessed. Here too Eriugena has been influenced by a Dionysian understanding of hierarchy and of hierarchical mediation of knowledge[11]. In Dionysius' system hierarchy stood for an ordered participation in a liturgical good or another good. Dionysius' notion of hierarchy is reworked by

---

[9] See PP V, 6818–6832, pp. 210–211, (= PL 122 1010B–C).

[10] The metaphysics of the God-world relationship which supports this is also heavily endebted to the Pseudo Areopagite, see H. A. MOONEY, "Some Observations on the Concept of Harmony in Pseudo-Dionysius Areopagita and John Scottus Eriugena," in: ELIZABETH A. LIVINGSTONE (ed.), *Studia Patristica, vol. XXIX*, Leuven: Peeters, 1997, pp. 304–309. This article argues that the distinction between God and world is upheld by both authors and that the accusation of pantheism raised against Eriugena is ungrounded.

[11] On this and on other matters future scholarship will benefit from the recent publication: PAUL ROREM. *Eriugena's Commentary on the Dionysian Celestial Hierarchy*, Toronto: Pontifical Institute of Mediaeval Studies, 2005, (= Studies and Texts; 150), esp. pp. 99–171. See too L. Michael Harrington's extensive introduction in: Ps. DIONYSIUS AREOPAGITA ET AL. *A Thirteenth-Century Textbook of Mystical Theology at the University of Paris. The Mystical Theology of Dionysius the Areopagite in Eriugena's Latin Translation with the Scholia translated by Anastasius the Librarian and Excerpts from Eriugena's Periphyseon*, Translation and Introduction by L. MICHAEL HARRINGTON, Paris, Leuven, Dudley: PEETERS, 2004, (= Dallas Medieval Texts and Translations; 4), pp. 1–38.

Eriugena through means of the biblical notion of the many mansions in the Father's house. The Irishman can thus arrive at his own concept of a plural participation in ultimate perfection and endowed knowledge of God.

### 1.3  Gregory of Nyssa

The theology of Gregory of Nyssa exerts its influence on Eriugena's interpretation of all three carriers of the appearing of God.

Gregory's emphasis on the incomprehensibility, not only of the divine essence, but of every individual essence, fertilises Eriugena's theory of the appearing of God in the world[12]. The created world is perceived as simultaneous laden with the meaning bestowed on it by its creator and, at the same time, mysterious. The mystery is rooted in the theocentric origin of all reality and the ensuing ontological depth which is ultimately elusive to the human intellect. The divine incomprehensibility has implications for the human search for the divine.

Our observation on the influence of Gregory of Nyssa on Eriugena's account of the appearing of God in the human creature centres on his interpretation of Gregory's *De hominis opificio* which Eriugena entitled *De imagine*. Here the extensive quotation from that work within *Periphyseon* suggests a substantial, if indeed as we shall argue, limited influence on Eriugena[13]. My thesis is that the two authors home in on a different human characteristic to which the human mirroring of the divine adheres and that the common ground between them consists in a similar identification of the motivation with which God creates the human in the divine image.[14]

Gregory selects different 'goods' for attention, the emphasis always falling on the human participation in all goods. Always insisting that the human reflects the plenitude of the goods inhering in the divinity, he nevertheless does single out one good and devote it particular attention. He asserts that one of these participated goods consists in being free from necessity, not being subjected to any physical power but having an independent will in one's decisions.[15] The special position assigned to freedom is confirmed in the *Oratio catechetica magna* where the gift of

---

[12] ERIUGENA develops his account of οὐσία and σύμβαμα interestingly enough naming Gregory of Nazianzus and Maximus Confessor as his sources PP I, 1245–1260, p. 43,(= PP I, PL 122, 471B–C). In connection with them he makes the point that οὐσία is unknowable not only to the senses but also to the intellect. It is known from certain 'circumstances' that it exists. He distinguishes between categories which are in the essence and ones which are predicated around it (circa). No one can define οὐσία in itself or say what it is PP I, 1911–1912, p. 63, (= PL 122, 487A). It is not defined as to what it is but that it is (*quid est / quia est*) PP I, 1917–1918, p. 63, (= PL 122, 487A–B).

[13] As many an interpreter of Eriugena knows or at least suspects, quotation is not necessarily the best indication of the assimilation and integration of another's position, see É. JEAUNEAU on the significance of quotation in Eriugena's texts: Pseudo-Dionysius, Gregory of Nyssa, and Maximus the Confessor.

[14] I have argued this in my article: The Notion of the Liberality of God in Gregory of Nyssa and Johannes Scottus Eriugena. What follows draws on the research presented in that article.

[15] See *De hominis opificio*, chapter 17, G. FORBES (ed.), p. 202.

being one's own master or mistress and having a free will is called that most beautiful and precious of goods.[16]

Eriugena gave accounts of the creation of the human in the image of God, in book two and in book four of *Periphyseon*. In both books he explicitly acknowledges his debt to Gregory's *De hominis opificio*[17]. Yet in neither major account of the creation of the human in the image of God does he focus his adoption nor his development of Gregory's position on this author's idea of freedom as pre-eminent in the mirroring of God[18]. However, in chapter eleven of *De hominis opificio* Gregory had presented another aspect of the human mirroring of the divine[19]. He had said that just as the prototype, God, is incomprehensible, so too is the image incomprehensible. In both his substantial accounts of the creation of the human it is this position which catches Eriugena's attention and which he creatively develops within his own synthesis. In his theology of God he develops the affirmation of our ignorance of the Divine infinity (a position which characterises Gregory's theology[20]) into an affirmation of the divine inability to comprehend what God is. In his anthropology Eriugena speaks of a radical disability of the human spirit to know what it is.

While both authors differ in their selection of the key aspect of the human mirroring of the divine, both see the creation of the human in the image of God as the crowning high-point of the divine liberality. I argue that both authors highlight the divine liberality or generosity as the moving force behind the creation of the human in the image of God. According to Eriugena the liberality of God is rooted

---

[16] See *Oratio catechetica magna*, E. Mühlenberg (ed.), in: *Gregorii Nysseni Opera*, Vol. III, part IV, (Leiden: 1996), p. 19, 18–21. In *De hominis opificio* freedom is not however presented as having an absolute precedence but a precedence through the role that it plays with respect to the other virtues. Freedom is pivotal because all genuine virtue is freely exercised. The importance of freedom comes from its function within the human fullness, the human plèroma which as a whole mirrors the divine plèroma. According to the system of Gregory the optimal exercise of freedom, the realisation of love, colours the whole human imaging of God. In the biblically oriented fifth chapter of *De hominis opificio,* Gregory refers to the first letter of John, (love comes from God and God is love), and argues that if love is missing in the human, then *all* aspects of the image of God in us are deformed. See GREGORY OF NYSSA, *De hominis opificio,* chapter 5, G. FORBES (ed.), p. 130.

[17] See for example PP II, 1929–1931, (= PL 122 585D), and PP IV, CCCM CLXIV, textual addition number 8, 32–33, p. 25, (= PL 122 758C).

[18] All the more surprising because in a different context in PP V Eriugena shows that he is aware that freedom belongs to the human nature as created in the image of God. In PP V, 4835–4838, p. 149, (= PL 122 966D) he can write: "*Si enim libertas naturae rationabilis ad imaginem dei conditae a deo data est – non enim imago dei ullis legibus detineri potuit coacta – …*" In *De diuina praedestinatione liber* human freedom had been the focus of Eriugena's attention and the status of the gift of freedom in the creation of the human in the image of God therefore received more explicit attention: see chapter four of *De diuina praedestinatione liber,* G. MADEC (ed.), p. 31, 153–164, (PL 122 373A–B).

[19] *De hominis opificio,* G. FORBES (ed.) pp. 156–158.

[20] See E. MÜHLENBERG, *Die Unendlichkeit Gottes bei Gregor von Nyssa. Gregors Kritik am Gottesbegriff der klassischen Metaphysik,* (= Forschungen zur Kirchen- und Dogmengeschichte; 16), (Göttingen: 1966).

in the divine perfection and fullness. He can call God 'the more than fullness and perfection': (*plus quam plenitudo et perfectio*).[21] Creation receives in abundance the gifts which descend from above from the Father of Lights, and flow out through all things from the widely flowing fullness of the divine goodness.[22] This notion of the divine liberality was one which he met in the writings of Gregory and which he made his own.[23].

Gregory's theology situates the fullness of grace and the fullest participation in the divine perfection in Jesus Christ. This aspect of his theology of pléroma has influenced Eriugena's theology of the appearing of God. In his Homily on the Prologue to John's Gospel he interprets the biblical words 'full of grace'[24]. He says these can be interpreted as applying to the humanity of the Word incarnate which receives the fullness of grace according to his humanity, since he is the head of the Church and the first-born of the universal creature, that is, of universal humanity, which in him and through him is cured and restored.[25] In his commentary on John's Gospel Eriugena describes how the Christian is progressively assimilated to Christ. This process is explicitly said to bring an increase of knowledge with it.

*Unusquisque enim fidelium, qualem in animo habuerit habitudinem per incrementa uirtutum, talem de christo habebit fidem per augmenta intellegentiarum. Et quotiens prioris uitae modis et inferioris moritur, et in altiores gradus subuehitur, totiens opiniones de christo, quamuis simplices, tamen in ipso et cum ipso morientur et in sublimiores de eo theophanias fide atque intelligentia prouehentur. Itaque in suis fidelibus christus cotidie moritur et ab eis crucifigitur, dum carnales de eo cogitationes, seu spirituales adhuc tamen imperfectas, interimunt, semper in altum ascendentes, donec ad ueram eius notitiam peruentant; ...*[26]

Eriugena even links this assimilation in virtue and knowledge to the concept of infinity, one which we have already mentioned as part of his debt to Gregory in the context of the theology of God. In this Christological assimilation too,

---

[21] PP I, 3172–3, p. 101, (= PL 122 516A).

[22] In the context of the return of all things to God Eriugena writes that the goods which human nature shall share *"sola diuina bonitatis largiflua plenitudine omnibus per omnia uniuersaliter inexhausta effusione manant"*, PP V, 3873–3874, p. 120, (= PL 122 946B).

[23] GREGORY OF NYSSA, *De hominis opificio*, chapter 17, G. FORBES (ed.), p. 202. ERIUGENA's Latin translation of this passage appears in PP IV, CCCM CLXIV, 2239–2248, p. 77, (= PL 122 795C–796A).
ERIUGENA himself argues that the Ps. DIONYSIUS too wrote at length of the divine goodness: *"De motu summe bonitatis ad seruanda, facienda, perficienda omnia, ipse Dionysius copiose disserit."* *Expositiones in ierarchiam coelestem*, J. BARBET (ed.), I, 192–193, p. 6, (= PL 122 131A–B). However, it is my opinion that the generosity of God as moving force behind the imaging of God in the creation of the human is an idea which is more developed in the writings of Gregory of Nyssa.

[24] "And the Word became flesh and dwelt among us, full of grace and truth; ..." John 1:14.

[25] *"Verbum quippe incarnatum, dominus noster Ihesus christus, plenitudinem gratiae secundum humanitatem accepit, quoniam caput ecclesiae est et primogenitus uniuersae creaturae, hoc est, totius uniuersaliter humanitatis, quae in ipso et per ipsum sanata et restaurata est."* Hom. JEAUNEAU (ed.), 23, 5–9, p. 310 (= PL 122 296A).

[26] Comm., XXXII, 31–42, É. JEAUNEAU (ed.), p. 182, (= PL 122 312A–B).

the notion of infinity plays a role: *infinitus enim infinite, etiam in purgatissimis mentibus, formatur.*[27]

## 1.4 Maximus

The most significant point of comparison between Johannes Scottus Eriugena and Maximus Confessor (in the context of their respective understandings of how God appears in the world) is a point of difference rather than a point of agreement. Maximus' theology includes the speculative position that the Logos would have become incarnate even if humans had not sinned[28]. Eriugena by way of contrast does not speculate on this. Although he does speak of the world being created in the Logos, he consistently speaks of the incarnation within a soteriological context alone.[29]

Maximus' influence on the theme of the appearing of God in the human person is confirmatory rather then inspirational: positions such as the fact that sexuality does not belong to the imaging of the divine, (a theme which Eriugena also encountered in Gregory of Nyssa) find confirmation in Maximus' theology. A textual edition points out that Maximus openly declares that the human, created in God's image and likeness, was without the difference of sex, and that the human is still without it to the extent that it is still in the image and likeness of the creator[30].

The influence of Maximus is most strongly felt in Eriugena's account of the appearing of God in Jesus Christ. The Christocentric definition of theophany which is inserted as an 'arch-stone' of Eriugena's theology of the appearing of God is radically indebted to Maximus.

Let us look at Eriugena's presentation of Maximus' position in *Periphyseon* book I:

*Ait enim theophaniam effici non aliunde nisi ex deo, fieri uero ex condescensione diuini uerbi, hoc est unigeniti filii, qui est sapientia patris, ueluti deorsum uersus ad humanam naturam a se conditam atque purgatam, et exaltatione sursum uersus humanae naturae ad praedictum uerbum per diuinum amorem.*[31]

---

[27] Comm., XXXII, 42–43, É. Jeauneau (ed.), p. 182, (= PL 122 312B). For an inspiring text in Gregory's writings see *De hominis opificio*, 21, (= PG 44, 201B).

[28] See E. Perl, Metaphysics and Christology in Maximus Confessor and Eriugena.

[29] The reason for this is probably Eriugena's respect for the Scriptures. The Scriptures set a limit to our conjectures about why God has acted in one way and not in another. It would be presumptuous to speculate on something not clearly indicated by the Scriptures. In Eriugena's opinion the scriptures speak of the incarnation within the context of the redemption. Maximus, who also rooted his theology in Scripture, obviously read some Scriptural texts differently.

[30] PP II, textual addition number 45, 216–225, p. 23, (= PL 122 541A–B).

[31] "For he [Maximus–H. M. ] says that theophany is effected from no other (cause) but God, but that it happens as a result of the condescension of the Divine Word, that is, of the only begotten Son Who is the Wisdom of the Father, downwards, as it were, upon human nature which was created and purified by Him, and of the exaltation upwards of human nature to the aforesaid Word by divine love." PP I, 296–301, p. 13, (= PL 122, 449A–449B), English from I. P. Sheldon-Williams, SLH VII, p. 53.

It is then astutely remarked that it is not only the incarnation of the Word which is in question here but also the theosis or deification of all humans. The text then continues:

*Ex ipsa igitur sapientiae dei condescensione ad humanam naturam per gratiam et exaltatione eiusdem naturae ad ipsam sapientiam per dilectionem fit theophania.*[32]

This whole passage[33] is a wonderful theology of the encounter between God and the human. When talking about the descent of God the categories are trinitarian: the only begotten Son; the wisdom of the father. They are markedly moral (*per dilectionem*) when talking about the ascent of the human. This theology of theophany deeply influenced Eriugena and is reflected in other passages of *Periphyseon* and in other writings where he explicitly confirms these thoughts as his own.[34]

## 2. Methodological reflection: Eriugena's academic methods

### 2.1 Eriugena's hermeneutic of the Scriptures[35]

Eriugena's first allegiance is to Holy Scripture: this attested to in the prayer which appears in the fifth book of *Periphyseon*.

*O domine Iesu, nullum aliud praemium, nullam aliam beatitudinem, nullum aliud gaudium a te postulo, nisi ut ad purum absque ullo errore fallacis theoriae uerba tua, quae per tuum sanctum spiritum inspirata sunt, intelligam. Haec est enim summa felicitatis meae finisque perfectae est contemplationis, quoniam nihil ultra rationabilis anima etiam purissima inueniet, quia nihil ultra est. Vt enim non alibi aptius quaereris quam in uerbis tuis, ita non alibi apertius inueniris quam in eis. Ibi quippe habitas et illuc quaerentes et diligentes te introducis, ibi spirituales epulas uerae cognitionis electis tuis praeparas, illic transiens ministras eis.*[36]

The wider context of the quotation makes clear that with the expression '*verba tua*' the Holy Scriptures are intended. This interpretation is also confirmed by the reference within the quotation to the inspiration of these words by the Holy Spirit.

Eriugena presents the interpretation of the depths of scripture as an arduous challenge in which however ratio, as a human faculty for appropriating scriptural

---

[32] "So from this condescension of the Wisdom of God upon human nature through grace, and the exaltation of the same nature to that same Wisdom through choice, theophany is brought about." PP I, 303–306, p. 13, (= PL 122 449B). English from I. P. SHELDON-WILLIAMS, SLH VII, p. 53.

[33] PP I, 296–306, p. 13, (= PL 122 449A–449B).

[34] "*Incomprehensibile quippe erat uerbum … Incarnatum uero quodammodo descendens mirabili quadam theophania et ineffabili et multiplici sine fine in cognitionem angelicae humanaeque naturae processit …*", PP V, 2376–2384, p. 75, (= PL 122 912C–D).

[35] I have also treated Eriugena's hermeneutic of Scripture and of the writings of the church fathers in an earlier article: HILARY MOONEY, Johannes Scottus Eriugena. Kreativer Umgang mit dem Erbe der Tradition.

[36] PP V, 6818–6828, p. 210, (= PL 122 1010B–C).

truth, rejoices. Thus at the start of the fourth book of *Periphyseon* using nautical imagery he writes:

*Tendenda uela nauigandumque. Accelerat nanque ratio perita ponti, nullas ueretur minas, nullos anfractus syrtesue cautesue formidat, cui delectabilius est in abditis diuini oceani fretibus uirtutem suam exercere, quam in planis apertisque otiosa quiescere, ubi uim suam non ualet aperire.*[37]

Again the context assures us that this and what immediately follow it are images for a difficult and controversial interpretation of holy scripture[38]. This interpretation of the nautical imagery is confirmed by patristic parallels. There immediately follows another image which Eriugena uses to illustrate the difficult and sometimes controversial interpretation of scripture: that of working a field. Here the agricultural cultivation stands for human reason undergoing development by rising to a fathomless challenge.

Yet it is not that scripture begrudges us its meaning: rather it challenges us to exercise our skill and to earn the reward: "*Neque hoc Spiritus sanctus inuidia voluit intelligendi (quod absit existimari), sed studio nostram intelligentiam exercendi, sudorisque in inuentionis praemii reddendi.*"[39]

Furthermore, however challenging the interpretation of scripture may be, the human may rely on God's help. Human Reason is not left unaided in this search for truth. Once more in nautical language we read:

*Diuina tamen clementia ducente et gubernante, prosperoque flatu diuini spiritus nostrae nauis carbasum implente, tutum inter haec rectumque iter carpentes ad portum quem petimus leni cursu liberi atque illaesi peruenturi sumus.*[40]

On this passage telling us of the divine clemency and the Holy Spirit's aid on the human journey, follows another passage in which a less specified grace of God is said to lead, help, work with and move *reason (ducente et adiuuante et cooperante et ad hoc mouente diuina gratia)* in a frequent and assiduous study of Holy Scriptures (*litterarum diuinarum*) until she may return and reach the contemplation of truth.[41]

The appropriation of the truth which is attained through extensive study of the scriptures is presented by Eriugena as a journeying, a journeying home. In each of

---

[37] PP IV, Jeauneau (ed.), CCCM CLXIV, 75–79, p. 4, (= PL 122 744A–B).

[38] See É. Jeauneau "Le symbolisme de la mer chez Jean Scot Érigène", in: idem, Études érigiènnes, Paris: Études Augustiniennes, 1987, pp. 289–296 (reprint of the article which first appeared in 1971), where, for example, on pp. 293/294 Jeauneau draws attention to similar imagery in the writings of the Pseudo-Dionysius, Maximus Confessor, Basil of Caesarea, Gregory of Nazianzus, and among the Latin fathers Ambrose and Jerome. Jeauneau distinguishes between the use of the symbol of the ocean in these authors for whom it represents a positively interpreted infinity, be this the infinite depths of God or the infinite depths of scripture, contrasting this with the negative use of the image of the sea in Augustine's writings. The use of the sea metaphor by Gregory the Great in whose writings the focus falls, not on the sea as such, but on the safe port to which the sea journey leads is also presented as a contrast to Eriugena's use.

[39] PP V, 6813–6815, p. 210, (= PL 122 1010B).

[40] PP IV, CCCM CLXIV, 70–74, p. 5, (= PL 122 744 A).

[41] PP IV, Jeauneau (ed.), CCCM CLXIV, 86–88, p. 5, (= PL 122 744B).

the pictures which he uses to convey this journey he emphasises the divine help to human reason on its odyssey.

The plurality of interpretations of Scripture and, accordingly, the plurality of theological positions which results from these nuanced interpretations, is, according to Eriugena, not only unavoidable but good. Eriugena roots this plurality in the infinity of God who communicates truth about God's self in the Scriptures.[42] He compares the plurality to the beauty of the innumerable variety of gleaming colours in a tiny point of a feather in a the peacock's tail:

> *Est enim multiplex et infinitus diuinorum eloquiorum intellectus. Siquidem in penna pauonis una eademque mirabilis ac pulchra innumerabilium colorum uarietas conspicitur in uno eodemque loco eiusdem pennae portiunculae.*[43]

Such an assertion raises, however, the difficult question of the *auctoritas* or status of one interpretation compared with that of others[44].

> *Omnis enim auctoritas quae uera ratione non approbatur infirma uidetur esse; uera autem ratio, quoniam suis uirtutibus rata atque immutabilis munitur, nullius auctoritatis astipulatione roborari indiget. Nil enim aliud uidetur mihi esse uera auctoritas, nisi rationis uirtute reperta ueritas et a sanctis patribus ob posteritatis utilitatem litteris commendata.*[45]

While Eriugena had characterised the authority of the Scriptures themselves as unwavering (*inconcussa*)[46], in the above quoted passage he states that the authority (of interpretations of the Scriptures) proceeds from the truth which the power of reasoning had discovered in the past. Eriugena does not highlight the *ratio* of the past as if it were a technical description of a particular autonomous human achievement. Even the functioning of reason is for him ultimately a form of receiving aided by divine grace[47]. One should not try to read the later distinctions between reason and faith, between human nature and grace back into the writings of Eriugena. It is important to grasp that in this context *ratio* indicates a human means of receiving truth which ultimately comes from divine wisdom. His systematic position tolerates no opposition between *ratio* and *auctoritas*:

---

[42] See PP III, 2953–2955, p. 102, (= PL 122 690B–C): "*Infinitus siquidem conditor sanctae scripturae in mentibus prophetarum spiritus sanctus infinitos in ea constituit intellectus. Ideoque nullius expositoris sensus sensum alterius aufert …*". Eriugena uses the notion of infinity to protect the ontological, linguistic and cognitive transcendence of God, presenting the divine infinity as an all embracing, and above all, as incomprehensible infinity: "*et incomprehensibili sua infinitate intelligit se excellere*" PP II, 2336, p. 98, (= PL 122 596D), English translation from I. P. SHELDON-WILLIAMS, SLH, IX, p. 161 "excels … by His incomprehensible Infinity".

[43] PP IV, CCCM CLXIV, 312–316, p. 13, (= PL 122, 749C).

[44] I have treated this matter in my article "Johannes Scottus Eriugena. Kreativer Umgang mit dem Erbe der Tradition".

[45] PP I, 3053–3059, p. 98, (= PL 122 513B–C). The Alumnus is speaking.

[46] PP III, 2176–2177, p. 76, (= PL 122 672C).

[47] In this context Eriugena does not sharply distinguish between *ratio* and *intellectus* as he does elsewhere.

*Vera enim auctoritas rectae rationi non obsistit, neque recta ratio uerae auctoritati. Ambo siquidem ex uno fonte, diuina uidelicet sapientia, manare dubium non est.*[48]

Furthermore, the argument that authority which is not confirmed by true reason is to be considered weak, is best interpreted as an invitation to discern. In each case the reader must discern just wherein the truth which an ecclesial interpreter of Scripture communicates consists, and what should be judged to be pastorally motivated 'wrapping'.

## 2.2 Eriugena and the plurality of theological authorities

Given the partiality of all truth and the plurality of interpretations of scripture what does Eriugena recommend as a method for dealing with diverging opinions?[49]

In the first place, arguing that the spectrum of opinions which can be sincerely held within the universal faith is broad, he proposes a course of discerning tolerance:

*Recte quippe ratiocinandi uia tenenda est, ut neque in dexteram neque in sinistram deuiare uideamur, hoc est, neque his quos summae ac sanctae auctoritatis esse catholica sanxit ecclesia detrahamus, neque eos quos simpliciter intellexisse cognouimus, quoniam intra catholicae fidei sinceritatem continentur, spernamus.*[50]

Secondly, he condemns 'narrowmindedness' as dangerous, arrogant and, above all, as contentious:

*Nostrum quippe sensum approbare aut eorum quos caeteros praecellere arbitramur, aliorum uero sensum reprobare, aut periculosissimum est, aut superbissimum, aut certe contentiosum.*[51]

At the end of his *Periphyseon* Eriugena entrusts it to a fellow scholar Wulfad asking him to correct what he finds lacking in it. As he relinquishes his main work from his hand he has a final word to say about the hermeneutic with which it is to be read: "... *unanimisque in caritate spiritus gratias universali omnium bonorum causae, sine qua nihil possumus facere, nobiscum referat, nulla reprehensionis libidine attractus, nullis facibus inuidiae succensus, quae sola prae caeteris uitiis caritatis et*

---

[48] PP I, 2975–2977, p. 96, (= PL 122 511B).

[49] Compare GUILIO D'ONOFRIO, "The *Concordia* of Augustine and Dionysius: Toward a Hermeneutic of the Disagreement of Patristic Sources in John the Scot's Periphyseon", in: BERNARD McGINN and WILLEMIEN OTTEN (ed.), Eriugena. East and West, pp. 115–140. See too J. C. MARLER, "Dialectical Use of Authority in the *Periphyseon*", in: BERNARD McGINN and WILLEMIEN OTTEN (ed.), Eriugena. East and West, pp. 95–113.

[50] PP IV, CCCM CLXIV, 3069–3074, p. 103, (= PL 122 814A–B). Eriugena does not however exclude the possibility and indeed the occurence of false opinions. These are then considered to be outside of the faith, or outside of the truth. Compare his comments on false (*falsae*) opinions in PP V, PL 122 970A.

[51] PP IV, CCCM CLXIV, 3076–3079, p. 103, (= PL 122 814A–B). The Alumnus is speaking.

*fraternitatis uinculum rumpere laborat.*"[52] Charity is the hermeneutic with which he hopes that others will read his work. This hermeneutic which he wishes from his reader is none other than the hermeneutic with which he himself has read other sources and integrated them within his work. He always sought the best, the useful in what they wrote. Similarly, charity is the motivation behind his attempts to accommodate and communicate his theology to the varying abilities to understand of his readership[53].

On this basis we can reconstruct what his advise to scholars baffled by a plurality of interpretations of the Bible would be. The tolerance demanded by charity should attend one's judgement of others and the plurality of scriptural interpretations will always be at hand.

Ever aware that what even the wisest human may produce is still darkness compared to the divine light, he concluded:

*'Vnusquisque in suo sensu abundet', donec ueniat illa lux, quae de luce falso philosophantium facit tenebras, et tenebras recte cognoscentium conuertit in lucem.*[54]

## 2.3  Eriugena's system as theology and philosophy

Eriugena has a sapiential understanding of truth: the truth which is derived form the holy Scriptures and the truth which we can affirm on the basis of our understanding of created nature are embraced within one overriding wisdom. The truth which we hold in common with true philosophers is a truth to be valued as such. In Eriugena's system faith does not contradict true philosophy. Faith is not an obstacle for those who philosophise piously:

*Iam inter nos non temere, ut censeo, ad purum est deductum omne quod de deo catholica fide approbante datur intelligi, de causa omnium similiter pie philosophantes oportere fateri.*[55]

---

[52] PP V, 7353–7370, pp. 226–227, (= PL 122 1021C–1022A), here 7357–7362, p. 227, (= PL 122 1022A).

[53] As already mentioned, Eriugena seems indebted to AUGUSTINE in *De doctrina christiana*, especially books one and four. Augustine there presents the aim of the interpretation and transmission of the bible as helping others to enjoy God with us (see *De doctrina christiana*, I, XXIX, 30, 1–28, J. MARTIN (ed.), p. 23). Biblical interpretation is an office of love and its end is to enable others to understand the Gospel's double precept of love of neighbour and of God (Mt. 22: 37–39, see *De doctrina christiana*, I, XXVI, 27, 5–11, J. MARTIN (ed.), p. 21). This understanding of the precept of love must then be acted upon "*Quisquis igitur scripturas diuinas uel quamlibet earum partem intellexisse sibi uidetur, ita ut eo intellectu non aedificet istam geminam caritatem dei et proximi, nondum intellexit*", (*De doctrina christiana* I, XXXVI, 40, 1–4, J. MARTIN (ed.), p. 29). The community of those who interpret the Scriptures is a community of co-operation in love. The interpreters help each other and receive help from each other in this mutual quest to love God: "*Velle tamen debemus, ut omnes nobiscum diligant deum, et totum, quod eos uel adiuuamus uel adiuuamur ab eis, ad unum illum finem referendum est.*" *De doctrina christiana*, I, 29, 30, 5–8, J. MARTIN (ed.), p. 23.

[54] PP V, 7391–7394, p. 228, (= PL 122 1022C).

[55] PP II, 2465–2468, p. 102, (= PL 599D–600A).

Within this sapiential understanding of truth, any apparent opposition between theology and philosophy disappears. Further, within wisdom, the truth of reason is seen as a ally embraced by the truth affirming virtue which faith is.

## 3. Systematic reflection: The appearing of God according to Eriugena

This thesis has reviewed Eriugena's writings on the appearing of God in all created reality, in the human creature and in Jesus Christ. How may we then characterise Eriugena's theology of the appearing of God? Is there a recurring pattern in the way in which he speaks of this phenomenon which may be noted in each of these three major contexts? It is the thesis of this investigation that in each context Eriugena's account of the appearing of God includes four key characteristics. Often these four key characteristics accrue to his use of the notion of theophany[56]. They are however also to be witnessed in his account of the appearing of God in the human created in the image of God where the term theophany is seldom explicitly mentioned.

### 3.1 The appearing of God in all reality

The distinction between knowing that God exists and not knowing what God is had established itself within certain Eastern theologies as an instrument for describing the possible extent, and the intrinsic limitation of human knowledge of God[57]. Eriugena too, steeped in the tradition of negative theology, uses this distinction but he inserts the insight within a new context[58]. Eriugena gives an account of the appearing of the infinite[59]. Creation is the work of the infinite and incomprehensible God and the divine works, although in themselves finite, let their maker appear. In his system creation is described as "theophanic": in creation the infinite God

---

[56] I have expressed similar views in my article: H. A. MOONEY, Infinitus enim infinite, etiam in purgatissimis mentibus formatur.

[57] See DEIRDRE CARABINE, The Unknown God, esp. p. 214 on Philo.

[58] Eriugena's theologia negativa may be considered in its genetic development. Thus the possibility of speaking about God's nature is more clearly restricted in *Periphyseon* than in his early work *De praedestinatione,* written before Eriugena undertook his extensive translations of the works of the Greek church fathers Ps. Dionysius and Gregory of Nyssa. See RENÉ ROQUES, "I. La symbolique de Jean Scot Érigène"; "II. Explication de textes érigéniens in pseudo-dionysiens" (conférences), École Pratique des Hautes Études. Section des sciences religieuses, Annuaire 1964–1965, Paris, 1964, pp. 121–125, p. 122 and BERNARD McGINN, "Negative Theology in John the Scot", in: *Studia Patristica* XIII (1975), pp. 232–238.

[59] The idea of the apparitional aspect of all creation has scriptural roots as Eriugena has pointed out: "*Atque ideo omnis creatura corporalis atque uisibilis sensibusque succumbens extremum diuinae naturae uestigium non incongrue solet in scripturis appellari.*" PP III, 2916–2918, p. 100, (= PL 122 689C).

appears[60]. In the third book of *Periphyseon* we read that every visible and invisible creature can be called a theophany, that is, a divine apparition.[61]

I intend to draw attention to the key characteristics of the appearing of God as it emerges in Eriugena's account of creation. Later the question whether these characteristics appear in the creational context alone, or whether they may be also observed in other contexts, may be addressed.

### 3.1.1 First key characteristic: 'because of the divine goodness'

The first aspect which emerges is the divine goodness which is the source of creation by the infinite and the revealing of the infinite alike. Asked why things were created out of nothing the speaker known as the Nutritor holds up a picture of the generosity of the subsisting good, which without any trace of envy, causes other beings to exist and which most abundantly distributes the individual goods and further, exercises its providence over all things[62].

The reason for creation may be expressed in more explicitly manifestational terms too: In a biblically oriented passage we read that God created out of nothing so that the extent and liberality of the divine goodness might be revealed and glorified through God's works: "*Propterea siquidem, inquis, omnia de nihilo facta sunt, ut diuinae bonitatis amplitudo et largitas per ea quae fecit et ostenderetur et laudaretur.*"[63] Eriugena's interpretation immediately includes the perception of this revelation and the ensuing praise which it inspires:

"*diuina bonitas ... omnia fecit, ut nulla creatura sit quae non, aut per se ipsam et in se ipsa aut per aliud, summum bonum non laudet.*"[64]

---

[60] See É. JEAUNEAU, Néant divin et Théophanie, p. 333; WERNER BEIERWALTES, Negati affirmatio: Welt als Metapher, pp. 265–266.

[61] "*Ideoque omnis uisibilis et inuisibilis creatura theophania (id est diuina apparitio) potest appellari.*" PP III, 2553–2555; (= PL 122 681A). On theophany compare the following studies: T. GREGORY, Note sulla dottrina delle "teofanie"; J. TROUILLARD, Érigène et la théophanie créatrice; IDEM, La notion de 'Théophanie' chez Érigène; É. JEAUNEAU, Néant divin et Théophanie; D. F. DUCLOW, Pseudo-Dionysius, John Scotus Eriugena, Nicholas of Cusa; RENÉ ROQUES, La symbolique de Jean Scot Érigène; IDEM, Explication de textes érigéniens in pseudo-dionysiens; R. HOEPS, Theophanie und Schöpfungsgrund; ROSEMANN, PHILIPP W. "Causality as concealing revelation in Eriugena: a Heideggerian interpretation", in: *American catholic philosophical quarterly* 79 (2005) 653–671; FALQUE, EMMANUEL. "Théophanie et Phénoménalité chez Scot Érigène", in: *Revue des sciences philosophiques et théologiques* 83 (2002) 387–421.

[62] See PP V, 4144–4154, p. 128, (= PL 122 952B) where the Nutritor suggests the following argument to the Alumnus: "*Alia ratio est, qua omnia de nihilo facta sunt. Summum bonum, quod a se ipso et in se ipso subsistens bonum est, non debuit abstinere a conditione bonorum, quae nec a semet ipsis nec in semet ipsis, sed ab ipso et in ipso bona sunt. Ac per hoc ex non existentibus existentia creauit, ne ueluti inuidiae reprehenderetur, retrahens se a substitutione eorum quae potuit substituere. Alioquin neque dominus esset, neque conditor naturarum, neque suorum bonorum copiosissimus et in nullo deficiens largitor, neque iustissimus meritorum iudex, neque omnium prouisor, si nil crearet.*"

[63] PP V, 4126–4128, p. 128, (= PL 122 951D).

[64] "The divine goodness ... created all things to this very end that there should be no creature

The selfless diffusion of the divine goodness is the source of creation and manifestation alike. Creation is the manifestation of the divine goodness, "for the divine goodness both will be active and will appear in all things"[65]. Eriugena expresses this as the becoming (in a particularly radical sense of becoming apparent) of God. The themes of the divine goodness which issues forth in creation, and self-manifestation through theophany are presented in a much cited passage from *Periphyseon* book III here reproduced in an abbreviated form:

*Summae siquidem ac trinae soliusque uerae bonitatis in se ipsa immutabilis motus et simplex multiplicatio et inexhausta a se ipsa in se ipsa ad se ipsam diffusio causa omnium, immo omnia sunt. ... Ambit ... omnia et nihil intra se est, in quantum uere est, nisi ipsa, quia sola uere est. Caetera enim, quae dicuntur esse, ipsius theophaniae sunt, quae etiam in ipsa uere subsistunt. ... Omne ... quod intelligitur et sentitur nihil aliud est nisi non apparentis apparitio, occulti manifestatio, negati affirmatio, incomprehensibilis comprehensio, ... infiniti diffinitio, incircumscripti circumscriptio, ...*[66]

### 3.1.2 Second key characteristic: 'with aesthetic mediation'

The second point is the radical aesthetic which inheres in this theophanic presentation of reality. It is good that the infinite appears, moreover it is good that God appears even in material beings. In a presentation of the difference between God, the cause of all things, and matter which Eriugena calls the unformed cause, Eriugena describes the end to which matter is created. Matter is said to be created to the end that those things which in themselves cannot be grasped by the senses, might by some means obtain a sensible appearance in it *"quae ad hoc creata est ut ea quae per se sensibus attingi non possent quodam modo in ea sensibiliter apparerent"*[67]. This is a very interesting presentation of the function of matter in apparitional, manifestational terms. The appearing to the senses is presented as a further good. This is presented as an absolute observation: there is no reference to the fall. It represents a thoroughly aesthetical position!

---

that does not either in itself and through itself, or through another, praise the Supreme Good."PP V, 4135–4144, p. 128, (= PL 122 952A–B).

[65] "*in omnibus bonitas diuina et operabitur et apparebit.*" PP V, 2634–2635, p. 82, (= PL 122 918B).

[66] "For the motion of the supreme and threefold and only true Goodness, which in Itself is immutable, and the multiplication of its simplicity, and Its unexhausted diffusion from Itself in Itself back to Itself, is the cause of all things, indeed is all things. ... It encircles all things and there is nothing within It but what, in so far as it truly is, is not Itself, for It alone truly is; for the other things that are said to be are Its theophanies, which likewise have their true subsistence in It. ... everything that is understood and sensed is nothing else but the apparition of what is not apparent, the manifestation of the hidden, the affirmation of the negated, the comprehension of the incomprehensible, ... the definition of the infinite, the circumscription of the uncircumscribed ..." PP III, 577–597, p. 22, (= PL 122 632D–633B) English translation from I. P. SHELDON-WILLIAMS, SLH XI, p. 59.

[67] PP I, 2471–2474, p. 80, (= PL 122, PL 122 500A).

No creature is excluded from this radical aesthetic. We already considered the text which states that there should be no creature that would not, either in itself and through itself, or through another, praise the Supreme Good[68]. The material realities, even those who are not possessed of senses or intellect offer God praise through their being the occasion of a perception of God for thinking creatures. In this sense they too praise God.

Eriugena's aesthetic is a radical theory of the appearing of God in creation. It includes the appearing of divine traces both in the intellectual and in the sensual orders. However, it is perhaps important to point out that Eriugena's aesthetic is not identical with a theory of the beautiful, where beauty is presented as an attribute of a particular selective category of beings. All reality lets the Infinite appear; this is Eriugena's aesthetic[69]. When he does speak explicitly of beauty (*pulchritudo, pulchrum*) it is nearly always in connection with the harmony of several or indeed of all beings[70].

### 3.1.3 Third key characteristic: 'from above'

A third point is the condescension of God which facilitates the theophanic appearing of the infinite. The appearing of the divine goodness is not an automatic "natural" diffusion. Eriugena presents it as a free condescension which aims at accommodating the intellectual limitations of the creature. Within his account of creation out of nothing in *Periphyseon* book three, he presents the theophanies as the appearing of the superessential nothing which God is. He here speaks of a certain ineffable condescension (*per condescensionem quandam ineffabilem*) by which the ineffable, incomprehensible and inaccessible brilliance of the Divine Goodness is beheld by the mind:

*Ineffabilem et incomprehensibilem diuinae bonitatis inaccessibilemque claritatem omnibus intellectibus siue humanis siue angelicis incognitam – superessentialis est enim et supernaturalis – eo nomine significatam crediderim, quae, dum per se ipsam cogitatur, neque est, neque erat, neque erit. In nullo enim intelligitur existentium, quia superat omnia. Dum uero per condescensionem*

---

[68] PP V, 4142–4144, p. 128, (= PL 122 952A–B).

[69] Compare REINHARD HOEPS in: Theophanie und Schöpfungsgrund, p. 190. In his very important and much read article "Negati affirmatio: Welt als Metapher" WERNER BEIERWALTES undertakes the task of clarifying the function of art using Eriugena's thought. However, Beierwaltes first deals with the metaphoric, theophanic function of the totality of Being and of the world as created (see "Negati affirmatio: Welt als Metapher", p. 269 and following); and, what is also of significance, he does not restrict Eriugena's aesthetic to an artistic moment.

[70] Compare WERNER BEIERWALTES, Negati affirmatio: Welt als Metapher, p. 272: "Gott als der creative Grund von Ähnlichen und Unähnlichen im Seienden insgesamt, also auch im Sein der Welt, begründet daher das harmonische oder einträchtige Zusammenbestehen (*concordia*) von Ähnlichem und Unähnlichem und damit von Gegensätzlichem überhaupt *als* die Schönheit von Welt: sie ist wie eine vielstimmige Melodie (*organicum melos*), in der weit Auseinanderliegendes und dissonant Erscheinendes aufgrund der rationalen Regeln der Musik doch einen Wohlklang (*dulcedo*) ergeben."

*quandam ineffabilem in ea quae sunt mentis obtutibus inspicitur, ipsa sola inuenitur in omnibus esse, et est, et erat, et erit.*[71]

The idea of condescension has roots in the writings of Maximus Confessor, as has been already mentioned.[72]

### 3.1.4 Fourth key characteristic: 'towards the infinite'

The fourth key aspect of the appearing of God to which I would like to draw attention is the earthly dialectic of finding God / and not finding God. Here Eriugena's own words in *Periphyseon* book five on the limited way that the infinite which is the end of human longing may be found, summarise the situation most aptly. Speaking of the end of the human search Eriugena states:

*Inuenit autem per theophanias, per naturae uero diuinae per se ipsam contemplationem non inuenit. Theophanias autem dico uisibilium et inuisiblilium species, quarum ordine et pulchritudine cognoscitur deus esse, et inuenitur non quid est, sed quia solummodo est, quoniam ipsa dei natura nec dicitur nec intelligitur. Superat nanque omnem intellectum lux inaccessibilis.*[73]

I have outlined how the appearing of the infinite Divinity is presented by Eriugena within the context of theophanic creation. Drawing the threads of what has been said together, I summarise: The ontological infinity of the unlimited divine nature finds expression in the all embracing divine superessence[74]. The corresponding cognitional infinity, the incomprehensibility is defended by the affirmation that even

---

[71] "I should believe that by that name is signified the ineffable and incomprehensible and inaccessible brilliance of the Divine Goodness which is unknown to all intellects whether human or angelic – for it is superessential and supernatural –, which while it is contemplated in itself neither is nor was nor shall be, for it is understood to be in none of the things that exist because it surpasses all things, but when, by a certain ineffable descent (*condescensionem*) into the things that are, it is beheld by the mind's eye, it alone is found to be in all things, and it is and was and shall be", PP III, 2541–2549, p. 88, (= PL 122 680D–681A), English from I. P. SHELDON-WILLIAMS, SLH XI, p. 167. From the following lines it is clear that Eriugena is here talking about the appearing of God in theophany: "*In quantum uero longius ordo rerum deorsum descendit, in tantum contemplantium obtutibus manifestius se aperit. Ideoque formae ac species rerum sensibilium manifestissimarum theophaniarum nomen accipiunt*". PP III, 2566–2569, p. 89, (= PL 122 681B).

[72] MAXIMUS often refers to this condescension: see Eriugena's Latin version of the *Ambigua ad Iohannem*: "*in ipsa diuina atque ineffabili condescensione mysteriorum notitiam declarauit*", *Ambigua ad Iohannem*, LXVII, 63–64, É. JEAUNEAU (ed.), CCSG 18, p. 257; corresponding to PG 91 1412A "ἀφράστῳ συγκαταβάσει".

[73] "It finds It through theophanies, but through the contemplation of the Divine Nature Itself it does not find it. Now by Theophanies I mean the species of all things visible and invisible, by the beauty and order of which it is made known that God exists, and it is found not *what* God is, but only *that* God is: for God's very nature is unknowable and unutterable, since the Inaccessible Light transcends every intellect," PP V, 2680–2686, p. 84, (= PL 122 919C–D).

[74] "*Creatrix uero totius uniuersitatis natura, quoniam infinita est, nullis finibus sursum uel deorsum concluditur. Ipsa siquidem ambit omnia et a nullo ambitur.*" "But the nature which creates the whole universe, being infinite, is not enclosed by and bound above or below, for it bounds all things and is bounded by nothing". PP III, 60–63, pp. 4–5, (= PL 122 620C), English from I. P. SHELDON-WILLIAMS, SLH, XI, p. 29.

through theophany God is not known as to what God is. God shines forth in the non-appearing depths of all beings. The revealing of the infinite God is good and God does not hesitate to appear even in material and animal beings. The infinite God who appears is free and good as expressed in the moral infinity of the infinitely good benefactor (*in nullo deficiens largitor*)[75] and the divine accommodating of the self-revelation, condescending to meet the needs of the observers.

### 3.2  *The appearing of God in Jesus Christ*

In another passage in this commentary on John's Gospel, Eriugena describes how the faithful knowledge of Christ is constantly purified. They leave behind a carnal and imperfect understanding of him. Progressing to ever higher forms of knowledge they approach the true knowledge of Christ.[76] Here we can observe how the encounter of the human with God is presented as an encounter *in* Christ. Eriugena here presents a vision of an ever increasing accommodation to Christ as model. It is a position which holds that moral progress is a prerequisite for the encounter with God in Christ. The infinite God is infinitely formed in the minds of those who have been purified.

He also writes that it is in the theophanies that God reveals himself to those who seek and love him. In the theophanies they are swept up *to meet Christ*.[77] Theophany is presented as encounter with Christ (*rapiuntur … obuiam christo*). It is an encounter granted to those who not only seek, (a possibility open to an intellectual irrespective of the virtue of their life,) but to those who love.

In the trinitarian and Christological texts, irrespective of whether they stress encounter with God in Christ, or encounter with Christ, the key aspects of Eriugena's theology of the appearing of God are preserved.

### 3.2.1  *The first key characteristic: 'because of the divine goodness'*

The divine goodness is now presented in terms of the persons of trinity who condescend to reveal themselves. In a treatment of the procession of the son from the Father in *Periphyseon* book II, Eriugena quotes and comments on Mt. 11:27 ("No one knows the father except the son and those to whom the son is willing to reveal him"). He situates this revelation within the context of a communal decision of the members of the blessed trinity to allow creatures to share in the knowledge of the father and the son and the spirit through the theophanies.[78]

---

[75] PP V, 4152, p. 128, (= PL 122 952B).

[76] "… *in suis fidelibus christus cotidie moritur et ab eis crucifigitur, dum carnales de eo cogitationes, seu spirituales adhuc tamen imperfectas, interimunt, semper in altum ascendentes, donec ad ueram eius notitiam perueniant; infinitus enim infinite, etiam in purgatissimis mentibus, formatur.*" Comm., I, XXXII, 38–43, É. Jeauneau (ed.), p. 182, (= PL 122 312A–B).

[77] Comm. I, XXV, 88–91, É. Jeauneau (ed.), p. 124, (= PL 122, 302B).

[78] See PP II, textual addtition number 83, 356–361, p. 43, (= PL 122 557D–558A).

### 3.2.2 *The second key characteristic: 'with aesthetic mediation'*

The encounter is with and in a risen human (and divine) person. Eriugena writes that the Word incarnate is our epiphania.[79] Eriugena seems to understand this objectively: Jesus is our epiphany in the sense that in him the triune God appears to us and addresses our senses: "… *uerbo uidelicet incarnato … nobis apparuit sensibusque corporeis comprehensibilem se fecit.*"[80]

### 3.2.3 *The third key characteristic: 'from above'*

The event of theophany involves the descent, indeed the condescension of the trinity to the needs of the human.

### 3.2.4 *The fourth key characteristic: 'towards the infinite'*

The ascent to Christ (or in Christ) in the theophanies in this life is never ending and in this way attended by the dialectic of finding and not finding God in Christ.

### 3.2.5 *Conclusion*

The structural isomorphism already witnessed between theophany in the context of creation, is thus preserved when theophany is used in a trinitarian and Christological context, be this in the sense of encounter with God in Christ, or encounter with Christ too. Moreover, the content of the concept of theophany appears increasingly in terms of discipleship and of seeking God with intellect and heart, and the Infinite whom one encounters becomes the beloved Christ in and to whom one undertakes the return.

### 3.3 *The appearing of God to the human creature: the subjective pole of the appearing of God*

Among the creatures presented by Eriugena within the 'hexaemeral' account in *Periphyseon* is the human. The special role of the human comes to the fore: the human is the pinnacle of creation, all creatures are created in the human. Eriugena approaches the uniqueness of the human in terms of cognition too. Not only is God revealed uniquely in the human created as *imago dei,* but the human creature itself consciously seeks to understand reality as a whole, and ultimately, God. The description of this conscious attending to God marks a turning point in the *Periphyseon,* marking the switch from *exitus* to *reditus,* from creation to return, ultimately to his

---

[79] PP V, 6506, p. 201, (= PL 122 1003C).
[80] PP V, 6507–6510, p. 201, (= PL 122 1003C–D).

account of God as the end of all things.[81] It is in terms of a cognitive return to God that Eriugena offers an etymology of the Greek term *anthropia:*

*Hanc rationem intuentes graeci humanitatem* ΑΝΤΡΟΠΙΑΝ *appellauere, hoc est* ΑΝΩ ΤΡΟΠΗΝ *(sursum uersus conversionem) uel* ΑΝΩ ΘΕΡΟΥCA ΟΠΙΑΝ *hoc est sursum seruans uisum.*[82]

The human is a creature which not only proceeds from the infinite God but turns back to this infinite God above it. This orientation to that above it takes place not only unconsciously, but consciously: the human turns towards that above in all ways open to it, including through its knowing, questioning, contemplating. Its destiny is to hold its gaze up to this infinite. This return is in fact an ongoing intellectual search for this infinite.

In this anthropologically oriented context one might expect Eriugena to provide us with details of the subjective experience of appropriating the appearing of God in general and of theophanic encounter in particular. In fact he offers us relatively little description of this[83]. I suggest that the purpose of most of Eriugena's subjectively oriented accounts of the appearing of God, even when used to indicate the conscious encounter with the infinite is not that of giving a psychological account of religious experience. He is rather concerned to communicate the theological structure of the appearing of God. I listed four key aspects of the appearing of God which recurred when this concept was used within the context of the appearing of God in creation and in and through Christ. These four aspects recur when texts from Eriugena's hand approach the conscious phenomenon of encounter with God.

Near the end of book V, at the close of *Periphyseon,* the Alumnus bursts into direct speech, addressing Jesus in a sincere prayer. He desires to understand the scriptures in order to find Jesus in them. This is described as the only blessedness which he asks for. Let us look at some of the key terms in the second half of this prayer. Speaking of the passing over which Jesus has prepared for His own, the Alumnus exclaims:

*Et quis est, domine, transitus tuus, nisi per infinitos contemplationis tuae gradus ascensus? Semper enim in intellectibus quaerentium et inuenientium te transitum facis. Quaereris enim ab eis semper, et semper inueniris, et non inueniris. Semper inueniris quidem in tuis theophaniis, in quibus*

---

[81] The pivotal role which the human plays in the switch from the *exitus* moment to the *reditus* of creation in *Periphyseon* has been particularly highlighted by W. OTTEN in: The Anthropology of Johannes Scottus Eriugena, esp. chapters 4 and 5.

[82] "It was because they understood this that the Greeks called humanity ἀνθρωπίαν that is, ἀνω-τροπίαν a turning towards what is above or ἄνω τηροῦσα ὀπίαν, that is, "holding the gaze aloft." PP V, 3655–3658, p. 114, (= PL 122 941C–D). English translation from J. J. O'MEARA / I. P. SHELDON-WILLLIAMS, Eriugena–Periphyseon (The Division of Nature), p. 619. The English is based on the Migne version of the text (PL 122) where Greek accents are provided.

[83] One can glean more details from an analysis of Eriugena's use of other key terms such as *theoria* and *contemplatio* and from his account of the stages in the return, the divisions in the human person and so on.

*multipliciter, ueluti in quibusdam speculis, occurris mentibus intelligentium te eo modo quo te sinis intelligi, non quid es, sed quid non es et quia es. Non inueniris autem in tua superessentialitate qua transis et exsuperas omnem intellectum uolentem et ascendentem comprehendere te. Ministras igitur tuis praesentiam tuam ineffabili quodam modo apparitionis tuae, transis ab eis incomprehensibili excelsitudine et infinitate essentiae tuae.*[84]

We find echoes of the four key aspects of the appearing of God already identified in Eriugena's object oriented account of this appearing in the contexts of creation and of revelation in Christ. It is the good God who initiates the encounter and ministers to the searchers. In the picture of ministering we recognise the divine accommodation which informed the divine condescension in creational theophany.

The context is once again seeking God, where the success and limitation of this search is expressed in the dialectic of both finding and not finding God. God is said to be found in the theophanies and yet the prayer reaffirms the infinite and incomprehensible transcendence of God. The search is an unending process of ever seeking and finding (the repetition of *semper*). Finally, the finding is mediated through the words of scripture, the assimilation of which involves sensual activity. The God who does not shy away from appearing in material creatures, does not shy away from appearing in particular words.

So much on the similarity between the encounter with God represented by this prayer and the key characteristics of creational and Christological apparition. We may observe that in addition to the common ground, certain traits are noticeably in the ascendant: The interpersonal context is becoming even more evident. The search itself is a search for a Thou, who reveals "himself" to "his" own. Thus it is presented in terms of an interpersonal encounter. The fruit of the encounter is not abstract knowledge but the experience of the divine presence (*praesentiam tuam*).

### 3.4 The appearing of God in the human created in the image of God

Eriugena strongly affirms the appearing of God not just *to* but *in* the human creature. I argue that his theology of the human created in the image of God is embraced within his theophanic scheme of the appearing of God. Granted he rarely uses the

---

[84] "And what is your passing over, O Lord, but an ascent through the infinite steps of Your contemplation? And ever do You open that way in the understandings of those who seek and find You. Ever are You sought by them and ever are You found, – and yet You are not found. You are ever found in Your theophanies in which You appear in the minds of those who understand You after a manifold mode, as in a number of mirrors, in the way in which You permit to be known not what You are, but what You are not; not what You are, but that You are; You are not found in Your superessential nature in which You pass beyond and exceed every understanding that desires to comprehend You and to ascend unto You. You grant unto Your own (*Ministras igitur tuis*) Your Presence by a mysterious manifestation of Yourself: You elude them by the infinite and incomprehensible transcendence of Your essence." PP V, 6828–6841, pp. 210–211, (= PL 122 1010C–D). Here the English translation of I. P. Sheldon-Williams / J. O'Meara, p. 700–701 has been modified by Hilary Mooney taking acount of Jeauneau's new critical edition of book five in CCCM CLXV.

term theophany in those passages where he is describing the human as created in the image of God. However, his tenet that every creature visible and invisible can be called a theophany must be so understood that it extends to the human creature too. The human creature certainly is not presented as less translucent of the divine than other creatures[85]. Furthermore, the inclusive interpretation is supported by the observation that each of the four characteristics of theophanic appearing recur in Eriugena's accounts of the particular case of theophany which (as I argue) the human is.

### 3.4.1 The first key characteristic: 'because of the divine goodness'

In the section on the *'imago dei'* theology of Eriugena we observed that God lets the human share in the divine perfection for no other reason than that God is good. God wishes to make participation in this goodness possible; the divine goodness freely initiates a generous giving. The divine generosity calls all beings out of nothing into existence, however the human creature, the creature which receives the greatest likeness to God, is particularly formed by this generosity. Only the human is created in the image of its creator. Thus the disclosure of God to the human in its imaging of the divine is rooted in this divine goodness. This has been treated in detail already. Here the role of the divine generosity in lavishly allowing the human to share in its perfection, and to thus image God for itself and for others, marks the first key characteristic which, as I argue, belongs to a theophanic account of the appearing of God.

### 3.4.2 The second key characteristic: 'with aesthetic mediation'

When the question arises why God created the human, whom God proposed to make in God's own image, in the genus of animal, the answer which Nutritor gives is that God wished so to fashion the human so that there might be one among the animals in whom God's image is expressly manifested[86]. God freely decides to appear not only in an intellectual other but in an other who includes a sensual aspect. This shows us that the imaging of the divine may be interpreted within an aesthetic of an appearing God, in this respect too, within a theophanic theology.

---

[85] See the Alumnus' remark in PP V, 3647–3652, p. 114, (= PL 122 941C): "*Si enim nos ipsos nosse et quaerere nolumus, profecto ad id, quod supra nos est, causam scilicet nostram, redire non desideramus. Ac per hoc in grabbato carnalis materiae morteque ignorantiae iacebimus. Nulla quippe alia uia est ad principalis exempli purissimam contemplationem praeter proximae sibi suae imaginis certissimam notitiam.*"

[86] PP IV, CCCM CLXIV, 860–864, p. 32, (= PL 122 763C): "*Et mihi sufficeret interroganti tibi quare deus hominem in genere animalium creauerit, quem ad suam imaginem facere proposuit, breuiter respondere: Quia ita uoluit eum condere, ut quoddam animal esset, in quo imaginem suam expressam manifestaret.*"

### 3.4.3 The third key characteristic: 'from above'

In the Alumnus' question why *an animal* images God, we sense the divine conde-scension behind this appearing. God is not only generous in creating the human in the divine image, this generous sharing may be understood as a condescension of God. The aspect of condescension is also to be witnessed in what I have called Eriu-gena's fifth approach to the mirroring of the divine where freedom as a mirroring feature is expounded. God condescends to call other free creatures into existence. God abandons the monopoly on freedom.

### 3.4.4 The fourth key characteristic: 'towards the infinite'

The fourth key aspect of theophanic appearing is the dialectic of finding and not finding God. At first sight, the phenomenon of imaging seems not to fit into this dialectic. 'Imaging' seems to name the positive alone, to name a perfect correspond-ence between image and imaged. Eriugena was, however, careful to point out that the prototype and its image differ in one thing only, that is, in the subject in which the perfection inheres. Thus in the human created in the image of God we have a signpost referring to another, referring to the Other who God is. The human encounters God as Other. The human can make progress in its perception of God as imaged in the human creature. Furthermore, the fact that many approaches can be taken to the human which is created in the image of God, implies that one ap-proach can complement the other. In this way too, by considering different facets of the imaging of God, we can grow in our perception of God. Finally, when we consider the imaging of God within the economy of creation, we grasp Eriugena's point that through an increase in virtue the basis for the mirroring of God in the human creature expands.

Thus in the context of the human created as '*imago dei*' too, a context where the term '*theophania*' is not evident, the four-fold theophanic structure seems neverthe-less to be the key to Eriugena's theology of the appearing of God.

### 3.5 Theophanic encounter with God

The theophanic structure of the cognitive encounter between God and the human, is the quintessence of Eriugena's theology of the appearing of God.

The contexts within which the term theophany itself is used are many. I argue that the use of the notion of theophany signifies an encounter-event characterised by four key characteristics listed above. So understood, we may speak of a *consistent* usage of the term theophania. The plurality of contexts within which it is used does not affect the *coherence* of the function of the term: it signals in creational as in Christological context a recurring pattern in the encounter of God and human.

I characterise Eriugena's theology of the appearing of God as theophanic, even those sections of his theology in which the word theophany does not occur. Had this study narrowly focussed on the verbal occurrence of the word 'theophan-' in all its forms then the study would be unable to account for the appearing of God in the human created in the image of God. Eriugena is a consistent thinker but he was certainly not a 'tidy' thinker. There is no one term which offers a key to his theology. However, by first reviewing how he actually speaks of the disclosure of God; then, in a second step, asking which term has the function of communicating the repetitive pattern found (in the case at hand the notion of theophany); and, finally, in a third step testing whether this pattern also occurs, (albeit anonymously) in those passages which speak of the appearing of God in the human person, one may indeed arrive at an adequate hermeneutic of the issue at hand.[87] The step in which we considered whether the notion of theophanic encounter can embrace the appearing of God in the human considered as created in the image of God is an important one. Through our affirmative response to the question we could avoid reading a breach into *Periphyseon*. Otten, for example, sees not just a turning point in book four of *Periphyseon* but the overthrowing of the theory of theophanic disclosure. By showing how the revealing of God in the human is embraced within the pattern of theophanic encounter, such a breach was not identified by our interpretation of Eriugena's writings.[88]

---

[87] We can compare the approach taken by G. Schrimpf in his Habilitationsschrift, Das Werk des Johannes Scottus Eriugena. He offers us a magnificent study of the *causae primordiales*, pp. 256–295, treating both the sources for this terminus, and its systematic contours. Problematic is however, in my opinion, when he tries to implement this one precise terminus as key to Eriugena's whole theology of the appearing of God: "*Der Begriff der Entstehungsgründe ist das geeignetste Instrument, um die gesamte Wirklichkeit als göttliche Erscheinung zu denken*", p. 288. I counter: this term is not the most suitable term for explaining the appearing of God in the human created in the image of God, or the appearing of God in Christ. These two facets of the appearing of God however belong to the whole picture which emerges from the Eriugenian corpus. Schrimpfs's study concentrates on Eriugena's Glosses on Martianus Capella, *De Nuptiis Mercurii et Philologiae*, namely his *Annotationes in Martianum*, on *De praedestinatione* and on *Periphyseon*. Neither the biblical commentaries of Eriugena nor his poetry receive extensive attention. Secondly, one has to be very precise about the sense in which *any* one term can serve as an instrument for explaining the appearing of God according to Eriugena. I argue that it is better to gather and record the recurring traits which occur in each context in which the author speaks of the disclosure of God. One may then better speak of a theology of the appearing of God and characterise this, than to identify an isolated instrument which must communicate so much in so many disparate settings.

[88] D. Ansorge does not experience a difficulty in finding the central '*Grundidee*' not only for one theme of *Periphyseon*, but indeed the Grundidee of the work as a whole. "*Darüberhinaus ist auch in den einzelnen Büchern selbst eine Sachlogik erkennbar, welche die vielfältigen Gedanken des Werkes als Entfaltungen einer nicht nur formal, sondern auch inhaltlich bestimmbaren Grundidee her verstehen läßt. Diese Grundidee ist Eriugenas Annahme, daß die Welt "Schöpfung" und alles Seiende Erscheinung Gottes als des schöpferischen Ursprungs von allem ist.*" p. 334; "*In stets neuen Anwegen bringt Eriugena in Periphyseon dasselbe zur Sprache: die Wirklichkeit, wie sie dem menschlichen Verstehen im Licht des christlichen Glaubens als Erscheinung ihres schöpferischen göttlichen Ursprungs erschlossen ist.*" p. 344. However, we must observe that his '*Grundidee*' is so widely formulated that it could characterise a vast number of theological works not just *Periphyseon* in particular. This diffuse character calls its analytic usefulness into question.

Has Eriugena presented us with an adequate account of the appearing of God? Several possible objections to his theory present themselves. He has been accused of pantheism and further, of denying the blessed an immediate vision of God in heaven. Further, he may be accused of representing heaven as an unending search. Let us address these objections.

The charge of pantheism may not be upheld[89]. The key to the argumentation against this reading is the basic tenet of historical interpretation that isolated texts must be interpreted within their context (that is within the whole of the literary work within which they occur) and against the background of the key historical sources inspiring them. Read on these terms, expressions such as the proposition that God will be all in all cannot be considered as expressing an inadequate distinction between God and the world in which God appears[90].

On the issue of what knowledge is granted to the blessed in heaven we may make the following observations. Interpreters of Eriugena's usage of the term *theophania* must constantly resist the temptation to turn theophany from the signpost for a structured encounter-event (a position which I find in accord with his writings) into a description of an object (a position which, in my opinion, is not supported by his writings considered as a whole)[91]. Neither in this life nor the next does one 'see' theophanies. One encounters God in theophany and the catalysts of that encounter may be any creature, the human creature in particular, or Jesus Christ. Only when one grasps this point may the texts which speak of theophanic knowledge in heaven accommodate each of Eriugena's two claims namely, in that first place, that no creature intervenes between God and us and, secondly, that the knowledge of God is *administered* to us in theophanies.[92]

Does Eriugena's strong emphasis on the infinity of God and our infinite search for God not run the risk of presenting heaven as 'search'[93] and not as a state of

---

[89] I have refuted the charge of pantheism in my article: H. Mooney, Some Observations on the Concept of Harmony.

[90] Compare W. Beierwaltes, "Marginalien zu Eriugenas 'Platonism'", in: H.-D. Blume and F. Mann (ed.), *Platonismus und Christentum. Festschrift für Heinrich Dörrie*, Münster, 1983, 64–74, (= Jahrbuch für Antike und Christentum Ergänzungsband, 10).

[91] On p. 231 of his excellent article "Eriugena and Aquinas on the Beatific Vision", in: W. Beierwaltes (ed.) Eriugena Redivivus, pp. 224–236, Dominic O'Meara makes a similar observation: "In Eriugena however theophany is not an intentional reality whereby we may know God. It is an independent reality, in fact God himself, as he shows himself to us."

[92] See PP V, 3658–3660, p. 114, (= PL 122 941D): "*Ad creatoris sui siquidem contemplationem, nulla alia interposita creatura, humanitas creata est.*"; PP V, 4689–4691, p. 145, PL 122 963C (*in phantasiis, … theophanias appellant, administrabitur*).

[93] For the biblical roots of the notion of the infinite search, a search occupying intellect and the deepest human longing, see Philippians 3, 13–14 "but one thing I do, forgetting what lies behind and straining forward to what lies ahead, (τοῖς δὲ ἔμπροσθεν ἐπεκτεινόμενος) I press on towards the goal for the prize of the upward call of God in Christ Jesus." Quoted from the RSV version, 1979: ἓν δέ, τὰ μὲν ὀπίσω ἐπιλανθανόμενος τοῖς δὲ ἔμπροσθεν ἐπεκτεινόμενος, κατὰ σκοπὸν διώκω εἰς τὸ βραβεῖον τῆς ἄνω κλήσεως τοῦ θεοῦ ἐν Χριστῷ Ἰησοῦ. This text played a significant role in the anthropology of Gregory of Nyssa. Gregory's anthropology, above all as it appeared in *De hominis opificio*, heavily influenced

'arrival'? Is this not problematic because then 'searching' or 'desiring' must be reconciled with the notions of 'fulfilment' and 'return'. Here we must first see what Eriugena actually says about heaven.

In the special return each blessed person is rewarded to the extent that they have lived virtuously in this life. In his interpretation of the parable of the wise and foolish virgins Eriugena is quick to point out that we should not imagine God offering some people less than others[94]. Using the image of the reception of light he points out that the divine light is in no way begrudging, holding back its light for itself. The light shines equally upon all but some turn away from the light. All are offered this light but, as will emerge in other texts, even the blessed receive this vision individually.

The presupposition which underpins this argument is that an infinite object makes possible an infinite number of perceptions of this object, and an infinite number of ways of returning to it. Eriugena implements the notion of the theophanies to accommodate this diversity. The contemplation of the truth is permitted to the blessed to different degrees. "For it shall appear to all, though not in the same measure but in an infinite number of ascents and descents of Theophany both to the righteous and to the unrighteous, but it shall appear to all; ..."[95] Eriugena's system emphasises that the divine infinity leads to an infinite diversity of experiences of finding God. The texts which place the infinite number of ascents within this context are numerous. For example in his commentary on John's Gospel he speaks of an infinite ascent *until the purged arrive* at the knowledge of him (Christ).[96] On the other hand I have only found the one text which seems to speak of an infinite search for God in heaven (PP V, PL 122 919D)[97]. It is perhaps significant that this

---

Eriugena. T. GREGORY too compares Gregory of Nyssa on the infinite outreaching of the human to God and Eriugena's anthropology see: Note sulla dottrina delle 'teofanie', pp. 86/87.

In Gregory's system the infinity of the search is implied, the unending reaching out to God. Eriugena emphasising a searching in this life and an 'arriving' or 'attaining' in the next. This difference in emphasis was pointed out to me by Prof. Werner Beierwaltes in a conversation on the eschatology of Gregory of Nyssa in comparison with that of Eriugena. For Eriugena's account of the human search for God I refer to ERIUGENA, *Expositiones in ierarchiam coelestem*, VI, 38–41, J. BARBET (ed.), p. 87–88: "*Quoniam infinitum est quod querit, necesse ut infinite querat, et quodammodo inueniat et quodammodo non inueniat: inueniat quidem ipsius theophaniam, non inueniat ipsius substantiam.*"

[94] PP V, 6900–6907, p. 213, (= PL 122 1012B–C).

[95] "*... non eodem modo, sed multiplicibus in infinitum diuinarum uisionum ascensionibus et descensionibus et iustis et iniustis apparebit, omnibus tamen apparebit, ...*" PP V, 4704–4707, p. 145, (= PL 122 964A), English from J. O'MEARA / I. P. SHELDON-WILLIAMS, Eriugena–Periphyseon (The Division of Nature), p. 645. This text was also of importance in the consideration of the hierarchic appropriation of the appearing of God in Jesus Christ.

[96] "*... semper in altum ascendentes, donec ad ueram eius notitiam perueniant; infinitus enim infinite, etiam in purgatissimis mentibus, formatur.*" Comm., I, XXXII, 41–43, É. JEAUNEAU (ed.), p. 182, (= PL 122 312B).

[97] PP V, 2687–2691, p. 84. It is interesting that in "Eriugena and Aquinas on the Beatific Vision" D. O'MEARA indeed ascribes this position to Eriugena, albeit, without criticising him for holding it: "In the beatific vision, furthermore, the absolute uncomprehensibility of God according to Eriugena and the consequent necessity of attaining the vision of God in theophanies give to this

text refers to the longing of the heavenly powers and not clearly of the human creature. In the face of this text it is not possible to decide conclusively the issue of whether Eriugena envisaged an infinite search on the part of all humans in heaven. I prefer to emphasise the many texts where the infinity of God in heaven is said to lead to an infinite number of ways of finding God than the one text which suggests that an infinite longing – *prospicere concupiscunt* [!] – continues in heaven.

Is Eriugena's account of the appearing of God *comprehensive* enough to explain contemporary religious experience? Here our answer must distinguish between explanation and description. As we have already pointed out, he does not offer us much which could be called psychological description of religious experience. Eriugena's writings, however, present a theological structure which can explain the encounter between the human and God whether that encounter takes place today or in the Carolingian past.

Finally, we may ask does Eriugena's account of the appearing of God adequately take the content or *message* of the Scriptures into account or does it stand in opposition to this? In the expository chapters of this study we have seen that his account of each carrier of the appearing of God is deeply rooted in a selection of scriptural verses which receive extended attention. For example Gen. 1:3 on the Logocentric rationality of the world in which God appears; Gen. 1:26–27 is central for his account of the appearing of God in the human person; his exposition of the Prologue of John's Gospel for the appearing of God in Jesus Christ[98]. We observe that Eriugena homes in, again and again, on a few select, scriptural verses which he constantly lets inspire his inquiries and confirm his conclusions. Scripture simultaneously sets the limits to his speculation. What has not been revealed to us in Scripture may not be taken as the subject matter of conjecture. Furthermore, after examining the wide spectrum of his writings, we may conclude that Eriugena certainly did not neglect that theme which, above others, must be regarded as a specifically scriptural notion, that is, the appearing of God in Jesus Christ.

Eriugena certainly understood his own academic undertaking as an interpretation of the words of Jesus.[99] It would be anachronistic to measure his use of these Scriptural passages against exegetical methods of today (if indeed this were possible in

---

vision a dialectical, progressive quality: even in this vision we will continue to search as we are led further and further in the theophanic contemplation of the hiddeness of God." p. 234. O'Meara refers to PP V, PL 122 1010C–D; 919C. In the first text I am not entirely convinced that a search for God *in heaven* is being affirmed. The context is understanding Jesus' words in the Scriptures, an activity usually assigned to our earthly life. The second text relies heavily on Gregory of Nyssa who certainly held that our search is infinite even in heaven. The question remains how completely Eriugena adopted this position. If one is to argue that he did adopt this notion from Gregory then I see a stronger indication of this in 2690–2691, p. 84, (= PL 122 919D) "*et uirtutes caelestes deum suum quaerunt, in quem semper prospicere concupiscunt ...*" than in the passage which preceeds this and to which O'Meara refers.

[98] Alternatively we could mention the fourth chapter of the letter to the Ephesians or indeed, Jn. 14: 2.

[99] See PP V, 6824–6826, p. 210, (= PL 122 1010C).

the light of the plurality of exegetical approaches current in the academic circles of the 21st century.) Whereas we might be tempted to criticise the selectivity of his use of Scripture, we must temper our criticism with the observation that he employed scripture only in combination with his reading of earlier theological sources. His particular sources were also selective, devoting some texts more attention than others. It was part of the theological method of his day to enter into dialogue with the interpretations of the past, expanding on the efforts of predecessors and amending them.

Perhaps after analysis and interpretation it is fitting to end by quoting a passage from Eriugena himself. Here, in an interpretation of the Gospel which inspired him so deeply, namely the Gospel of John, we observe Eriugena's parallel use of the biblical image 'mansions' (μοναί) and the conceptual notion of theophany. This passage communicates how theophany is much more than an intermediary cognitive object which one confronts in one's search for God, how it is much more than a ontological coalescence of God and world, and how theophanic encounter involves not only an infinite searching in this life, but an infinite number of ways of finding God in the next. In the following text the biblical imagery conveys something of the room for encounter which theophany is; it simultaneously offers us an envisagement of the homecoming to the many mansions in which the heavenly father appears.

*Unusquisque enim secundum suae sanctitatis atque sapientiae celsitudinem ab una eademque forma quam omnia appetunt, uerbum dico, formabitur. Ipsa nanque de seipsa loquitur in euangelio: 'In domo patris mei mansiones multae sunt', se ipsam domum patri appellans. Quae, dum sit una eademque incommutabilisque permaneat, multiplex tamen uidebitur his quibus in se habitare largietur. Nam unusquisque, ut diximus, unigeniti dei uerbi notitiam in seipso possidebit, quantum ei gratia donabitur. Quot enim numerus est electorum, tot erit numerus mansionum. Quanta fuerit sanctarum animarum multiplicatio, tanta erit diuinarum theophaniarum possessio.*

PP I, 270–280, p. 12, (= PL 122 448C–D)

# Epilogue

A insint féin ar Fhlaitheas Dé,
Ag sin oileán gach éinne,
An Críost atá ina fhuil ag scéith
An casadh tá ina bhréithre.

Is macasamhail dá oileán féin
Oileán seo Bharra Naofa,
An Críost a bhí ina fhuil ag scéith
An phúcaíocht ait i ngéagaibh.

A personal perception of God's heaven,
That is each one's island, one's retreat,
The Christ that in his blood is bleeding
Gives shape and purpose to his speech.

The island where lived the sainted Barra
Is an image of each man's island soul,
The Christ that in his blood was bleeding
Is the hauntings in the branches we behold.*

---

* Verses from Seán Ó Ríodáin's modern Gaelic poem about the holy island of the sixth century monk Finbarr (also known as Barra): Oileán agus Oileán Eile (An Island and Another Island), quoted from Declan Kiberd / Gabriel Fitzmaurice, (ed.), *An Crann faoi Bhláth (The Flowering Tree)*. Contemporary Irish Poetry with Verse Translations, Dublin, Wolfhound Press, 1991, pp. 26–27.

# Bibliography
## (sources consulted)

This selective bibliography lists the literature most relevant to the theme handled in this study. Both the writings of Johannes Scottus Eriugena and secondary literature on these writings have been collected in MARY BRENNAN, *Guide des études érigéniennes. Bibliographie commentée des publications 1930–1987* and complemented by GERD VAN RIEL, "A Bibliographical Survey of Eriugenian Studies 1987–1995", in idem et al., (ed.), *Iohannes Scottus Eriugena. The Bible and Hermeneutics,* pp. 367–400; GERD VAN RIEL "Eriugenian Studies 1995–2000," in: JAMES MCEVOY, MICHAEL DUNNE (ed.), *History and Eschatology in John Scottus Eriugena and his time,* pp. 611–626.

## Abbreviations

| | |
|---|---|
| CCSL | = Corpus Christianorum, Series Latina |
| CCSG | = Corpus Christianorum, Series Graeca |
| CCCM | = Corpus Christianorum, Continuatio Mediaevalis |
| CSEL | = Corpus Scriptorum Ecclesiasticorum Latinorum |
| GCS | = Die Griechischen Christlichen Schriftsteller |
| GNO | = Gregorii Nysseni Opera |
| LMA | = Lexikon des Mittelalters |
| LThK | = Lexikon für Theologie und Kirche |
| MGH | = Monumenta Germaniae Historica |
| PL | = Migne, Patrologia Latina |
| PG | = Migne, Patrologia Graeca |
| PTS | = Patristische Texte und Studien |
| R. S. V. | = Revised Standard Version of the Bible |
| SC | = Sources Chrétiennes |
| SLH | = Scriptores Latini Hiberniae |
| TRE | = Theologische Realenzyklopädie |

## Works of Johannes Scottus Eriugena

*Eriugena Periphyseon (The Division of Nature),* translation by INGLIS P. SHELDON-WILLIAMS, revised by JOHN O'MEARA, Montréal: Bellarmin / Washington: Dumbarton Oaks, 1987.

*Glossae Divinae Historiae. The Biblical Glosses of John Scottus Eriugena,* edited with an intro-duction by JOHN J. CONTRENI and PÁDRAIG P. Ó NÉILL, Florence: SISMEL-Edizioni del Galluzzo, 1997.

*Ioannis Scotti Eriugenae Carmina,* MICHAEL HERREN (ed.), Dublin: School of Celtic Stud-ies / Dublin Institute for Advanced Studies, 1993, (= Scriptores Latini Hiberniae, XII).

*Iohannis Scoti Eriugenae. Expositiones in Ierarchiam Coelestem,* JEANNE BARBET (ed.), Turn-hout: Brepols, 1975, (= Corpus Christianorum Continuatio Mediaeualis, 31).

*Iohannis Scotti Annotationes in Marcianum,* CORA E. LUTZ (ed.), Cambridge, Massachusetts: The Mediaeval Academy of America, 1939, reprint 1987. Le Commentaire érigénien sur Martianus Capella, De nuptiis Lib. I, d'après le manuscrit d'Oxford Bodl. Lib. Auct. T. 2. 19, fol. 1–31, ÉDOUARD JEANEAU (ed.), in: *Quatre thèmes érigéniens* (Conférence Institut d'Études médiévales Albert-le-Grand 1974) Montréal / Paris: Vrin, 1978, pp. 101–186.

*Iohannis Scotti De diuina praedestinatione,* GOUVEN MADEC (ed.), Turnhout: Brepols, 1978, (= Corpus Christianorum. Continuatio Mediaeualis L).

*Iohannis Scotti Eriugenae Periphyseon (De Diuisione Naturae) Liber Primus; Liber Secundus; Liber Tertius,* INGLIS P. SHELDON-WILLIAMS, LUDWIG BIELER (ed.), Dublin: The Dublin Institute for Advanced Studies, reprint 1978, first published 1968; 1972; 1981, (= Scriptores Latini Hiberniae, vols. VII, IX, XI). *Iohannis Scotti Eriugenae Periphyseon (De Diuisione naturae) Liber Quartus,* ÉDOUARD JEANEAU (ed.), with the assistance of MARK A. ZIER, Dublin: The Dublin Institute for Advanced Studies, 1995, (= Scriptores Latini Hiberniae, XIII).

*Iohannis Scotti Eriugenae Periphyseon, Liber Primus; Liber Secundus; Liber Tertius, Liber Quar-tus, Liber Quintus, Editionem nouam a suppositiciis quidem additamentis purgatam, ditatam uero apppendice in qua uicissitudines operis synoptice exhibentur,* ÉDOUARD JEANEAU (ed.) Turnhout: Brepols, 1996; 1997; 1999; 2000; 2003 (= Corpus Christianorum Continuatio Mediaeualis, vols. CLXI, CLXII, CLXIII, CLXIV, CLXV).

*Jean Scot Érigène, De la division de la nature (Periphyseon),* Livre I.-IV, FRANCIS BERTIN, (trans.), Paris: Presses Universitaires de France, 1995–2000.

*Jean Scot. Commentaire sur l'évangile de Jean,* ÉDOUARD JEANEAU (ed.), Paris: CERF, 1972, (= Sources Chrétiennes, 180).

*Jean Scot. Homélie sur le Prologue de Jean,* ÉDOUARD JEANEAU (ed.), Paris: CERF, 1969, (= Sources Chrétiennes, 151).

*Joannis Scoti Opera,* HEINRICH. J. FLOSS (ed.), in: JACQUES P. MIGNE (ed.), *Patrologia Latina* 122, Paris: 1853 and 1865.

JOANNIS SCOTUS, *Versio operum S. Dionysii Areopagitae,* in: JACQUES P. MIGNE (ed.), *Patro-logia Latina,* 122.

*John Scottus Eriugena. Treatise on Divine Predestination,* MARY BRENNAN, (trans.), Notre Dame: University of Notre Dame Press, 1998, (= Notre Dame Texts in Medieval Cul-ture, 5).

"Le '*De Imagine*' de Grégoire de Nysse traduit par Jean Scot Érigène", MAÏEUL CAPPUYNS, (ed.), in: *Revue de théologie ancienne et médiévale* 32 (1965) 205–262.

*Maximi Confessoris Ambigua ad Iohannem, iuxta Iohannis Scotti Eriugenae Latinam interpreta-tionem,* ÉDOUARD JEANEAU (ed.), Turnhout: Brepols / Leuven: Leuven University Press, 1988, (= Corpus Christianorum Series Graeca, 18).

*Maximi Confessoris Quaestiones ad Thalassium, una cum latina interpretatione Ioannis Scotti Eriugenae,* CARL LAGA and CARLOS STEEL (ed.), Turnhout: Brepols, 1980; 1990, (= Corpus Christianorum Series Graeca, 7; 22).

*Widmungsbrief zu De Praedestinatione,* ERNST DÜMMLER (ed.), in: Monumenta Germaniae historica Epist. V 630 and following.

*Widmungsbriefe zu den Übersetzungen des Ps. Dionysius und des Maximus Confessor,* ERNST DÜMMLER (ed.), in: Monumenta Germaniae historica Epist. VI 158–162.

## Other Ancient and medieval authors

AMBROSIUS. *De paradiso,* KARL SCHENKL (ed.), 1897, CSEL 32, 1

AMBROSIUS. *Exameron,* KARL SCHENKL (ed.), 1897, CSEL 32, 1

AMBROSIUS. *Expositio euangelii secundum Lucam,* MARC ADRIAEN (ed.), 1957, CCSL 14

ANASTASIUS BIBIOTHECARIUS. *Epistola ad Carolum,* 1853, PL 122.

AUGUSTINUS. *Confessiones,* LUC VERHEIJEN (ed.), 1981, CCSL 27.

AUGUSTINUS. *De civitate dei,* BERNHARD DOMBART, ALFONS KALB (ed.), 1955, CCSL 47, 48.

AUGUSTINUS. *De doctrina christiana, De vera religione,* JOSEPH MARTIN (ed.), 1962, CCSL 32.

AUGUSTINUS. *De Genesi ad litteram,* JOSEPH ZYCHA (ed.), 1894, CSEL 28, 1

AUGUSTINUS. *De ordine,* PIUS KNÖLL (ed.), 1922, CSEL 63.

AUGUSTINUS, *De ordine,* WILLIAM. M. GREEN, (ed.), 1970, CCSL 29

AUGUSTINUS. *De trinitate,* WILLIAM J. MOUNTAIN (ed.), FR. GLORIE (assistance), 1968, CCSL 50.

AUGUSTINUS. *De uera religione,* KLAUS-DETLEF DAUR (ed.), 1962, CCSL 32.

AUGUSTINUS. *In Iohannis euangelium tractatus,* RADBODUS WILLEMS (ed.), 1954, CCSL 36.

BASIL. *Homiliae in Hexaemeron,* STANISLAS GIET (ed.), ²1968, SC 26 [bis].

BOETHIUS. *De institutione arithmetica,* GOTTFRIED FRIEDLEIN (ed.), Leipzig: Minerva, first published 1867, reprint 1966

*Biblia Sacra iuxta vulgatam versionem,* Stuttgart: Deutsche Bibelgesellschaft, ³1983.

C. IULIUS VICTOR. *Ars Rhetorica,* REMO GIOMINI and MARIA SILVANA CELENTANO (ed.), Leipzig: BSB B. G. Teubner Verlagsgesellschaft, 1980.

CICERO, M. TULLIUS. *De inuentione,* THEODOR NÜSSLEIN (ed.), Düsseldorf: Artemis & Winkler Verlag, 1998.

EPIPHANIUS. *Ancoratus,* KARL HOLL, PAUL WENDLAND (ed.), Leipzig: Hinrichs, 1915–1922, GCS 25.

GREGORY OF NAZIANZUS. *Orationes 27–31,* PAUL GALLAY (ed.) Maurice JOURJON (collaboration), 1978, SC 250.

GREGORY OF NYSSA. *De hominis opificio,* in: *Sancti Patris Nostri Gregorii Nysseni Basilii Magni fratris quae supersunt omnia,* Vol.I, GEORGE H. FORBES, (ed.), Burntisland: Pitsligo, 1855, p. 102–318

GREGORY OF NYSSA. *De Vita Moysis,* HUBERTUS MUSURILLO (ed.), 1964, GNO VII/I.

GREGORY OF NYSSA. *Grégoire de Nysse. La vie de Moïse ou Traité de la perfection en matière de vertue,* introduction et traduction de JEAN DANIELOU, S.J., Paris: Édition du Cerf, 1955.²

GREGORY OF NYSSA. *Gregory of Nyssa: Dogmatic treatises, etc.,* HENRY AUSTEN WILSON, trans., Nicene and Post-Nicene Fathers, second series, vol. 5, Peabody, Massachusetts: 1995, first published in 1893.

GREGORY OF NYSSA. *Oratio catechetica magna,* E. MÜHLENBERG (ed.), in: GNO III/IV,

HEIRIC OF AUXERRE. *Vitae S. Germani Commendatio, MGH, Poetae Latini aevi Carolini, (III),* LUDWIG TRAUBE (ed.), Berlin: 1896, (= Poetae Latini Medii Aevi, 3).

MARTIANUS CAPELLA. *De nuptiis Philologiae et Mercurii,* ADOLF DICK (ed.), Leipzig: Teubner, 1925.

MARTIANUS CAPELLA. *De nuptiis Philologiae et Mercurii,* JAMES WILLIS (ed.), Leipzig: Teubner, 1983, (= Bibliotheca Scriptorum Graecorum et Romanorum Teubneriana).

MARTIANUS CAPELLA. *Martianus Capella and the Seven Liberal Arts.* Vol. I The Quadrivium of Martianus Capella. Latin Traditions in the Mathematical Sciences 50B.c.-A.D. 1250 by WILLIAM HARRIS STAHL. With a Study of the Allegory and the Verbal Disciplines by RICHARD JOHNSON with E.L. BURGE. New York: Columbia University Press, 1971, (= Records of Civilization: Sources and Studies, 84,1).

MARTIANUS CAPELLA. *Martianus Capella and the Seven Liberal Arts.* Vol. II The Marriage of Philology and Mercury trans. by WILLIAM STAHL, RICHARD JOHNSON with E.L. BURGE. New York: Columbia University Press, 1977, (= Records of Civilization: Sources and Studies, 84,2).

MAXIMUS CONFESSOR. *Ambigua ad Thomam una cum Epistula secunda ad eundem,* BART JANSSENS (ed.), 2002, CCSG 48.

MAXIMUS CONFESSOR. *Maximi Confessoris Ambigua ad Iohannem, iuxta Iohannis Scotti Eriugenae Latinam interpretationem,* ÉDOUARD JEAUNEAU (ed.). 1988, CCSG 18.

MAXIMUS CONFESSOR. *Quaestiones ad Thalassium,* Carl Laga (ed.), 1980, CCSG 7.

ORIGENES. *De principiis* HENRI CROUZEL, MANLIO SIMONETTI (ed.), 1978, SC 252.

PHILO OF ALEXANDRIA. *De opificio mundi,* LEOPOLD COHN, PAUL WENDLAND (ed.), Berlin: Reimer, 1896.

PHILO OF ALEXANDRIA. *Philon d'Alexandrie. De Vita Mosis, I–II, introduction, traduction et notes,* ROGER ARNALDEZ, CLAUDE MONDÉSERT, JEAN POUILLOUX, PIERRE SAVINEL (ed.), Paris: Éditions de CERF, 1967, (= Les œuvres de Philon d'Alexandrie, 22).

PHILO OF ALEXANDRIA. *Philo in ten volumes, (and two supplementary volumes),* FRANCIS H. COLSON, and GEORGE H. WHITAKER, (trans.), vol, I, London: Heinemann Ltd, 1966.

PLATO. *Timaeus,* according to Calcidius in: Timaeus a Calcidio translatus commentarioque instructus, ed. JAN HENDRIK WASZINK, (POVL J. JENSEN collaboration), London: In Aedibus Instituti Warburgiani, Leiden: Brill, 2a edition, 1975, (= Corpus Platonicum medii aevi, Plato latinus vol. IV).

PLOTINUS. *Opera I–III,* PAUL HENRY and HANS-RUDOLF SCHWYZER (ed.), Oxford, ³1984 (Vol. I); 1977 (vol. II); 1982 (Vol. III).

PLOTINUS. *Plotinus with an English translation by A.H. Armstrong,* vol V, (Enneads V. 1–9), ARTHUR H. ARMSTRONG (trans.), Cambridge: Harvard University Press / London: William Heinemann Ltd, 1984, (= The Loeb Classical Library, Vol. 444).

PROCLUS. *Commentarium in Platonis Parmenidem,* VICTOR COUSIN (ed.), Hildesheim: Olms, 1961, (reprint of 1864 edition from Paris; = Procli Philosophi Platonici Opera inedita, 3).

PROCLUS. *Latin translation: Commentaire sur le Parménide de Platon. Traduction de Guillaume de Moerbeke,* Tome II: Livres V à VII et Notes marginales de Nicolas de Cusa, CARLOS STEEL (ed.), Leuven: Univ. Press, 1985.

PROCLUS. *Opera inedita quae primus olim e codd. mss. Parisinis Italicisque vulgaverat nunc secundis curis emendavit et auxit Victor Cousin,* VICTOR COUSIN (ed.), Paris, 1864 (reprint: Hildesheim, 1961), 617–1258.

PROCLUS. *Proclus' Commentary on Plato's Parmenides,* GLENN R. MORROW, JOHN M. DILLON (trans.), JOHN M. DILLON (intro., notes), paperback printing, with corrections, Princeton: Princeton University Press, 1992.

PROCLUS. *Proclus. The Elements of Theology. A revised text with translation, introduction and commentary,* ERIC R. DODDS (ed.), Oxford: Oxford University Press, ²1963, reprint 1977.

PRUDENTIUS TRECENSIS EPISCOPUS. *De Praedestinatione contra Erigenam,* JACQUES P. MIGNE (ed.), 1881, PL 115.

Ps. DIONYSIUS AREOPAGITA et al. *A Thirteenth-Century Textbook of Mystical Theology at the University of Paris. The Mystical Theology of Dionysius the Areopagite in Eriugena's Latin Translation with the Scholia translated by Anastasius the Librarian and Excerpts from Eriugena's Periphyseon,* Translation and Introduction by L. MICHAEL HARRINGTON, Paris, Leuven, Dudley: PEETERS, 2004, (= Dallas Medieval Texts and Translations; 4).

Ps. DIONYSIUS AREOPAGITA. *De coelesti hierarchia.* GÜNTHER HEIL (ed.), 1991, PTS 36.

Ps. DIONYSIUS AREOPAGITA. *De divinis nominibus,* BEATE R. SUCHLA, (ed.), 1990, PTS 33.

Ps. DIONYSIUS AREOPAGITA. *De mystica theologia, and Epistulae,* ADOLF MARTIN RITTER (ed.) 1991, PTS 36.

Ps. DIONYSIUS AREOPAGITA. *Pseudo-Dionysius. The Collected Works.* COLM LUIBHEID, translation, New York, Mahwah: Paulist Press, 1987.

*Recueil des Actes de Charles II le Chauve Roi de France,* I, GEORGES TESSIER (ed.), Paris: Imprimerie Nationale, 1943.

REMIGIUS Lugdunensis Episcopus, *Liber de tribus Epistolis,* JACQUES P. MIGNE (ed.), 1852, PL 121.

*Septuaginta. Vetus Testamentum Graecum,* vol. 1, Genesis, JOHN W. WEVERS (ed.), Göttingen: Vandenhoeck & Ruprecht, 1974.

*Vetus latina. Die Reste der Altlateinischen Bibel,* vol. 2, Genesis, BONIFATIUS FISCHER (ed.), Freiburg: Herder, 1951.

## Secondary literature

ABRAHAM, WILLIAM J. "Revelation Reaffirmed", in: Paul Avis (ed.), *Divine Revelation,* pp. 201–215.

ALLARD, GUY-H. (ed.). *Jean Scot écrivain. Actes du IVe colloque international. Montréal 28 août– 2 septembre 1983.* Montréal / Paris: Cahiers d'études médiévales. Cahier spécial 1, 1986.

ALLARD, GUY-H. *Johannis Scoti Eriugenae Periphyseon Indices Generales,* Montréal: Institut d'études médiévales, Université de Montréal / Paris: Librairie Philosophique J. Vrin, 1983.

ALLARD, GUY-H. "La structure littéraire de la composition du *De diuisione naturae*", in: O'Meara, *The Mind of Eriugena,* pp. 147–157.

ALLENBACH, JEAN. et al. *Biblia patristica. Index des citations et allusions bibliques dans la littérature patristique.* Vol. 1–6, Paris: Éditions du Centre National de la Rechereche Scientifique, 1972–1995.

ALONSO, JOAQUÍN MARÍA. "Teofania y visión beata en Escoto Eriugena", in: *Revista Española de Teología* 10 (1950) 361–389; 11 (1951) 255–281.

ANGENENDT, ARNOLD. *Das Frühmittelalter,* Stuttgart: Kohlhammer, 1995².

ANSORGE, DIRK. "Origines und Eriugena. Eine Vorstudie zur Rezeptionsgeschichte", in: *Theologische Quartalschrift* 176 (1996) 192–204.

ANSORGE, DIRK. *Johannes Scottus Eriugena. Wahrheit als Prozeß. Eine theologische Interpretation von "Periphyseon".* Innsbruck: Tyrolia Verlag, 1996, (= Innsbrucker theologische Studien, 44).

ARMSTONG, ARTHUR H. *An Introduction to Ancient Philosophy,* London: Methuen & Co., ³1977.

AUTY, ROBERT et al. (ed. and advisers). *Lexikon des Mittelalters,* München: Deutscher Taschenbuch Verlag, 9. vols., paperback edition, 2002.

AVIS, PAUL (ed.). *Divine Revelation,* London: Darton, Longman and Todd Ltd., 1997.

GERHARD KRAUSE, GERHARD MÜLLER et al. (ed.), *Theologische Realenzyklopädie,* Berlin: Walter de Gruyter, 1976–2007

BAUER, MARTIN. "Nachwort", in: *Dionysiaca* (Faksimile-Neudruck der zweibändigen Ausgabe von Brügge 1937 in 4 Bänden), Vol. 4 Stuttgart, Bad Cannstatt 1989, pp. 1668–1675.

BEATRICE, PIER FRANCO. "*Quosdam Platonicorum Libros.* The Platonic Reading of Augustine in Milan", in: *Vigiliae Christianae* 43 (1989) 248–281.

BEIERWALTES, WERNER. (ed.). *Begriff und Metapher. Sprachform des Denkens bei Eriugena. Vorträge des VII. Internationalen Eriugena-Colloquiums. Werner-Reimers-Stiftung Bad Homburg 26.–29. Juli 1989,* Heidelberg: Carl Winter Universitätsverlag, 1990, (= Abhandlungen der Heidelberger Akademie der Wissenschaften, Philosophisch-historische Klasse; Jg. 1990, Abh. 3).

BEIERWALTES, WERNER. (ed.). "Das Problem des absoluten Selbstbewußtseins bei Johannes Scotus Eriugena", in: *Platonismus in der Philosophie des Mittelalters.* (= Wege der Forschung, CXXVII), Darmstadt: 1969, pp. 484–516, (reprinted from *Philosophisches Jahrbuch* 73 (1965–66) 264–282).

BEIERWALTES, WERNER. *Denken des Einen. Studien zur Neuplatonischen Philosophie und ihrer Wirkungsgeschichte.* Frankfurt / Main: Klostermann, 1985.

BEIERWALTES, WERNER. "Deus est Veritas. Zur Rezeption des griechischen Wahrheitsbegriffs in der frühchristlichen Theologie", in: *Pietas. Festschrift für Bernhard Kötting,* (ed.) ERNST DASSMANN and KARL SUSO FRANK, JAC.E 8, Münster: Aschendorff, 1980, pp. 15–29.

BEIERWALTES, WERNER. "Duplex theoria. Zu einer Denkform Eriugenas", in: W. Beierwaltes, (ed.) *Begriff und Metapher,* pp. 37–64.

BEIERWALTES, WERNER. "Einheit und Dreiheit", in: IDEM, Eriugena. Grundzüge, pp. 204–256.

BEIERWALTES, WERNER. "Eriugena. Aspekte seiner Philosophie", in: idem, *Denken des Einen,* pp. 337–367.

BEIERWALTES, WERNER. *Eriugena. Grundzüge seines Denkens,* Frankfurt: Klostermann, 1994.

BEIERWALTES, WERNER. *Eriugena Redivivus. Zur Wirkungsgeschichte seines Denkens im Mittelalter und im Übergang zur Neuzeit. Vorträge des V. Internationalen Eriugena-Colloquiums Werner-Reimers-Stiftung Bad Homburg, 26.–30. August 1985,* Heidelberg: Carl Winter Universitätsverlag, 1987.

BEIERWALTES, WERNER (ed.). *Eriugena. Studien zu seinen Quellen. Vorträge des III. Eriugena-Colloquiums Freiburg im Breisgau, 27.–30. August 1979,* Heidelberg: Carl Winter Verlag, 1980, (= Abhandlungen der Heidelberger Akademie der Wissenschaften, Philosophisch-historische Klasse; Jg. 1980, Abh. 3).

BEIERWALTES, WERNER. *Identität und Differenz,* Frankfurt: Klostermann, 1980.

BEIERWALTES, WERNER. "Marginalien zu Eriugenas 'Platonism'", in: H.-D. BLUME and F. MANN (ed.), *Platonismus und Christentum. Festschrift für Heinrich Dörrie,* Münster, 1983, 64–74, (= Jahrbuch für Antike und Christentum Ergänzungsband, 10).

BEIERWALTES, WERNER. "Negati Affirmatio: Welt als Metapher. Zur Grundlegung einer mittelalterlichen Ästhetik durch Johannes Scotus Eriugena", in: RENÉ ROQUES, *Jean Scot Érigène et l'histoire de la philosophie,* pp. 263–276.

BEIERWALTES, WERNER. "Plato philosophantium de mundo maximus", in: Idem, Eriugena. Grundzüge, pp. 32–51.

BEIERWALTES, WERNER. *Proklos. Grundzüge seiner Metaphysik,* Frankfurt: Klostermann, ²1979, (= Philosophische Abhandlungen; vol. 24).

BEIERWALTES, WERNER. Review of Riccati dissertation in: *Mitteilungen und Forschungsbeiträge der Cusanus-Gesellschaft* 17 (1986) 272–277.

BEIERWALTES, WERNER. *Selbsterkenntnis und Erfahrung der Einheit. Plotins Ennead V 3. Text, Übersetzung, Interpretation, Erläuterung,* Frankfurt: Klostermann, 1991.

BEIERWALTES, WERNER. "The Revaluation of John Scottus Eriugena in German Idealism", in: JOHN J. O'MEARA and LUDWIG BIELER (ed.), *The Mind of Eriugena,* Dublin: Irish University Press, 1973, pp. 190–199.

BERSCHIN, WALTER. "Greek elements in medieval latin manuscripts", in: MICHAEL W. HERREN and SHIRLEY A. BROWN, *The Sacred Nectar of the Greeks,* pp. 85–104.

BERSCHIN, WALTER. "Griechisches bei den Iren", in: HEINZ LÖWE (ed.), *Die Iren und Europa im früheren Mittelalter,* Stuttgart: Klett-Cotta, vol. 1, 1982, (= Veröffentlichungen des Europa-Zentrums Tübingen: Kulturwiss. Reihe), pp. 501–510.

BIELER, LUDWIG. "Observations on Eriugena's commentary on the Gospel of John: A second harvest", in: RENÉ ROQUES (ed.), *Jean Scot Érigène et l'histoire de la philosophie,* pp. 235–241.

BIELER, LUDWIG. "Remarks on Eriugena's Original Latin Prose", in: JOHN J. O'MEARA and LUDWIG BIELER (ed.), *The Mind of Eriugena,* pp. 140–146.

BINCHY, DANIEL A. "The Passing of the Old Order", in: BRIAN O' CUIV, *The Impact of the Scandinavian Invasions on the Celtic-speaking Peoples c. 800–1100 A.D. Introductory Papers read at Plenary Sessions of the International Congress of Celtic Studies held in Dublin, 6–10 July, 1959,* Dublin: Institiúid Ard-Léinn, 1975, pp. 119–132.

BINDING, GÜNTHER. "Anselm von Canterbury", in: *LMA,* vol. I, 1980, pp. 680–687.

BISCHOFF, BERNHARD. "Das griechische Element in der abendländischen Bildung", in: *Mittelalterliche Studien. Ausgewählte Aufsätze zur Schriftkunde und Literaturgeschichte,* vol. II, Stuttgart: Anton Hiersemann, 1967, pp. 246–275.

BISCHOFF, BERNHARD. "Irische Schreiber im Karolingerreich", in: RENÉ ROQUES, *Jean Scot Érigène et l'histoire de la philosophie,* pp. 47–57.

BISCHOFF, BERNHARD. *Mittelalterliche Studien. Ausgewählte Aufsätze zur Schriftkunde und Literaturgeschichte,* vol. II, Stuttgart: Anton Hiersemann, 1967, pp. 246–275.

BISCHOFF, BERNARD. "Wendepunkte in der Geschichte der lateinischen Exegese im Frühmittelalter", in: BERNARD BISCHOFF, *Mittelalterliche Studien. Ausgewählte Aufsätze zur Schriftkunde und Literaturgeschichte, T. 1,* Stuttgart: Hiersemann, 1966, pp. 205–273.

BLUMENTHAL, UTA-RENATE (ed.). *Carolingian Essays. Andrew W. Mellon Lectures in Early Christian Studies.* Washington, D.C.: The Catholic University of America Press, 1983.

BÖHM, THOMAS. "Adnotationes zu Maximus Confessor und Johannes Scottus Eriugena," in: WALTER HAUG and WOLFRAM SCHNEIDER-LASTIN, (ed.), *Deutsche Mystik im abendländischen Zusammenhang. Neu erschlossene Texte, neue methodische Ansätze, neue theoretische Konzepte.* Kolloquium Kloster Fischingen 1998, Tübingen: Max Niemeyer Verlag, 2000, pp. 51–60.

BÖHM, THOMAS. *Theoria, Unendlichkeit, Aufstieg. Philosophische Implikationen zu De Vita Moysis von Gregor von Nyssa,* Leiden: Brill, 1996.

BÖHM, THOMAS. "Unbegreiflichkeit (lat. incomprehensibilitas)" in: *Historisches Wörterbuch der Philosophie,* JOACHIM RITTER, KARLFRIED GRÜNDER and GOTTFRIED GABRIEL (ed.), völlig neubearbeitete Ausgabe des "*Wörterbuchs der Philosophischen Begriffe*" von Rudolf Eisler, vol. II, U–V, Basel: Schwabe & Co., pp. 112–115.

BOMMERSHEIM, PAUL. "Johannes Scottus Eriugena und die Dynamik des Nordens", in: *Deutsche Vierteljahresschrift für Literaturwissenschaft und Geistesgeschichte* 21 (1943) 395–416.

BOŠNJAK, BRANKO. "Dialektik der Theophanie. Über den Begriff der Natur bei J. S. Eriugena", in: *La Filosofia della Natura nel Medioevo* (Atti del terzo congresso internazionale di filosofia medioevale, Passo della Mendola (Trento) 31 agosto - 5 settembre 1964), Milano: 1966, pp. 264–271.

BRENNAN, MARY. *Guide des études érigéniennes. Bibliographie commentée des publications 1930–1987/A Guide to Eriugenian Studies. A Survey of Publications 1930–1987,* Fribourg: Éditions Universitaires Fribourg Suisse, 1989, (= Vestigia. Études et documents de philosophie antique et médiévale; vol. 5).

BRENNAN, MARY. "Materials for the Biography of Johannes Scottus Eriugena", in: *Studi Medievali,* 3. ser. 27 (1986) 413–460.

BROX, NORBERT. "Fragen zur «Denkform" der Kirchengeschichtswissenschaft", in: *Zeitschrift für Kirchengeschichte* vol. 90, 4. 28 (1979) 1–21.

BRUEREN, RAINIER. "Die Schrift als Paradigma der Wahrheit. Gedanken zum Vorbegriff der Metaphysik bei Johannes Scotus Eriugena", in: WERNER BEIERWALTES, (ed.), *Begriff und Metapher,* 187–201.

BRUEREN, RAINIER. *Metafysiek in meervoud: de godsidee en de vraag naar waarheid bij Scotus Eriugena en Hegel,* (Dissertation Nijmegen, 1990), Enschede: Sneldruk Enschede, 1990.

BÜRKLE, HORST, CHRISTOPH DOHMEN, THOMAS SÖDING, JOHANN MAIER, WERNER SCHLÜSSLER, JÜRGEN WERBICK. "Offenbarung", in: *LThK,* vol. 7, col. 983–995.

CANTÓN ALONSO, JOSÉ LUIS. "Intelecto y teofanía en Escoto Eriúgena", in: *Actas del I Congreso Nacional de Filosofía Medieval,* Saragossa: Ibercaja, 1992, 213–225.

CAPPUYNS, MAÏEUL O. S. B. *Jean Scot Érigène. Sa vie, son oeuvre, sa pensée,* Louvain: Abbaye du Mont César and Paris: Desclée de Brouwer, 1933, (= Universitas Catholica Lovaniensis. Dissertationes ad gradum magistri in Facultate Theologica consequendum conscriptae, Series II. Tomus 26).

CARABINE, DEIRDRE. "*Apophasis* and Metaphysics in the *Periphyseon* of John Scottus Eriugena", in: *Philosophical Studies* 32 (1988–90) 63–82, Dublin.

CARABINE, DEIRDRE. *John Scottus Eriugena,* Oxford: Oxford University Press, 2000.

CARABINE, DEIRDRE. *The Unknown God. Negative Theology in the Platonic Tradition:* Plato to Eriugena, Louvain: Peeters Press, 1995, (= Louvain Theological & Pastoral Monographs; 19).

CENTRE D'ÉTUDES DES RELIGIONS DU LIVRE, PARIS, PAUL VIGNAUX (ed.), *In principio. Interprétations des premiers versets de la Genèse,* Paris: Études augustiniennes, 1973.

CHARLES-EDWARDS, THOMAS M. *Early Christian Ireland,* Cambridge: Cambridge Universtiy Press, 2000.

CHRISTLIEB, THEODOR. *Leben u. Lehre des Johannes Scotus Erigena in ihrem Zusammenhang mit der vorhergehenden und unter Angabe ihre Berührungspuncte mit der neueren Theologie,* Gotha: Besser, 1860.

COLISH, MARCIA L. "Carolingian Debates over *Nihil* and *Tenebrae:* A Study in Theological Method", in: *Speculum* 59 (1984) 757–795.

COLISH, MARCIA L. "John the Scot's Christology and Soteriology in Relation to his Greek Sources", in: *Downside Revue* 100 (1982) 138–51.

COLSON, FRANCIS H. and GEORGE H. WHITAKER. *Philo in ten volumes* (and two supplementary volumes), Vol, I, London: Heinemann Ltd, 1966.

CONTRENI, JOHN J. *Carolingian Learning, Masters and Manuscripts,* London: Variorum Reprints, 1992.

CONTRENI, JOHN J. "Masters and Medicine in Northern France during the Reign of Charles the Bald", in: MARGARET GIBSON and JANET NELSON, *Charles the Bald,* pp. 333–350.

CONTRENI, JOHN J. "The Biblical Glosses of Haimo of Auxerre and John Scottus Eriugena", in: *Speculum* 51 (1976) 411–434.

CONTRENI, JOHN J. *The Cathedral School of Laon from 850–930. Its Manuscripts and Masters,* Munich: Bei der Arbeo-Gesellschaft, 1978, (= Münchener Beiträge zur Mediävistik und Renaissance-Forschung, 29).

CONTRENI, JOHN J. "The Irish 'Colony' at Laon during the time of John Scottus", in: R. ROQUES, *Jean Scot Érigène et l'histoire de la philosophie,* pp. 59–67.

M. CRISTIANI. "Lo Spazio e il Tempo nell'Opera dell'Eriugena",in: *Studi medievali,* 3rd series, 14 (1973), 39–136.

COPLESTON, FREDERICK. *A History of Philosophy, Vol 2 Medieval Philosophy, Part 1 Augustine to Bonaventure,* New York: Image Books, Doubleday & Company, 1962.

CROUSE, ROBERT D. "*Primordiales Causae* in Eriugena's Interpretation of Genesis: Sources and Significance", in: GERD VAN REEL, CARLOS STEEL, JAMES MCEVOY, (ed.), *Iohannes Scottus Eriugena. The Bible and Hermeneutics,* pp. 209–220.

CROUSE, ROBERT D. "The Meaning of Creation in Augustine and Eriugena", in: ELIZABETH A. LIVINGSTONE (ed.), *Studia Patristica XXII. Papers presented to the Tenth International Conference on Patristic Studies held in Oxford 1987,* Leuven: Peeters Press, 1989, 229–234.

DALY, GABRIEL. "Revelation in the Theology of the Roman Catholic Church", in: PAUL AVIS (ed.), *Divine Revelation,* London: Darton, Longman and Todd Ltd., 1997, pp. 23–44.

DEMPF, ALOIS. "Johannes Eriugena und die Metaphysik der Karolingerzeit", in: Idem., *Metaphysik des Mittelalters,* Teil 1, München: R. Oldenbourg, 1971 (= reprint of edition from 1934).

DICK, ADOLFUS. *Martianus Capella,* Leipzig: Teubner, 1925.

DILLON, JOHN. "The Roots of Reason in John Scottus Eriugena", in: *Philosophical Studies* (Ireland) (1991–2) 25–38.

DOHMEN, CHRISTOPH. "Offenbarung II. Biblisch-theologisch: 1. Altes Testament", in: *LThK,* vol. 7, col. 985–6.

D'ONOFRIO, GIULIO. "Disputandi disciplina. Procédés dialectiques et *logica vetus* dans le langage philosophique de Jean Scot", in: GUY-H. ALLARD (ed.), *Jean Scot écrivain,* pp. 229–263.

D'ONOFRIO, GIULIO. "The *Concordia* of Augustine and Dionysius. Toward a HERMENEUTIC OF THE DISAGREEMENT OF PATRISTIC SOURCES IN JOHN THE SCOT's *Periphyseon*", IN: BERNARD McGinn and WILLEMIEN OTTEN (ed.), *Eriugena: East and West,* pp. 115–10.

D'ONOFRIO, GIULIO. "Über die Natur der Einteilung. Die dialektische Entfaltung von Eriugenas Denken", in: WERNER BEIERWALTES, *Begriff und Metapher,* pp. 17–38.

DRÄSEKE, Johannes. *Johannes Scotus Erigena und dessen Gewährsmänner in seinem Werke De Divisione Naturae libri V,* Leipzig: Dieterich'sche Verlags-Buchhandlung, 1902 (= Studien zur Geschichte der Theologie und der Kirche; 9/2).

DROBNER, HUBERTUS R. *Bibelindex zu den Werken Gregors von Nyssa.* Paderborn: Kamp 6. H. R. Drobner, 1988.

DRONKE, PETER. "Theologia veluti quadam poetria: quelques observations sur la fonction des images poétique chez Jean Scot", in: RENÉ ROQUES (ed.) *Jean Scot Érigène et l'histoire de la philosophie,* pp. 245 -252.

Duclow, Donald F. "Denial or Promise of the Tree of Life? Eriugena, Augustine and Genesis 3:22b", in: Gerd Van Riel, Carlos Steel, James McEvoy (ed.), *Iohannes Scottus Eriugena. The Bible and Hermeneutics*, pp. 221–238.

Duclow, Donald F. "Dialectic and Christology in Eriugena's *Periphyseon*", in: *Dionysius* 4 (1980) 99–118.

Duclow, Donald F. "Gregory of Nyssa and Nicholas of Cusa: infinity, anthropology and the via negativa", in: *Downside Review* 92 (1974) 102–108.

Duclow, Donald F. "Isaiah meets the Seraph. Breaking ranks in Dionysius and Eriugena?", in: Bernard McGinn and Willemien Otten (ed.), *Eriugena East and West*, pp. 233–252.

Duclow, Donald F. "Pseudo-Dionysius, John Scotus Eriugena, Nicholas of Cusa: An Approach to the Hermeneutic of the Divine Names", in: *International Philosophical Quarterly* 12 (1972) 260–278.

Duclow, Donald F. "The Hungers of Hadewijch and Eckhart", in: *The Journal of Religion* 80 (2000) 421–441.

Duclow, Donald F. "Virgins in paradise. Deification and Eschatology in 'Periphyseon' V, in: Guy-H. Allard (ed.), *Jean Scot ecrivain*, pp. 30–49.

Dulles, Avery. *The Assurance of Things Hoped for. A Theology of Christian Faith*, New York / Oxford: Oxford University Press, 1994.

Dunn, James D. G. "Biblical Concepts of Divine Revelation", in: Paul Avis (ed.), *Divine Revelation*, pp. 1–22.

Dutton, Paul E. "Eriugena the Royal Poet", in: Guy-H. Allard (ed.) *Jean Scot Écrivain*, pp. 51–80.

Dutton, Paul E. Review of G. Schrimpf, *Das Werk des Johannes Scottus Eriugena im Rahmen des Wissenschaftsverständnisses seiner Zeit*, in: *Journal of the History of Philosophy* 23 (1985) 253–4.

Eicher, Peter. *Offenbarung. Prinzip neuzeitlicher Theologie*, Munich: Kösel Verlag, 1977.

Enders, Markus *Natürliche Theologie im Denken der Griechen*, Frankfurt: Knecht, 2000, (= Fuldaer Hochschulschriften; 36).

Falque, Emmanuel. "Théophanie et Phénoménalité chez Scot Érigène", in: *Revue des sciences philosophiques et théologiques* 83 (2002) 387–421.

Fabricius, Cajus and Daniel Ridings. *A Concordance to Gregory of Nyssa*, Göteborg: Acta Universitatis Gothoburgensis, 1989, (= Studia Graeca et Latina Gothoburgensia L).

Festugière, André-Jean. *Personal Religion among the Greeks*. Berkeley / Los Angeles: University of California Press, 1954.

Fitzmyer, Joseph A. "Pauline Theology", in: Raymond Brown et al. (ed.), *The new Jerome Biblical Commentary*, Englewood Cliffs, New Jersey: Prentice-Hall, revised edition, 1990, (first published 1969 under the title *The Jerome Biblical Commentary*), Part Two, pp. 1382–1416

Flasch, Kurt. *Das philosophische Denken im Mittelalter. Von Augustin zu Machiavelli*. Stuttgart: Philipp Reclam jun, 1987.

Ganz, David. "The Debate on Predestination", in: Margaret T. Gibson and Janet L. Nelson, *Charles the Bald*, pp. 353–373.

Gersh, Stephen and Dermot Moran (ed.). *Eriugena, Berkeley, and the Idealist Tradition*, Notre Dame: Notre Dame University Press, 2006.

Gersh, Stephen. *From Iamblichus to Eriugena. An Investigation of the Prehistory and Evolution of the Pseudo-Dionysian Tradition*, Leiden: Brill, 1978, (= Studien zur Problemgeschichte der antiken und mittelalterlichen Philosophie; VIII).

GERSH, STEPHEN and BERT ROEST (ed.), *Medieval and Renaissance Humanism. Rhetoric, Representation and Reform,* Leiden: Brill, 2003, (= Brill's Studies in Intellectual History; 115).

GERSH, STEPHEN. *Middle Platonism and Neoplatonism. The Latin Tradition,* 2. vols., Notre Dame: University of Notre Dame Press, 1986.

GERSH, STEPHEN. "Omnipresence in Eriugena. Some Reflections on Augustino-Maximian Elements in Periphyseon", in: WERNER BEIERWALTES, *Eriugena. Studien zu seinen Quellen,* pp. 55–74.

GERSH, STEPHEN. Review of John J. O'Meara, *Eriugena,* in: *Speculum* 66 (1991) 218–221.

GERSH, STEPHEN. "The Structure of the Return in Eriugena's Periphyseon", in: WERNER BEIERWALTES, *Begriff und Metapher,* pp. 108–125.

GIBSON, MARGARET T. AND JANET L. NELSON (ed.). *Charles the Bald: Court and Kingdom. Papers based on a Colloquium held in London in April 1979,* Oxford: BAR, 1981, (= BAR International Series 101).

GNILKA, CHRISTIAN. *Der Begriff des 'rechten Gebrauchs',* Basel: Schwabe & Co AG, 1984. (= *CRHSIS. Die Methode der Kirchenväter im Umgang mit der antiken Kultur,* 1)

GODMAN, PETER. "Latin poetry under Charles the Bald and Carolingian Poetry", in: MARGARET T. GIBSON and JANET L. NELSON (ed.), *Charles the Bald: Court and Kingdom. Papers based on a Colloquium held in London in April 1979,* Oxford: BAR, 1981, (= BAR International Series 101) pp. 293–309.

GOODENOUGH, ERWIN R. *An Introduction to Philo Judaeus.* Lanham, MD: University Press of America, ²1986, (= Brown Classics in Judaica).

GOODENOUGH, ERWIN R. *By Light, Light. The Mystic Gospel of Hellenistic Judaism,* Amsterdam: Philo Press, 1969, (reprint of 1935 edition).

Görres-Gesellschaft. Grundfragen der kirchengeschichtlichen Methode – heute. Internationales Symposion des Römischen Institutes der Görres-Gesellschaft in Rom 1981, in: *Römische Quartalschrift für Altertumskunde und Kirchengeschichte* 80 (1985) 1–258.

GREGORY, TULLIO. "Note sulla dottrina delle 'teofanie' in Giovanni Scoto Eriugena", in: *Studi medievali* 3a ser. IV (1963) 75–91.

GREETHAM, DAVID C. "Édouard Jeauneau's edition of the 'Periphyseon' in light of contemporary editorial theory", in: *American Catholic Philosophical Quarterly* 79 (2005) 527–548.

HANVEY, JAMES. "Conclusion: Continuing the Conversation", in LAURENCE. P. HEMMING (ed.), *Radical Orthodoxyy? A Catholic Enquiry,* pp. 149–171

HARBISON, PETER. "Irland. A. Materielle Kultur und Kunst", in: *LMA,* vol. V, 1991, col. 652–654.

HARBISON, PETER. "Irland. C. Monastisches und kirchliches Leben", in: *LMA,* vol. V, 1991, col. 660–662.

HAUER, JAKOB WILHELM. "Der nordische Geist im christlichen Frühmittelalter", in: *Deutscher Glaube* 4 (1937) 394–405.

HEINE, RONALD E. *Perfection in the Virtuous Life. A Study in the Relationship Between Edification and Polemical Theology in Gregory of Nyssa's De Vita Moysis,* Philadelphia, 1975.

HEINZER, FELIX and CHRISTOPH SCHÖNBORN (ed.). *Maximus Confessor. Actes du Symposium sur Maxime le Confesseur, Fribourg, 2–5 Septembre 1980, Fribourg,* Suisse: Éditions Universaires, 1982, (= Paradosis, XXVII).

HEMMING, LAURENCE P. (ed.). *Radical Orthodoxy–A Catholic Enquiry?,* Aldershot: Ashgate, 2000.

HERREN, MICHAEL. "Eriugena's Aulae 'Aulae Sidereae', the 'Codex Aureus', and the Palatine Church of St. Mary at Compiègne", in: *Studi Medievali,* ser. 3 28 (1987) 593–608.

HERREN, MICHAEL. "The Commentary on Martianus Attributed to John Scottus: its Hiberno-Latin Background", in: GUY-H. ALLARD, *Jean Scot Écrivain*, pp. 265–286.

HERREN, MICHAEL W. and SHIRLEY ANNE BROWN. *The Sacred Nectar of the Greeks. The Study of Greek in the West in the Early Middle Ages*, Exeter: Short Run Press, 1988, (= King's College London Medieval Studies; 2).

HJORT, PEDER. *Johan Scotus Erigena oder von dem Ursprung einer christlichen Philosophie und ihrem heiligen Beruf*, Copenhagen: 1823

HÖDL, LUDWIG. "Artes liberales, III. Bedeutung für die scholastische Philosophie und Theologie", in: *LMA*, vol. I, 1980, col. 1061–1062.

HOEPS, REINHARD. *Das Gefühl des Erhabenen und die Herrlichkeit Gottes. Studien zur Beziehung von philosophischer und theologischer Ästhetik*, Würzburg: Echter, 1989.

HOEPS, REINHARD. "Theophanie und Schöpfungsgrund. Der Beitrag des Johannes Scottus Eriugena zum Verständnis der *creatio ex nihilo*", in: *Theologie und Philosophie* 67 (1992) 161–191.

HOLTZ, LOUIS. "Grammairiens irlandais au temps de Jean Scot: quelques aspects de leur pédagogie", in: RENÉ ROQUES (ed.) *Jean Scot Érigène et l'histoire de la philosophie. Laon 7–12 juillet 1975*, pp. 69–78.

HUBER, JOHANNES. *Johannes Scotus Erigena. Ein Beitrag zur Geschichte der Philosophie und Theologie im MA*, Munich: Lentner, 1861.

JAEGER, WERNER. *Die Theologie der frühen griechischen Denker*. Stuttgart: W. Kohlhammer Verlag, 1953.

JEAUNEAU, ÉDOUARD. "Appendice III Allegoria, Mysterium, Sacramentum, Symbolum", in: ÉDOUARD JEAUNEAU (ed.), *Jean Scot. Commentaire sur l'évangile de Jean. Introduction, texte critique, traduction, notes et index*. Paris: CERF, 1972, (= Sources Chrétiennes 180), pp. 397–402.

JEAUNEAU, ÉDOUARD. "De l'art comme mystagogie. (Le Jugement dernier vu par Érigène)," in: Yves CHRISTE (ed.), *De l'art comme mystagogie. Iconographie du Jugement dernier et des fins dernières à l'époque gothique. Actes du Colloque de la Fondation Hardt tenu à Genève du 13 au 16 février 1994*, Poitiers: Université de Poitiers, Centre national de la recherche scientifique, Centre d'études supérieures de civilisation médiévale, 1996, pp. 1–8.

JEAUNEAU, ÉDOUARD. *Études Érigéniennes*. Paris: Études Augustiniennes, 1987.

JEAUNEAU, ÉDOUARD. "Heiric d'Auxerre disciple de Jean Scot", in: DOMINIQUE IOGNA-PRAT, etc., *L'école carolingienne d'Auxerre*, Paris: Beauchesne, 1991, pp. 353–370.

JEAUNEAU, ÉDOUARD. "Jean Scot et la métaphysique des nombres", in: WERNER BEIERWALTES, *Begriff und Metapher*, pp. 126–141.

JEAUNEAU, ÉDOUARD. "Jean L'Érigène et les Ambigua ad Iohannem de Maxime Le Confesseur", in: FELIX HEINZER and CHRISTOPH SCHÖNBORN (ed.), *Maximus Confessor. Actes du Symposium sur Maxime le Confesseur, Fribourg, 2–5 Septembre 1980, Fribourg*, Suisse: Éditions Universaires, 1982, (= Paradosis, XXVII), pp. 343–364.

JEAUNEAU, ÉDOUARD. "Jean Scot et la métaphysique du feu" in: ÉDOUARD JEAUNEAU, *Études érigéniennes*, Paris, 1987, pp. 299–319.

JEAUNEAU, ÉDOUARD. "La division des sexes chez Grégoire de Nysse et chez Jean Scot Érigène", in: WERNER BEIERWALTES (ed.). *Eriugena. Studien zu seinen Quellen*, pp. 33–54. Reprint in *Études Érigéniennes*, pp. 343–364.

JEAUNEAU, ÉDOUARD. "L'édition du livre IV du Periphyseon", in: CLAUDIO LEONARDI and ENRICO MENESTÒ (ed.), *Giovanni Scoto nel suo tempo*, pp. 469–486

JEAUNEAU, ÉDOUARD. "Le Cogito érigénien", in: *Traditio. Studies in Ancient and Medieval History, Thought, and Religion*, 50 (1995) 95–100.

JEAUNEAU, ÉDOUARD. "Le symbolisme de la mer chez Jean Scot Érigène", in: ÉDOUARD JEAUNEAU (ed.), *Études Érigéniennes,* 287–296.

JEAUNEAU, ÉDOUARD. "Le thème du retour", in: JEAUNEAU (ed.), *Études Érigéniennes,* 365–394.

JEAUNEAU, ÉDOUARD. "Néant divin et théophanie", in: ALAIN DE LIBERA et al. (éd*.), Langages et philosophie. Hommage à Jean Jolivet,* Paris: Vrin, 1997, pp. 331–337.

JEAUNEAU, ÉDOUARD. "Pseudo-Dionysius, Gregory of Nyssa, and Maximus the Confessor in the Works of John Scottus Eriugena", in: UTA-RENATE BLUMENTHAL (ed.), *Carolingian Essays,* pp. 137–149.

JEAUNEAU, ÉDOUARD. *Quatre Thèmes Érigéniens. Conférence Albert-le-Grand 1974.* Montréal: Institut d'études médiévales Albert-le-Grand / Paris: Librairie J. Vrin, 1978.

JEAUNEAU, ÉDOUARD and PAUL E. DUTTON. *The Autograph of Eriugena,* Turnhout: Brepols, 1996, (= Corpus Christianorum, Autographia Medii Aeui, 3).

JEAUNEAU, ÉDOUARD. "The Neoplatonic Themes of *Processio* and *Reditus* in Eriugena", in: *Dionysius* 15 (1991) 3–29.

KALDENBACH, GISELA. *Die Kosmologie des Johannes Scottus Eriugena. Versuch einer Interpretation seines philosophischen Hauptwerks: De divisione naturae libri V unter kosmologischem Grundaspekt,* München: UNI–Druck, 1963.

KAPRIEV, GORGI. "Eodem sensu utentes? Die Energienlehre der 'Griechen' und die causae primordiales Eriugenas," in: *Theologische Quartalschrift* 180 (2000) 289–307.

KASPER, WALTER et al. (ed.). *Lexikon für Theologie und Kirche,* Freiburg: Herder, ³1993–2001.

KAULICH, WILHELM. *Das spekulative System des Johannes Scotus Erigena,* Prag: Gerzabek, 1860.

KAULICH, WILHELM. *Die Entwicklung der scholastischen Philosophie von Johannes Scotus Erigena bis Abälard,* Prag: Tempsky, 1863.

KAVANAGH, CATHERINE. "Eriugenian developments of Ciceronian topical theory", in: STEPHEN GERSH and BERT ROEST (ed.), *Medieval and Renaissance Humanism,* pp. 1–30.

KELLY, JOSEPH F. "Hiberno-Latin Theology", in: HEINZ LÖWE, *Die Iren und Europa,* vol. 2, pp. 549–567.

KERN, WALTER et al. (ed.). *Handbuch der Fundamentaltheologie, vol. 2, Traktat Offenbarung,* Tübingen: Francke Verlag, second revised edition, 2000, (= UTB für Wissenschaft / Große Reihe).

KERN, WALTER. "Zur theologischen Auslegung des Schöpfungsglaubens", in: *Mysterium Salutis,* vol. II, Einsiedeln: Benziger, 1967, pp. 464–544.

KIBERD, DECLAN & GABRIEL FITZMAURICE (ed.). *An Crann faoi Bhláth (The Flowering Tree),* Dublin: Wolfhound Press, 1991.

KING-FARLOW, JOHN. "From Dionysius to Eriugena: a bridge for voluntarism or 'divine freedom'?", in: *Laval théologique et philosophique* 48 (1992) 367.

KLOOS, KARI. "Seeing the Invisible God: Augustine's Reconfiguration of Theophany Narrative Exegesis", in: *Augustinian Studies* 36 (2005) 397–420.

KÖPF, ULRICH. "Dogmengeschichte oder Theologiegeschichte?", in: *Zeitschrift für Theologie und Kirche,* 85 (1988) 455–473.

KREMER, KLAUS. "Dionysius Pseudo-Areopagita oder Gregor von Nazianz? Zur Herkunft der Formel 'Bonum est diffusivum sui'", in: *Theologie und Philosophie* 63 (1988) 579–585.

KREUZER, JOHANN. "Weisheit bei Eriugena. Vom Nichtwissen Gottes", in: TILMAN BORSCHE and JOHANN KREUZER (ed.), *Weisheit und Wissenschaft,* München: Wilhelm Fink Verlag, 1995, (= Schriften der Académie du Midi, 2).

LATOURELLE, RENÉ. *Theology of Revelation,* New York: Alba House, 1966 (Expanded translation of Théologie de la Révelation, Bruges: Desclée de Brouwer, 1963).

LE BOURDELLÈS, R. "Connaissance du grec et méthodes de traduction dans le monde carolingien jusqu'à Scot Érigène", in: RENÉ ROQUES (ed.), *Jean Scot Érigène et l'histoire de la philosophie,* pp. 117–123.

LEONARDI, CLAUDIO and ENRICO MENESTÒ (ed.). *Giovanni Scoto nel suo tempo. L'organizzazione del sapere in età carolingia. Atti del XXIV Convegno storico internazionale, Todi, 11–14 ottobre, 1987,* Spoleto: Centro Italiano di studi sull'alto medioevo, 1989, (= Atti dei Convegni dell'Accademia Tudertina e del Centro di studi sulla spiritualità medievale, Nuova serie; 1).

LEONARDI, CLAUDIO. "Martianus Capella et Jean Scot. Nouvelle Présentation d'un vieux problème", in: GUY-H. ALLARD, *Jean Scot Écrivain,* pp. 187–207.

LEVINE, PHILIP. "Two early Latin versions of St. Gregory of Nyssa's περὶ κατασκευῆς ἀνθπῶπου", in: *Harvard Studies in Classical Philology,* LXIII (1958) 473–492.

LEYS, ROGER, S. J. *L'Image de Dieu chez Saint Grégoire de Nysse. Esquisse d'une doctrine,* Bruxelles: L'Édition Universelle, 1951, (= Museum Lessianum–Section théologique; 49).

LIEBESCHÜTZ, HANS. "The Place of the Martianus *Glossae* in the Development of Eriugena's Thought", in: JOHN J. O'MEARA, LUDWIG BIELER (ed.), *The Mind of Eriugena,* pp. 49–58.

LINDBECK, GEORGE. *The Nature of Doctrine: Religion and Theology in a Postliberal Age,* London: SPCK, 1984.

LONERGAN, BERNARD J. *Insight. A Study of Human Understanding,* FREDERICK E. CROWE (ed.), 5. ed., revised and augmented, Toronto: University of Toronto Press, 1992, (Collected Works of Bernard Lonergan; 3).

LONERGAN, BERNARD J. *Verbum. Word and Idea in Aquinas,* FREDERICK E. CROWE (ed.), Toronto: University of Toronto Press, 1997, (= Collected Works of Bernard Lonergan; 2).

LOUTH, ANDREW. *Denys the Areopagite,* London: Geoffrey Chapman, 1989.

LÖWE, HEINZ (ed.). *Die Iren und Europa im früheren Mittelalter,* Stuttgart: Klett-Cotta, 2 vols. 1982, (= Veröffentlichungen des Europa-Zentrums Tübingen: Kulturwiss. Reihe).

LUTZ, CORA E. (ed.). *Iohannis Scotti Annotationes in Marcianum.* Cambridge, Massachusetts: The Mediaeval Academy of America, 1939.

MADEC, GOULVEN. *Jean Scot et ses auteurs. Annotations érigéniennes,* Paris: Études Augustiniennes, 1988.

MARENBON, JOHN. *Early Medieval Philosophy (480–1150). An Introduction.* Revised edition, London: Routledge, 1988.

MARENBON, JOHN. *From the Circle of Alcuin to the School of Auxerre. Logic, Theology and Philosophy in the Early Middle Ages,* Cambridge: Cambridge University Press, 1981.

MARENBON, JOHN. "John Scottus and the 'Categoriae Decem'", in: WERNER BEIERWALTES (ed.), *Eriugena. Studien zu seinen Quellen,* pp. 117–134.

MARENBON, JOHN. "Wulfad, Charles the Bald and John Scottus Eriugena", in: M. GIBSON and J. NELSON, *Charles the Bald,* pp. 375–383.

MARLER, Jack C. "Dialectical Use of Authority in the *Periphyseon*", in: *Eriugena. East and West,* 95–113.

MARTELLO, CONCETTO. *Simbolismo e Neoplatonismo in Giovanni Scoto Eriugena,* (= Symbolon. Studi e testi di filosofia antica e medievale, dir. F. Romano; 5), Università di Catania, 1986.

MARTIN, FRANCIS X. and JOHN A. RICHMOND (ed.). *From Augustine to Eriugena. Essays on Neoplatonism and Christianity in Honor of John O'Meara,* Washington D. C.: The Catholic University of America Press, 1991.

MARTINET, SUZANNE. "Aspect de la ville de Laon sous Charles le Chauve", in: RENÉ ROQUES, *Jean Scot Érigène et l'histoire de la philosophie,* pp. 23–36.

MAY, GERHARD. "Die grossen Kappadokier und die staatliche Kirchenpolitik von Valens bis Theodosius", in: GERHARD RUHBACH (ed.), *Die Kirche angesichts der Konstantinischen Wende,* Darmstadt: Wissenschaftliche Buchgesellschaft, 1976, (= Wege der Forschung, 106).

McCUE, E. C. "The Point of Departure of Johannes Scottus Eriugena", in: *The Modern Schoolman* 12 (1954) 19–21.

McEVOY, JAMES and MICHAEL DUNNE (ed.). *History and Eschatology in John Scottus Eriugena and his Time,* Leuven: Leuven University Press, 2002, (= Ancient and Medieval Philosophy. De Wulf-Mansion Centre, Series 1; vol. 30).

McEVOY, JAMES J. "John Scottus Eriugena. Recent Works of Consultation", in: *Philosophical Studies* (Ireland) (1988–90) 83–98.

McEVOY, JAMES J. "'Reditus omnium in superessentialem unitatem'. Christ as universal Saviour in Periphyseon V", in: CLAUDIO LEONARDI and ENRICO MENESTÒ (ed.), *Giovanni Scoto nel suo tempo. L'organizzazione del sapere in età carolingia. Atti del XXIV Convegno storico internazionale, Todi, 11–14 ottobre,* 1987, Spoleto: Centro Italiano di studi sull'alto medioevo, 1989, (= Atti dei Convegni dell'Accademia Tudertina e del Centro di studi sulla spiritualità medievale, Nuova serie; 1), pp. 365–381.

McGINN, BERNARD and WILLEMIEN OTTEN (ed.) *Eriugena. East and West. Papers of the Eighth International Colloquium of the Society for the Promotion of Eriugenian Studies, Chicago and Notre Dame 18–20 October 1991,* Notre Dame, Indiana: Univ. of Notre Dame Press, 1994, (= Notre Dame Conferences in Medieval Studies; V).

McGINN, BERNARD. "Eriugena Mysticus", in: CLAUDIO LEONARDI and ENRICO MENESTÒ (ed.), *Giovanni Scoto nel suo tempo,* pp. 235–260.

McGINN, BERNARD J. "Negative Theology in John the Scot", in: *Studia Patristica* 13, Berlin: Akademie Verlag, 1975, (= Texte und Untersuchungen zur Geschichte der altchristlichen Literatur, 116), 232–238.

McGINN, BERNARD J. "The Negative Element in the Anthropology of John the Scot", in: *Jean Scot Érigène et l'histoire de la philosophie,* 315–326.

McKITTERICK, ROSAMOND. "The Palace School of Charles the Bald", in: MARGARET GIBSON and JANET NELSON, *Charles the Bald,* pp. 385–400.

Mc NALLY, ROBERT E. *The bible in the Early Middle Ages,* Westminster (Maryland): Newman Press, 1959.

McNAMARA, BRIAN, S. J. Emanation and return. A study of the relations between the Creator and man in the later work of Johannes Eriugena, (= unpublished doctoral dissertation submitted to the Faculty of Theology, St. Patrick's College Maynooth), 1983.

McNAMARA, BRIAN, S. J. "The Ascent to Truth. Methodological Factors in the Writings of John Scotus Eriugena", in: *Milltown Studies* (1985) 1–31.

MEISSNER, HENRIETTE M. *Rhetorik und Theologie. Der Dialog Gregors von Nyssa De anima et resurrectione,* Frankfurt / Main, Bern, New York, Paris: Peter Lang, 1991, (= Patrologia. Beiträge zum Studien der Kirchenväter; 1).

MEREDITH, ANTHONY. *The Cappadocians,* London: Chapman: 1995, (= Outstanding Christian Thinkers).

MILBANK, JOHN. "Knowledge. The theological critique of philosophy in Hamann and Jacobi", in: JOHN MILBANK, CATHERINE PICKSTOCK and GRAHAM WARD (ed.), *Radical Orthodoxy,* pp. 21–37

MILBANK, JOHN, CATHERINE PICKSTOCK and GRAHAM WARD (ed.), *Radical Orthodoxy. A New Theology*, London: Routledge, 1999.

MOONEY, HILARY A. "Der goldene Leuchter. Die ekklesiale Vermittlung der Offenbarung nach Johannes Scottus Eriugena", in: JOHANNES ARNOLD; RAINER BERNDT; RALF M. W. STAMMBERGER (ed.): *Väter der Kirche. Ekklesiales Denken von den Anfängen bis zur Gegenwart. Festgabe zum siebzigsten Geburtstag von Hermann-Josef Sieben*, Paderborn: Schöningh, 2004, pp. 49–67.

MOONEY, HILARY A. *"Infinitus enim infinite, etiam in purgatissimis mentibus formatur: Die Struktur der Begegnung mit dem unendlichen Gott nach Johannes Scottus Eriugena,"* in: JAMES McEVOY and MICHAEL DUNNE (ed.), *History and Eschatology in John Scottus Eriugena and his Time*, Leuven: Leuven University Press, 2002, (= Ancient and Medieval Philosophy. De Wulf-Mansion Centre, Series I; vol. 30), pp. 463–486.

MOONEY, HILARY A. "Johannes Scottus Eriugena. Kreativer Umgang mit dem Erbe der Tradition", in: *Freiburger Universitätsblätter*, 146 December, 1999, pp. 39–51.

MOONEY, HILARY A. "Some Observations on the Concept of Harmony in Pseudo-Dionysius Areopagita and John Scottus Eriugena," in: ELIZABETH A. LIVINGSTONE (ed.), *Studia Patristica, vol. XXIX.* Leuven: Peeters, 1997, pp. 304–309.

MOONEY, HILARY A. "The Notion of the Liberality of God in Gregory of Nyssa and Johannes Scottus Eriugena", in: MAURICE F. WILES, EDWARD J. YARNOLD, PAUL M. PARVIS (assistance) (ed.), *Studia Patristica, vol. XXXVII, papers presented at the Thirteenth International Conference on Patristic Studies held in Oxford 1999*, Leuven: Peeters, 2001, pp. 207–211.

MORAN, DERMOT. "Pantheism from John Scottus Eriugena to Nicholas of Cusa", in: *New Scholasticism* 64 (1990) 131–152.

MORAN, DERMOT. *The Philosophy of John Scottus Eriugena. A Study of Idealism in the Middle Ages*, Cambridge: Cambridge University Press, 1989.

MORTLEY, RAOUL. *From Word to Silence I. The Rise and Fall of Logos*, Bonn: P. Hanstein, 1986, (= Theophaneia; 30).

MÜHLENBERG, EKKEHARD. *Die Unendlichkeit Gottes bei Gregor von Nyssa. Gregors Kritik am Gottesbegriff der klassischen Metaphysik*, Göttingen: Vandenhoeck & Ruprecht, 1966, (= Forschungen zur Kirchen- und Dogmengeschichte, 16).

NAUTIN, PIERRE. "Genèse I, 1–2, de Justin à Origène", in: CENTRE D'ÉTUDES DES RELIGIONS DU LIVRE, PARIS, PAUL VIGNAUX (ed.), *In principio. Interprétations des premiers versets de la Genèse*, pp. 61–94.

NOACK, LUDWIG. *Johannes Scotus Erigena. Sein Leben u. seine Schriften, die Wissenschaft u. Bildung seiner Zeit, die Voraussetzungen seines Denkens u. Wissens u. der Gehalt seiner Weltanschauung*, Leipzig: Koschny, 1876.

Ó CRÓINÍN, DÁIBHÍ. *Early Medieval Ireland 400–1200*, London: Longman, 1995.

Ó CRÓINÍN, DÁIBHÍ. and GEARÓID MAC NIOCAIL. "Irland. B. Allgemeine und politische Geschichte", in: *LMA*, vol. V, 1991, pp. 654–660.

O' CUIV, BRIAN (ed.). *The Impact of the Scandinavian Invasions on the Celtic-speaking Peoples c. 800–1100 A.D. Introductory Papers read at Plenary Sessions of the International Congress of Celtic Studies held in Dublin, 6–10 July, 1959*, Dublin: Institiúid Ard-Léinn, 1975.

O'MEARA, JOHN J. "Eriugena's Use of Augustine in his Teaching on the Return of the Soul and the Vision of God", in: RENÉ ROQUES (ed.), *Jean Scot Érigène et l'histoire de la philosophie*, pp. 191–200.

O'COLLINS, GERALD. *Retrieving Fundamental Theology. The Three Styles of Contemporary Theology*, London: Geoffrey Chapman, 1993.

O'DALY, GERALD. "Dionysius Areopagita", in: *TRE*, vol. VIII, pp. 772–780.

OHLIG, K.-H. *Fundamentalchristologie. Im Spannungsfeld von Christentum und Kultur,* München: Kösel, 1986

OLLIG, HANS-LUDWIG. Review of G. Schrimpf, *Das Werk des Johannes Scottus Eriugena im Rahmen des Wissenschaftsverständnisses seiner Zeit,* in: *Theologie und Philosophie* 58 (1983) 105–107.

O'MEARA, DOMINIC J. "Eriugena and Aquinas on the beatific vision", in: WERNER BEIERWALTES (ed.), Eriugena redivivus, pp. 224–236.

O'MEARA, DOMINIC J. "L'investigation et les investigateurs dans le 'De divisione naturae' de Jean Scot Érigène", in: *Jean Scot et l'histoire de la philosophie,* pp. 225–233.

O'MEARA, DOMINIC J. Review of É. Jeauneau (ed.), *Ambigua ad Iohannem, iuxta Iohannis Scotti Eriugenae Latinam interpretationem,* in: Speculum 66 (1991) 445–446.

O'MEARA, DOMINIC J. "The Concept of Natura in John Scottus Eriugena (De divisione naturae Book I)", in: *Vivarium* XIX(1981) 126–145.

O'MEARA, DOMINIC J. "The Problem of Speaking about God in John Scottus Eriugena", in: UTA-RENATE BLUMENTHAL, *Carolingian Essays,* pp. 151–167.

O'MEARA, DOMINIC J. *The Structure of Being and the Search for the Good,* Aldershot: Ashgate, 1999, (= Variorum Collected Studies Series, CS629).

O'MEARA, JOHN J. *Eriugena.* New York: Clarendon Press, Oxford University Press, 1988.

O'MEARA, JOHN J. "Magnorum Virorum Quendam Consensum Velimus Machinari" (804B). Eriugena's use of Augustine's De Genesi ad litteram in the Periphyseon", in: WERNER BEIERWALTES (ed.), *Eriugena. Studien zu seinen Quellen. Vorträge des III. Eriugena-Colloquiums Freiburg im Breisgau, 27.–30. August 1979,* Heidelberg: Carl Winter Verlag, 1980, (= Abhandlungen der Heidelberger Akademie der Wissenschaften, Philosophisch-historische Klasse; Jg. 1980, Abh. 3), pp. 105–116.

O'MEARA, JOHN J. and LUDWIG BIELER (ed.). *The Mind of Eriugena. Papers of a Colloquium Dublin, 14–18 July 1970,* Dublin: Irish University Press, 1973.

O'NÉILL, PÁDRAIG. "The Old-Irish Words in Eriugena's Biblical Glosses", in: GUY-H. ALLARD, *Jean Scot Écrivain,* pp. 287–297.

OTTEN, WILLEMIEN. "Eriugena's *Periphyseon*. A Carolingian Contribution to the Theological Tradition", in: *Eriugena. East and West,* pp. 69–93.

OTTEN, WILLEMIEN. "In the shadow of the divine: negative theology and negative anthropology in Augustine, Pseudo-Dionysius and Eriugena," in: *The Heythrop Journal* 40 (1999) 438–455.

OTTEN, WILLEMIEN. "Some Perspectives in Eriugenian Studies. Three Recent Publications", in: *Freiburger Zeitschrift für Philosophie und Theologie* 37 (1990) 515–526.

OTTEN, WILLEMIEN. *The anthropology of Johannes Scottus Eriugena.* Leiden: Brill, 1991, (= Brill's studies in intellectual history).

OTTEN, WILLEMIEN. "The Dialectic of the Return in Eriugena's *Periphyseon*", in: *Harvard Theological Review* 84 (1991) 339–421.

OTTEN, WILLEMIEN. "The Influence of Eriugenian Thought: Report on the International Eriugena Colloquium, Bad Homburg, 26–30 August 1985", in: *Studi Medievali,* 3. ser. 27 (1986) 461–473.

OTTEN, WILLEMIEN. "The Interplay of nature and man in the 'Periphyseon' of Johannes Scottus Eriugena, in: *Vivarium* 28 (1990) 1–16.

OTTEN, WILLEMIEN. "The Texture of Tradition. The Role of the Church Fathers in Carolingian Theology", in: Irena Backus, *The Reception of the Church Fathers in the West.,* 2 vol., vol. 1 From the Carolingians to the Maurists, Leiden: Brill, 1997, pp. 3–50.

PACHAS, JOSÉ ANTONIO. "Influencia de Gregorio de Nisa sobre Juan Escoto Eriúgena: aproximación a partir del "Periphyseon", in: *Teología y vida* 45 (2004) 539–563.

PANNENBERG, WOLFHART. *Systematische Theologie,* vol. I Göttingen: Vandenhoeck & Ruprecht, 1988.

PATSCHOVSKY, ALEXANDER. "Dionysius Areopagita", in: *LMA* 3 (1986) 1076–1087.

PEISKER, CARL HEINZ. *Evangelien-Synopse der Einheitsübersetzung,* Wuppertal und Kassel: Oncken Verlag and Stuttgart: Verlag Katholisches Bibelwerk, 1983.

PÉPIN, JEAN. "*Mysteria* et *Symbola* dans le commentaire de Jean Scot sur l'évangile de Saint Jean", in: JOHN J. O'MEARA and LUDWIG Bieler, *The Mind of Eriugena,* pp. 16–20.

PERGER, MISCHA VAN. "Wie Maximus Confessor und Augustinus die Theophanie verstanden: zu Eriugena, 'Periphyseon' I 449A–450B," in: *Freiburger Zeitschrift für Philosophie und Theologie* 46 (1999) 35–51.

PERL, ERIC D. "Metaphysics and Christology in Maximus Confessor and Eriugena", in: *Eriugena. East and West,* pp. 253–279.

PIEMONTE, GUSTAVO. "L'expression quae sunt et quae non sunt. Jean Scot et Marius Victorinus", in: GUY- H. ALLARD (ed.), *Jean Scot écrivain,* p. 81–113.

PIEMONTE, GUSTAVO. "Notas sobre la 'Creatio de nihilo' en Juan Escoto Eriugena", part 1, *Sapientia,* 23 (Buenos Aires, 1968) 37–58

PIEMONTE, GUSTAVO. "Some distinctive theses of Eriugena's Eschatology in his Exegesis of the Gospel according to St. Matthew", in: JAMES MCEVOY and MICHAEL DUNNE (ed.), *History and Eschatology in John Scottus Eriugena and his Time,* Leuven: Leuven University Press, 2002, (= Ancient and Medieval Philosophy. De Wulf-Mansion Centre, Series 1; vol. 30), pp. 227–242.

PIEMONTE, GUSTAVO. "Recherches sur les 'Tractatus in Matheum' attribués à Jean Scot", in: G. VAN RIEL, C. STEEL, J. MCEVOY (ed.), *Iohannes Scottus Eriugena: The Bible and Hermeneutics,* pp. 321–350.

PRÉAUX, JEAN. "Jean Scot et Martin de Laon en face du *De Nuptiis* de Martianus Capella", in: RENÉ ROQUES (ed.), *Jean Scot Érigène et l'histoire de la philosophie. Laon 7–12 juillet 1975,* Paris: Éditions du Centre National de la Recherche Scientifique, 1977, (= Actes du Colloque International N° 561, Colloques Internationaux du Centre National de la Recherche Scientifique), pp. 161–170.

PREUSS, HORST DIETRICH, Offenbarung II. Altes Testament, in: *TRE,* vol. XXV, pp. 117–128

REYNOLDS, P.L. Review of Dermot Moran, *The Philosophy of John Scottus Eriugena: A Study of Idealism in the Middle Ages,* in: *Speculum* 66 (1991) 208–210.

RICCATI, CARLO. "'Processio' et 'explicatio' chez Jean Scot et Nicolas de Cues", École Pratique des Hautes Études, Section Sciences religieuses, *Annuaire* XC (1981–82) 495–497, Paris: 1982.

RICCATI, CARLO. *'Processio' et 'Explicatio'. La doctrine de la création chez Jean Scot et Nicolas de Cues,* Naples: Bibliopolis, 1983, (= Instituto Italiano per gli studi filosofici, Serie Studi VI).

RICHÉ, PIERRE. "Charles le Chauve et la culture de son temps", in: RENÉ ROQUES, *Jean Scot Érigène et l'histoire de la philosophie,* pp. 37–46.

RICHÉ, PIERRE. *Écoles et enseignement dans le Haut Moyen Age de la fin du Ve au milieu du XIe siècle,* Paris, 1979.

RICHÉ, PIERRE. *Education and Culture in the Barbarian West from the Sixth Through the Eighth Century,* trans. J.J. Contreni, Columbia, S.C.: University of South Carolina Press, 1978.

RIEL, GERD VAN, CARLOS STEEL and JAMES MCEVOY (ed.). *Iohannes Scottus Eriugena. The Bible and Hermeneutics,* Leuven: Leuven University Press, 1996.

ROQUES, RENÉ. "Allocution de M. René Roques", in: *Jean Scot Érigène et l'histoire de la philosophie,* pp. 13–18.

ROQUES, RENÉ. "Genèse 1, 1–3 chez Jean Scot Erigène", in: CENTRE D'ÉTUDES DES RELIGIONS DU LIVRE, PARIS, PAUL VIGNAUX (ed.), *In Principio. Interprétations des premiers versets de la Genèse,* pp. 173–212.

ROQUES, RENÉ. "Jean Scot Érigène", in: MARCEL VILLER et al. (ed.), *Dictionnaire de spiritualité. Ascetique et mystique. Doctrine et histoire,* Paris: Beauchesne, 1937–1995, vol. 8, 735–761.

ROQUES, RENÉ (ed.). *Jean Scot Érigène et l'histoire de la philosophie. Laon 7–12 juillet 1975,* Paris: Éditions du Centre National de la Recherche Scientifique, 1977, (= Actes du Colloque International Nº 561, Colloques Internationaux du Centre National de la Recherche Scientifique).

ROQUES, RENÉ. "I. La symbolique de Jean Scot Erigena", "II. Explication de textes érigéniens et pseudo-dionysiens", (conférences), *École Pratique des Hautes Études. Section des sciences religieuses. Annuaire 1964–65 Tome LXXII,* Paris: 1964, pp. 121–125.

ROQUES, RENÉ. *Libres sentiers vers l'érigénisme,* Rome: Edizioni dell'Ateneo,1975, (= Lessico intellettuale europeo 9).

ROQUES, RENÉ. "I. Théophanie et nature chez Jean Scot Erigène "; "II. Explication de quelques passages du De divisione naturae", (conférences), *École Pratique des Hautes Études. Section des sciences religieuses. Annuaire 1966–67 Tome LXXIV,* Paris: 1966, pp. 162–167.

ROQUES, RENÉ. "I: Théophanie et nature chez Jean Scot Erigène"; "II. Explication de textes érigéniens et pseudo-dionysiens", (conférences), *École Pratique des Hautes Études. Section des sciences religieuses. Annuaire 1965–66 Tome LXXIII,* Paris: 1965, pp. 156–161.

ROQUES, RENÉ. "'Valde artificialiter'. Le sens d'un contresens", in: *Libres sentiers vers l'Érigènisme,* pp, 45–98.

ROREM, PAUL. *Pseudo-Dionysius. A Commentary on the Texts and an Introduction to Their Influence,* Oxford: Oxford University Press, 1993.

ROREM, PAUL. *Eriugena's Commentary on the Dionysian Celestial Hierarchy,* Toronto: Pontifical Institute of Mediaeval Studies, 2005, (= Studies and Texts; 150).

ROSEMANN, PHILIPP W. "Causality as concealing revelation in Eriugena: a Heideggerian interpretation", in: *American catholic philosophical quarterly* 79 (2005) 653–671.

RUDNICK, ULRICH. *Das System des Johannes Scottus Eriugena. Eine theologisch-philosophische Studie zu seinem Werk.* Frankfurt-Bern-New York-Paris: Peter Lang, 1990.

SAVVIDIS, KYRIAKOS. *Die Lehre von der Vergöttlichung des Menschen bei Maximos dem Bekenner und ihre Rezeption durch Gregor Palamas,* St. Ottilien: EOS Verlag, 1997, (= Veröffentlichungen des Instituts für Orthodoxe Theologie; vol. 5).

SCHMITZ, JOSEF. "Das Christentum als Offenbarungsreligion im kirchlichen Bekenntnis", in: Walter Kern et al. (ed.), *Handbuch für Fundamentaltheologie,* Tübingen: Francke Verlag, second revised edition 2000, (= UTB für Wissenschaft / Große Reihe), pp. 1–12.

SCHRIMPF, GANGOLF. *Das Werk des Johannes Scottus Eriugena im Rahmen des Wissenschaftsverständnisses seiner Zeit. Eine Hinführung zu Periphyseon,* Münster: Aschendorff, 1982, (= Beiträge zur Geschichte der Philosophie und Theologie des Mittelalters, Neue Folge, 23).

SCHRIMPF, GANGOLF. "Der Beitrag des Johannes Scottus Eriugena zum Prädestinationsstreit", In: H. Löwe, (ed.) *Die Iren in Europa* Vol. II, pp. 819–865.

SCHRIMPF, GANGOLF. "Die Sinnmitte von "Periphyseon"", in: RENÉ ROQUES (ed.) *Jean Scot Érigène et l'histoire de la philosophie. Laon 7–12 juillet 1975,* pp. 289–305.

SCHRIMPF, GANGOLF. "Die systematische Bedeutung der beiden logischen Einteilungen (*divisiones*) zu Beginn von *Periphyseon*" in: CLAUDIO LEONARDI and ENRICO MENESTÒ (ed.), *Giovanni Scoto nel suo tempo*, pp. 113–151.

SCHRIMPF, GANGOLF. "Johannes Scotus Eriugena", in: *LMA* 5 (1991) 602–605.

SCHRIMPF, GANGOLF. "Johannes Scotus Eriugena", in: *TRE* 17 (1988) 156–172.

SCHRIMPF, GANGOLF. "Johannes Scottus Eriugena und die Rezeption des Martianus Capella im karolingischen Bildungswesen", in: WERNER BEIERWALTES (ed.), *Eriugena. Studien zu seinen Quellen*, pp. 135–148.

SCHRIMPF, GANGOLF. "Zur Frage der Authentizität unserer Texte von Johannes Scottus' 'Annotationes in Martianum'", in: JOHN J. O'MEARA and LUDWIG BIELER (ed.), *The Mind of Eriugena*, pp. 125–139.

SCHÜSSLER FIORENZA, FRANCIS. *Foundational Theology. Jesus and the Church,* New York: Crossroad, 1986.

SCHWYZER, HANS-RUDOLF. "Plotin", in: GEORG WISSOWA et al. (ed.), *Paulys Realencyclopädie der klassischen Altertumswissenschaft,* Vol. XXI, Stuttgart: Druckenmüller, 1951, col. 471–592.

SELLS, MICHAEL A. *Mystical Languages of Unsaying,* Chicago: Chicago University Press, 1994.

SHELDON-WILLIAMS, INGLIS P. "A Bibliography of the Works of Johannes Scottus Eriugena", in: *Journal of Ecclesiastical History,* 10 (1959) 198–224.

SHELDON-WILLIAMS, INGLIS P. "A List of Works doubtfully or wrongly attributed to Johannes Scottus Eriugena", in: *Journal of Ecclesiastical History* 15 (1964) 76–98.

SHELDON-WILLIAMS, INGLIS P. "Eriugena and Citeaux", in: *Monastica* 19 (1977) 75–92.

SHELDON-WILLIAMS, INGLIS P. "Eriugena's Greek Sources", in: JOHN J. O'MEARA, LUDWIG BIELER, *The Mind of Eriugena*, pp. 1–15.

SHELDON-WILLIAMS, INGLIS P. "The Greek Platonist Tradition from the Cappadocians to Maximus and Eriugena", in: ARTHUR Hilary ARMSTRONG *The Cambridge History of Later Greek and Early Medieval Philosophy,* Cambridge: University Press, 1970², 425–533.

SIEBEN, HERMANN JOSEF, "Die 'res' der Bibel. Eine Analyse von Augustinus, De doctrina christian I–III", in: *"Manna in deserto": Studien zum Schriftgebrauch der Kirchenväter,* Köln: Koinonia-Oriens, 2002, (= Edition Cardo; 92), pp. 267–294.

SILONIS, RAPHAELE LÓPEZ, S. J. *La dialectica de las antinomias y de las teofanias en la teoria del conocimiento de dios de escoto erigena. Excerpta ex dissertatione ad Lauream in Facultate Philosophica Pontificiae Universitatis Gregorianae,* Madrid: 1967.

SOLIGNAC, AIMÉ. "Exégèse et métaphysique. Genèse I, 1–3 chez saint Augustin", in: CENTRE D'ÉTUDES DES RELIGIONS DU LIVRE, PARIS, Paul Vignaux, *In principio. Interprétations des premiers versets de la Genèse,* pp. 153–171.

SOMMERVILLE, ROBERT. "Pope Nicholas I and John Scottus Eriugena", in: *Savigny-Stiftung: Zeitschrift der Savigny-Stiftung für Rechtsgeschichte. Kanonistische Abteilung,* 114 (1997) 67–85.

SOUTHERN, RICHARD W. *Western Society and the Church in the Middle Ages,* (= The Penguin History of the Church, Vol. 2). London: Penguin 1990, first published by Pelican, 1970.

STAUDENMAIER, FRANZ ANTON. *Johannes Scotus Erigena und die Wissenschaft seiner Zeit. Mit allgemeinen Entwicklungen der Hauptwahrheiten auf dem Gebiete der Philosophie und Religion, und Grundzügen zu einer Geschichte der speculativen Theologie,* vol. 1, Frankfurt / Main: Andreäische Buchhandlung, 1834.

STEEL, CARLOS. "The Tree of the Knowledge of Good and Evil", in: G. VAN RIEL, C. STEEL, J. MCEVOY (ed.), *Iohannes Scottus Eriugena. The Bible and Hermeneutics,* pp. 239–255.

STOCK, BRIAN. "In search of Eriugena's Augustine", in: WERNER BEIERWALTES (ed.), *Eriugena. Studien zu seinen Quellen,* pp. 85–104.

STOCK, BRIAN. "'Intelligo me esse'. Eriugena's 'Cogito'", in: *Jean Scot Érigène el l'histoire de la philosophie,* pp. 327–334.

STOCK, BRIAN. "The Philosophical Anthropology of Johannes Scottus Eriugena", in: *Studi Mediaevali,* 3ª Serie, 8 (1967) 1–57.

STRAUSS, GERHARD. *Schriftgebrauch, Schriftauslegung und Schriftbeweis bei Augustin,* Tübingen: Mohr, 1959, (= BGBH 1).

SUCHLA, BEATA REGINA. "Wahrheit über jeder Wahrheit. Zur philosophischen Absicht der Schrift 'De divinis nominibus' des Dionysius Areopagita", in: *Theologische Quartalschrift* 176 (1996) 205–217.

TESSIER, GEORGES (ed.). *Recueil des Actes de Charles II le Chauve Roi de France,* vol. I, Paris: Imprimerie Nationale, 1943.

*Thesaurus Linguae Graecae # E,* University of California, Irvine, 1999

THONNARD, FRANÇOIS-JOSEPH. "La notion de 'nature' chez saint Augustin. Ses progrès dans la polémique antipélagienne", in: *Revue des Études Augustiniennes* 11 (1965) 239–265.

THUNBERG, LARS. *Microcosm and Mediator. The Theological Anthropology of Maximus the Confessor,* Lund: Gleerup, 1965, (= Acta Seminarii Neotestamentici Upsaliensis 25).

TOMASIC, THOMAS MICHAEL. "The Logical Function of Metaphor and Oppositional Coincidence in the Pseudo-Dionysius and Johannes Scottus Eriugena", in: *The Journal of Religion* 68 (1988) 361–376.

TRACY, DAVID. "The Uneasy Alliance Reconceived. Catholic Theological Method, Modernity, and Postmodernity", in: *Theological Studies* 50 (1989) 548–570.

TRESCHOW, MICHAEL, WILLEMIEN OTTEN, WALTER HANNAM (ed.), *Divine creation in ancient, medieval, and early modern thought. Essays presented to the Reverend Robert D. Crouse,* Leiden: Brill, 2007, (= Brill's Studies in Intellectual History; 151)

TROUILLARD, JEAN. "Eriugène et la théophanie créatrice", in: J. J. O'Meara and L. Bieler (ed.), *The Mind of Eriugena,* pp. 98–113.

TROULLARD, JEAN. "La notion d''analyse' chez Érigène", in: *Jean Scot et l'histoire de la philosophie,* pp. 349–356.

TROUILLARD, JEAN. "La notion de 'théophanie' chez Erigène", in: S. Breton et. al. *Manifestation et révélation,* Paris: Éditions Beauchesne, 1976, pp. 15–39, (= *Philosophie* I).

TROUILLARD, JEAN. "Procession néoplatonicienne et création judéo-chrétienne", in: *Neoplatonisme, mélanges offert à Jean Trouillard,* Les cahiers de Fontenay N° 19.20.21.22, Fontenay aux Roses: e. n.s, 1981, pp. 1–30.

ULRICH, FERDINAND. "Cur non video praesentem? Zur Implikation der 'griechischen' und 'lateinischen' Denkform bei Anselm und Scotus Eriugena", in: *Freiburger Zeitschrift für Philosophie und Theologie* 22 (1975) 70–170.

VAN RIEL, GERD. "A Bibliographical Survey of Eriugenian Studies 1987–1995", in: GERD VAN RIEL et al. (ed.), *Iohannes Scottus Eriugena. The Bible and Hermeneutics,* pp. 367–400.

VAN RIEL, GERD. "Eriugenian Studies 1995–2000," in: JAMES MCEVOY, MICHAEL DUNNE (ed.), *History and Eschatology in John Scottus Eriugena and his time,* pp. 611–626.

VIGNAUX, PAUL. *La pensée au moyen âge,* Paris: 1948, = *Philosophie au moyen âge,* Paris: Colin, 1958, pp. 16–21, (Trans. *Philosophy in the Middle Ages,* London: Burns & Oats, 1959, pp. 17–24.).

VISCHER, LUKAS, and D. LERCH. "Die Auslegungsgeschichte als notwendige theologische Aufgabe", in: *Studia Patristica* 1 (1957) 414–419, (= TU 63).

WALLACE-HADRILL, JOHN M. *The Frankish Church,* Oxford: Clarendon Press, 1983, pp. 241–257.

WALTER, PETER. *Theologie aus dem Geist der Rhetorik. Zur Schriftauslegung des Erasmus von Rotterdam.* Mainz: Grünewald, 1991.

WEINER, SEBASTIAN FLORIAN. *Eriugenas negative Ontologie,* Amsterdam / Philadelphia: B. R. Grüner, 2007, (= Bochumer Studien zur Philosophie; 46).

WEISSNER, GERNOT, HORST DIETRICH PREUSS, BRIGITTE (RIVKA) KERN-ULMER, HORST BALZ, EILERT HERMS, "Offenbarung", in: HORST BALZ et al. (ed.), *Theologische Realenzyklopädie, vol. XXV, Ochino-Parapsychologie,* Berlin: Walter de Gruyter, 1995, 109–210

WEISWEILER, HEINRICH. "Die Ps-Dionysiuskommentare 'In coelestem hierarchiam' des Scotus und Hugo von St. Victor", in: *Recherches de théologie ancienne et médiévale* 19 (1952) 26–47.

WESTRA, HAIJO JAN (ed.). *From Athens to Chartres. Neoplatonism and Medieval Thought. Studies in Honour of Edouard Jeauneau.* Leiden: E. J. Brill, 1992, (= Studien und Texte zur Geistesgeschichte des Mittelalters, 35).

WHITELOCK, DOROTHY, ROSAMOND MCKITTERICK and DAVID DUMVILLE (ed.). *Ireland in Early Mediaeval Europe. Studies in Memory of Kathleen Hughes,* Cambridge: Cambridge University Press, 1982.

WILLIS, JAMES. *Martianus Capella,* Leipzig: BSB B.G Teubner Verlagsgesellschaft, 1983, (= Bibliotheca Scriptorum Graecorum et Romanorum Teubneriana).

WIMBUSH, VINCENT L. and RICHARD VALANTASIS, (with the assistance of GAY L. BYRON, WILLIAM S. LOVE). *Asceticism,* Oxford: Oxford University Press, 1995.

WIORA, WALTER. "Das vermeintliche Zeugnis des Johannes Eriugena für die Anfänge der abendländischen Mehrstimmigkeit", in: *Acta musicolica* 43 (1971) 33–43.

WOHLMAN, AVITAL. "John Scottus Eriugena, a Christian philosopher", in: *American Catholic Philosophical Quarterly* 79 (2005) 635–651.

YATES, FRANCES A. *Lull & Bruno. Collected Essays, Vol. I.* London: Routledge & Kegan Paul, 1982.

YATES, FRANCES A. "Lull, Raymond, Bl.", in: *New Catholic Encyclopedia,* Vol. 8, pp. 1074–1076.

YATES, FRANCES A. "Raymond Lull and John Scotus Eriugena", in: *Journal of the Warburg and Courtauld Institutes* 23 (1960) 1–44, reprinted in FRANCES A. YATES, *Lull & Bruno. Collected Essays, Vol.* I, London: Routledge & Kegan Paul, 1982.

ZACHHUBER, JOHANNES. *Human Nature in Gregory of Nyssa, Philosophical Background and Theological Significance,* Leiden: Brill, 2000, (= Supplements to Vigiliae Christianae, Vol. XLVI).

ZIMMERMANN, ALBERT. Review of Gangolf Schrimpf, *Das Werk des Johannes Scottus Eriugena im Rahmen des Wissenschaftsverständnisses seiner Zeit,* in: *Archiv für Geschichte der Philosophie* LXVI (1984) 101–3.

ZINTZEN, CLEMENS. (ed.). *Die Philosophie des Neuplatonismus,* Darmstadt: Wissenschaftliche Buchgesellschaft, 1977.

# Index of Biblical References

# Index of Ancient and Medieval Persons

Maximus (Confessor) xii, 10, 14, 20, 21, 38,
   51, 56, 57, 64, 65, 66, 68, 70, 80, 81, 82,
   87, 89, 90, 99, 100, 102, 111, 121, 123, 126,
   152, 153, 162, 165, 168, 169, 171, 175, 178,
   181, 186, 190, 193, 195, 203, 218, 219, 222,
   226, 227, 228, 233, 235, 236
Michael, II Byzantine emperor 37

Nicholas (of Cusa) 14, 15, 19, 138, 200, 219,
   222, 225, 231, 233
Nicholas, I Pope 235

Origen 10, 59, 219, 231

Pardulus (of Laon) 26, 32, 33
Philo 10, 48, 49, 136, 199, 219, 223, 226
Plato 7, 22, 52, 62, 219, 222, 223

Plotinus 6, 7, 8, 9, 22, 65, 94, 219, 222, 235
Porphyry 8, 22, 46, 48
Proclus 7, 10, 22, 45, 46, 65, 94, 219, 220,
   222
Prudentius 27, 31, 220

Ratramnus (of Corbie) 32
Raymund (Lull) 237
Remigius 26, 32, 220

Theodosius 230
Theodulf 37, 48

Valens 230

Wulfad 21, 16, 39, 197, 229

# Index of Modern Persons

# Index of Subjects

The table of contents provides access to many major themes. By way of complement, this index covers selected major themes whose treatment might not otherwise be readily and accurately localised.

# Beiträge zur historischen Theologie
Herausgegeben von Albrecht Beutel

## Alphabetical Index

*Dietz, Thorsten:* Der Begriff der Furcht bei Luther. 2009. *Volume 147.*

*Drecoll, Volker Henning:* Die Entstehung der Gnadenlehre Augustins. 1999. *Volume 109.*

*Elliger, Karl:* Studien zum Habakuk-Kommentar vom Toten Meer. 1953. *Volume 15.*

*Evang, Martin:* Rudolf Bultmann in seiner Frühzeit. 1988. *Volume 74.*

*Friedrich, Martin:* Zwischen Abwehr und Bekehrung. 1988. *Volume 72.*

*Gestrich, Christof:* Neuzeitliches Denken und die Spaltung der dialektischen Theologie. 1977. *Volume 52.*

*Gräßer, Erich:* Albert Schweitzer als Theologe. 1979. *Volume 60.*

*Graumann, Thomas:* Die Kirche der Väter. 2002. *Volume 118.*

*Grosse, Sven:* Heilsungewißheit und Scrupulositas im späten Mittelalter. 1994. *Volume 85.*

*Gülzow, Henneke:* Cyprian und Novatian. 1975. *Volume 48.*

*Hamm, Berndt:* Promissio, Pactum, Ordinatio. 1977. *Volume 54.*

– Frömmigkeitstheologie am Anfang des 16. Jahrhunderts. 1982. *Volume 65.*

*Hammann, Konrad:* Universitätsgottesdienst und Aufklärungspredigt. 2000. *Volume 116.*

*Hoffmann, Manfred:* Erkenntnis und Verwirklichung der wahren Theologie nach Erasmus von Rotterdam. 1972. *Volume 44.*

*Holfelder, Hans H.:* Solus Christus. 1981. *Volume 63.*

*Hübner, Jürgen:* Die Theologie Johannes Keplers zwischen Orthodoxie und Naturwissenschaft. 1975. *Volume 50.*

*Hyperius, Andreas G.:* Briefe 1530–1563. Hrsg., übers. und komment. von G. Krause. 1981. *Volume 64.*

*Jacobi, Thorsten:* „Christen heißen Freie": Luthers Freiheitsaussagen in den Jahren 1515–1519. 1997. *Volume 101.*

*Jetter, Werner:* Die Taufe beim jungen Luther. 1954. *Volume 18.*

*Jørgensen, Theodor H.:* Das religionsphilosophische Offenbarungsverständnis des späteren Schleiermacher. 1977. *Volume 53.*

*Jung, Martin H.:* Frömmigkeit und Theologie bei Philipp Melanchthon. 1998. *Volume 102.*

*Käfer, Anne:* „Die wahre Ausübung der Kunst ist religiös". 2006. *Volume 136.*

*Kasch, Wilhelm F.:* Die Sozialphilosophie von Ernst Troeltsch. 1963. *Volume 34.*

*Kaufmann, Thomas:* Die Abendmahlstheologie der Straßburger Reformatoren bis 1528. 1992. *Volume 81.*

– Dreißigjähriger Krieg und Westfälischer Friede. 1998. *Volume 104.*

– Das Ende der Reformation. 2003. *Volume 123.*

*Kleffmann, Tom:* Die Erbsündenlehre in sprachtheologischem Horizont. 1994. *Volume 86.*

– Nietzsches Begriff des Lebens und die evangelische Theologie. 2003. *Volume 120.*

*Klein, Michael:* Westdeutscher Protestantismus und politische Parteien. 2005. *Volume 129.*

*Koch, Dietrich-Alex:* Die Schrift als Zeuge des Evangeliums. 1986. *Volume 69.*

*Koch, Gerhard:* Die Auferstehung Jesu Christi. ²1965. *Volume 27.*

*Koch, Traugott:* Johann Habermanns „Betbüchlein" im Zusammenhang seiner Theologie. 2001. *Volume 117.*

*Köpf, Ulrich:* Die Anfänge der theologischen Wissenschaftstheorie im 13. Jahrhundert. 1974. *Volume 49.*

– Religiöse Erfahrung in der Theologie Bernhards von Clairvaux. 1980. *Volume 61.*

*Korsch, Dietrich:* Glaubensgewißheit und Selbstbewußtsein. 1989. *Volume 76.*

*Korthaus, Michael:* Kreuzestheologie. 2007. *Volume 142.*

*Kraft, Heinrich:* Kaiser Konstantins religiöse Entwicklung. 1955. *Volume 20.*

*Strom, Jonathan:* Orthodoxy and Reform. 1999. *Volume 111.*

*Tietz-Steiding, Christiane:* Bonhoeffers Kritik der verkrümmten Vernunft. 1999. *Volume 112.*

*Thumser, Wolfgang:* Kirche im Sozialismus. 1996. *Volume 95.*

*Trelenberg, Jörg:* Augustins Schrift *De ordine.* 2009. *Volume 144.*

– Das Prinzip „Einheit" beim frühen Augustinus. 2004. *Volume 125.*

*Voigt, Christopher:* Der englische Deismus in Deutschland. *2003. Volume 121.*

*Voigt, Friedemann:* Vermittlung im Streit. 2006. *Volume 140.*

*Wallmann, Johannes:* Der Theologiebegriff bei Johann Gerhard und Georg Calixt. 1961. *Volume 30.*

– Philipp Jakob Spener und die Anfänge des Pietismus. ²1986. *Volume 42.*

*Waubke, Hans-Günther:* Die Pharisäer in der protestantischen Bibelwissenschaft des 19. Jahrhunderts. 1998. *Volume 107.*

*Weinhardt, Joachim:* Wilhelm Hermanns Stellung in der Ritschlschen Schule. 1996. *Volume 97.*

*Werbeck, Wilfrid:* Jakobus Perez von Valencia. 1959. *Volume 28.*

*Weyel, Birgit:* Praktische Bildung zum Pfarrberuf. 2006. *Volume 134.*

*Wittekind, Folkart:* Geschichtliche Offenbarung und die Wahrheit des Glaubens. 2000. *Volume 113.*

*Ziebritzki, Henning:* Heiliger Geist und Weltseele. 1994. *Volume 84.*

*Zschoch, Hellmut:* Klosterreform und monastische Spiritualität im 15. Jahrhundert. 1988. *Volume 75.*

– Reformatorische Existenz und konfessionelle Identität. 1995. *Volume 88.*

*ZurMühlen, Karl H.:* Nos extra nos. 1972. *Volume 46.*

– Reformatorische Vernunftkritik und neuzeitliches Denken. 1980. *Volume 59.*

*For a complete catalogue please write to the publisher*
*Mohr Siebeck • P.O. Box 2030 • D–72010 Tübingen/Germany*
*Up-to-date information on the internet at www.mohr.de*